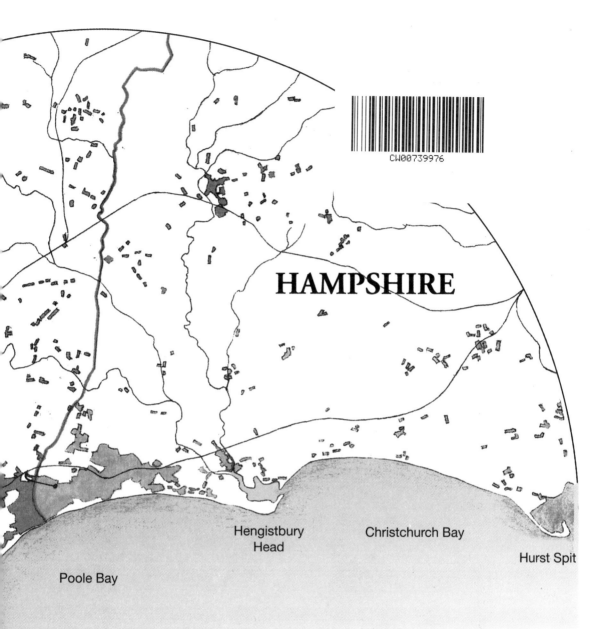

HAMPSHIRE

Hengistbury
Head

Christchurch Bay

Hurst Spit

Poole Bay

udland Bay

wanage Bay

Bournemouth Area c.1915.

*General extent of Conurbation and
Built-Up areas c.1915; road networks,
municipal parks and cemeteries excluded.*

The Natural History
of Bournemouth
and the
surrounding area

Written by members of the
Bournemouth Natural Science Society

Edited by Ray Chapman BSc (Hons)

First published in Great Britain by Wessex Books for the Bournemouth Natural Science Society
2009

Copyright © The Bournemouth Natural Science Society 2009

ISBN 978-1-903035-32-0

A copy of the CIP data for this book is available from the British Library

Designed and produced for the BNSS by Wessex Books, Salisbury SP4 0HD

Jacket designed by KF:D LTD

Design © Wessex Books 2009

Printed and bound in India

Foreword

Aged ten my bible was Smith's *New Naturalist* on 'British Reptiles'. I was snake mad and spent every available summer minute sneaking around the ditches of the Lower Itchen in Hampshire, pillow case in pocket bagging Grass Snakes. I had seen Adders, but frustratingly only when rambling with my parents who rudely forbade me from catching any! When I couldn't get out I read and re-read Smith's account of a 'plague of Smooth Snakes' in Bournemouth and after much nagging I was taken there to see for myself 'that it's no longer a place for snakes'. Walking through the manicured Winter Gardens there was no more disappointed young herpetologist in the land. I sat on a bench and strained to imagine those halcyon heaths of yesteryear, had an ice-cream and went home. I've never been one for nostalgia .

That's why I really admire the pragmatic attitude encompassed within the Zoology and Wildlife Conservation in Bournemouth sections in this book – it so intelligently accepts the changes distant and recent. The area has changed, and it will still, but it's not all bad and the people of this area have a recognised stake and say in its future. Okay, the Smooth Snakes (which I later caught up with and found pretty uninspiring!) have gone, but now the beautiful Green and Wall Lizards are slowly spreading and if the eco-fascists, who want to purge anything purported to be 'non-native' can be held at bay, these creatures will flourish and with a flash of their brilliant green scales perhaps excite some youngster who steals behind the Boscombe beach huts, and instil a real and lifelong interest in wildlife. But perhaps most worrying of all is that the reality of this vision is more endangered than all the area's vulnerable habitats and their species.

The 1914 edition which this supersedes was the product of a small legion of good amateur naturalists and the UK has a fine tradition for cultivating this 'species'. Indeed, as this current volume shows enough survive with the skills, energy and dedication to produce a thoroughly comprehensive and valuable update on the region's flora and fauna. But aren't we all getting old, nudging nearer to that great nature reserve in the sky, and when was the last time you saw a kid with a pillow case desperately trying to find a vestige of heather amongst the geranium beds in the municipal parks? Look, we've got the data, we've done the science, we've come up with a model for conservation and we've made some progress. These pages prove it, but we have to fight harder to protect what we love, and we have to use our passion to spark a similar desire in new generations of the Bournemouth Natural Science Society. Failure to do so will seed changes that pragmatism will not protect and maybe lead to the evolution of a sterile new species of naturalist whose trade is learned in the virtual world. Call me old fashioned, but I think that this book has come from hearts, not hard-drives.

Chris Packham
Naturalist and Broadcaster 2009

It is almost one hundred years since the first edition of the *The Natural History of Bournemouth and the Surrounding Area* described the wealth of wildlife and habitats found in the area. In that time many changes have taken place. The twentieth century saw huge losses of habitats because of development, forestry and change in agricultural practice. Perhaps the most significant loss is the huge reduction in area of the heathlands that then surrounded Bournemouth and Poole.

Direct human pressure on the natural environment has increased enormously. There are now many more people, many more cars and the coast and countryside are now important recreational and tourism resources. We have also come to realise that wildlife and the natural environment make a vital contribution to our quality of life. Nature is good for people and regular contact with nature improves our general health and well being. Making room for wildlife is vital particularly in urban areas where many people have little opportunity to visit the countryside. We must improve green spaces and create wildlife corridors that enable wildlife to live alongside people and also let people experience nature.

In 1914 the focus of naturalists was to record, describe and often to collect species in order to expand our knowledge of the variety of life on Earth. Conservation was then limited to the protection of isolated pockets of wildlife. While it is still very important to protect rare and declining species and habitats the emphasis has now shifted. The conservation sector promotes the integration of wildlife and habitats with human activity in living landscapes and living seas that enable people to live healthy and prosperous lives and also allow wildlife to flourish.

The new edition of *The Natural History of Bournemouth and the Surrounding Area* provides an important historical picture of the area's wildlife and habitats at the start of the twenty-first century. It also reminds us that we are fortunate to live in a place that is rich in wildlife and that we have a responsibility to protect that wildlife for the future.

Dr Simon Cripps, Chief Executive, Dorset Wildlife Trust

Bournemouth Centenary 2010

Bournemouth 2010 is a year long celebration of the bicentenary of the founding of Bournemouth. The history chapter inside reflects on some of the changes that have been seen during that time.

Contents

Map showing places mentioned in the text

Subscribers

The following people subscribed to the book in advance of publication. The Book Committee would like to thank them for their commitment which gave us encouragement to continue with the project.

Rex Bale & Hilary Barton
David Bird
P. Booth
Michael Broadey
Rosemary Broadey
Professor James Bullock
Mr K A Butt
Mr G T E Cadbury
Sara Cadbury
Margaret Carpenter
Jan Chambers
Ray Chapman
John Chudley
Mr A J Cooper
Vera Copp
James Court
John Cresswell
Phred Crossby
Patrick Cushley
Richard Davies
Pushka Deiana
Judith & Mike Downing
Stephen Durant

Margaret Dyos
Mrs M V Evelyn
Mike Faherty
Tricia Farrington
Vivien Goodwin
Jenny Gurden
Marion Hancock
Miss M D Hillyer-Cole
Geoffrey Hood
Pamela Hood
Alison Hunt
David Jenkins
Eric Johnson
Anne Joliffe
Maureen Keates
Anne King
Lesley Lamb
Michael Lanham
Steve Limburn
Jonathan McGowan
Suzy Moores
James Morris
Steven Moult

Enid Nixon
Beryl Parramore
Winston Peters
Jennie Philips
Keith & Eileen Rawlings
Suzette Reeve
Mr R B Reid
Victoria S Richards
Brian Rowed
Tony Ruth
Gordon Seward
Margaret Seward
Mike Skivington
Andrew Smith
Derek Stockbridge
John Street
Graham Teasdill
Mary Thornton
Mary Tiller
Nicola Wadsworth
Kenn Williams

Abbreviations

AONB	Area of Outstanding Natural Beauty
BSBI	Botanical Society of the British Isles
BNSS	Bournemouth Natural Science Society
BP	Before the Present
DEFRA	Department of Environment, Food and Rural Affairs
DERC	Dorset Environmental Records Centre
DWT	Dorset Wildlife Trust
HCT	Herpetological Conservation Trust
LNR	Local Nature Reserve
NNR	National Nature Reserve
RSPB	Royal Society for the Protection of Birds
SNCI	Site of Nature Conservation Interest
SSSI	Site of Special Scientific Interest
WWF	World Wildlife Fund

Introduction

Ray Chapman

The Coat of Arms of Bournemouth

Quarterly argent and azure, a cross flory between, a lion rampant holding between the paws a rose in the first and fourth quarters, six martlets two two and two in the second, and four salmons naiant and in pale in the third, all counterchanged.

Crest: On a Wreath of the colours upon a Mount vert a Pine Tree proper in front four roses fessewise or.

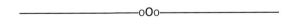

Bournemouth's complex coat of arms, granted on 24 March 1891, reflects aspects of the town's origins and its natural history.

The cross flory is taken from the arms attributed to King Edward the Confessor: the whole district in the midst of which Bournemouth stands was originally a Royal Estate belonging to him. The predominant colours of blue and yellow suggest sea and sand. The four salmon represent the River Stour which marks the boundary between Bournemouth and Christchurch. The roses carried by the lions come from the arms of Hampshire of which Bournemouth was formerly part. The martlets may be regarded as sand martins representing the cliffs. The roses under the crest symbolise the town's parks and gardens, whilst the pine tree highlights one of the prominent species in the town, used in the eighteenth century to provide resin for violin bows and also reputed to add to the health-giving properties of the town's air. All of these features are summarised in the motto – 'Beauty and Health'.

There are, of course, many books about Bournemouth and the surrounding area, its history, industry, archaeology and natural history. This one is somewhat different because it covers all of these topics but attempts to integrate them and consider the interactions between them which result in the beautiful area in which we live.

In 1914 the Society published a book titled *The Natural History of Bournemouth and Surrounding District*. It was written by various members and covered all of the natural history topics plus geology and archaeology. It was sold at Horace G Commin, 100 Old Christchurch Road and at Bright's Stores Ltd, The Arcade for the amazing price of 2/6d (12.5p). The Society has considered producing an up-to-date version for some time and the book you are reading is the outcome.

USING THE BOOK

This book is intended for the general reader with an interest in natural history but not necessarily any experience, although it is hoped that the more knowledgeable reader will find much of interest. We have attempted to cover an area within a 15 mile radius of Bournemouth but, of course with such a large and varied area some must only be lightly touched upon. We are fortunate in this area to have such a wealth of flora and fauna, together with a diverse geology and benign climate that are the framework for the former. The chapters all stand alone although to gain a real understanding of the natural history in our area it is recommended that all are read at some time. We have tried not only to record the various species currently present in the area but also to look back and consider some of the changes that have occurred and some that may happen in the future as the many pressures on the area and the climate grow.

The geology chapter details the way that the area has developed. The history of Bournemouth outlines its development and relationship to the natural history as it has grown and shows how easily we could have lost all of the wonderful areas that are still left for us to enjoy. The chapters covering the fauna and flora are presented in the usual order although in some cases divided into areas to show the variation in ecology.

The common names of species are given first in bold with the scientific name following; the index includes both. Words in the glossary are also shown in bold for the first usage in each chapter.

Dimensions where given are in metric rather than using the cumbersome method of showing both. 1 cm = 0.39 inch, 1 inch = 2.54 cm.

As this book does not go into great detail of most of the species it is recommended that use is made of the accompanying reading and references lists. Most of the publications mentioned are available from local libraries.

If it is intended to follow some of the walks included it is suggested that appropriate 'tools of the trade' are used such as binoculars, geology and ordnance survey maps, a hand lens and a note book to record the things that are seen and when and where. The Society will always be interested in any unusual sightings.

It is important if undertaking a field trip that the Countryside Code is adhered to and that there is right of way on any land entered. Inclusion in this volume does not signify public right of way. If collecting fossils in West Dorset the fossil Code of Conduct asks that any unusual find be notified to the authorities; Charmouth Heritage Centre will supply the details. Additionally if fossil collecting along the coast, care should be taken to avoid cliff falls and rising tides. Fossils should only be collected from the beach or fallen blocks not from *in situ* locations.

THE AUTHORS

All of the authors are members of the BNSS and have spent many years pursuing their subjects, most of them are not professional natural historians but are experienced in their chosen field.

ROSEMARY BROADEY *Ornithology* I am a member of both the RSPB and Dorset Bird Club, and, of course, the Bournemouth Natural Science Society. I have arranged the Ornithology Programme of Lectures and Field Meetings at the Society since 2003.

SARA CADBURY *Mycology* I was born, bred and educated in Bournemouth and worked at the Ordnance Survey in Southampton. I now live on our farm in the New Forest, from where I am able to follow my interests in wildlife, botany and mycology. I have been a member of the

British Mycological Society for many years, am a founder member of the Hampshire Fungus Recording Group, and a member of the Association of British Fungus Groups from its inception.

JOHN CRESSWELL DIP ARCHAEOLOGY HNC *History* Born and bred in Bournemouth, I worked as a technical/scientific illustrator at Christchurch. Then in London I engaged in archaeological digs, moving into local history after an eye injury. Returning to Bournemouth in 2000 after taking early retirement, I have concentrated on learning about Bournemouth's early history as well as doing practical nature conservation work. I am the BNSS Curator.

PHRED CROSSBY *Archaeology* I started a career in science and engineering in the late 1950s. Then in the early 1970s started helping in rescue archaeology; with excavations, etc. I have continued to study and interest myself in archaeology ever since.

WENDY CROSSBY *Ornithology* My parents sparked my interest in the natural world with walks, sightings and information. I belong to the RSPB, BNSS and WWT. Ornithology is my favourite occupation in this diverse area.

JUSTIN DELAIR *Geology* I am the author, sometimes with fellow professionals, of over 50 popular, educational or technical publications concerning geology, geomorphology and palaeontology, having in the process enjoyed a long-standing association with Bournemouth and its environs. Aspects have included quarrying and commercial geology, natural drainage and coastal erosion, fossil faunas and the early history of their study in Britain.

MIKE DOWNING *Botany* A graduate in Electrical Engineering, my working life was split between design, manufacturing and customer technical support. My interest in natural history began as a teenager living near to the Pennine moors but it was not until I retired that I had the opportunity to develop this interest upon joining BNSS. Since 2006 I have enjoyed planning field meetings for the Botany Section.

MARGARET EVELYN *Botany* A teenage passion for Botany lay dormant until meeting the wonderful Bob Lees at BNSS. His enthusiasm, encouragement and patience helped me with the learning process which will stay with me for, I hope, many years to come.

JONATHAN McGOWAN *Zoology* I am a self taught naturalist and have lived in various places in Dorset. I have been involved with local ecological and conservation issues since the late 1970s, and worked for conservation bodies. I have lectured, photographed, painted, recorded and written about local wildlife, and taught in the field. I am the zoology section chairman for BNSS. Lately I have been involved in 'big cat' research with local studies into the non-native cat phenomenon having been involved in television and radio programmes. I am currently writing a book on the subject.

MARY THORNTON *Marine* I was fortunate to study botany, marine botany and freshwater ecology at the University College of North Wales, Bangor from 1967–74. I have remained interested in science, conservation of the environment and the dissemination of natural history knowledge.

RAY CHAPMAN *Editor* Trained as an aeronautical engineer my working life was in various engineering disciplines. In later years I became interested in the natural sciences, particularly geology, which I spend most of my time on since retirement.

In addition to the authors thanks must be given to the proof readers, members who vetted the writing and the reviewers of the chapters. Enid Nixon and John Street who were also committee members throughout the programme carried out the major part of the proof reading.

HISTORY OF THE BOURNEMOUTH NATURAL SCIENCE SOCIETY

The Bournemouth Natural Science Society (BNSS) was formed in 1903 by a group of Bournemouth people with an interest in the Natural Sciences. There had been two previous Societies in Bournemouth with similar aims. The first, the Bournemouth Natural History Society, was started about 1868 and existed until around 1882 when its activities ceased. The next was started around 1884 and was known as the Bournemouth Scientific and Antiquarian Society. It functioned until 1896 when it too became defunct. Some of the members of this Society tried to resurrect the activities of these earlier organisations; they used to meet in each other's houses to read scientific papers. The first minutes of a Committee meeting are dated 2 November 1903 which is when the Society could be said to have really started. The name at this stage was the Bournemouth and District Society of Natural Science. At the end of the Society's first year there were 112 members, 77 men and 35 women. During that year 18 lectures were given. There were just five sections compared to the 12 functioning today. The society met at first in private homes until in 1906 a rented room above Thick's Boot Shop, 122, Old Christchurch Road was taken. Lectures were given at various halls around Bournemouth. In 1909, with larger premises required, a move was made to Granville Chambers at Richmond Hill.

By the end of 1912 the membership was 400 (346 in 2008) and the need to house the ever growing collections meant that larger premises were desperately needed. These were found in the new Municipal College building in the form of a large ground floor room. These premises were used until 1919 when at the end of the Great War space was required for the expansion of technical education.

A major move was now made with the purchase of 39 Christchurch Road where the Society remains today. The princely sum of £3000 was raised from the members by debentures to purchase and refit the house. Work began in September 1919, the formal opening was on 7 February 1920. Ten years later it was felt that the lecture room was not large enough and a large lecture hall was added to the premises. This is still in use today and the original lecture room is now known as the Museum Room. The house is today a Grade 2 listed building and houses the collections in a series of rooms together with IT facilities and the usual offices.

39 Christchurch Road

THE GARDEN, Ray Gibbs

The site was originally part of the native heathland with Scots Pine trees and heathers. The pines were felled mainly in the period 1940–60, having succumbed to storm damage.

It was probably developed as a garden in the late 1870s when the house was built, but it is not until 1923 that documentary evidence has been found.

The Bournemouth Natural Science Society purchased the house and grounds in 1919 and from that date to the present the garden has been developed by its members with occasional professional help, being planted not just with the more common trees, shrubs and herbaceous plants, but also with rare and less common ones.

Being formerly heathland, the acidity in the soil provides ideal growing conditions for **calcifuge** plants. Among those in the garden are Rhododendrons, Azaleas, various Heathers, Skimmias and Camellias. The garden has hardly changed in character since 1923, although parking spaces in front of the house have increased considerably, with the previously gravelled area being laid to tarmacadam. In 1959, a strip of land on the western side of the garden was sold off to produce additional income.

In February 1976, the house acquired Grade 2 listed building status and the garden became a conservation area with all the trees over a certain size having preservation orders placed on them. Unfortunately, over the years, some shrubs, for example the **Bay Laurels**, *Laurus nobilis*, and *Griselinias* have been allowed to grow into large trees and as a result were blocking light from and depriving of nutrients some of the less common trees and shrubs. Consequently, several Bay Laurels have recently been cut down to create more space.

Among the trees of particular interest are, at the front of the house, an **Indian Bean Tree**, *Catalpa bignonioides*, with heart shaped leaves and white flowers in summer and a **Maidenhair Tree**, *Ginko biloba*, whose leaves are widely used as a herbal remedy. At the rear of the house on the eastern side is a *Paulonia sp.*, whose spectacular foxglove-like flowers appear in May. Also, growing in the lawn is a **Dawn Redwood**, *Metasequoia sp.* Discovered in a Chinese temple in 1941, the tree was introduced to Britain in 1948. Unlike most conifers, it loses its feathery foliage in winter. This attractive tree is found in several ornamental gardens throughout Britain, but is still relatively rare.

There is a wide variety of shrubs in the garden, many of which have been donated by members over the years. Of particular interest are the scented winter flowering shrubs such as **Winter Daphne**, *Daphne odora, Osmanthus burkwoodii*, **Witch Hazel**, *Hamamelis mollis*, and *Mahonia sp.* Among the summer flowering shrubs and trees, one of the most the most striking is the **Chilean Fire Bush**, *Embothrium coccineum*. In early summer masses of tubular red flowers appear and give the impression of being on fire. Also worth a mention is the **Bottle Brush**, *Callistemon sp.* This Australian shrub is characterised by its red or purple flower heads, each flower having a long bristle-like stamen which gives the overall appearance of a bottle brush. Growing in the lawn is a *Cornus kousa*. Unlike the popular Dogwood, this large shrub produces masses of white four petalled flowers in early summer.

The island bed immediately behind the house has a small ornamental pond at the centre. Despite its size, it provides a habitat for a variety of fresh water invertebrates. 'Pond dips' are organised on BNSS open days and are proving very popular with young people. Among the species found in the pond are fresh water shrimps, water boatmen, cyclops, water fleas, clams and snails. There are also at least three different species of flatworm. In early spring, large amounts of frog spawn are laid by mating frogs. It is hoped in the near future to create a larger wildlife pond at the rear of the garden to encourage a wider range of animals, for example, newts, frogs and various insect larvae.

The policy for the garden in the future is to be more wildlife friendly and to this end a number of hibernation and nesting boxes have been installed at appropriate locations for hedgehogs, amphibians and birds. A bird box with an observation camera has recently been installed on the western side of the building and every spring nesting blue tits can be observed on a TV screen situated in the Museum room.

LOOKING FORWARD

From its inception the objective of the Society has been to study, research and discuss all aspects of the natural sciences. Proceedings have been published every year since 1908 with interesting papers and descriptions of lectures and field trips. Lectures are held at least twice a week given by members or outside experts in a wide variety of subjects, not necessarily limited to Natural Science. Additionally there are field trips to local areas of geological, botanical, ornithological and zoological interest with visits to further afield places taking place at regular intervals; study groups are also held using items from the collections to illustrate the topics.

The collections are a major facet of the Society; they have been collected from many sources. Members bring things that interest them as well as donating their own collections. Other organisations and private individuals have donated significant items over the years and some objects have been purchased.

There is a large collection of birds and bird eggs on display in the museum. Although the collecting of such items is not carried out today, in the days that it was there was little option if close study of animals and birds was to be conducted. We retain such things for their scientific value and study. Similarly there are large collections of insects, butterflies and moths. The ability to study a case of variants of a single species is invaluable to the entomologist and we are sometimes asked to provide specimens to other organisations for research.

Possibly less contentious are the shell collections, (although again collection of exotic species is now discouraged or prohibited), both local and foreign with some beautiful examples. The geology collection has some excellent items including the Dent collection of Barton fossils highly rated when purchased by the Society to retain them in the area. It was described by Mr. Henry Keeping, curator of the museum at Cambridge, as 'one of the best in the world – probably only equalled by the Edwards Collection in the British Museum and the one in the Sedgwick Museum at Cambridge'. Report by Sir Daniel Morris, 1914.

The botany collection contains specimens dating back for many years all neatly preserved and documented. The archaeology exhibits include many finds from around the area with many fine Neolithic hand axes and other tools. There is also a collection of Egyptian artefacts, the Grenfell Collection, including a mummy in its sarcophagus. The mummy has been CAT scanned and a model of the head may be seen in the hall.

There have been many well known members of the Society over the years. Probably the most notable was Alfred Russel Wallace, the co-author with Charles Darwin of the original papers on the origin of species presented to the Linnaean Society.

PROMINENT PAST PRESIDENTS OF THE
BOURNEMOUTH NATURAL SCIENCE SOCIETY

1903-04	John Elmes Beale,	Mayor of Bournemouth.
1909-10	Dr Arthur Smith Woodward, FRS, FLS, FGS	Director of Geology, Natural History Museum.
1910-11	Dr Dukinfield H. Scott, MA, LLD, FRS, FLS, FGS	President Linnaen Society.

Ray Lankester

1911-13	Sir E. Ray Lankester, KCB, MA, LLD, FRS, FLS	Director of Natural History, Natural History Museum.
1913-16	Sir Daniel Morris, KCMC, JP, MA, DSc, DCL, FLS	Assistant Director Royal Botanic Gardens Kew.
1920-21	Lt Col Sir David Prain CMG, CIE, FRS	Director Royal Botanic Gardens Kew.
1926-28	Heywood Sumner, FSA	Archaeologist, Illustrator.
1929-30	Prof Frederick Orpen Bower, DSc, FRS	Regius Prof. of Botany, University of Glasgow.
1934-35	Sir Frank Watson Dyson KBE, MA, DSc, LLD, FRS, FRAS	Astronomer Royal.
1938-39	Prof Geoffrey Hale Carpenter, MBE, DM, FLS, FZS, FRES	President Entomological Society.
1964-65	Dame Kathleen Lonsdale, DBE, DSc, FRS	President British Association for the Advancement of Science.

Kathleen Lonsdale

1967-68 Prof Frank Hodson,   Professor of Geology Southampton University.
         PhD, BSc, FGS   President Section C British Association.

The Society has, over the years, tried to be at the forefront of scientific and natural history thinking and techniques. Papers and lectures given have reflected this and records have been kept of the wildlife and the changes to the environment and countryside over the last one hundred years. As we move into the next century of the existence of Bournemouth we will continue to do so. To this end we are continuing and strengthening our links with other organisations in the area and involving ourselves with the discussions and actions being taken to preserve the environment and the open spaces of our area for future generations. Our programme is to include keynote lectures by prominent speakers and our study groups will debate today's issues and problems. Our regular field trips will continue to record the condition of our flora and fauna as well as local conditions. Steps are being taken to make the museum more accessible to the public by increasing the number of times that it is open. The Society is a registered charity and as such we shall continue to meet our charitable objectives of providing educational opportunities for the general public.

We hope that you enjoy this book and that it will lead you further into the world of natural history. The Society members are always available for advice when the Museum is open or will answer an e-mail or letter sent to the Society:

Bournemouth Natural Science Society
39, Christchurch Road
Bournemouth
BH1 3NS
Tel: (01202) 553525
E-mail: contact@bnss.org.uk
Web-site: www.bnss.org.uk

The Society thanks Chris Packham for his support in contributing the foreword. His interest in and dedication to natural history is, of course, well known. Our grateful thanks to the Dorset Wildlife Trust whose support and encouragement together with a substantial financial donation are much appreciated. This book was in part prompted by the Bournemouth Bicentenary. We would like to thank the Bournemouth 2010 committee for supporting us with a financial grant. My thanks again to the authors, proof readers, reviewers and all people who contributed to the publication. My gratitude to Jane Drake of Wessex Books for her patience, advice and support and extreme effort to produce a fine looking book. Any errors and omissions remain mine.

Ray Chapman, Editor

1 History & Archaeology

John Cresswell
Phred Crossby

In the preface to the original 1914 book, the Mayor, Alderman McCalmont Hill, remarked that Bournemouth was unhindered by a history. Presumably he was unaware that a few years earlier there had been magnificent celebrations for its Centenary. To understand properly the natural history of the Bournemouth area, some overview is necessary of how it has been shaped by the forces of nature and mankind. Even our most treasured natural spots are purely artificial. This volume is not the place for a detailed description of the 2 million years leading up to the present day, but this and the following section attempt to provide a background to the landscape and environment we enjoy today.

After the end of the Eocene some 34 million years ago, there is little geological evidence in the area until the Pleistocene started 1.8 million years ago. It is the start of the modern period with flora and fauna for the most part little different from that we recognise today. The landmass that was to become the British Isles was still part of the European continent's north-western fringe. It was a period of extremes of weather, with thousands of years of such severe cold that the polar ice cap extended across much of northern Eurasia and North America. These periods are called Glacials and several such cyclic events occurred interspersed with times of warmth termed Interglacials. Although the ice sheets did not reach as far south as to cover the Bournemouth area, the permanent permafrost would have decimated all but the hardiest of organisms. With each warm period a new and varying suite of flora and fauna was to migrate northwards. Sites elsewhere in Britain have yielded lions, elephants and hippos, as well as deer and smaller animals for these periods.

Our present understanding is that Mankind originated in Africa, perhaps being forged by the climatic changes affecting the world generally. A fairly advanced form called *Homo erectus* emerged in north-east Africa around 2 million years ago. It walked upright, had a reasonably sized brain, about 75 per cent of modern man, and carried a stone toolkit with a characteristically lanceolate-shaped, all-purpose implement. Often called hand-axes or bifaces, they could be used for digging up plants, butchering carcases, or making holes. Although the fossil evidence is still sparse, the 'calling card' of this culture is found extensively across the Old World. In fact, Bournemouth is demonstrably one of the richest areas in the British Isles for hand-axes, with over 1200 recorded. By 780,000 years ago man had evolved into the more advanced and larger brained *Homo heidelburgensis*. A recent date from the archaeological site of Boxgrove has yielded his presence in Britain some 500,000 years before the present (BP). Bournemouth's hand-axes have been individual finds uncovered during house building rather than rigorous scientific excavation; a recognition of a single distinctive shape of stone at the expense of locating any associated material. Borough Surveyor, John Scott, amassed a collection, marking his specimens with district and depth in soil but, alas, no exact provenance as the general logic in archaeology was that depth was equatable with age. Typology – how shapes altered over time – is marginally helpful in that Bournemouth has produced all the recognised forms of hand-axes from crude, pointed, ovate, cleaver to **ficron**, and including the later S-shaped cutting edge. Sizes range from 10 cm to over 18 cm. Many are of iron-stained flint. These must cover a time scale of nearly half a million years.

It should be mentioned that a couple of examples of Clactonian flakes c400,000 years old have come from Winton. These are crude cutting tools of arbitrary shapes and may be earlier than the hand-axes. ('Clactonian' is named after Clacton-on-Sea where this culture was first identified and does not refer to the seat of origin. The hand-axes belong to the Acheulian culture – from St Acheul in France – but much earlier specimens are found in East Africa.)

It is significant that most of the Bournemouth hand-axes have been found in terrace gravels of the River Stour. The Stour, with the Avon, and even the Bourne, have been active rivers for millions of years. They once conjoined with the rivers to the east to form a larger Solent River which cut its way eastwards in land protected from the sea by the high ridge of Chalk that stretched from Purbeck to the Isle of Wight. A million years ago, the Stour meandered lazily across its lower stretches. As it did so, flint nodules collected from its more energetic upper levels were deposited as it shifted course, building up floodplains. In the 'Ice-

Paleoliths from the Bournemouth Gravels

Age' sequence described above, this would have occurred during an Interglacial. Animals of all kinds would have visited the river to drink and bathe. Here they were most vulnerable to predators, including man. That so many hand-axes were found in former floodplains of the Stour suggests most are the discarded remnants of an animal kill and its dismemberment. Other evidence such as wooden spears and bones have not survived the acid conditions of the gravels. During the following Glacial, the sea levels lowered as the water cycle fed the growing ice caps. The Stour needed to cut downwards to meet the sea: it acted like an aggressive juvenile, leaving its former floodplain high above it. The release of the water with the melting of the ice again raised the sea level. Again the river meandered and created a new floodplain, and Nature re-enacted its life and death dramas. This new floodplain was lower than the earlier. With the cycle repeating itself subsequently, an established river has written its history in the landscape with fragments of floodplain hanging along the valley as a series of terraces with those at the top being the oldest and those nearer the present level being the youngest. Each relict floodplain thus acts as a dating container for any enclosed artefact (assuming it had not been eroded from earlier levels). It is a 'Relative' form of dating, and not an 'Absolute' date stamp. They are notoriously difficult to work out – especially since the Stour terraces are now built on – but it would indicate that the main distribution of the Bournemouth hand-axes occurred during the Hoxnian and Ipswichian Interglacials and warm phases in between, i.e. ranging from 430,000 to 117,000 BP overall although they were also redeposited through post glacial flooding.

With the Last (Devensian) Glaciation, which started around 117,000 BP, there are new men on the landscape. Africa had disgorged its latest contribution to history – *Homo sapiens* – around 60,000 BP. The new species was to flood the world, both Old and New, bringing language, art and fire. By the time it reached north-west Europe it came in two varieties: Neanderthal Man *H.s.neanderthalensis*, and *H.s.sapiens*, which was to prevail as ourselves. The Neanderthals came with a new flint toolkit, called today the Mousterian. A few examples have been recovered from the Bournemouth area but conditions would have been quite cold. An offshoot of the culture, called the Levalloisian, characterised by the manufacture of hand-axes as flakes from a specially shaped core, is also represented in Bournemouth by a couple of specimens.

By now, the climate was improving. A new geological period – the Holocene – began around 10,000 BP. Neanderthals had previously mysteriously disappeared, despite having a larger brain than Modern Man who was to remain until the present day. The normal route of immigration to Britain had altered. The direct south-north route had been flooded by the English Channel. This had resulted from the breaching of the Dover–Calais Chalk ridge during the Anglian Glacial around 450,000 BP. Plants, animals and Man were obliged to scramble across the sinking North Sea Basin from eastern Europe. The mammals, especially, have demonstrated this origin. The rising sea level was assisted by the sinking of the south of England as the weight of the glaciers on Scotland diminished, adjusting the buoyancy of the land mass – a process called **isostacy**. The British Isles became islands as early as 7000 BP. Apart from flying creatures and birds, Britain was 'closed'. It is worth mentioning here the other breach in the Chalk. Since the Alpine **orogeny**, the Upper Cretaceous beds were squeezed into a vertical 'spine' from Purbeck across to the Isle of Wight. The Chalk, especially, was resistant, forming a 400 metre thick buffer against the sea from the soft Tertiary beds to the north. At a time still yet to be exactly established, the Channel cut through the barrier, utilising the course of the Frome and Piddle Rivers, and the marine assault against the coasts of firstly Poole Bay, then Christchurch Bay, began. The Needles and Old Harry Rocks still bravely resist further erosion.

After the latest Glacial, animals invaded Britain including roe and red deer, elk, **aurochs**, boar, wolf, brown bear, as well as a whole range of shrews, rodents and mustelids.

It was not long before man followed this game. The Upper Palaeolithic Creswellian peoples seemed typical cavemen and made for the high limestone areas in the country. In the Bournemouth region there is a later hunters' site at Hengistbury Head, dating from 12,500 BC. It is one of only four open air sites of this date found in Britain. Although the climate was still cool, there was sufficient game to be killed. They had a toolkit of bladelets, straight-backed blades and tanged points. No animal bones were preserved at the site.

Hengistbury Head

Hengistbury Head was first known to have been occupied, albeit on a temporary basis, in the Upper Palaeolithic (late Old Stone Age). The evidence of flint tools included **end scrapers**, **burins**, backed blades, **bladelets** and **shouldered points**. The site overlooked a wide coastal plain and with the river systems to the north was ideal as a residential hunting site for groups tracking migratory game.

The early Mesolithic (Middle Stone Age), when the Head is assumed to be more than twenty kilometres from the sea, also had a base with an assemblage of flint tools. The tools found include **microliths**, end scrapers and small **denticulates**, all suggesting the hunting of small game, with no evidence of burins, axes or adzes.

The early Neolithic finds, of leaf-shaped flint arrow heads, suggests hunting with no evidence of occupation at Hengistbury until the Late Neolithic at about 2000 BC. At that time people were living on the headland at Warren Hill and the lower slopes. The material discarded includes Grooved Ware decorated pottery, flint scrapers, knives, borers, arrowheads, polished axes, and whetstones. All suggesting many activities in this area. Hengistbury is considered one of the most important known Late Neolithic sites in Wessex.

The Bronze Age (1500–600 BC) had an extensive occupation site on the flank of Hengistbury overlooking Christchurch harbour.

The Iron Age was the period of great activity at Hengistbury Head. The Head becomes protected by a length of palisaded double dykes across its neck. This protected area became a spacious anchorage for overseas trade and control of the river routes into Wessex. The harbour settlement expanded around and after 100 BC, with evidence of trade including wine amphorae from western Italy and unusual blocks of raw purple and yellow glass. Also there is evidence of pottery from Brittany, numerous coins of western France (Armorica) and artefacts from northern Britain. The Breton boats carried both Mediterranean and local products, to and from France via the Channel Islands where British (Durotrigian) coins from Wessex have been found.

Excavations also discovered evidence of exports from Hengistbury, which included iron, copper alloy, gold, silver, Kimmeridge shale and grain. Cattle, in the form of salt beef and hides, are also believed to be exported to the continent. Indeed, the Greek geographer Strabo around the start of the first millennium wrote that corn, cattle, gold, silver, hides, slaves and hunting dogs were exported from Britain.

Prior to the Roman invasions Hengistbury was the port-of-trade involved in major exchanges. New technologies were introduced through Hengistbury Head, shown by some wheel turning of pottery as well as imported pottery and the turning of Kimmeridge shale for ornaments and jewellery. In addition silver-rich lead from the Mendips was having the silver extracted at Hengistbury by a cupellation process. Cupellation involved heating the silver-lead alloy to 1100°C when the lead oxidises to litharge and can be removed as a scum on the surface of the molten metal. The process is repeated until only the silver is left. The litharge can be reduced if required to recover the lead.

Presumably as a result of Caesar's campaigns the trade links declined after the middle of the first century BC. This was partly due to the suppression of the Bretons and also to new exchange systems in eastern Britain supported by Roman roads between the Channel ports and the Rhine and south via Lyons to the Mediterranean. But occupation continued as evidenced by metalled roads and palisaded enclosures, with amphorae from Italy and Spain showing a reduced but continuing Atlantic trade route.

However after the invasion of AD 43 Hengistbury seems to revert to little more than an agricultural village.

Mesolithic men used a core and blade technique to produce a microlithic tool assemblage. They, too, were hunter-gatherers occupying the Christchurch Harbour region with sites at Hengistbury Head and Stanpit. A scatter of individual flints have been found widely across the Bournemouth area, including a few tools made of Portland Chert. This would suggest links with the important Mesolithic settlement on Portland. The toolkit included several tranchet axes and picks, which would have been used for hacking down vegetation, but it would have been small scale – for food, making huts, etc. Susan Palmer has noted that such finds in our local coastal region are presently in those which are now fairly barren except for shrubs, giving access to search for artefacts. The scrapers, blades and microlithic points (which could be hafted on arrow shafts) all indicate a hunting economy. Red deer and boar were favoured prey, with roe deer and aurochs also on the menu. It would seem the red deer of the period were 50 per cent larger than present specimens.

A couple of thousand years or so after the retreat of freezing climate, the landscape had blossomed. Botany textbooks give the typical succession of: moss – grass – scrub – Scots pine and silver birch – ending in full 'climax' mixed deciduous woodland. Along the central southern coast, the dominant tree of the woodland was lime. Received wisdom has this sylvan idyll slashed away by the area's next group of incomers. In view of what was to become today's most precious habitat – heathland – there must also have existed at that time wide swathes of heather and gorse. Britain, isolated from the mainland, could not have evolved such an elaborate ecosystem dependent on heath *in vacuo*. An obvious reservoir would have been the New Forest area, for instance, although the paucity of the Mesolithic may also suggest poor vegetation generally.

Man's first major impact on the ecology of the planet came with the adoption of agriculture. No more the vagaries of gathering or the chase: by planting grain and domesticating animals, there could be a supply of food always on hand. Between 9000 and 4000 BC, the Neolithic culture spread as a slow wave across Europe from its Middle East origin. It is typified by the slash and burning of woodland to make clearings for fields. An addition to the toolkit was the polished stone axe. Hafted into a wooden handle, it has been demonstrated to be a quick despatcher of medium-sized trees. Controlled fire then removed the more obstinate vegetation. (This 'slash and burn' technique continues in the rainforests today.) Microscopic examination of pollen from Neolithic sites provides a clue with the sudden decline in the elm pollen – the tree's shoots make good fodder for cattle. Mammal evidence shows a grassland fauna of field and water voles.

The Neolithic peoples impressively made their mark on the chalk highlands of Wiltshire. For the next few millennia, the coastal regions were peripheral to what was happening on Salisbury Plain, but the distribution of finds is still extensive in the Bournemouth area. A Neolithic burial mound existed just a few yards away from the BNSS's premises until destroyed, unexcavated, by the building of Berkeley Mansions in 1930. In 1932 a skull was found embedded in peat in Longham Meadow, which John Cameron has described as Neolithic. BNSS funded an excavation of another long barrow in Castle Lane in 1936, from which came Windmill Hill pottery. Charcoal evidence from the site yielded oak, hazel and hawthorn. A dish-quern was found in 1927 on Charminster Hill demonstrating that grain was being grown and ground for flour.

Over the years members of the Society have mapped the local discoveries. It is a hall of fame which includes: William Wallace (son of Alfred Russel), Heywood Sumner, Henry Bury, and John Calkin. Hard evidence comes in the many finds of flint tools and, more interestingly, with the polished axe heads of stone from elsewhere which demonstrate a long-distance trade.

The following Bronze Age is equally well represented in the Bournemouth area. Again, the burial mounds are prominent on the Chalk, such as along the Dorset Ridgeway across the Isle of Purbeck. However, the local heathlands are dotted with many round barrows. In Bournemouth alone there were over a hundred. The barrows at Hengistbury Head were targeted by Bushe-Fox in 1911–12 with a quite scientific excavation; others across Dorset would have fallen victim to Victorian amateur plunderers out for an afternoon's adventure; but many have been swept away by the expanding urbanisation, remembered only by occasional place or street names. The acid soils were not conducive to preserving skeletons, but we have considerable amounts of the fragile Bronze Age pottery. Flint tools abound, especially barbed-and-tanged arrowheads, clusters of finds have been made around King's Park, Redhill, Wick, Southbourne and Hengistbury Head, Jumpers and in Poole Harbour. These are testimony to hunting practices continuing over what appears to have been heathland. At the same time, an absence of these arrowheads – such as at Kinson – might indicate settlement. Important perforated stone maceheads occur made of sandstone and other alien stone. A gold torque was found in 1852 in a barrow at St Catherine's Hill. Indeed, the main concentration of finds is over the sandy Eocene beds of the area that include St Catherine's Hill. At Wimborne, a diagonal NE–SW swathe of London Clay might well have supported a dense forest, pierced here by two valleys of the Stour, and at Fordingbridge by the Avon. J Bernard Calkin in 1952 eloquently argued that Wiltshire was supplied through Christchurch using tracks across the heathlands emerging through these valleys into Cranborne Chase and towards Salisbury Plain, respectively. Our area would have played a pivotal role in the development of the important Wessex Culture.

Referring to the period between 2000 and 700 BC as the Bronze Age immediately indicates that metal tools are now being used. Bronze – an alloy initially of copper and arsenic, later tin or sometimes zinc – was again discovered by the emerging civilisations in the Middle East. Its ability to be moulded into robust tools and weapons made it superior to the old stone tools, although these continued to be used in humbler occupations for several millennia to come. The introduction of weapons on the archaeological scene marks a darker side. Were the Beaker folk, whose characteristic pottery can be traced migrating across the Atlantic coastal countries, bringing culture and gifts, or were they savagely enforcing a new regime? However, the continuation of Stonehenge and other henge monuments would suggest a peaceful transition.

The local Middle and Late Bronze Ages are dominated by Deverel–Rimbury pottery, so named after two sites just outside our area. These people did not leave any physical memorial to their presence on the landscape. However, they must have lived in sizeable settlements because of their large cemeteries. These were not with ostentatious monuments, but as each cremation took place, the **sintered** bone was scraped up and put in a bucket-shaped urn, and this inserted in the ground. Whole collections of these cremations have been found across Bournemouth called 'urnfields' because they sit like turnips planted in a field. Redbreast Hill, Moordown, yielded some 97 urns. Another famous grave yard was the urnfield found at Pokesdown in 1926/7. The Red House Museum and BNSS have examples of the numerous urns recovered. Another urnfield was dug at Stapehill in 1967–9. One intact urn with sintered bone was dug up by a BNSS member at St Catherine's Hill in 1918 and is on display at the Society's museum.

The subsequent Iron Age spread across Britain from around 700 BC. There seems to be an origin in Central Europe, both culturally and linguistically. Since these people co-existed and traded with literate Romans, we know they spoke a Celtic tongue, allied to the modern Welsh language. Whilst sharing many characteristics, Britain was covered in a rash of quarrelsome tribes keeping themselves separate. Bournemouth stood roughly at the boundary of two tribes: the Atrebates in the east, and the Durotriges in the west. A few high hills within each tribal area were turned into seats of refuge surrounded by a series of defensive ramps and ditches. They are termed hill forts and in troubled times the farmers would herd the animals and take their valuables to the forts for security. Such forts in our area include Badbury Rings, Dudsbury, and there were smaller fortified hills dotted around. An important variation was the promontory fort at Hengistbury Head, where a double bank and ditch was thrown across the isthmus. As scheduled Ancient Monuments, some of the larger hill forts have enabled wildlife to flourish. Badbury Rings and Hengistbury Head are SSSIs now doubly protected by English Heritage and Natural England.

Badbury Rings

Badbury Rings are 330 ft high enclosing 7 hectares and are the remains of an Iron Age hillfort, consisting of three ramps each 15m high, with a simple flanking earthwork on one side of the entrance. It was created by digging a ditch in the chalk and piling the spoil on the bank of the ditch doubling the height of the defensive works. It is dated from 800 BC to AD 43. Its use was terminated by the arrival of *Legio II Augusta* commanded by Vespasian.

Four Roman roads converge just north of the fort; two roads crossing would perhaps be a more modern view. Dorchester to Old Sarum and Bath to Hamworthy. They intersect a quarter mile north at Pamphill and without doubt they do deviate to pass close by Badbury or follow pre-existing routes focusing on the hill fort. Now, looking at the roads differently we have the Old Sarum–Badbury–Lake Farm–Hamworthy road which is the original supply road of the 2nd Augustan, when it first established a fort at Lake Farm, being built on a grand scale right from the start. Called Ackling Dyke as it crosses Cranborne Chase with a splendid **agger** easily visible and offering splendid walks in some places.

The whole area around Badbury has had considerable use through time. Late Neolithic sites, difficult to find on the ground as areas were often reused in later periods, such as the Bronze Age. Such evidence exists for late Neolithic occupation below a Bronze Age enclosure south of Badbury Rings from 3000 to 1500 BC. South and west are ancient field systems. Just outside the western defences of the Rings are Bronze Age barrows and a further group one mile northwest, with two more on King Down one mile northeast.

A Roman settlement lies nearby at one and a half miles east and a Roman fort half a mile west at Crab farm Shapworth on the Roman road to Dorchester. In addition the Hansworth Roman villa is two miles north of the Rings. Yet more was to be discovered recently at Crab Farm.

It has been a view for some time that Salisbury Plain and Cranborne Chase form an area of 900 square miles with virtually no villas although peasant farmsteads and villages abound. The area should favour small towns but none are known. This was thought to represent an Imperial Domain with heavy exaction of grain or tax due to some slight to the Empire. As a result it was believed a minor settlement in the late Iron Age at Badbury was little more than a roadside market in the early Roman occupation possibly due to a religious site then common at cross roads. The Great West Road from London to Dorchester runs for 130 km across Wessex without going near a town. However, at each of 3 major crossroads (30 km apart) minor market settlements grew.

However the discovery in 1976 by Norman Field of the supposed Auxiliary fort at Crab Farm led to further research by Martin Papworth. The fort is now accepted as the citadel in the centre of a substantial town with origins in the Iron Age. Not a planned town with a street grid, but developing gradually into a large settlement not fully defined but covering an area greater than twenty-five hectares.

The town could be the one in the Antonine Itinerary known as Vindocladia lying on the road linking Sorviodunum (Old Sarum) with *Durnovaria* (Dorchester). The modern village of Shapwick, mentioned in the Domesday book, is likely to be a direct but scaled down descendant of the Iron Age settlement. Perhaps the future will show our 900 square miles as not so empty after all.

Hill Forts

In Wessex there is reason to believe that old hill forts were brought back into use as defence against Saxon raiders, as by AD 440/450 Wessex was flanked by Saxon settlements to the northeast and the southeast. There is some evidence that during the sixth century battles were fought with Saxons at or close to hill forts. It is recorded by Gildas (a sixth-century Celtic monk) that a great British victory occurred at Mount Badon around the start of the 6th century (Gildas was probably born around that time). The possibility of it being at Badbury Rings exists (Jackson, 1958), suggesting that Badbury was 'Baden' of King Arthur fame with the defeat of the Saxons at the famous battle of *Mons Badonicus* circa AD 518.

Refined smelting techniques, reaching higher temperatures, enabled iron to be extracted from ore. Much harder than bronze, it gave an edge to its users. Swords and spears were obvious 'improvements', but craftsmanship in a whole range of metalwork was exquisite, with Celtic art still appreciated today. Pottery was now wheel-thrown in several forms with some wheel finished.

Calkin has identified Early Iron Age sites at Hamworthy, Corfe Mullen, Strouden Farm, Bargates – and Hengistbury Head. For many centuries, Christchurch Harbour was used for trading, serviced from an extensive settlement behind the double dykes of Hengistbury Head. Protected behind this, the people engaged in a large trading operation with the growing Roman Empire. From 100 BC to the conquest of AD 43, wine – especially – was imported, perhaps in exchange for slaves. It may be assumed that the local iron ore was smelted or traded. A mint has been claimed for the site with over 3000 coins found, but no actual evidence of minting has been found.

The Romans successfully invaded Britain in AD 43 and had extended their territory as far as Exeter (*Isca*) within 5 years. The major local Civitas Capital was *Durnovaria* (Dorchester) with forts at Badbury (*Vinocladia*) and Lake Farm. Christchurch Harbour was bypassed in favour of Poole, where mining activities of the various rocks of the Isle of Purbeck took place. There were isolated villas at Rockbourne and Hemsworth, this latter excavated by Henry Le Jeune of the BNSS in its early days.

Pottery kilns were excavated by Heywood Sumner in the New Forest, where clays from the Eocene beds produced a domestic ware. Termed Romano–British ware these late third to fourth century kilns are being described as foreign import technology. For much activity during this period it is difficult to distinguish between maker or user, although the natives were obviously more numerous. Black burnished ware was produced around Poole from the Iron Age to the fifth century BC. Other industries involved were at Purbeck, the mining of stone and the manufacture of black shale bracelets and furniture and at Hamworthy, the processing of salt. The famous Roman roads, for the most part, skirted our area. Any produce was manhandled or taken by packhorse to the nearest contacts.

Even before the Romans left Britannia in AD 410, the coasts were being attacked by men from north central Europe. Saxons, Jutes and Angles were just some of the people marauding across the Empire's boundaries. To ward off the threat, several forts were erected along the eastern coasts of Britain, but with Visigoths at the gates of Rome, the Legions were forced to depart, leaving their colony to the mercy of the barbarians. The transition varied from place to place. The Jutes seem to have been the main invaders along the southwest coast, establishing themselves in the Isle of Wight and the New Forest area around the Solent. Local folklore has the chiefs Hengist and Horsa invading Bournemouth. It is a mythology still promulgated by local place names (but strangely, *not* Hengistbury Head). Bokerley Dyke along Cranborne Chase held off the Saxons, but they were mainly interested in going westward. A strong British presence existed in the Isle of Purbeck.

In 495 the Saxons, Cerdic and his son Cynric, pushed their way up the Avon valley. Twenty four years later they established a foothold in a battle of Cerdicsford (Charford) near Downton, just outside our area. The new empire was called Wessex – the implication being that it belonged to the West Saxons, supplanting or oppressing the indigenous Romano–British population.

But from around 700, much of Wessex was English, with Saxons converting to Christianity. The centre of power was at Winchester, which under Alfred became the capital. An early local settlement in our area was at Christchurch, which was then called Tweoxneam or Twynham meaning '[place] between the streams'.

The later half of the first Millennium was a time of much strife, not least with the incursions of the Danes, which Alfred finally quelled in 896 although they kept returning. Many institutions were built but little remains from our area. Wareham still retains earthen defences on three sides of the town. There was probably a Saxon foundation to the church at Christchurch, and also a fortified settlement on the hill of Corfe Castle. It was at the latter that King Edward the Martyr was murdered by his step-mother in 978. Iford has been identified as Yattingaford where the forces of Edward the Elder met those of Ethelwald in 901.

Although the map is littered with Anglo-Saxon names – the many 'hams', 'tons' and 'fords' – there seems little impact by the invaders on the natural landscape.

In 1086, the Norman King William ordered a complete inventory of his new kingdom. The resulting *Domesday Book* is as breath-taking in its detail as it is frustrating in the interpretation. Most of Hampshire (in which Bournemouth once was) has been analysed. We can see that Twynham had 39 houses occupied by 32 villeins, 18 bordars, 4 radmen, 3 coliberts and 3 serfs, but such figures only give an order of magnitude. We can note the number of watermills along the Avon, and that some supplied eels. There were 4½ fisheries along the Stour.

We can also note that the Avon Valley was quite settled along its length, rich in meadows and pockets of woodland. The woods were less important as a source for timber than for **swine** pannage (the eating of acorns and beech mast) in the autumn. Ringwood could thus support 189 swine. We may also lay to rest the Medieval Chronicles' calumny that King William evicted people from the New Forest so that it could go to waste in order for him to hunt without hindrance. It was already so desolate that ploughs could not operate economically because of the poor soil. The New Forest plays a large part in our history. William established it in 1079: according to *The Anglo-Saxon Chronicle*, for the deer and enacted laws therewith, so whoever killed a hart or a hind should be blinded. As he forbade killing the deer, so also the boars. He also appointed concerning the hares that they should go free. King William Rufus died in the New Forest, either accidentally or assassinated for increasing the death penalty. Although there was some relaxation by Henry III, the laws remained until James I. It was then a strange concept that a human could 'own' an animal. Hart and hind referred to red deer. Buck and doe was once specific to roe deer – until the Normans introduced fallow deer into their parklands to be hunted. Such animals had been present in the Hoxnian Interglacial, and there were some doubtful records since, but it would seem the Normans obtained their breed from the Mediterranean. Wolves also existed since the killing of two was rewarded by King John in 1210. Charles II was the last monarch to hunt in the Forest.

The Normans were also responsible for another animal that was to shape our landscape: the coney. The term 'rabbit' originally referred to the young which were regarded as a delicacy. These were often released on islands where they could not escape – nor damage crops. Could sandy Warren Hill across Christchurch Harbour have provided a convenient supply for the Norman dinner tables at Twynham?

Domesday provided a picture of settlement which – apart from the dramatic growth of Bournemouth centuries later – is not dissimilar to the pattern today. 1066 saw the last successful invasion of England by a foreign power, and the rural areas – especially – enjoyed a certain stable, rustic idyll untouched by national strife or a need to supply more than required.

It should come as no surprise that Medieval documents confirm our conception of the Dorset forests. Records can give glimpses of 500 ash trees and 2000 maples being cut from East Holme for repairs at Corfe Castle by the Constable in 1278, and 8 large oaks taken from Holt Forest to make a bridge also at Corfe Castle in 1356, or that 6 roe deer were given by the king in 1232 to stock up his park at Bere. Later in the sixteenth century Holt Forest was recorded as having several hundred large oaks – ideal for building up the supply of naval ships.

The Isle of Purbeck had a status of forest, chase or warren at different periods. Medieval deer parks are also recorded at Canford, Lytchet Matravers, Kingston Lacy and Tarrant Rushton. Such exclusion zones would have preserved their ecology, whilst outside the common folk eked out a living from the land.

The division between the chalk uplands and the clay and sand lowlands, the Chalk–Cheese boundary follows the Cretaceous–Eocene unconformity on the western periphery of our area. The grazing of sheep would have been on the limestone hills, whilst in the lowlands the concentration would have been on cattle and dairy produce. The native local cheese is Blue Vinney, the name coming from an ancient word for 'mould' suggesting a quite early date for its production. Horses would have been used as heath-croppers in both Dorset and Hampshire. Commoners in the New Forest would also have had permission to graze their ponies, and by the thirteenth century there were round-ups called Drift to weed out poor stock.

The church grew strong in early medieval times: there was a priory at Christchurch, and a nunnery at Tarrant Crawford. Wimborne Minster was founded early in the eighth century, with Saint Cuthburga commencing her rule as Abbess in 705. The religious communities would have held sizeable grounds in order to be self-sufficient.

Expansion of habitations was savagely curtailed as the Black Death swept its way across the area from its footfall at Melcombe Regis in 1348. The towns of Wessex were especially struck by the plague with estimates of a third or half of the population dying. Whether transmitted by flea-carrying black rats, or humans, the former is now found infrequently across the area. Other animals which succeeded were sheep as abandoned fields were enclosed and turned to pasture, with a single shepherd requiring less manpower than crops. The lords of the manors were often compelled to enclose some of the common fields to ensure the agricultural regime. Some landowners profited by the new circumstances and a spate of fine manor houses arose, Cranborne having quite an early foundation.

The Civil War affected the region although local skirmishes and sieges had only a small effect on population numbers. However, what have become national monuments suffered. In 1644 Col Hardress Waller took Christchurch without loss of blood. Corfe Castle withstood a longer siege in 1643, but in 1646, the war coming to an end, the castle was taken by treachery and the defences destroyed, providing the area with its magnificent ruin.

The period of peace that followed, and the growth of trade abroad enabled fortunes to be made. Whilst the gulf between rich and poor widened, those with money could display their wealth in large houses and estates unfettered by the need for fortifications. Grand houses were built profusely across the landscape, bringing exotic shrubbery and unusual animals which sometimes escaped into the surrounding countryside. Kingston Lacy was built 1663/5 for Sir Ralph Bankes to replace his slighted Corfe Castle. The approach from Blandford is graced by the famous avenue of beech trees. St Giles, rebuilt in 1650 on an earlier pile, Charborough Park, and Crichel House built in the eighteenth century are other examples of large houses surrounded by parks and gardens. They have contributed to the landscape and also have allowed a certain refuge to wildlife as the areas outside are developed or farming intensified.

Access to these country estates demanded a better transport system with better roads. Turnpike roads cross the country. One such was the Poole, Wimborne and Cranborne Trust established in 1756 with roads linking Poole with Dorchester, Salisbury, Ringwood and Southampton, the latter road passing through Bourne Bottom, crossing the Stour at Iford.

Stage coaches despatching vital mail also doubled as provision for universal travel. Heavy goods were still transported by coastal shipping. Poole, Lymington and Southampton were ports but also ship-building centres. The forest hinterland would be source for timber for boat construction. Poole had already a long history as a trading port, replacing Melcombe Regis in the mid-fifteenth century as the only officially recognised sea port in Dorset. Some hundred years later, a connection with Newfoundland brought in salted cod and oil. And in the sixteenth and seventeenth centuries, a ceramic trade grew up based on clays dug around Poole Harbour. Other Eocene clays were used for the rustic Verwood pottery. In the Bournemouth area the cliffs were dug for ferrous sulphate. It was used for tanning, and other uses. Both Alum Chine and Boscombe contributed to this copperas manufacture. Purbeck marble had been quarried since the fourteenth century and continued in the seventeenth century for use in church monuments which lost favour after the Reformation, but stone was still shipped out of Swanage at a rate of 50,000 tons a year at the end of the eighteenth century. However, the local geology never lent itself to the main thrusts of the Industrial Revolution when it burst onto the rest of England in the late eighteenth century.

Other locals undertook a more lucrative but risky life. Smuggling was rife throughout the eighteenth and nineteenth centuries. The desolate coastline of Hampshire lent itself to the secretive landing of boats with contraband. Christchurch Creek was used continuously. After the Battle of Mudeford in 1784, the victor smugglers were allowed to keep 500,000 litres of spirits and about 35,000 kg of tea. From West Moors, Isaac Gulliver acted with apparent immunity at the end of the eighteenth century, dying a rich and venerated citizen.

The need for self-sufficiency brought about by the European wars, demanded better agricultural methods. Land once regarded as 'waste' was enclosed and brought into use. Each field needed demarcation and miles of hedges were planted, both denying and (albeit unintentionally) providing habitat for wildlife.

Land became available for those with new wealth, no longer the preserve of the aristocracy, yet the Lords of the Manors replicated their betters as they climbed their respective social ladders. Huntin', shootin', and fishin' was as much their scene. Persecution of deer, foxes and otters by hunts grew with the new landed gentry, and the creation of game reserves for partridges and pheasants for shoots gave them the entré into higher society. By 1800, the rigid social order was beginning to change. Engineers and scientists were bringing about technological revolutions and new ways of life. This quiet Dorset backwater would not remain untouched.

Kimmeridge

The first BNSS book gives a brief mention of Kimmeridge shale discs, known as coal money (from W. A. Miles, 1820), but by then recognized as the waste products of lathe turned objects producing armlets, bracelets and charms for the Roman world.

In Neolithic times Kimmeridge shale was used to make ornaments and functional items such as spindle whorls. Shale beads of that period are known to have reached Gloucestershire indicating that they were used for trade.

'Coal Money'

During the Iron Age it is thought that only a limited industry existed. Excavation carried out on an Iron Age dwelling and shale workings support the above theory. The coming of the Romans changed the scale, expanding the industry using lathes with flint tool blades.

A long continuity of the Roman industry is supported by evidence of eleven known sites during the Roman period. The shale products have been found throughout the Empire. These included shale bowls, dishes, slabs used as trays, table legs (animal head and claw) used in making a popular Roman three legged table. The shale when smoothed and polished with beeswax looks very similar to Jet. Excavation of a Roman villa, at Dewlish in Dorset, revealed shale sheets lining the cold plunge bath.

Romano–British grave skeletons show shale rings sometimes worn above the elbow as well as the wrist, known as Armlets. In addition both the shale and a red to biscuit coloured strata at Kimmeridge have been used as tesserae in mosaics.

No further record of Kimmeridge minerals used on a large scale is known until the end of the sixteenth century when Lord Mountjoy and Sir William Clare started extracting alum, with shale used as the fuel for the process. A pier and dock was built around 1610 to support the trade. The early extraction of alum was terminated using legal action by holders of the 'alum monopoly'. Following on from the above Sir William and Abraham Bigo constructed a glassworks in 1617 producing green glass drinking vessels from silica fuelled by the shale. The remains of a furnace with a glass melt in a crucible of ball clay have been discovered as evidence of the industry. The glass business was closed in 1623 by court action as a monopoly to sell glass in London had been infringed.

Later remains mainly from the nineteenth century show extensive extraction of bituminous shale with cliff quarrying and adits into extensive underground workings. A new pier was constructed by the Bituminous Shale Co (1848), fed by tramways to ship the shale to Weymouth, for distillation into gases, oils, paraffin wax, naphta and by-products of varnish, dyes and fertilizer. Paris was supplied with shale from the 1860s for gas production until 1878. Mining continued until 1890, then was replaced by cement-making exploiting lime rich marls fuelled by shale and closing in 1900.

Tramways used to cover Purbeck for many mineral industries and the remains of railway lines lying over the cliff at Kimmeridge are considered to be one of these. However, an alternative view is that the rails are the remains of a moving gunnery target laid running north east used in the Second World War.

Industry at Kimmeridge has changed but is still flourishing, as oil extraction continues from the mid-twentieth century to the present day, albeit from much deeper strata than the ancient shale industries. The working of the nodding donkeys being well known landmarks at Kimmeridge.

Nodding Donkey

Another landmark is the Clavell tower, built by the Revd John Clavell in 1830 using yellow stone from the beach and then clad in cement. The coastguard used it for a time as a lookout point. Its recent claim to fame came when painted black and used in the television adaptation of PD James' novel *The Black Tower*. The tower has recently been dismantled and rebuilt 25metres back from the cliff edge to avoid collapsing because of cliff erosion.

Graves found at Kimmeridge and Studland contained skeletons of beheaded women with the head between the knees. A third century coin of Carausius (AD 287–293) was in one excavated near a Roman shale workshop. Interestingly, at an Inn near Wareham hangs a sign of a headless woman carrying her head under her arm. The Inn is called the 'Silent Woman', indicating a long held tradition of quiet women in the Purbeck.

Clavell's Tower

RECENT HISTORY OF THE BOURNEMOUTH CONURBATION

The beginning of the nineteenth century marks the moment when Bournemouth was born and becomes centre-stage to our story. In the previous chapter we have examined some of the climatic, natural and human influences on the landscape. The pace of change had been slow, almost accidental. The next two hundred years brought with it such alterations that some may yet be unstoppable.

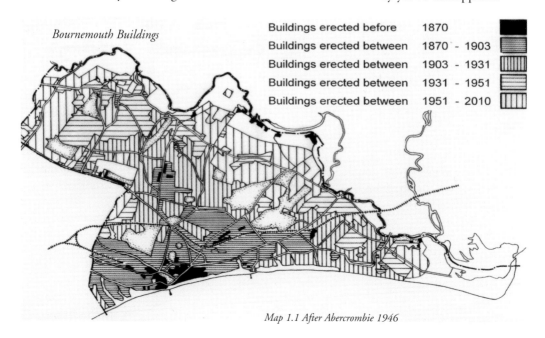

Bournemouth Buildings

Buildings erected before	1870	■
Buildings erected between	1870 - 1903	
Buildings erected between	1903 - 1931	
Buildings erected between	1931 - 1951	
Buildings erected between	1951 - 2010	

Map 1.1 After Abercrombie 1946

The first Ordnance Survey map of 1811, with its exquisite draughtsmanship, is a virtual 'snap shot' of this early stage. Poole and Christchurch had both grown around their respective harbours and were the largest towns along the south-west coast, nuzzling the south-east and south-west corners of Dorset and Hampshire, respectively. Both were towns with long histories, well-established. Dotted around the map are smaller towns; market towns like Ringwood, Fordingbridge, Wimborne Minster, Wareham, a boat-building town like Lymington, Swanage still a fishing town but soon hoping to capitalise on the new craze for sea-bathing, and the small town around Corfe Castle. The Census Returns of 1801 for these places give an indication of their size.

Poole	5801	Christchurch	3773	Ringwood	3222
Wimborne Minster	3039	Lymington	2378	Fordingbridge	2335
Wareham	1627	Swanage	1382	Corfe Castle	1344

A network of roads and paths linked these towns and the many villages and hamlets peppered across the area and microhabitats of the manor houses. Population was mainly low, and life was without too many expectations. The economy was mainly rural with little industry. Fields were enclosed and close to the sites of habitation; beyond there existed spaces referred to as 'downs' (some 18 in our area), 'heaths' (33), 'commons' (11), and 'woods' (7). They all played some role in the rural life but for the most part were ignored, allowing nature to take its course. However, changes were already taking place. Isaac Taylor had in 1759 produced maps showing the Dorset heathland of which the later Ordnance Survey would suggest some 30 per cent had already disappeared. The New Forest had its inclosures, but only Ringwood Forest gives indications of deliberate planting.

The main administrative unit was the parish. Christchurch was the important parish of the area with fingers of influence along the coasts and river banks and the fringes of the New Forest. Holdenhurst had its own though subsidiary parish, encompassing some of its neighbouring hamlets along the southern Stour bank. These villages of Wick, Iford, Throop and Holdenhurst retained a certain independence until being swallowed up in later expansions of the borough of Bournemouth. Kinson, too, had an old foundation and that retained independence until 1931.

With the wars against Napoleon, the British government looked favourably at means of ensuring good supplies of essential crops. In 1801 a General Inclosure Act was passed easing the way for land to be made available for better cultivation. For centuries the land that was to become Bournemouth was the westerly portion of the Parish of Christchurch. It was known as the Liberty of Westover – the name being a corruption of 'West of the River Stour'. It had existed as a separate Hundred since the sixteenth century. A stagecoach route linked Christchurch with the equally ancient town of Poole, and there was a scatter of individual houses in the desolate landscape. The lands to the north were quite fertile and of value, but the higher lands towards the coast were heathland wastes. This latter consisted of some 5100 acres.

Following the initial Act, the Christchurch Inclosure Act was passed 4 May 1802. It provided for the Commonable Lands to be divided into small parcels of very little value, partly covered with furze and heath, to be sold off. Some cottagers were concerned for their **turbary** rights and some recompense was given, with the occupants of 86 cottages in the district being allowed to cut turf for fuel on five turbary commons which were set aside – and which we shall revisit later. Despite the delay, selling started in January 1803 and was completed within a couple of years. Land was sold off for expenses, and some land allocated for roads and gravel pits for their maintenance.

The main buyers were five gentlemen of money: Sir George Ivison Tapps, William Dean, the Earl of Malmesbury, William Driver and Philip Norris. In total the sale of 1258 acres realised just over £4000. The buyers were probably uncertain what to do with the unpromising land. Tapps did see some potential and started planting up various plots with Scots pines, *Pinus sylvestris*, as a cash crop – for pit props and as timber for ships, both desperately required in the fight against Napoleon. He was later to add Maritime pine, which was to be symbolised on Bournemouth's crest. [John Young (1999) made the interesting point that had Common Rights prevailed, there would be no Bournemouth – but an important nature reserve like Dunwich Common in Suffolk.]

Lewis Tregonwell, a captain in the Watch, stationed at Mudeford was attracted to the wooded valley of the Bourne stream and decided to set up home there. He moved into the district in September 1810, first occupying an inn on the Poole–Christchurch road, then moved into a new house two years later. Over the next few years he had built a few cottages, offering them to friends to partake of the almost private bathing beach. Thus Bournemouth came into being.

In 1835, Tregonwell's neighbouring Lord of the Manor, Sir George Gervis, was granted a private Act whereby he was empowered to spend some £5000 to improve his land. Benjamin Ferrey designed villas and parks and envisaged Bournemouth's new direction. With the co-operation of the second Lord Malmesbury, Gervis cleared the undergrowth of the eastern banks of the Bourne stream, laid out walks and planted thousands of exotic ornamental shrubs. It was later to be called Westover Gardens, being completed by 1850.

The Bournemouth Board of Commissioners was established in the wake of an 1856 Improvement Act. The population of Bournemouth may be extrapolated as about 1100. The town then being considered as that area within a mile radius from the Belle Vue Hotel. The Commissioners zealously put schemes into action. The valley of Bourne Stream was drained, the waters embanked and the banks laid out as pleasure gardens in 1873.

The nearby Cranbourne Gardens had opened in 1862. To the existing Scots pines, were added Maritime and Monterey Pines, rhododendrons were imported in their thousands, and – presumably – Holm Oaks. All were suited to the acid soils and the mild south coast climate. Bournemouth was to be later called 'The Evergreen Valley'.

The first streets of Bournemouth were laid out by Christopher Creeke, who abhorred straight roads. By mid-century the Christchurch–Poole road was still the main artery and horse-drawn omnibuses and Mail coaches plied. The railway line from London to Dorchester laid out in the 1850s skirted the north of Bournemouth, and the nearest station was at Holmsley (opened 1857). An extension to the railway system of a branch from Ringwood to Christchurch and thence to Bournemouth East, opened in 1870. This was followed by an extension from Poole to Bournemouth West Station in 1874.

The building of the first jetty in 1856 (later a more substantial pier in 1861), allowed sea-borne traffic. Bournemouth became accessible to the wider world. Already recognised as a watering place for the middle classes, the advent of the Bank Holiday Act 1871 meant that Londoners could now descend for cheap day trips, spending up to 8 hours in 'sunny Bournemouth'. As the years passed, and longer holidays were granted, more came to Bournemouth. The impact on the town was the improvement of its public gardens and other leisure facilities; and as many decided to stay, there was the increasing provision for housing.

In a modern climate dominated by environmental issues, voiced by dozens of local, national and international organisations, it may seem difficult to appreciate the Victorian lack of concern about the natural world. Nature was considered bountiful and subservient to Man, as provided by Genesis, I, 26. There was a growing fascination in natural objects, and during the nineteenth century, the leisured middle class took to collecting shells, birds' eggs, butterflies, seaweeds, flowers, and stuffed animals and birds. Although the first and second Earls of Malmesbury enjoyed the sport of shooting birds from the sky over their estate at Hurn, they also stuffed the skins and displayed them in their home. William Hart was a Christchurch 'preserver of animals', whose shooting activities provided many a visitor with a similar case of birds fit for their parlour as a souvenir from Bournemouth. Whether animal or plant, the rarer specimens were the most sought. Only late in the century did Hart ponder why some birds seemed less common than previously.

The 1880s showed a sharp increase in building and an expansion of the town's footprint. Nationwide this urbanisation needed to include green space if the problems of industrial slums were not to be repeated. Urban parks became the pride of every Victorian township. Central Bournemouth had its Pleasure Gardens for some years, and other parcels of lands such as Dean Park and Horseshoe Common were given for organised sport.

The heath fringes were being encroached upon. The Bournemouth Park Lands Act, 1889 authorised certain open spaces for the recreation and enjoyment of the public. The five areas were considered as turbary, previously allowing commoners the right to remove heath for fuel. The respective owners were quite willing to relinquish – with compensation – spaces which were later to become Meyrick Park (opened in 1894), King's Park (1902), Queen's Park (1902), Seafield Pleasure Gardens (1928) and Redhill Common (1920s). For the most part these areas were used for sport, especially golf, which required certain management regimes, yet trees and shrubs provided some natural aspects.

To the west, Poole had long been agitating for a public park. Lord Wimborne generously offered some land along Parkstone Bay in 1885, and the 40 acre Poole Park was duly opened by the Prince of Wales 18 January 1890. The same day, Parkstone Recreation Ground of 3 acres was also opened by the royal visitors.

To the east, Christchurch between the Stour and Avon Rivers had large expanses of common land. Much remains as public open space. The most popular and immediate to the town is the Quomps. This is a small 5 acre meadow pasture, its name meaning swampy. It is known from eighteenth century records when grazing rights were exercised. In 1909, Lord Malmesbury handed over his rights to the Town Council for the site to be a recreation ground.

The Central Gardens in Bournemouth were extended along the length of the Bourne stream. The original bridge over the brook enlarged to become part of the Square. Both Upper and Lower Gardens have continued to have added exotic trees and shrubs, not least palms. Colourful flower beds are to be expected, with neat mown lawns to impress the visitors. The natural content was as artificial as the tinted postcards, with imported white peacocks, and, in 1922, the grey squirrel. Recreation, here, was of a refined style – promenading, sitting, listening to the band.

Other formal gardens had been created across Bournemouth, such as Boscombe Chine, Shelley Park and Argyll. The Chines became protected – especially Alum Chine after mid-century ravages along its slopes by geologists. These valleys and ancient routes to the shore were supplemented by cliff-edge paths. Another green factor is the cemeteries. God's Acre at St Peter's Church was running out of grave space by the 1870s. After long deliberations, Wimborne Road Cemetery was acquired and the first interment was made in 1878. East Cemetery followed in 1897, with North and Kinson Cemeteries opening in the 1930s. Such cemeteries were landscaped and maintained for appearances. Yews, weeping willows and other symbolic trees were planted, together with a certain predilection for Chilean Pines. Locked at night, little used during the day, these cemeteries have become refuges for wildlife.

On 27 August 1890 Bournemouth received a charter to become a Municipal Borough which was greeted with much rejoicing. The Board of Commissioners was replaced by a Council, elected in November of the same year. One of its first considerations was the adoption of its motto; *Pulchritudo et Salubritas* – 'Beauty and Health'. The beauty came from the natural environment, and the health followed from being surrounded by it. The new Municipal Borough was now 2593 acres, compared with 1140 acres when the Board of Commissioners was formed. Hampshire County Council had been established under the Local Government Act of 1888, and Bournemouth was now entitled to some representative control of County affairs. Later, in 1900, Bournemouth became a County Borough, which enabled the acquisition of Winton, Moordown, Pokesdown and Southbourne, and some other districts the following year.

One of the more important decisions the Council made was to embark on an undercliff drive. It had been argued about for many years. There were those who thought the golden cliffs added to the beauty of the shore as much as their continual erosion added to the beach. Those more conscious of the loss of their real estate, favoured a protection against the wave action. In 1907 the first section of seawall was opened to the east of the pier, allowing promenaders an easy walk along the front. At stages over the century, other stretches of promenade were added along almost the complete length of the Bournemouth coastline. The sandy cliffs did disappear – under a carpet of vegetation. This has provided a new habitat for Bournemouth, and whilst denying one to the sand martins, the plants create a marvellous wildlife corridor along its length, and are the home to exotics, some desirable, others less so. Paradoxically, Hengistbury Head and its vulnerable isthmus are presently denied protection. In the mid-nineteenth century a John Holloway assumed possession of ironstone boulders along the coast where they had fallen from the cliffs at Warren Head. Along with other mining activities here, these 'doggers' were carted away for smelting. It is estimated that as a result of this loss of protection to the base of the cliffs, some third of the width of the Head was subsequently eroded away. The installation of a long groyne in 1937 helped stabilise the situation, but the geological exposure in the cliffs has been deemed so unique, that English Nature/Natural England has decreed that erosion should be allowed to continue. Elsewhere along the coast, the Tertiary beds are similarly unprotected, although Barton-on-Sea has had to make some provision to protect its soft clays.

Open spaces on the fringes of the towns were places of informal activity and large gatherings. Christchurch had a long established market which was held on Portfield, the ground near Bargates. Later it was developed as a recreation ground, but part was turned into a public garden with special attention to the planting of New Zealand trees and shrubs, marking its connection with the other Christchurch on South Island.

Team sports like cricket and football grew in popularity in the nineteenth century. In the case of burgeoning Bournemouth, many of the itinerant young artisan-builders no doubt knocked a ball around at recognised sites. These grounds – especially East Common on Holdenhurst Road – would also serve for travelling fairs and circuses. Better roads and improved means of transportation favoured the growth of visitations by large companies, as opposed to the casual buskers. Mid-century adverts can trace the itinerary of circuses around the area, visiting a new town every day. The Councils would also avail themselves of these large parks and other open spaces for civic celebrations. The lavish Coronation events of 1902 took place at Meyrick Park, as did a Military Tattoo in 1908. It also held the large 1910 Centenary carnival parade. In conjunction with these Centenary celebrations, the land to the west of Hengistbury Head was used for an International Aviation Meeting, the first of its kind in Britain. A two-mile course was laid out across the fields for the primitive aircraft. Later, the site was seriously considered as an aerodrome for Bournemouth. However, during the subsequent war, the Royal Flying Corps used Ensbury Park, which was then enlarged into an aerial race course until 1919, and thereafter for the racing of cars, horses and greyhounds.

Meanwhile, both cricket and football had gained a growing passive audience. Dedicated grounds were provided to which professional teams would gravitate. Dean Park was created as a multi-sports arena in 1871, and was to become the local home for Hampshire County Cricket Club. Later, King's Park was made available in 1902 to the Boscombe Football Club. In time, a series of stadiums was built to house the Cherries.

As new schools were built in the interwar period they were invariably provided with extensive playing fields, enabling children to become healthily active. During the 1980s competitive sport was eschewed, and the Government allowed straitened school budgets to be relieved by the selling off of playing fields to developers. But the management regimes of all games' pitches and golfing greens entailed the removal of 'pests' like moles and leatherjackets, so they were generally regarded by ecologists as green deserts.

Removal of regarded pests often became fanatical crusades. The Churchwarden Accounts of Holdenhurst in the eighteenth century relate to polecats, sparrows, rooks and stoats, in return for pence for their pelts. Brusher Mills, of the New Forest, specialised in killing adders, ending with a formidable tally by the time he died. Nearer home, at the beginning of the twentieth century, reptile-killing forays across the undeveloped heaths of Bournemouth made strange pastimes. During the Second World War local foxes were persecuted by those keeping chickens and rabbits to supplement their meagre diet. After the War, it was the rabbits' turn to be a pest, and during the 1950s, a biological war was waged with the introduction of myxomatosis. It was an agonising death to rabbits across the country. Although some survived to form new colonies, new strains or deliberate re-introductions occasionally afflict rabbits in our area.

As development engulfed the countryside and all it contained in the 1880s, warning bells sounded in various quarters. In 1895 'The National Trust for Places of Historic Interest or Natural Beauty' was registered under the Companies Act. Its impact locally did not happen until Brownsea Island was taken over in 1962. The Dorset Wildlife Trust has undertaken a great deal of the nature conservation work, not least ensuring the survival of the last southern pocket of red squirrels. The National Trust received a large boost to its properties in 1981 with the death of Ralph Bankes, indeed it was the Trust's largest bequest. It consisted of Kingston Lacy, Corfe Castle and Godhurston Manor, as well as important sites such as Badbury Rings, Studland Heath, and Nine-barrow Down. With its positive attitude, the Trust is caring for a range of Dorset habitats.

The early decades of the twentieth century saw more enlargement of Bournemouth, with the absorption of the previous outlying villages. Remaining intervening fields were swallowed up by new estates. Hengistbury Head would have presented a major single development had Gordon Selfridge fulfilled his castle dream: fortunately for posterity, the land was re-sold to Bournemouth Council in 1930.

During the Second World War parks, fields and allotments were put into service for providing food. Young townswomen joined the Landgirls scheme, helping with ploughing up football pitches and parklands, as well as working on local farms. As part of 'Dig for Victory' gardens grew vegetables rather than flowers. Air raid shelters were erected on communal parks. A side issue was the removal of cast-iron railings round many local parks to be melted down for armaments. These emergency activities no doubt had some damaging psychological impact on the perception of open spaces. 'Unnecessary' journeys into the countryside being unacceptable, and limited access to the beaches, would have curtailed botanising and other naturalising. The thin volumes of the wartime BNSS Proceedings also speak of limited observation.

At the end of hostilities Sir Patrick Abercrombie prepared a joint plan for the conurbation of Bournemouth, Poole and Christchurch. The total population was estimated as being some 220,000. The war effort had produced pockets of industry across the area, mainly around the periphery of the conurbation, and it was felt these should be maintained, or other areas designated as appropriate. The airfields at Hurn and Christchurch were especially developed by Vickers and De Havillands, respectively, for the manufacture of aircraft until the collapse of the industry around 1960. The airfield at Hurn was retained and is now classed as an International Airport.

Poole, with its military and industrial installations, received some attention by the Luftwaffe during the War. Some 82 buildings were completely destroyed and around 5000 (about 25 per cent) had some damage. Earlier, in 1937, nearly 800 houses – mainly in Old Town – had been condemned. The Council decided it would require some 4000 houses to meet the growing population.

Bournemouth survived relatively intact at the end of the War. Only infrequently was it a target and the final tally was 75 properties totally destroyed, 171 necessitating demolition, 675 seriously damaged but capable of repair, and some 9000 with minor damage. Some cleared spaces were given over to prefabricated houses – temporary buildings, although some were to remain for many years longer than intended. Houseboats were allowed along the Stour. But there was a will to provide homes, again, 'fit for heroes'. The post-Abercrombie plans outlined increased expansion with the map of Bournemouth covered with hatched areas, especially on the previously unbuilt fringes on the west, north and east of the borough. Lack of building materials delayed anything less than urgent repairs and development.

The expansion of open spaces in Bournemouth was especially mentioned by Abercrombie as being important to the town as a place of health and recreation, whether for holiday-makers or retired persons, both of which would likely increase. The plans proposed an increase in public open space by a third to 1624 acres. Some of this would be done by compulsory purchase.

In the 1930s, Hengistbury Head was considered ripe for development. The Brightlands Estate was started at the western end as early as 1928, and a long, wide avenue was laid out with sewers and services as far east as Double Dykes, appropriately named 'Broadway' but known locally as 'The Landing Strip'. It promised much prestigious development, but even at the start of the War, the only building constructed was 'The Saxon King' pub to await its influx of customers, whose blue-tiled roof stood out, isolated amongst green fields. A post-war, predominantly bungalow, development quickly expanded along Broadway until the new local residents, thinking enough was enough, agitated and achieved Green Belt status for the eastern portion of the Head in the 1950s. The general concept of Green Belt was pioneered in the UK in 1930, after pressure from the Council for the Preservation of Rural England and other organisations. The Town & Country Planning Act, 1947, allowed local authorities to establish Green Belt. Bournemouth took the opportunity to extend protection along the length of the Stour flood plains. The conurbation presently has the fifth largest of the 14 designated Green Belts in England.

Many of these peripheral areas, detached from habitation, were to suffer from being refuse tips in the 1940/50s. The realisation of heavy metals and other toxins leaching from domestic waste into the river was not greatly understood, although the Holdenhurst sewage works was often cited as polluting the river. The landfill altered the landscape, destroying marshland habitat, although presumably without protest. In the mid-1970s farmland was drained at Muscliff, and the course of the Stour was altered at Redhill to increase better flow of the waters. Such alterations were later to be blamed for flooding further down the river.

During the 1950s there came an increasing concern at Man's effect on the planet. On a less global scale, new agricultural practices were affecting wildlife. The BNSS Chairman of Entomology, W Cox, was probably echoing a general view when he suggested in 1958 that Lepidoptera were becoming scarcer from the widespread use of weed killers and insecticides.

By 1958 county naturalist trusts were forming across Britain. It was a movement that took some by surprise. These were different from the usual societies; they were proactive trusts acquiring and holding land as nature reserves. Norfolk had led the way in 1926, but the Hampshire and Isle of Wight Naturalists Trust was not formed until 1960. The Dorset Naturalists Trust was formed a year later. These formed under the aegis of the SPNC, and collectively changed their names to 'wildlife trusts' during the 1980s.

The post-war expansion in use of the motor car was both good and bad. It enabled families to explore the countryside, giving access to the New Forest, the chalk downs, etc. It was an independence that reduced the need for public transport. Some of the early victims were the rural bus routes, the loss of which meant even greater need of cars. It was a downward spiral.

New roads were needed to cater for this growth in traffic. Swathes were cut through the countryside, such as the Christchurch Bypass (in 1958) and the Bournemouth–Ringwood Spur Road (in 1960s). Counter to this, many railway tracks were torn up during the Beeching regime, and locally the Ringwood line was removed which created corridors through the western Forest. Where trains still ran, a later benefit was the use of diesel-electric locomotives instead of steam. No longer was there a need to regularly burn the embankments as a precaution against cinder-generated fires. The sloping sides were ideal habitats. Long-purged seeds could now flourish, and the fox had safe entry into the heart of the towns, where they are now firmly in residence, fed by litter louts and concerned individuals.

Further afield, it is now realised that the Bovington tank-testing ranges on the western fringes of our area have become nature havens, mostly untroubled by human activity apart from the occasional shell-burst. The Ministry of Defence recognises this serendipitous outcome and now positively assists with protection on many of its sites.

The car-borne excursionists can now be contained within compounds with leisure facilities with an environmental message. Moors Valley Country Park started life when East Dorset District Council purchased 82 acres in 1984. With a 9-hole golf course, narrow gauge railway, play area and visitor centre, the first phase opened in 1988. More acreage was added with new attractions later. With 750,000 attendances a year it has become one of the most popular parks in the south of England. With such sites the environmental aids become partially or wholly self-funding, thereby ensuring economic survival. The District Council is also responsible for some two dozen other sites – such as Parley and Poor Commons – and a Countryside Action Group of volunteers helps conservation work on them.

Hengistbury Head was released from defence use after the War, and returned to being a popular spot for recreation. It was commonplace for cars to be driven all over the site, eroding both the flora and the archaeology. Various restraints were brought in, backed by its designations as a Site of Special Scientific Interest, a Scheduled Ancient Monument and a Local Nature Reserve in 1990, with parts also being designated as an Environmentally Sensitive Area, Special Area of Conservation and a Site of Nature Conservation Interest. Rangers were employed to maintain the site, and the first Management Plan was produced in 1989. Some years earlier – in 1964 – an Outdoor Education and Field Studies Centre was opened on Christchurch Harbour. Its sailing activities were the more visible, but there was an important environmental aspect. The Head has maintained a valued site for field studies with coachloads of schoolchildren visiting from all over the south of England. The Centre was also the focus of the wildlife recording activities. Hengistbury Head is a complex site with six important habitat types, not least its heathland.

In 1992, the United Nations convened a World Summit at Rio de Janeiro. Its purpose was to ensure that the planet was to survive into the twenty-first century and be sustainable for future generations. 150 nations signed up agreeing to a raft of measures to effect this. The major concept was 'thinking globally; acting locally', giving the opportunity to make the changes necessary to every individual, every authority, every business, every country. It is referred to as 'Agenda 21'. The towns in our conurbation began their responses around 2000. Bournemouth adopted a Partnership scheme, since called 'Bournemouth 2026', which has attracted a membership of some 200 businesses, voluntary groups and service-providers, collectively working towards a sustainable town. Both Poole and Christchurch retained the Local Agenda 21 appellation for their action team. The underlying aim is to involve every individual into ensuring a viable future for the planet. With steering committees, working groups and forums, a dialogue of information and consensus is being developed.

One major factor from Rio was the government's production of the UK Biodiversity Action Plan (UK BAP) in 1994. Later, in 2002, a Biodiversity Strategy for England was launched, by which biodiversity was to be included in the policies of every public sector organisation.

In Dorset a partnership of 35 councils, environmental bodies, service providers and businesses, under the aegis of the Dorset Wildlife Trust, came together with the common aim to reverse the ecological decline with collaborative action. The Dorset Biodiversity Strategy appeared in 2003 as a ten-year project to highlight priority habitats and species.

The Bournemouth Environment Forum took some of the biodiversity aspects for inclusion into the Community Strategy. Ramifications of this are now producing a major project to monitor the wildlife of the Bournemouth parks and open spaces. This will be done with the help of the various Friends groups which have sprung up. The long decline in local parks during the 1970/80s as a result of low funding by local authorities across Western Europe in general, with the removal of park-keepers and the replacement of dedicated ground staff through Compulsory Competitive Tendering, has driven local communities to champion their local parks. 'Friends of' groups channel local opinion to the Council for improvements and actually undertake practical work. They have now become partners with the local authority and able to attract outside monies which the Councils cannot. A good local example has been the rise of the Friends of Boscombe Chine Gardens in 2002. It was a time of controversy about what trees needed removal, but also the time for applying for a Heritage Lottery Fund grant of £1.5 million for a major refurbishment of the Gardens, returning some of the Victorian elegance and including provision for improved wildlife habitat. It is now one of ten Green Flags the Bournemouth Council receive from the former Civic Trust for parks of high quality.

The Council compiled a Green Space Strategy in 2006 to cover parks and countryside to allotments, cemeteries, playing fields and verges. Some 18 per cent of the borough's land area, most of which is green space, is managed by Leisure Services. The document was designed to focus on the needs of residents and how to sustain the spaces both financially and ecologically. It was recognised that the growth in the provision of flats has increased the concrete footprint and reduced the amenity space for each housing unit. It is therefore important to ensure public open space remains available.

The single storey bungalow was land-hungry and needed to be set in a large garden to enhance the extravagance. Several locations proved ideal for these more expensive homes. Estates were carved out of former field sites, especially to the north of the borough. Green Belt was then seen as potential estates. In 1988, even the WWF – not normally involved with local enquiries – was moved to counter plans for housing on heathlands in the Ringwood and Wareham areas. Some 4500 homes were planned for St Leonards. This was just one site amongst the House Builders Federation objective to build 49,000 new homes in Dorset. Other targets were some 200 acres in Throop and Holdenhurst where there could be 4500 new homes. Green Belt was coming under threat.

Containing the living was one thing, another threat was from the dead, as Kinson Cemetery in 1989 sought to encroach on the nearby Common. Champions arose for both Kinson and Turbary Commons to fight such despoliation. A Dorset Heathland Forum, then a new group made up of county and local authority representatives, opposed the plans. A Dorset Heathland Strategy was adopted to protect the remaining pockets of the once-extensive habitat: some 85 per cent had been lost during two centuries. Dorset claimed the finest heaths in Europe, with a unique, if generally poorly appreciated flora and fauna. The Herpetological Conservation Trust was formed to protect the generally dismissed snakes and lizards and amphibia. Their work has aided knowledge of the animals and their requirements. An Urban Heaths Partnership is locally championing the heaths and endeavouring to protect this fragile habitat against their use by humans, not least by crazes of arson and quad bikes. Building close to heathland is being discouraged to lessen the human impact.

In the postwar period, farming has been squeezed out of the urban boroughs as former fertile fields are replaced with housing estates. There have been new demands on agricultural methods. Modern combine harvesters have necessitated larger fields and the removal of intervening hedgerows. Use of pesticides and fertilisers have leaked into the water systems.

New crops such as oilseed rape, which suddenly became popular in the 1970s, have made up a quarter of the sown fields, and the resultant overspill of seeds have made rape a common naturalised wild flower. A similar tale comes with American mink, farmed for its skins for the fur trade. Animals released from a Ringwood farm by animal rights activists in the 1990s, moved down the waterways and were found in Christchurch and elsewhere within a few weeks, where they are now part of the local fauna.

The Wildlife & Countryside Act, 1981, made it illegal to uproot any wild plant without permission from the owner. 'Plants' included also algae, fungi and **bryophytes**, but the collection of fungus for culinary purposes still poses legal problems. This Act also brought in far greater powers than the earlier Protection of Birds Act of 1954: killing of a larger range of birds and the collecting of eggs was severely punished.

English Nature was set up in 1990 to be responsible for the protection of the country's natural environment. Its brief covered not only the land with its flora and fauna, but also aquatic environments, geology and soils. In 2006, it amalgamated with the Countryside Agency and the Rural Development Service to be called Natural England. It was able to award the status of Sites of Special Scientific Interest and Areas of Outstanding Natural Beauty (AONB), but with the anthropocentric requirements of enjoyment and access rather than any necessarily intrinsic importance. It is the 'sustainable use of the natural environment'. In our area there are many clusters of SSSIs, and most of the Isle of Purbeck and Cranborne Chase are AONB. The conurbation is less blessed with woodland. Added regulations come from the European Union, the most important being the Conservation (Natural Habitats) Regulations 1994.

From Old Harry Rocks westwards to east Devon, the cliffs were designated a UNESCO World Heritage Site in 2001. This 95 miles (153 km) stretch of coastline provides an almost complete geological sequence through the Mesozoic period. Although mostly marine in origin, these sedimentary rocks were deposited during the time when dinosaurs reigned on earth, and has been nick-named 'The Jurassic Coast'. It is one of only a few geological sites to be protected by international legislation. Important educational possibilities come with this. Also wildlife can benefit from such protection. Durlston Country Park is a 'gateway' to the Jurassic Coast, although it was established in the 1970s by Dorset County Council. In June 2008 it received the status of National Nature Reserve from Natural England. It contains downland, sea cliffs – and the offshore waters are a Marine Research Area.

On the other side of Bournemouth, the New Forest gained National Park status on 1st March 2005. It was Britain's eighth National Park, but the first in the south east of England. The New Forest had seen a number of changes during the intervening years since the Royal Navy rape of timber in the early seventeenth century. Plantations were deliberately created later and these encroached on Commoners' rights. In 1877, the New Forest Act provided for a court of ten Verderers with six Agisters to regulate activity. However, the exigencies of the First World War caused the felling of broadleaf trees and their replacement by conifers. The Forestry Commission took control in 1923 of the Crown lands which make up most of the New Forest. This has been a benign situation. Alun Michael, the Minister of Rural Affairs at the time of National Park deliberations, stated the New Forest could not be a museum of landscape but would have to be a living place. Again, an anthropocentric viewpoint, but driven by having to persuade the public that their taxes spent on caring for the environment gave them some return. The Forestry Commission, originally established in 1919 to expand Britain's forests and woodlands, is now providing more access to the Forest, creating car parks, and walks, and educating the public. There are still around 3000 ponies freely wandering the Forest and the surrounding villages. These are a great attraction to visitors, but often become victims of night-time traffic.

The New Forest

Geology and Environment: The Forest occupies a central position on the Eocene Oligocene strata – lying in the downfold of the chalk of the Hants basin. The strata consists of mainly soft sands and clays, sediments laid during the Tertiary era. Overlying are Pleistocene gravels, some left as plateaus in the Forest.

The valley gravels are 'economic' aggregates – washed and graded for concrete. Plateau gravels contain clays worked dry and used for sub-base layers for roads, drives, and footpaths. Plateau gravels have been worked on the Western edge of the Forest on private heaths – Rockford common, Ibsley common, Gorley hill – these workings mutilate open heath scenery creating a conflict of industry with amenity, with restoration being difficult.

The soils tend to be more acid in the North; thus leading to the concentration of past agriculture in the South. Still today there is a greater diversity of flora in the Southern heaths and bogs.

The Forest consists of a series of eroded benches or plateaus; the highest in the North (Telegraph Post 175 m), the South less than 63 m. In the North stream erosion has left a series of high ridges separated by wide steep sided U shaped valleys. In the South and East plateaus are 15/46 m with a gentle slope to the Solent, less fragmented by drainage, forming an expansive undulating plain.

Impoverished soils with acid tolerant heathers and grassland are a major feature today. But widespread relics of former agriculture on the heaths suggest they were once productive. Pollen analysis shows heaths arose after early woodland cover was destroyed by early farming. In the valleys and folds of the Forest bogs or mires exist. These lowland bogs are a rare feature of Western Europe forming a unique if somewhat subtle environment.

The afforestation by the Crown has led over the centuries to a conflict of interest between the needs of the Crown for hunting and forestry and that of the commoners for livestock pasture. In the last century commoners' rights have been well recognized, with the canalizing of some Forest rivers to improve drainage and the drainage of the bogs, coupled with many decades of drier seasons, all helping to extend grazing areas. However, at the same time increasing recognition of the Forest as a public amenity and latterly as an important natural environment has recently led to a reversal of the above processes. Now rivers are being brought back to their original meandering routes and water is being drained back into the bogs, so the flora and fauna of the Forest is being preserved as it was under afforestation. Unfortunately the reversal is too late for many species now gone from the Forest.

The full effects of climate change are yet to be seen. However, all scenarios show increased precipitation and rises in temperature may be from 0.1 to 0.3 degrees centigrade per decade, noting that Britain's last continuous snow patch near Ben MacDhui melted in 1933. We may yet see changes to the flora, including the mix of trees normal for the Forest. Already we have once-rare visiting birds now breeding in the area.

By 8000 BP the ice had retreated from north of the Thames, woodland spreads and fauna such as red deer, *Cervus elephas*, wild ox, or aurochs, *Bos premigenius*, and wild boar, *Sus scrofa*, appear. Pollen analysis from the Forest peat shows that the emerging vegetation sequence starts with pine, willow and birch, followed by hazel, elm, ash and alder, and finally beech and pedunculate oak. The upper Palaeolithic (late Old Stone Age) is replaced by the Mesolithic hunter-gatherers, with scarce evidence on heathlands but they are widespread: some arrowheads and fine points for fish spear barbs are surface finds on Beaulieu Heath. It is believed that limited deforestation was used to offer grazing for game.

A hundred years ago the *Handbook of Bournemouth* mentioned a few Bronze Age barrows, the Roman pottery industry and the death of William Rufus; followed by dismissing the Forest from further discussion.

Neolithic *c*3200–1800 BC: Deforestation starts in earnest in Britain, with settled agriculture and burning off the forests. Cereal cultivation and livestock had arrived. However, Neolithic settlements are rare on heathland in Britain and the New Forest is no exception. A few arrowhead finds suggest the Forest was used for hunting.

Bronze Age, *c*1800–500 BC: In the New Forest the first major forest clearances seem to be in the Bronze Age with little evidence for Neolithic settlement. Progressive clearance with reduction of woodland and extension of heaths continued into modern times although reduced from the eleventh century onwards with changes restricted and controlled usage as it became a Royal Forest.

In the past pre-historians mainly looked at barrows, hill forts and later Roman kilns, early land use was not investigated. The archaeologist, Heywood Sumner, (a famous member of the Society) believed poor soils precluded farming, yet his fieldwork (1920–30) recorded many earthworks. The numerous Bronze Age barrows on the Southern heaths conflicted with his belief in low level agriculture. Field work by Passmore and Jones (1961–66) listed numerous abandoned enclosures and field systems. These vary from nineteenth century, to medieval and back to much earlier.

Abundant evidence of Middle Bronze Age and Late Bronze Age occupation is supported by pollen analysis of lowland heaths which show signs of cultivation. The destruction of woodland was followed by cereal cultivation which moved to other areas as soil nutrients were exhausted, thus changing the woodland to the heathland we would recognize today. (It is worth noting that upland moorlands such as Dartmoor were also created by man.) There is further evidence of Bronze Age occupation of the Forest with boiling mounds seen as crescent or kidney shaped piles of calcined flints found near streams. These were heated in hearths and the heated stones then placed in the pot to help cook the food. A Bronze Age pot was found in one boiling mound during excavation. The Ordnance Survey record 176 Bronze Age barrows in the Forest. Sumner recorded a further 133 around Bournemouth. The Bronze Age farmers let in the weather! The soils were reduced by rain, and then the Forest became a land of coarse grasses, bracken and heather. The process of podzolisation goes along with changes from deciduous to heather moor. Pollen analysis shows the following cycle: deciduous woodland ? grassland (cereals) ? grass heath ? heather.

Iron Age 500 BC–AD 43: Evidence of the Iron Age is sparse compared to the Bronze Age suggesting that soil fertility had already dropped. Cultivation was now no longer viable in most of the Forest. It has been suggested that the clearance of woodland started in the Mesolithic to increase grazing for game, continued in the Neolithic, culminating with increased Bronze Age farming.

Iron Age occupation is shown by a 'few' enclosures, hill forts and the first cart burial found in the UK (Hatchet Moor). Hill forts can be found such as Tatchbury Mount which is 9 m above its surroundings with a double /triple entrenchment, Malwood Castle with a square bank and ditch, also Castle Hill on the western edge of the Forest overlooking the Avon valley near Fordingbridge. Other minor and potential forts have been recorded.

Roman AD 43–410: The Romans used a more sophisticated agriculture and supported a larger population in Britain. Land cleared and cropped by primitive techniques had lost its nutrients and was no longer worth cultivating on a large scale by the Romans.

Roman occupation of the Forest appears confined to the pottery industry, sites for this are mainly at Latchmoor Brook, Dickens Water, Ashley Hole valleys, and outliers near Burley. The need for replenishment of wood for charcoal and fresh clay deposits may explain the large number of kilns in the Forest caused by a move to fresh productive ground. It was however a large long-standing industry existing

5¼ inches high. Brown, with white pattern.

Light Brown. 4¼ inches high.   Brown Ware. 4¼ inches high.

Red patterns on bases of fawn-coloured pottery. Diameters, 4 inches.

Examples of Pottery found in the New Forest, Hampshire.

New Forest pottery (Revd J Pemberton)

mainly through the third and fourth centuries AD. The products known as New Forest Ware are found over many regions of Britain. The nearest known settlement is to the East of the Forest at Nursling (Onna), with some remnant of a road heading into the Forest.

Settlement: *Domesday Book* provides the earliest historical evidence. Not all the Forest has poor soils as is reflected in the modern settlement patterns; which start from Saxon times onwards. Little is known or recorded after the end of the Roman period in the Forest until the Normans. *The Anglo-Saxon Chronicle* refers to a battle between the British and the Saxons in the late fifth early sixth centuries, with a landing by Cerdic and the defeat of the British at Downton. It implies that the Avon valley was the area of action on the western edge of the Forest. Place names in the Forest, apart from obvious later names such as Beaulieu (beautiful place), are of Germanic origin with settlements on more fertile sites which form the basis of settlement and permanent agricultural patterns in the Forest today.

Early Saxons treated infertile wild lands as common hunting grounds. Emergence of the aristocracy reduced free rights of the chase as late Saxon Kings reserved the chase of the deer for themselves. Restrictions were more vigorous under Norman forest law. The area was afforested by 1086 (1079 the official date) initially with extreme penalties, later becoming lenient, together with various privileges to be known as the Rights of Common (note: registration of land with common rights claimed as published in 1858 is the written basis of common rights today).

Roman kiln (Heywood Sumner)

The New Forest was declared a Royal hunting preserve in AD 1079: The fauna included red and fallow deer, wild boar and small game. Royal hunting lasted for a long time with six hunting lodges (thirteenth to fifteenth centuries) identified. Charles II was the last King to hunt in the Forest and in 1666 he and Nell Gwyn stayed in the lodge now known as the New Park Manor hotel. In fact, it seems five out of the six lodges are currently hotels having passed through the stage of gentleman's country residences. Beaulieu was the area containing King John's hunting lodge circa 1199, but lies outside our area of interest. Under Queen Victoria the Deer Removal Act of 1851 finally finished the Forest as a hunting preserve.

The *Domesday Book* states 'In Nova Foresta et Circa Ea' (In the New Forest and around it) were 102 holdings, many on the periphery of today's Forest. Most were on the terrace soils of the Avon valley and between Christchurch and Lymington. The total population exceeded 2000. Many sites were reduced in value due to becoming part of the Royal Forest known as 'afforestation'. Except for 21 sites some level of depopulation occurred during the period 1066–1086 and then it is believed that this was followed by a slow re-occupation.

Many of the above alleged lost settlements are represented today by names of farms and localities but not settlements or parishes. Examples: Sloden SU210130 and Eyeworth Lodge SU225145. Also the sites of many Roman kilns are in this area suggesting that the lost villages had a long history. Very little evidence has been found to support the 'lost settlement' argument.

Afforestation did not necessarily mean the land became Crown property but the King could subject other mens' land to Forest Law, so that it could not be enclosed or cultivated; even free range pastoral use came under restrictions. However, Commoners' rights of pasture became established with cattle, ponies, sheep and common mast (pigs in the pannage season) able to wander onto the King's land and the royal deer allowed to wander onto other mens' land.

The heaths would be readily colonized by holly, oak, hawthorn, etc. Even the most nutrient-deficient soils are colonized by acid-tolerant birch and Scots pine. However the development of scrub to woodland is inhibited by the browsing and grazing of deer and stock assisted by controlled burning.

One viable industry for 'waste land' since mediaeval times to the mid twentieth century has been warrening. Pillow mounds are now considered evidence of artificially aided rabbit warrens and many were recorded on the western side of the Forest, now destroyed by gravel working. However, there is evidence of pillow mounds in the Forest near the fine seventeenth century house Moyles Court.

Military: At the extreme south-east edge of the area we cover, at the seaward end of a spit, lies Hurst Castle extending out from Milford on Sea. It defends the western approaches to the Solent. The oldest element is an artillery fort completed by Henry VIII in 1544. This attractive building was updated in 1803 to include stronger vaulted ceilings to support the weight of new cannon. The basement roof was also strengthened to protect the magazine. By 1870 it had become one of Palmerston's Follies, acquiring enormous armoured wings to house 38-ton rifled guns. In 1893 the massive guns were augmented by a battery of quick-firing guns emplaced outside the East wing. It was garrisoned in both World Wars as part of the coastal artillery defence.

The Alternative Fireplace: The First World War saw a harvest of needed timber and the Portuguese Fireplace near Highland Water is a reminder of the troops stationed in the forest for collecting timber. The gunpowder factory at Eyeworth, near Fritham, increased production. A turf covered powder store is still visible in one of the fields in the area.

Hurst Castle Cannon Proof Vaulting

Mr Ray Powell from Dorset tells the following concerning his uncle Harry Higgins. Harry was a gunner before the Great War and after completing his time in the Royal Artillery he emigrated to Canada. From October 1914 onwards Canada sent troops to Britain. These included The Princess Patricia's Light Infantry composed of former British soldiers. Among these was Harry, now with logging experience, assigned to the Forest with others. Whether he worked alongside the Portuguese or separately is not known at this time. At the end of the war Harry married Mary Legg, Ray's maternal aunt, and settled in Poole. Harry, well remembered for his practical abilities, told in detail of an enormous fireplace he had once built in the corner of the hut where he billeted because of the severe winter in the Forest. The 'corner' aptly fits the construction of the existing fireplace. The mystery remains, was it built by the Portuguese or by a very cold soldier called Harry?

The Second World War saw a large number of airfields built in the Forest mainly to support tactical operations leading up to and during the invasion of Europe. The control tower at Ibsley

Portugese Fireplace

*Ibsley Wartime
Control Tower*

is a remaining feature of that time.

Ashley Walk became a major bombing range that is still pock marked with bomb craters and includes many features one of which is a slightly scaled down replica of the German U-Boat pens with a two metre thick ferro-concrete roof, now covered to resemble a giant tumulus and shown as such on OS Maps.

At the National Record Centre Kew can be found map references for Allied tanks that became bogged down during exercises in the mires but had vanished by the time the recovery crews turned up a few days later.

The evolution of the Forest from a Royal hunting preserve to its current status

Statute 1224: For the Drift of the Forest – Drift is used to improve stock and weed out poor ponies, a term still used today for the pony round-ups.

Pressure from landowners led to the Charta de Foresta 1217: extensive disafforestation allowing legal enclosures and cultivation under license from the Crown.

In 1279 a legal boundary was established for the Forest, placing many holdings outside the Forest and Forest law – mainly unchanged until modified by the New Forest Act 1964.

67,000 acres of crown land is prevented from reclamation or cultivation. Successive acts of Parliament since 1698 provided for enclosure of land for timber – today 19,600 acres of statutory silvicultural enclosures exist with not more than 17,600 acres fenced at any one time. Also approximately 2,300 acres of absolute freeholds of the Crown with 44,500 acres as common grazing of heath, bog and woodland exists.

From the fifteenth century interest changed gradually from deer preservation to timber production as England moved to become a maritime nation.

After the sixteenth century timber for the Navy became of growing importance with early enclosures to protect timber. This created legal conflict between Commoners and the need for timber which went on for hundreds of years. This was caused initially by growing yew for bows, raw wood for charcoal for smelting of marine fittings, and finally large timbers for shipbuilding. The next three Acts indicate how the Commoners' pasture is reduced and unprotected, followed by further Acts to redress the balance.

1483 first Act to encourage tree growing. Naval enclosures caused a fear that a forest with no pasture would ensue.

1698 Act dedicated a further 6,000 acres to trees (today two-thirds is open to grazing and one-third timber production).

1851 Deer Removal Act confirmed that the Crown no longer protected the deer but large scale enclosures of timber. This Act was followed by the formation of the New Forest Commoners' Defence Association and the New Forest Association.

1847 The railway arrives linking Southampton with Dorchester thus opening the Forest as a leisure amenity. Gerald Lascelles, Deputy Surveyor (1880–1915), thought that the New Forest should be a national park for amenity rather than the growing of timber,

1877 The above associations petition the Government leading to the Act of 1877; Crown enclosures became subject to regulation and control with only 16,000 acres fenced and a permanent 44,000 acres for the Commoners free of restrictions.

1923 Management of the Forest passed to the Forestry Commission. The public criticized the intent of the Commission to replace hard wood stands with conifers. The protection of ancient and ornamental woodland became of public concern.

1949 The Act of 1949 included many recommendations for protecting the Forest for all. The Forest experienced increasing damage to tracks and livestock from the motor car. In 1963 there was an accident every day.

1964 Act and the 1949 Act govern the Forest today and many believed that with such acts protecting the Forest and its management there was no need for the forest to officially become a National Park. The 1964 Act included the fencing of major routes and the provision of underpasses for the animals.

However the Forest is now designated a National Park and we wait with interest to discover what difference it will make.

At the turn of the century, the 2001 Census showed populations of Poole, Bournemouth and Christchurch being 138,288, 163,444 and 44,869, respectively. Bournemouth has come to outgrow its older neighbours. The land between has filled with housing and all its paraphernalia. It is regarded as a conurbation. Several times during the 20th century it acted thus, and several times discussion moved towards creating a unified authority. Poole fought against such a proposal after the Abercrombie plan, wishing to preserve its identity in a bid for County Borough status. With the inclusion as part of the South West Region Assembly, the discussion has again arisen although the three boroughs became more united against a perceived imposed threat.

The politics behind this need not be discussed here. From a wildlife point of view, this conurbation sits as a black blob amongst some of the finest habitat in Britain, if not the world. The Dorset Environmental Records Centre was established in 1976. Like the other nation-wide county recording units, it is an independent organisation designed to collect data relating to the whole of Dorset, using contemporary sources and researching earlier records.

Recent decades have seen the rise of specialist groups dealing with bats, deer, butterflies, otters, badgers – even plant galls. Field work is increasingly being done by professionals and experts. Whilst groups like the Christchurch Harbour Ornithological Group produce such important work, the amateur still provides valuable input. Many a species distribution map shows a void at the conurbation in an otherwise sea of dots. There is a need to adjust our focus and familiarise ourselves with our urbanised flora and fauna neighbours. A start is being made to recognise the value of urban wildlife and to record what is on our doorstep. Dorset Wildlife Trust in 2005 established its Urban Wildlife Programme. There are a number of factors driving and influencing this. Urban wildlife trusts are slowly growing – Avon, London, etc. Their conservation role complements the knowledge gained by the more passive observer. Dorset Wildlife Trust's Urban Programme, based at Corfe Mullen, encourages a more active understanding of the conurbation wildlife. Allied to the organisation is a joint project with Bournemouth University to survey the wildlife of local green spaces, using teams of specialised experts working with interested amateurs.

The past two hundred years has been a journey of wildlife appreciation, from sporting quarry, or at least tolerance, to objects of concern and understanding. There exists a wide audience wanting to learn more about the natural world around them. Bournemouth is privileged by its location which impinges on a variety of beautiful habitats and amazing ecosystems. The average person needs guides through this wonderful world of life to stimulate their interests. At a time when societies themselves are becoming endangered species, there is an important role still left to the broadly-based natural history societies still extant which, as enshrined in the rules of the BNSS, seek to promote 'interest in and knowledge of the Natural Sciences'. The present volume hopes to do just that.

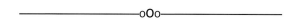

Maps

2 Geology

Justin Delair

TOPOGRAPHY

Even a cursory glance at the topography (the surface landscape), of the Bournemouth area (see the map on p. v) shows it to be surprisingly varied, itself the principal cause of the great interest it has held for the naturalist, past and present. This variety is spread somewhat unevenly across the four distinct regions into which the area can be conveniently divided.

The largest region (Area 1) includes all of the country inland of the coast fronting Poole and Christchurch bays eastwards of an imaginary line drawn between Lytchett Minster in the south and Edmondsham in the north. This region thus encompasses all the terrain up to that line west of the River Avon and all that part of the New Forest falling within the area's eastern sector.

Extending more or less uninterruptedly for roughly equal distances north, east, and west of Bournemouth's municipal boundaries, generally low-lying gently undulating territory typifies the region's present topography. This has been excavated locally to form shallow valleys by the larger rivers (Avon, Stour, Allen, etc.), all streams emanating from sources beyond the area's far north western limits. Together with numerous lesser streams, these rivers represent the region's main surface drainage system. In the east the New Forest rivers are relatively minor streams, in few cases directly connected to the rivers just alluded to. As explained later, they have none the less influenced aspects of the past developments of the New Forest's present topography.

The small, though still quite extensive region westwards of the above mentioned Lytchett Minster/Edmondsham line (Area 2), is generally more elevated and characterised by a landscape of low chalk hills. It also includes the picturesque valleys of the upper reaches of the Allen and Stour rivers, along with much of the country known to naturalists and antiquarians as Cranborne Chase.

The next region (Area 3) lies west-south-west of Bournemouth proper. It includes island-strewn Poole Harbour, England's largest natural marine haven, and all the rather flat neighbouring heathland extending southwards to the lowest flank of the striking Purbeck Hills and eastwards to Studland Bay. It is noteworthy for the coastal sand dunes occupying the northern extremity of Studland Peninsula bordering Shell Bay, for the area's only sizeable natural inland body of water, the Little Sea, on the same peninsula, and for the fact that, except for the Frome, every river and stream traversing it flows due north into Poole Harbour. Though once far greater, a point amplified later, the comparatively insignificant east-flowing River Frome enters the Harbour from the west close to the historic town of Wareham.

Our final region (Area 4) embraces the range of the Purbeck Hills from Handfast Point, or The Foreland, in the east to Povington Hill (207 metres above mean sea level) in the west, as well as all the less elevated land southwards to the scenically impressive and often precipitous coastline between Kimmeridge Bay and Ballard Down north of Swanage Bay. This lower topography is generally hillier than that of the three preceding regions, marked by steep narrow valleys at many places plunging seawards between the cliffs.

Apart from the Corfe River draining northwards through the Corfe Gap, into our third region, and the short River Swan flowing eastwards to Swanage Bay every other stream in Area 4, all very minor ones at that, flows southwards to the cliff-girt coast.

GEOLOGY

The success of animals and plants at exploiting given terrestrial or marine habitats is unquestionably dependent not only on the habitat's geographical setting, but also on its prevailing annual weather cycle, and its geological under-pinning. Precisely such factors have produced the natural conditions associated with the Bournemouth area's present faunal and floral inhabitants. Changes to environmental regimes inevitably affect continuing suitability for pre-existing faunal and floral organisms.

Although geological or geomorphological activities often initiate such changes they can arise either separately or jointly, abruptly or slowly, or even from quite other causes (e.g. artificial canalization or diversion of formerly natural streams, unplanned pollution, or from accidents – such as invasion of mudlands by *Spartina* grass). Habitats, therefore, can be modified abruptly and severely, or over longer periods and less acutely.

Examples of all these effects have occurred at various times in Bournemouth's geological past, sometimes surprisingly recently, and mostly as the outcome of geological changes of significance.

On considering the area's geology more fully, it will be helpful at the outset to note that geological strata is commonly classified, mapped, and studied as solid or drift geology.

Solid geology is a term used to differentiate strata (e.g. Sandstone or Chalk) deposited antecedent to the later erratic accumulation upon them of scattered superficial deposits (e.g. gravels or soils). These latter are appropriately termed drift. Both solid and drift geology are well represented in the Bournemouth 'area'.

In the following account solid deposits are often referred to simply as 'rocks', irrespective of whether they are genuinely hard (consolidated) limestones, sandstones, or ironstones, or softer (unconsolidated) clays, sands, or grits.

Many of the rocks we shall consider contain fossils. These, often of great variety, provide valuable insights into the environmental conditions under which the rocks containing them were deposited. They show what the climates must have been like and where now long-vanished contemporary continents, islands and coastlines apparently once existed. They also reveal what kinds of life forms inhabited these bygone lands and seas. The various kinds of fossils met with will be briefly assessed relative to the rocks hosting them, thereby corroborating that organic evolution has indeed responded down the long corridor of time to ever-changing environmental conditions.

The area's oldest rocks date from late Jurassic times, approximately 150 million years ago, and occur in the Isle of Purbeck (Area 4). Its youngest rocks, of late Eocene age, laid down about 35 million years ago, are met with around Milford on Sea (Area 1).

Exposures of the area's very earliest rocks occur in the cliffs and foreshore ledges at Kimmeridge Bay (Area 4). They consist of alternating bands of limestones and clays, which were initially deposited as sediments on an ancient sea floor. These rocks are collectively termed and mapped as the Kimmeridge Clay; and despite the lower bands of limestones and clays not being visible at the bay, the complete series, observable further west, is known to attain a thickness of 500 m.

Embedded in these rocks, which were deposited on the floor of a warm, muddy sea, are the fossilised remains of countless late Jurassic animals. These are mostly marine organisms, commonest of all are the coiled shells of ammonites, distant relatives of today's squids and the nautilus. Examples of large crushed ammonites can be found on some of the foreshore ledges at low tide. There also are the remains of smaller shelled creatures, crabs and marine worms together with the bony remnants of extinct species of fish and enormous aquatic reptiles such as ichthyosaurus, plesiosaurus, pliosaurus and marine crocodiles. Rarer discoveries have included water-borne teeth and bones of land dwelling dinosaurs and flying pterosaurs. These finds demonstrate that dry land had not been far distant.

Kimmeridge ledges looking west

The Kimmeridge Clay is a celebrated source rock for the oil reserves in the North Sea, and there is enough of the organic matter that forms the basis of oil in the rocks that some parts of the cliff have caught fire in the past. Despite this, the oil pumped from greater depths by the 'nodding donkey' on the nearby cliffs comes from the Lower Jurassic Lias and the reservoir is the Middle Jurassic Cornbrash about 320 m below the cliffs.

The Kimmeridgian beds dip slowly eastwards, past Hounstout Cliff and Rope Lake Head, before finally disappearing below the surface on the west side of St Aldhelm's Head.

The next oldest strata are the Portlandian series which, directly overlying the Kimmeridgian beds, mark the shallowing of the marine conditions that characterised late Jurassic times. They consist of sands and clays (the Portland Sands), underlying fine limestones (the Portland Stone), deposited in comparatively shallow water. Although taking their name from the Isle of

Hounstout Cliff from St Albans Head

Portland (many miles west of the Bournemouth area), in Purbeck the Portland beds actually reach a greater thickness (73 m), outcropping eastwards along the coast from Hounstout Cliff to Durlston Head. Good inland exposures occur in quarries at Coombe Bottom and St Aldhelm's Head.

While the architectural merit of Portland stone is reviewed elsewhere, here we highlight the abundance in it at several horizons of interesting assemblages of marine invertebrate fossils, and particularly the enormous size of certain ammonites. Most of the previously noticed Kimmeridgian vertebrate groups were still represented, but more rarely and by different species, as the Portland sea was far shallower than the Kimmeridge sea, with the pure limestones having formed in areas of shallow, warm sand bars, conditions not unlike the Bahamas today.

Purbeck rocks – alternating successions of limestones, shales, and sandy marls overlie the Portland beds, and reach a thickness of 120 m at Durlston Bay. About 140 million years old, they exemplify shallow-water and terrestrial deposits accumulated under **lacustrine** and lagoonal conditions created by the withdrawal of the earlier Portlandian sea. Occasionally deposits left by transient marine incursions also occur, indicating that land was generally low-lying and characterised by numerous seasonal water courses, mudflats and salt pans. The latter, induced by high evaporation, implies a continuance of warm temperatures.

Purbeck rocks are well seen in the coastal cliffs from St Aldhelm's Head to Peveril Point on Swanage Bay's south shore, and in numerous inland quarries before the Purbeck beds themselves disappear in the north below the younger Wealden beds.

The sequence of rocks exposed at Durlston Bay is world famous as it contains the **type section** of the Purbeck strata as well as the boundary separating the Jurassic and Cretaceous periods (Table 2.1), although its exact position within the sequence is still under debate.

GEOLOGICAL TIME-SCALE				
ERA	PERIOD	EPOCH	Start Million years ago.	Duration Million years
Cainozoic	Quaternary	Holocene	0.01	0.01
		Pleistocene	1.81	1.8
	Neogene	Pliocene	5.3	3.5
		Miocene	23.8	18.5
	Palaeogene	Oligocene	33.7	9.9
		Eocene	55	21.3
		Palaeocene	65	10
Mesozoic	Cretaceous	Late		77
		Early	142	
	Jurassic	Late		64
		Middle		
		Early	206	
	Triassic	Late		42
		Middle		
		Early	248	
Palaeozoic	Permian	Late		42
		Early	290	
	Carboniferous	Late		64
		Early	354	
	Devonian	Late		63
		Middle		
		Early	417	
	Silurian	Late		26
		Early	443	
	Ordovician	Late		52
		Middle		
		Early	495	
	Cambrian	Late		50
		Middle		
		Early	545	
Precambrian	Proterozoic		2500	1505
	Archean		3800	1300
	Hadean		4600	800

Table 2.1 Geological Timescale

An overview of the commercial exploitation of the celebrated 'Purbeck Marble' and other associated limestones is provided later.

Fossils are prolific, mostly comprising fresh and brackish water invertebrates, but while particular forms may abound at a specific horizon, they may be scarce in adjacent ones; other animals may be restricted to just a single isolated horizon. Near the base of the Purbeck rocks are levels with fossil soils containing the stumps and trunks of coniferous trees, many partly overgrown by algae that lived in the warm swampy conditions.

Especially important are the crustaceans known as ostracods, and molluscs dominate several horizons. Predictably, marine creatures like ammonites and belemnites are absent, although the sea-urchin *Hemicidaris purbeckensis* flouts this rule. Insects and the isopod *Archaeoniscus* occur commonly at a number of horizons.

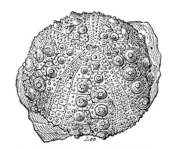

Hemicidaris Purbeckensis, E. Forbes.
Middle Purbeck.

Fig 2.1 Hemicidaris purbeckensis

Of outstanding interest is the remarkable range of fossil vertebrates found in these rocks. These include rare fishes peculiar to Purbeck conditions, remnants of some of the earliest true frogs, a unique series of dwarf crocodiles, the only known occurrence of Purbeckian ichthyosaurs and a unique early rhynchocephalian *Homoeosaurus*, an unusually large long-necked pterosaur, at least two apparently miniature dinosaurs, various primitive ground lizards, and many full-sized turtles, all complementing a population of some of the oldest known mammals. Some of these have been named *Plagiaulax*, *Amblotherium*, *Triconodon*, and *Peralestes*. They belonged to four long extinct mammalian orders ancestral to the living marsupials and other primitive mammals of more recent development. Even fossil egg-shells have been found.

Fossilised footprints and tracks of two- and four-legged dinosaurs occur in these rocks together with plant remains. Of the latter conifers and cycads (tree ferns) predominate. An interesting exception is *Chara*, a stonewort placed botanically between the algae and the **bryophytes**. It exemplifies the immense antiquity of such plants.

The following 15 or so million years saw continuing marine recession and a rejuvenation of pre-existing rivers. This resulted in the creation of a large shallow freshwater basin across much of southern England. Huge quantities of river-borne detritus were discharged into this basin to a thickness, at Swanage, of 716 m. Deposited as bands of clay, shales,

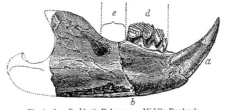

Plagiaulax Becklesii, Falconer. Middle Purbeck.
Right ramus of lower jaw, magnified two diameters.
a. Incisor. *b, c*. Line of vertical fracture behind the pre-molars. *d*. Three pre-molars, the third and last (much larger than the other two taken together) being divided by a crack. *e*. Sockets of two missing molars.

Fig 2.2 Plagiaulax becklesii

marls, sands, and coarse grits, and known as the Wealden formation, these rocks blanketed the preceding Purbeck beds. In our area these deposits are confined to Area 4 south of the Purbeck Hills (Map 2.1).

Map 2.1 Geology locations

Commercial exploitation of these beds has been limited to brick-making at Godlingston, and, briefly in the nineteenth century, to harvesting ironstone concretions at Swanage Bay.

Fossils of freshwater invertebrates and fishes, and land and aquatic reptiles occur in these Wealden beds, alongside primitive mammals like those in the Purbeck rocks. Like those of insects, remains of conifers and numerous kinds of tree-ferns occur in considerable abundance. The climate was evidently tropical or subtropical.

About 120 million years ago, the ocean again invaded the land and, as a shallow sea, drowned the low-lying Wealden landscape, depositing upon it a basal bed of pebbles followed by sands, shales and multi-coloured clays. Together these deposits comprise the Lower Greensand.

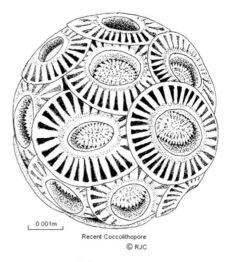

0.001m

Recent Coccolithopore
© RJC

Fig 2.3 Coccolithopore

As with the Gault and Upper Greensand deposits (reviewed below), those of the Lower Greensand formation are restricted to a narrow strip of land on the southern flanks of the Purbeck Hills. They are best viewed at their seawards end in Punfield Cove on the northern shore of Swanage Bay. Lesser exposures of them occur at Corfe and nearby Challow, although they nowhere attain any great thickness.

Varied marine fossils occur profusely, the commonest being lamellibranchs (bivalves) and gastropods. Ammonites, crustaceans, the teeth of sharks, and worm-bored wood are also met with; such evidence confirms that the climate remained warm.

Overlying the Lower Greensand are, in ascending order, the Gault clays and Upper Greensand. formations. These accumulated on the floor of a deepening sea, sometimes to a thickness reaching 58 m.

A band of quartz or lydite pebbles everywhere prominently mark the juncture of the Gault with the Lower Greensand. The best Gault exposures again appear at Punfield Cove while those of the Upper Greensand near the base of nearby Ballard Cliff.

The Gault clays are black and organically rich, but comparatively unfossiliferous, whereas the sands of the Upper Greensand are much paler grey-green glauconitic deposits containing phosphate nodules and a profusion of fossils. Oysters and spiral worm tubes are exceedingly common at some horizons, with other fossils such as ammonites, sea urchins and shark teeth being seen at some levels. As plant fossils are scarce it has been suggested that, due to marine expansion, land was more distant.

The next 30 million years or so witnessed the steady accumulation on the sea floor of the Chalk formation. Chalk (Latin *Creta*) thereby gives the Cretaceous Period (Table 2.1) its distinctive name.

This sea (christened Tethys by geologists) drowned vast tracts of land as it spread as far as the Americas, Russia, Australia, and New Zealand. It was home to countless marine organisms and algae composed of minute coccolithopores, which, when they died and sank to the sea floor, accumulated over long periods to form the Chalk deposits. Locally, these deposits occur along the coast between Ballard Cliff and Studland. The visible upper stretches of the Purbeck Hills (the boundary of our Areas 3 and 4) likewise consist of Chalk, which, as a wide-ranging deposit, does not reappear in the Bournemouth area except in Cranborne Chase (Area 2). The geomorphological portion of this chapter (pp 53–54) explains the cause of this apparent hiatus.

Not all the known Chalk beds even occur in our area. The uppermost (latest) Chalk deposits were eroded away before the lowest (first) rocks of the following Tertiary (Cainozoic) Era were laid down. Thus, in the cliffs west of Handfast Point fronting Studland Bay, where the Chalk and these Tertiary deposits meet, is an unconformity, a depositional phenomenon of rare occurrence in the Bournemouth area.

Almost exclusively marine, Chalk fossils include sponges, sea-urchins, bivalve shells, ammonites, belemnites, a great array of fishes, and large swimming reptiles contemporary with the last dinosaurs resident on more distant dry land. All imply the

Unconformity, Studland

prevalence of a warm climate. At some localities Chalk has been dug commercially for lime burning and other purposes.

Commencing about 65 million years ago, the earlier part of the Tertiary Era (Table 2.1) is intimately associated with the Hampshire Basin (Map 2.2) and well represented in the Bourne-mouth area.

The Hampshire Basin resulted from an early Tertiary uplift of the Earth's surface concomitant with a widespread retreat of the sea, the surviving waters of which, in southern England, were confined to the newly formed basin.

Meteorologically eroded sediments from these recently uplifted land areas were carried by rivers and deposited as

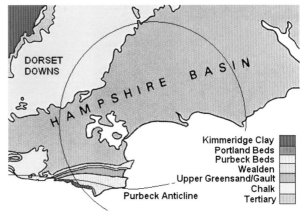

Map 2.2 Hampshire Basin

detritus on the basin's floor. The volume of this detritus was often high. The basin's shoreline frequently advanced and receded locally, causing rivers to alter course, deepen, become shallow, or bifurcate. It also caused offshore mud and gravel bars to form and affect marine circulation as the rate and volume of detrital deposition and the frequency, lateral extent, and physical composition of specific sediments repeatedly changed. This is characteristic of Tertiary strata throughout the Bournemouth area.

The area's lowest (oldest) Tertiary rocks, the Reading Beds, are best seen at Studland, although inland exposures of them occur near Wimborne and around Cranborne. Overall their thickness varies from 15–30 m. They are notable for a basal sandy clay containing brown ironstone and a profusion of blackened rolled flints derived from the eroded underlying Chalk. Mottled clays and multi-coloured sands overlie this basal bed.

Approximately 60 million years ago another marine incursion caused the Reading Beds to be covered by 30 m of sands and clays known as the Basement Bed of the London Clay. That stratum, and the Reading Beds, once regarded as separate early formations of the Eocene Period, are now considered to be different aspects of the preceding Palaeogene Period (Table 2.1).

The Basement Bed is generally sandy, and locally crowded with remains of *Ditrupa* (a fossil marine worm) and fish otoliths.

Overlying the Basement Bed is the London Clay proper. It is the lowest (oldest) deposit of the Eocene Period, which began about 55 million years ago. It reached a thickness of around 100 m in a well-boring at Christchurch, but is appreciably thinner elsewhere, being just 27.4 m thick at Verwood. Generally it is a bluish-grey clay containing scattered septarian nodules, and is thought to be a marine deposit. Despite yielding fossilised plant fragments at Studland, a nearly complete uncrushed turtle at Verwood, and occasional fossils elsewhere of crabs, gastropods and bivalves, it is not very fossiliferous. The climate was evidently wet and subtropical.

The London Clay is capped by the Poole Formation (previously termed the Bagshot Beds), mostly deposited by rivers draining from the west, although several brief marine incursions also contributed to its creation. The constituent rocks are well developed in the Purbeck heathlands south and south-west of Poole Harbour (Area 3), and comprise a mixture of clays, silts, and cross-bedded sands. These were recently divided into eight sequences identified by separate local names.

Of the named sequences, the lowest (oldest) is the Broadstone Sand (formerly known as the Redend Sandstone). It occurs prominently in the cliffs at Redend Point fronting Studland Bay, where iron oxides have coloured coarse river sands bright yellow and red in seemingly random fashion through pyrite oxidation. Clay, hosting subtropical plant stems and leaves, occurs in the cliffs to the north,

Red End Point, Studland Bay looking N

while the cliffs still further north consist of consolidated blown sand.

Much of the Purbeck heath's surface is covered by a coarse pebbly iron-stained grit consolidated after deposition. Known today as the Parkstone Sand, it was formerly called the Agglestone Grit. Its maximum thickness is some 11 m, and it has been used sporadically as building stone. Two outcrops on Godlingston Heath, known as the Agglestone and Puckstone respectively, have, through being linked to local myth, highlighted this grit in popular folklore for centuries.

Agglestone Rock. P Climenson 1906

Agglestone Rock. R Chapman 2008

As the text states the Agglestone is formed from an iron-stained consolidated sandstone which at one time formed a hard layer on the surface. Now generally eroded away it had left many small pieces littering the heathland and a smaller stone called the Puckstone as well as the Agglestone. The pebbly grit was deposited by a large eastward flowing river some 45 million years ago. The Agglestone is perched on a conical mound of sand which has been protected by the rock the erosion process having left the rock standing. Hardy, 1910, had a different explanation. He believed that the area had been extensively quarried for building material and for hand mill stones; the quarrying had left the Agglestone behind. Up until 1970 the rock stood in an anvil like position but erosion of the sand mound caused it to tilt into the position that it exhibits today. Hardy had also predicted that this would happen, he also suggested that it may have been a Logan Stone. This is a suspended stone that may be rocked by pushing as occurs in Cornwall and Scotland.

There is of course the local explanation referred to in the text:

'Myths … are often found attached to erratic blocks of stone. Thus, one of a somewhat analogous character is current in relation to that remarkable mass of ferruginous sandstone known as 'the Agglestone,' in the Isle of Purbeck.

The country people say of it that his Satanic majesty (who is often a very important personage in these capricious freaks) was one day sitting on the Needles Rocks, Isle of Wight, whence espying Corfe Castle in the distance, he took the cap from his head and threw it across the sea, with the intent of demolishing that structure.

But it would appear that he had over-estimated his powers of jactation, for the missile fell short of its mark, and there it stands to this day on Studland Heath, a monument of disappointed malice, a wonder to the peasantry, and a theme of antiquarian conjecture.

Notes and Queries, March 3rd 1866

The object of the Devil's displeasure is sometimes differently given as Old Harry Rocks, Studland church or Salisbury Cathederal. The rock has also been called 'The Devil's Anvil' for obvious reasons looking at the old picture.

The Agglestone is easily reached across the heath from Studland Village and it makes for a very pleasant walk with some beautiful views with interesting geology and natural history.

Succeeding the Agglestone Grit is a series of current-bedded sands and clays known as the Bournemouth Freshwater Series, thought by some geologists to partially overlap the next geological rocks, the Bracklesham Beds. The Bournemouth Freshwater Series overlie the Agglestone Grit south of Poole Harbour (Area 3) and on that haven's north shore, commence at Sandbanks and continue eastwards along the coast, via the chines, to the lift east of Bournemouth pier (Area 1). They also extend inland for a considerable distance beyond Poole. The Series represent a complex mixture of yellow and white sands and 'pipe' clays, all arranged as lens-shaped deposits, up to some hundreds of yards wide, overlapping one another vertically.

Some of these overlapping deposits have recently been individually differentiated and separately named, as, for example, the Parkstone Clay, the Creekmoor Sand and Clay, and as the Branksome Sand. This arrangement better reflects the freshwater lake and **braided river** conditions under which they accumulated, both contemporaneously and successively, hence their frequent lens-like character.

Between the late eighteenth and early twentieth centuries around Poole, Wareham, and the north-western outskirts of Bournemouth, these clays were dug for the manufacture of pottery, sundry earthenware products, and bricks, while their use in producing thin-stemmed clay smokers' pipes, imparted to them their distinctive popular name, The Pipeclay.

Boscombe Sands E of Bournemouth Pier

These and other excavations then at Corfe, and elsewhere on the Purbeck heathlands, led to scientifically notable discoveries of the remains of fan-palms, ferns, *Aralia*, *Liquidambar*, and other tropical plants. Similarly, during late Victorian times, a rich and varied harvest of ancient woods, leaves, and seeds, along with insect remains, came to light in these deposits near Branksome Dene Chine, evidence confirming a continuance of tropical conditions in the Bournemouth area.

Canford cliffs looking N

Deposits previously recorded simply as 'Bagshot Beds' underlie obscuring vegetation clothing large tracts of the New Forest (Area 1), especially its western districts. Here they occupy a long stretch running from Ringwood, via Burley, to Holmsley. This obscuration unfortunately precludes their ready correlation with any of the aforementioned Poole Formation sequences or Freshwater Series, a difficulty also affecting the clays formerly excavated at Verwood for pottery making. None the less, whatever their exact identities, these obscured New Forest deposits have long directly influenced local drainage and floral colonisation.

The next rocks of Eocene age are those known collectively as the Bracklesham Beds. In the Bournemouth area the lowest (oldest) of these are the Bournemouth Marine Beds, which, today, are best seen in the cliff exposures at East Cliff. From that point they dip gently east before eventually disappearing at beach level near the site of the former Southbourne pier.

Dark clays mixed irregularly with yellow and grey sands comprise these beds, some of which, however, are not marine but freshwater sediments deposited under deltaic conditions. Vertically curved features in some of the freshwater sandy layers indicate that they originally existed as sandbanks in some of the ancient delta river channels.

Botanical fossils include ferns, *Eucalyptus*, and, at Honeycombe Chine, fruit of the stemless palm *Nipa*. Animal fossils mostly belong to marine creatures characteristic of subtropical climates.

Boscombe Sands, ancient seashore deposits, overlie the Bournemouth Marine Beds. First visible in the upper cliff east of Bournemouth pier, they dip eastwards to finally vanish beneath Warren Hill on Hengistbury Head. These sands consist of irregular seams of unfossiliferous yellow and white sands mixed with shingle deposits of well rolled flints. The latter probably represent off-shore shoals or shingle bars.

At Hengistbury these sands are coloured black, grey and white, and yield remains of *Sequoia* trees. The low cliffs immediately west of Hengistbury Head become, for a distance of around 50 m, wholly composed of coarse flint gravel. Typically river deposits, the apparent significance of these gravels is discussed on p 57.

Capping Hengistbury's Boscombe Sands are the Hengistbury Beds themselves. Confined to the Head they, too, dip gently eastwards. Opinions have varied

Honeycombe Chine

as to whether they are classifiably the latest (youngest) deposits of the Bracklesham Beds as a whole or the lowest (oldest) of the following Barton Formation. Current views incline to the latter.

The lowermost Hengistbury Beds are olive-green sandy clays resting upon a basal layer of flint pebbles. By way of contrast, the higher Hengistbury rocks display many alternating thin seams of pale chocolate or dark grey clay and sands enclosing bands of ironstone nodules. Fossil remains of sharks and crocodiles occur in some of these beds, but are usually very poorly preserved. Sometimes containing flattened tree stems, the nodules were once mined commercially, an activity that unwittingly exacerbated erosion of the Head itself. The sands and clays of the Hengistbury beds contain several beds rich in the burrows of crustaceans. These can be seen to be lined with pellets of sand to stop them collapsing in the soft sediment.

Fig 2.4 Nipa Palm Fruits

Long subject to debate, the Creechbarrow Beds of Creechbarrow Hill, 4 km west of Corfe in Purbeck (Area 4), are now generally regarded as the Bournemouth area's youngest Bracklesham Beds deposits. The hill is exclusively composed of clays, sands with bands of flints, and layers of hard and soft limestones. Collectively these deposits attain a thickness of about 10 m, and everywhere show rapid lateral variation.

Gravel Bed in low cliffs by the Double Dykes

Creechbarrow's fossils are of great interest. Gastropods, for example, are relatively common, whereas lamellibranchs are less so; and mammals exhibit an unexpected range. The latter include primitive carnivores, insecti-vores, **artiodactyls**, rodents, hippomorphs, marsupials, and ancestral primates (monkeys, e.g. *Adapis, Heterophys, and Microchoerus*). These creatures enjoyed a warm climate. Some of these animals suggest that the Creechbarrow deposits yielding them may even be of Bartonian age.

Hengistbury Head looking NNW

Although some modern borehole logs partially redress matters, knowledge of inland exposures of alleged Bracklesham Beds deposits is comparatively poor, and largely derives from imperfect pre-Second World War records of now inaccessible or inactive clay and brick-pit workings. It is now seldom possible to accurately correlate formerly exposed deposits with specific Bracklesham Beds horizons better seen at the aforementioned coastal localities. None the less, Bracklesham Beds rocks extend far inland and were once observable at St Catherine's Hill, Neacroft, Watton's Ford, Poulner, Cripplestyle, Ogden's Purlieu, and numerous other places scattered across Area 1. Like the Bagshot Beds, they have influenced local drainage and the development of particular botanical assemblages there from time immemorial.

The next deposits are those of the Barton and Solent Formations. Pre-eminently, but not solely, of marine origin, they are outstandingly exposed in the cliffs fronting Christchurch Bay between Cliff End 1 km east of Mudeford, and Paddy's Gap near Milford on Sea, via Highcliffe, Barton on Sea, and Hordle. All the many constituent beds, which at Barton are as much as 67.5 m thick dip to the east before disappearing at beach level at Paddy's Gap. Temporary inland exposures at Keyworth and other places west of Lymington confirm that these beds continue subterraneously as far as and beyond the Bournemouth area's eastern limits, and westwards at least as distant as New Milton, Bransgore, Markway Hill, Stony Cross, Ringwood, and Crow, either in or adjacent to the New Forest proper.

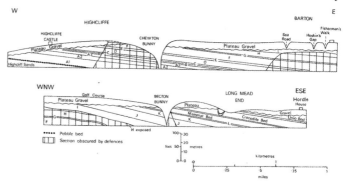

Fig 2.5 Cliff section between Mudeford and Milford on Sea

In ascending order, the most important of these beds are the Highcliffe Sands, the Barton Beds (long since usefully divided into Lower, Middle, and Upper), and the Lower Headon Beds. Of these, the Highcliffe Sands and the Lower Barton Beds are jointly known as the Highcliffe Member of the Barton Formation, the Middle Barton Beds as the latter's Naish Member, the Upper Barton Beds as its Becton Sand Formation, and the Lower Headon Beds as its Headon Hill Formation.

The Highcliffe Sands, which thinly overlie the Hengistbury Beds on Hengistbury itself, recur in full at Highcliffe as buff and white sands having fine seams of 'pipe' clay near their base. These indicate deposition in a shallow sea.

Capping the Highcliffe Sands are the greenish and bluish sandy clays of the Lower Barton Beds which contain ironstone nodules.

Fossil marine invertebrates, including the foraminifer *Nummilites*, together with fish otoliths, sharks' teeth and the rare turtle *Patanemys* have been found in these beds. These show that a deeper sea existed then.

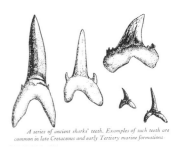

A series of ancient sharks' teeth. Examples of such teeth are common in late Cretaceous and early Tertiary marine formations

Fig 2.6 Shark Teeth

The Middle Barton (Naish Member) rocks are primarily successive deposits of glauconitic sands and brownish-grey sandy clays featuring intrusive bands of cement stones (septaria). These, and the character of the immense number and range of fossils yielded by these deposits, apparently reflect shallower marine conditions. Of the fossils, especially prevalent are gastropods, such as *Athleta*, *Turritella* and *Hippochrenes*. Bivalves, exemplified by *Cardium*, *Callista* and *Corbula*, along with sharks' teeth, fish vertebrae, and turtle bones, are likewise notably abundant. Typically these fossils are extremely well preserved, and many of the shells could easily be mistaken for modern sub-tropical species.

Zeuglodon

The Eocene beds at Barton are justly famous not merely for the numbers and variety of their fossils but also for the great rarity of some of them. Remains found there of *Basilosaurus* are a prime example.

Also known as *Zeuglodon* or *Zygorhiza*, *Basilosaurus* was one of the earliest known whales. The first bones of this archaic mammal were discovered at Barton in Victorian times by, it appears, the Dent family who owned property near the site of the 'Pebble Beach Restaurant' on Barton's present sea-front. These, along with the rest of the Dents' fine collection of Bartonian fossils, were acquired in 1912 by the Society, in whose museum they may still be inspected.

Remains since found elsewhere of more completely preserved generally similar Eocene whales show that *Basilosaurus* had a body longer and slimmer than those of modern whales, and may have reached an overall length of 15 or more metres. Its nostrils were located much nearer the front of its skull than those of living whales, and its jaws were equipped with the teeth of a powerful predator. Fig 2.7.

The ancestry of these animals is not yet certainly known, but they were evidently quite common in the late Eocene seas; a fact suggesting that fossils casting a fuller light on their origins must still await discovery in the earlier Tertiary deposits.

Fig 2.7 Basilosaurus (Zeuglodon) After R Kellog 1936

Basilosaurus (Zeuglodon): a 16.5 m long skeleton of this primitive whale found in North America last century, clearly illustrating the animal's principal characteristics. Only isolated detached bones of *Basilosaurus* occur (occasionally) in the Bournemouth area.

A limestone band composed of **comminuted** shells separates the Naish Member deposits from the overlying Upper Barton (Becton Member) Beds. The lowest of these is a thick bluish-grey sandy clay called the Chama Bed, crowded with bivalve fossils like *Glycymeris*, *Crassatella* and *Chama* itself, and those of gastropods such as *Pollia*. Above this lies a much thicker wholly unfossiliferous deposit of white and yellow sand which, at Becton Bunny, is superseded by greyish-brown clays enveloping both marine and estuarine bivalves and gastropods; and capping these are pale sands containing only brackish-water representatives of these shells. The final, uppermost, deposit of the Becton Member is a 1.2 m thick black clay hosting much fossil wood.

Throughout the accumulation of the Becton Member deposits, the sea clearly became ever shallower as much of the old Hampshire Basin silted-up and shorelines advanced towards the latitude of today's cliffs. These developments heralded the continental conditions that were to typify the remainder of Eocene times. The climate, though still a warm one, was evidently somewhat cooler and drier.

Although formerly regarded as Oligocene rocks, the Lower Headon Beds of the Totland Bay Member, and those of the shortly to be reviewed Solent Formation (see Table 2.1), are now classed as terminal Eocene deposits. The Eocene Period ended about 33 million years ago.

Clearly seen in the cliffs between Becton Bunny and Paddy's Gap, these deposits, especially at

Hordle Cliff – the very first Eocene locality (anywhere!) to receive serious attention from naturalists during geology's embryonic (eighteenth century) era – consist mainly of unconsolidated brackish or freshwater sands and clays (sometimes containing ironstone nodules) accumulated during a regime of interconnecting lakes and river estuaries. Inevitably these deposits vary in linear extent and thickness, may be lens-like or partially overlap one another.

At Hordle Cliff, where they are 25 m thick, the Lower Headon Beds are renowned for their abundance and variety of fossils. Despite the presence of interesting invertebrate fossils (chiefly bivalves and gastropods) throughout these beds, of decidedly greater import are the primitive mammals. They are akin to those noted from Creechbarrow (p 47), met with in the lowest deposit (aptly styled the Mammal Bed). Similarly, the following Leaf Bed yields the leaves and seeds of at least 50 species of ancient swamp-forest plants. Some of the species closely resemble montane plants still flourishing in southern China.

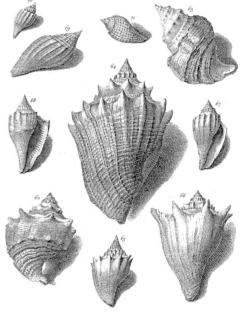

The appropriately named overlying sandy Crocodile Bed likewise contains a notable subtropical fauna of extinct fishes, frogs, lizards, snakes, crocodiles, alligators, turtles, early birds, and yet more mammals. Higher deposits feature lignite seams and, in the topmost Rodent Bed, remains of ancestral rodents like *Adelomys* and *Theridomys*.

Some of the woodcuts of the first collection of Eocene shells found at Hordle Cliff

Now inaccessible inland exposures, apparently of Lower Headon deposits, once existed at Efford, Lymore, and Thorney Hill (Area 1), at each of which bricks and tiles were manufactured early in the twentieth century. Commercial foreshore and sea-bed collecting of the ironstone nodules also previously occurred off Hordle Cliff.

Finally, the Solent Formation, mainly unconsolidated sands and clays comprising the Middle and Upper Headon Beds (formerly called the Headon Member), occur as sub-surface deposits in region 1 of the Bournemouth area. As stated in outmoded texts, they were formerly accorded an Oligocene age (Table 2.1). Knowledge of these beds largely derives from scattered modern **borehole logs** and bygone inland exposures in long-abandoned clay and brick pits at Burley, Purlieu, and Poors Common north of Bransgore. The few fossils known from these localities indicate that these deposits had primarily accumulated under fluviatile and marsh conditions.

As with the Bagshot, Bracklesham, and Barton rocks, those of the Solent Formation underpin sizeable, if irregular, tracts of the western New Forest and have contributed to the natural development of its surface drainage and vegetational cover.

While evidence outside the Bournemouth area indicates that Oligocene, Miocene, and Pliocene rocks were indeed deposited within the area, subsequent erosion and other natural events preceding the Pleistocene Period (Table 2.1) ensured their removal. Today they are partially represented by discontinuous remnant sheets of surface gravels and occasional sarsens – examples of superficial drift deposits.

Drift Deposits

Geologically much younger than the solid rocks just considered, drift deposits date from the two latest divisions of Earth history, i.e. Pleistocene and Holocene (Recent) times (Table 2.1), when climates in the Bournemouth area had cooled significantly. Unconformably blanketing solid rocks in all four of our regions, the drift, in the guise of gravels, gritty clays, loams, and earths, varies locally in extent, composition, and thickness due to the undulating surface of the subjacent terrain. Down the years, separate studies and differing classifications have been made of these unconsolidated deposits, sometimes in conjunction with the area's geomorphology. The principal gravel groups, briefly reviewed below, have been individually termed as Clay-with-Flints, Angular Flint Gravel, Plateau Gravel, and Valley (Terrace) Gravel. These resulted from different processes occurring at different times.

The oldest of these appears to be the Clay-with-Flints. Spread as disconnected patches over the surface of the Chalk uplands in Purbeck (Area 4) and parts of Cranborne Chase (Area 2) they are structureless accumulations of chocolate-coloured or red-dish clay containing unworn flints, rounded flint pebbles, and quantities of Eocene sand. The accumulations, as at West Creech Hill, can reach a thickness of 10 m or more, although elsewhere they are generally considerably less.

Also scattered as small patches over the area's higher Chalk outcrops are irregular masses of smashed angular flints, again in association with quantities of sand or gritty clay. These form the Angular Flint Gravel, which some geologists believe is a variant of, or coeval with, the Clay-with-Flints accumulations. Only a few patches occur in our area near Steeple and, debatably, at Rye Hill near Edmondsham.

Almost entirely composed of subangular flints, rounded flints, and pebbles from eroded Eocene deposits, the Plateau Gravel is seemingly of late Pleistocene age and partly of fluviatile origin. In the Bournemouth area it irregularly covers the high grounds between the river valleys in and around Bournemouth itself, e.g. Canford and Wallis Down, and in the western sector of the New Forest, e.g. Vereley Hill and Wilverley Plain. It also caps the cliffs from Highcliffe to Milford on Sea, apparently occurs on Brownsea Island in Poole Harbour, and occupies two small patches in Purbeck, one near West Bucknowle, the other a small knoll near Encombe.

Prior to the development of the river valleys Plateau Gravel is widely believed to have mantled virtually the entire Bournemouth 'area'.

Valley (Terrace) Gravel is essentially redeposited Plateau Gravel washed down from adjacent higher ground during the formation of the above valleys. In many valleys immense volumes of this gravel accumulated on the valley slopes and floors, often as well defined 'terraces'. some of which are now up to 15 m above existing river levels. Long extracted commercially, some of the exhausted resultant gravel pits now serve as wildlife sanctuaries, e.g. the series at Blashford northwards of Ringwood. Interestingly, these gravel accumulations cannot have accrued under existing conditions as they underlie, and thus predate, the alluvium being deposited by the present rivers.

Large to very large smooth subangular blocks of sandstone, known as Sarsens, are occasionally found in gravel accumulations. Their main interest lies in their apparent origin as portions of a formerly extensive Eocene sandstone deposit later removed by erosion and transported to their present scattered locations by powerful water movements. Locally, specimens have been found at Moordown, Upper Parkstone, Milford on Sea, Pokesdown, and other places.

Superficial Deposits

As well as the drift gravels, other superficial deposits, by being present in the Bournemouth area deserve mention here. These are the Head and Coombe (Combe) Rock deposits, the Brickearths, Loess, Blown Sands and Tufa and the Alluvia and Peat.

Head occurs haphazardly as weathered and disintegrated angular rock debris on the inter-valley high grounds and valley slopes and bottoms of our area. It sometimes interbeds with or passes laterally into adjacent gravels, effects believedly resulting from 'downhill' movement by solifluction (sludge creep). Discoveries of Ice Age mammals (mammoth and woolly rhinoceros) in typical Head deposits, as at Encombe suggest its formation under cold and wet conditions during late Pleistocene times.

Closely related to Head is the Coombe Rock. This occurs as structureless masses of chalk-rubble and flints in a chalky or clayey paste not infrequently weathered into a stony loam. Coombe Rock occurs sporadically on Chalk slopes and dry-valley floors, where it can be as much as 5 m thick. It is also sometimes associated with Brickearth deposits. Instances of Coombe Rock reportedly occur in dry Chalk valleys near Cranborne (Area 2).

Brickearths are light brownish loams composed of ferruginous clays containing mixed quartz and flint sand fragments and sometimes gravelly seams and scattered flints. Some depositions represent solifluction flows on hill slopes, others wind-blown Loess-like accumulations, and yet others apparently river-flood deposits. They occur discontinuously at several localities in the Bournemouth area, often influencing the character of overlying soils. Occasionally remains of Ice Age animals are met with in these deposits which indicate their late Pleistocene origin.

Loess is a generally similar deposit to Brickearth comprising well graded but unstratified (mainly) siliceous wind-blown particles, which, at some localities, exhibit vertical jointing. Although its geographical distribution is irregular, detailed studies during the 1910s confirmed that small unconnected patches of it occur in the western New Forest and neighbouring districts. Loess appears to date from late glacial times or a little later.

Another **Aeolian** deposit is Blown Sand. In our area it manifests as sand dunes, e.g. those on the South Haven Peninsula north and east of the Little Sea, as sand hills, e.g. at Sandbanks and Southbourne and as supra-tidal sand spits, e.g. on the Hengistbury Head shore of Mudeford Run. Essentially unstable, such deposits repeatedly change volume and physical configuration. They are of modern (Holocene) origin.

Tufa is a name given to a spongy or cellular deposit formed, mainly in limestone regions, by deposition from solutions of calcium bicarbonate at or around springs by water which has traversed limestone strata. Such deposits can rapidly preserve organisms they envelop, and can quickly enlarge in extent. A celebrated example of this has occurred at Blashenwell near Corfe (Area 4). As much as 3 m thick, it has yielded the remains of numerous modern land and freshwater snails, and the leaves of oak, hazel, and elm. Its date has been set in the wet Mesolithic episode of mid-Holocene times. Tufa formation no longer occurs at Blashenwell.

Alluvium is a still on-going deposit of varying width and thickness produced by modern rivers and, as banked-up features, by the sea around estuaries. It usually consists of fine, unconsolidated muds derived from natural 'washings' of the rocks and superficial deposits in the stream basin concerned.

In the Bournemouth area the largest accumulations of alluvium occur in the Frome, Stour, and Avon valleys, where they have slowed the original river flows. Around Poole Harbour Alluvium merges into Peat. Peat is directly associated with inland Alluvial deposits, occurring as wide tracts on locally depressed marshy ground. At such places the Peat can reach considerable depths and enclose trunks of ancient trees, as in Cranborne Chase, and in the Luscombe and Stour valleys. Elsewhere, associated submerged peats and tree stumps occupy the sea bed off Bournemouth pier.

Soils

The last of the surface deposits requiring consideration here are the soils which unevenly blanket virtually every square metre of the entire Bournemouth 'area'. Some ancient soils (palaeosoils), such as Loess and Brickearth, have already been mentioned, the oldest being the highly mineralised 'soil' beds of Purbeck age. Here we focus on their modern equivalents.

Natural, as against artificially 'improved', modern soils vary widely, not merely compositionally but often rapidly in terms of lateral extent. Such disparity is typical of the Bournemouth area.

During correlations of soils with, say, land drainage, natural vegetation, or agricultural endeavour, allowance should be made for the characteristics of individual soil 'types' special to the districts concerned. Soil profiles must be considered first.

The lowest or deepest levels of 'natural' soils necessarily repose on the bed-rock of a given locality, and, to some degree, are usually saturated. At those levels conditions are constantly reducing (not oxidising), and the soil sometimes suffers locally from impeded drainage. These soils are often referred to as Gley or Glei. In the soils immediately above the Gley, reduction and oxidation alternate, commonly imparting a mottled appearance to the soils.

The soil levels capping those just noted are normally the driest, permitting the maximum downward movement of water, and the greatest amount of leaching and oxidation.

When combined, these three soil profiles are typically those of a Podsol. Podsols are characteristic of areas enjoying cool-temperate humid climates and conditions suitable for well developed leaching.

Three main 'types' of soil occur in the Bournemouth 'area'. These are Sandy Soils, Loamy Soils (loams), and Clay Soils. Each possesses different drainage qualities. Of these Sandy Soils, containing 60 per cent or more sand and less than 10 per cent clay, tend to drain 'too easily' and are predominantly dry and generally afford less 'hold' for large rooted vegetation. Such soils are present in our Purbeck region (Area 4). Loamy Soils, retaining sand and clay in almost equal amounts, exhibit 'balanced drainage' and support a more varied flora. Clay Soils, composed of far more clay than sand, are normally poorly drained and in wet weather, become sticky or viscous. A comparatively limited number of different plants successfully thrive on them.

Considerable research has been done on the soils of the New Forest sector of our area, but only patchily elsewhere due to extensive local urbanisation. Consequently, no detailed comprehensive map of the area's soils has yet been issued. As a challenging though less than foolproof exercise interested botanists should, through field observation, be generally able to ascertain underlying soil 'types' from the kinds of plant cover naturally flourishing in pedologically unmapped localities.

GEOMORPHOLOGY

This branch of natural history primarily concerns the accurate description and interpretation of our present scenery or natural land relief. In our area scenery ranges from terrestrial features like hills and plateaux to valleys and coastlines. Its interpretation involves the causes (folding, tilting, elevation, depression, or dislocation) of the creation of those features. It also involves the sea's periodic drowning or erosion of both dry-land and submarine surfaces resulting in, or coeval with, the evolution of natural land drainage regimes.

The framing of a precise temporal sequence of such developments is crucial to any rational interpretation of the foregoing. It explains why land relief sometimes bears little relation to underlying lithospheric (crustal) structure. Associated bygone climates have likewise been pertinent as one of the keys to understanding the ever-changing procession of now-fossil plants and animals met with down the long corridor of Bournemouth's geological past.

Here we take a closer look at these elements, in some cases briefly mentioned on previous pages, insofar as they have affected the Bournemouth area's geological record. As highlighted below, nearly all the larger topographic features just listed have resulted from large-scale movements of Earth's crust.

Little needs to be added to previous statements about the origin and present distribution of the area's Mesozoic rocks, except that the youngest of them, the Chalk, suffered severe denudation in late Cretaceous times. Several hundred vertical metres of the upper Chalk, sometimes including whole zones were eroded then, providing surviving Chalk surfaces with undulating or pitted appearances. Very powerful forces were required to produce these effects, suggesting to some that they were caused by the **KT** event which allegedly brought the Mesozoic Era and much of its life to a sudden end.

But irrespective of its actual genesis, no doubt exists that this denudation preceded the accumulation of the first (oldest) Tertiary deposits (Table 2.1). At many places (Studland for example) the hollows and undulations are filled by the lithologically very different Reading Beds deposits containing typical Chalk flints. Flints are especially common in undisturbed upper levels of the Chalk. This late Cretaceous disturbance was also marked by a widespread retreat of the old Tethyan Sea and a general crustal uplift of land areas – both preludes to the birth of the Hampshire Basin.

Although in early Tertiary times (say 60 to 40 million years ago) land areas and seas repeatedly rose and fell by modest amounts on at least six occasions, essentially stable subtropical conditions prevailed throughout the Basin, with deposits accumulating within it on virtually the same horizontal plane as the underlying denuded Chalk surface. Rivers then were seemingly east-flowing.

The final phase of Eocene deposition saw a slow but steady withdrawal of the sea and the advent of cooler continental conditions, which were continued in the following Oligocene Period.

No rocks dating from the Oligocene or subsequent Miocene and Pliocene periods (Table 2.1) occur today in the Bournemouth area. That is because, if any were deposited, they and extensive portions of the older Eocene and Palaeocene deposits were removed by a global event known as the Alpine Orogeny or Alpine storm. A massive pan-continental crustal disturbance erupting in early Miocene times (about 25 million years ago), it caused among other effects, the uplift of many mountain ranges, widespread volcanic activity, and, as now believed, the initiation of the Antarctic ice cap.

Many familiar scenic features of the Bournemouth area date from that event. It was responsible for the 85–90° tilted uplift of the Mesozoic rocks now represented by the Purbeck Hills and neighbouring coastal Purbeck scenery (Area 4), and the accompanying removal of the Tertiary deposits which, until then, had overlain both them and the Chalk of Cranborne Chase (Area 2), as discussed below.

The pressures during this upheaval were so acute that colossal portions of the uptilted Chalk were dislocated as faults. A famous example, best viewed from the sea, occurs at Ballard Down.

The elongated east–west trough or valley-like low country between the Purbeck Hills in the south and the higher ground of Cranborne Chase and northwards to Salisbury Plain, resulting from these violent crustal movements, naturally formed a drainage basin. Early on this was occupied by an east-draining river flowing across territory

The Ballard Down Fault looking E

destined in its lower reaches to become the Solent. Geologists know this as the Solent River. The present River Frome is a surviving stretch of this ancient stream. Temperate climates had evidently replaced the previous warm ones.

Some 14 million years ago, during the Miocene, aerial erosion of our area's inland terrain led to the development there, as far north as Salisbury and east as Dorchester, of a peneplain.

A peneplain is typically the end-product of a cycle of land erosion occurring under humid conditions. It indicates that such erosion had been active across this inland tract since the time of the Alpine Orogeny.

Certainly by around 12 million years ago, this erosional process had worn down formerly noteworthy physiographic structures on the peneplain to relative insignificance. Their remnants, not preserved in the Bournemouth area, were subsequently drowned, along with the whole of our area except Purbeck, by a high-level marine invasion by, as styled by some, the 'Calabrian Sea'.

This sea inundated some localities now as much as 210 m above Ordnance Datum (OD), and obliterated many prexisting drainage systems in the north and east of the huge tract flooded.

Although land is known to have existed to the north and east of our 'area', the precise extent of the 'Calabrian Sea' is still uncertain. By late Pliocene times, however, it was in retreat and, about 3 million years ago had withdrawn completely.

Across the Hampshire Basin successive stages in the sea's recession were marked by a series of marine gravels. Consistently occupying constant heights above OD, these are distinct from the river-valley gravels, and are known as Terrace Gravels. Different names distinguish different terraces, several of which occur prominently at or near Bournemouth. Collectively their deposition spanned thousands of years.

At many places these gravels exhibit evidence of 'cold-weather' deposition, when Siberian 'permafrost' conditions were the norm. Natural frost structures, together with Brickearths,

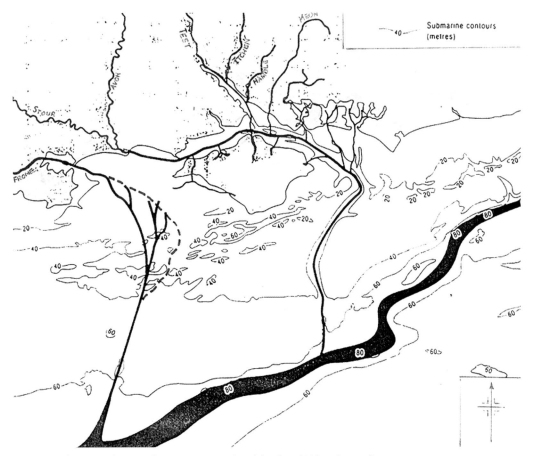

Map 2.3 The pre-Holocene Solent river system. (Bridgland and Velegrakis et al)

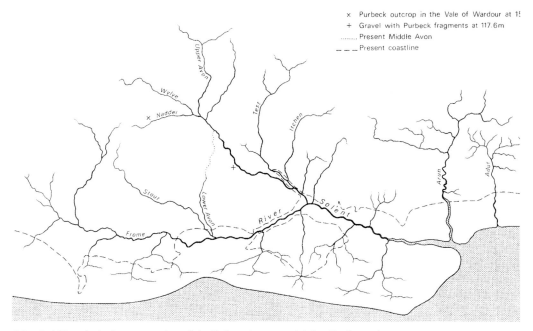

Map 2.4 Hypothetical reconstruction of the 'Solent river system' (after Reid 1902)

Coombe Rock deposits, fossil ice wedges, and, near Edmondsham, a swallow-hole or **doline**, indicate that these gravels were distributed under peri-glacial conditions by great successive melt-water floods occasioned by thawing ice-sheets north of our area. Flowing southwards, these floods poured over the unconsolidated stony flint-ridden rocks of the long drowned Pliocene peneplain material. In the process they removed up to an estimated 10.5 m of peneplain strata, depositing the constituent grit and stones higgledy-piggledy often as unstratified Terrace Gravels. Although at some places they are stratified (e.g. east of Chewton Bunny). The youngest of these gravels date from around the beginning of Holocene times, approximately 10,000 years ago but some of the older deposits may have resulted from sub-aerial erosion during Pliocene times and subsequent redeposition as 'gravel terraces' by late or post-glacial river action.

In the Bournemouth area these gravels occur abundantly at numerous places, such as Sleight, Wimborne, Wareham, Sway, and Barton on Sea, where many metres of them cap the coastal cliffs. They have long been, and still are, locally excavated for a wide variety of commercial purposes, both on land and, as dredged **aggregates**, from Christchurch Bay's sea bed.

The onset of Holocene times heralded a period of warmer weather generally like today's. Scenically, however, our area differed noticeably from that now familiar to us, while sea-level, in the English Channel, was appreciably lower.

Coevally, Bournemouth's famous chines were minor surface melt-water run-off channels which, though first formed in glacial late Pleistocene times, did not acquire their present widths and depths until approximately 5,000 years later, i.e. in Mid-Holocene times.

The Solent Valley was just that. Continuous dry land extended southwards from our present coastline east and west to the Isle of Wight and the Isle of Purbeck, and to a line of low chalk hills, known as the Wight/Purbeck Ridge, that united the two 'islands' between the Needles and Old Harry Rocks. The nearest chalk stack is called the Pinnacle. Records of submerged offshore stumps of ancient trees indicate that the New Forest formerly spread across this terrain well south of today's coastline. Poole Harbour, and Studland, Poole, and Christchurch bays did not exist then, and very probably Swanage Bay did not either (Map 2.4).

Traversing the Solent Valley, the Solent River (p 56) was previously believed to have flowed eastwards between the New Forest and the Isle of Wight before debouching into the English Channel southeast of the island. Accordingly, all the Bournemouth area rivers and streams were credited with having been tributaries of it, the old river gravels possibly appearing anomalously in the Eocene cliffs just west of Hengistbury Head (p 46) being taken by some to mark where the River Stour had formerly turned south to join the Solent River.

Recent researches, however, show that the Solent River passed through a gap in the Wight/Purbeck Ridge to reach the English Channel, while the river previously interpreted as the Solent River's eastern extension was really an eastern, now drowned, stretch of the Avon. Today the Avon and Stour jointly enter the sea immediately north of Hengistbury Head at Mudeford (Map 2.3).

Old Harry Rocks, Purbeck looking NE

All that changed when, following the severence of the British Isles from mainland Europe, rising sea levels in the English Channel, about 5,000 years ago, enabled the sea to flood through the gap in the Wight/Purbeck Ridge and inundate most of the Solent Valley to submerge most of its ancient river system. The aforementioned bays and Poole Harbour were born then, as was a still active cycle of erosion involving the coast between Sandbanks and Milford on Sea. Among other effects erosion has lost Hengistbury Head a good third of its original bulk. This cycle has caused extensive and often surprisingly rapid erosion of the unconsolidated cliff deposits along this coastal stretch. These losses have been intensified by the added seepage within the cliffs of seawards-draining onshore waters.

This seepage is especially serious in the low cliffs of Wealden strata fronting Swanage Bay, and elsewhere (as in Area 4) it is the main cause of the sporadic landslips occurring along coasts of solid Mesozoic (Portlandian and Purbeckian) rocks.

Marine agencies, however, are primarily responsible for eroding the sea cliffs around Handfast Point, where small sea-caves have been excavated and 'stacks' detached from the mainland. Old Harry Rocks are famous examples of the latter. Photographs of these rocks taken 100 or more years ago clearly show how rapid chalk erosion can be. It is also very much ongoing, for it was only in 1896 that one of these stacks, Old Harry's Wife, was demolished by the sea.

Erosion of Tertiary deposits has generated other effects – new coastal features at several

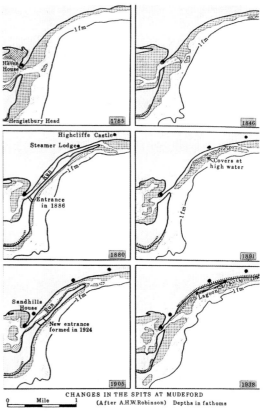

Fig 2.9 Changes in the spits at Mudeford

localities by marine currents. These include sand or shingle spits, sand dunes, and shingle banks.

Among these are the dunes of Shell Bay, those now largely lost to urbanisation at Sandbanks (Area 3) and Sandhills near Southbourne, and those on the north-east shore of Hengistbury Head adjacent to Mudeford Run (Area 1). In repeatedly changing extent and shape, the latter have received special attention, as have the dunes next to the Little Sea on the South Haven Peninsula.

The famous shingle spit at Hurst (Area 1), catastrophically breached on several past occasions, has slowly moved position eastwards over the past few hundred years. Evidence suggests that the New Forest Danestream, which now reaches the sea via Sturt Pond at Keyhaven, formerly did so west of the present spit before the Pond was formed.

All these coastal developments have involved the reassembly of eroded on-shore material by a combination of longshore drift and tidal activity. Critically, longshore drift has a naturally predominant eastwards direction of movement. All these dunes and spits are presently sited on east-facing shorelines. Offshore shingle banks, such as the Dolphin Bank and the celebrated Shingles south-west of Hurst Spit, are further submarine features produced through re-assembly of previously eroded onshore sediments by marine action. Although apparently permanent, such banks repeatedly increase and decrease in extent and size, and certainly post-date the mid-Holocene drowning of the old Solent Valley.

This brief overview of the Bournemouth area's geological and geomorphological past unmistakably demonstrates how, by underpinning all local organic activity, geology forms the base upon which the entire natural history of Bournemouth and its environs has been enacted from time immemorial and that, through the changes it is still undergoing, it will continue to influence the area's future natural history to a similar degree.

Fig. 24. After J. Chaffey

Fig 2.11 Studland dune complex (After J Chaffey 2000)

From Camden's Britannia, 1607.

From Avery's survey, 1721.

Fig 2.10 Four old maps of the South Haven Peninsula

From Isaac Taylor's map, 1765.

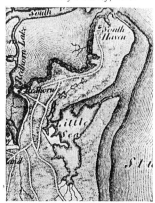

From the Ordnance Survey of 1811.

3 Mycology

Sara Cadbury

The area covered by this book has several important and varied habitats for fungi to grow and thrive. Some of these areas have been better recorded by mycologists, both amateur and professional, than others. For example the New Forest has been well recorded over the last century and thus may rather overshadow the remaining areas.

The woodlands of both coniferous and deciduous trees, the heathlands and the grassland areas are the most important places for the sheer variety and profusion of fungi, but the open spaces and the parks and gardens of the urban areas, the sand dunes of Studland Bay and the chalk downlands of Dorset are all good 'fungi hunting' places.

There have been many name changes in mycology in the years since the last book was published. Some fungi have been moved into another genus and some have changed their species name – and some have changed both their genus and species name.

This is all due to our better understanding and knowledge of fungi with improved microscopes and techniques. With increased information now obtained from their DNA, it was found that some specimens had been incorrectly classified.

At the commencement of the twenty-first century, the British Mycological Society and Natural England commissioned two eminent experts to give English names to all the common species of fungi.

This comprehensive list is now easily available to all and the English names are now printed in all good field guides alongside the Latin names. Besides the fact that this makes a potentially 'difficult' subject easier for the interested amateur, it also prevents the increase in the proliferation of confusing English names.

Every year, in our area alone, there are still several species of fungi that have never been recorded in the area previously. More people are now out foraying than ever before with a greatly increased knowledge of the subject, huge enthusiasm and with the help of a variety of excellent field guides that have recently been published.

Gone are the days when Victorian ladies were horrified by the **Stinkhorn fungus**, *Phallus impudicus*, because of its smell and phallus-like appearance, and when the likes of Beatrix Potter could not find the courage to draw it, and Charles Darwin's daughter donned gloves, and went out to collect all she could find and burn them !

We are indeed fortunate to have the New Forest so near to Bournemouth – it being one of the most outstanding areas for fungi in this country. The variety of habitat, actually in the New Forest itself, provides a huge diversity of fungi – with its broadleaved and conifer woods, wet and dry heath, alder and willow bogs, dry and wet lawns.

The British Mycological Society, which was founded in 1896, had its first New Forest foray from Lyndhurst (which was easily accessible by train) in 1899 and its second one in 1916 – with an emphasis on macro

Common Stinkhorn

rather than micro fungi. Their recording and forays in the area have continued, gradually increasing in regularity, until the present day.

Fungi are dependent on different vegetation types and on both living and dead plant material, with some exceptions. They tend to show their fruiting bodies predominately in the Autumn (like apples on a tree) so are then more obvious, but their root system,or mycelium, is in the substrate (the ground or wood) all the year round. So the Autumn is generally accepted as the 'best' time to find fungi –because the 'biggest and the best' are then most obvious. However a good example of a Spring fruiting mushroom is the **St George's Mushroom**, *Calocybe gambosa*, which is edible, and fruits abundantly all over our area in the grass, beside paths, tracks, woods and carpark edges, and sometimes in great profusion if conditions are right. It is even named after the time of year! – St. George's Day – 23 April.

In the deciduous woodlands, perhaps the largest, most obvious and the longest lasting, are the 'shelf-like' bracket fungi which grow on living or dead, standing or fallen, tree trunks. The brackets themselves may be very large indeed – some up to half a metre across and just as hard as the wood on which they grow, and they have pores rather than gills, underneath the cap. The most common one is the **Artist's fungus**, *Ganoderma australe*, and it is probably the largest one too, but a similar looking one called *Ganoderma applanatum* has never been recorded in the New Forest, in spite of the fact that there appear to be many suitable oak trees, although it is common in other parts of the country.

Artist's Fungus

Chicken of the Woods

The **Chicken of the Woods**, *Laetiporus sulphureus*, is a very visible fungus that must be mentioned in oak woods, since it can easily be spotted from a good distance away, any time from Spring to Autumn. In its prime, it has layered tiers of large fan-shaped fruiting bodies that are brightly coloured orange/yellow that can cover as much as a metre on the tree trunk. It is also one of the few fungi that will flourish on **Yew**, *Taxus*. It is only an annual fungus although it can still be recognised for what it is when it is a dirty cream colour and crumbling sadly as it lies broken on the leaf litter under the host tree, many months later.

A much smaller bracket fungus, with thinner 'shelves' but very common and just as tenacious, is the **Turkeytail**, *Trametes versicolor*, which is also an annual, and grows in layered tiers of lovely muted shades of brown and black – which are reminiscent of turkeytails!

A rare annual bracket fungus is the **Oak polypore**, *Piptoporus quercina*, which has been found on only one site in the New Forest so far. A near relative the **Birch polypore**, *Piptoporus betulina*, is often found and evident on many of the mature birch trees, both living and dead.

Old beech woods are particularly rich in fungal species – both on the ground and on the trees. The beautiful **Porcelain fungus**, *Oudemansiella mucida*, is common with its white translucent cap and gills, as are the **Oyster mushroom** family, *Pleurotus*, most of which are edible. Many rare fungi that appear as flat sheets,

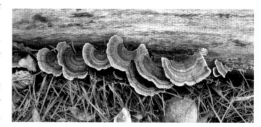

Turkeytail

or resupinate, can be a mycologist's dream but may prove to be rather uninteresting to the casual observer.

The amazing and rare *Hericium* genus of fungi, the **Tooth fungi**, which have spines or teeth instead of gills, are a New Forest speciality and are a sight to behold, as they protrude from the wood in apparently large fluffy lumps – and they are even edible too!

Since the disappearance of the elm tree from the countryside in England, it has been very pleasing to now sometimes find a fungus formerly frequent on elms, that has found a new home on beech, elm and sycamore trees in the New Forest. It is the beautiful pinky apricot coloured **Wrinkled Peach**, *Rhodotus palmatus*, which has managed to adapt happily to an alternative substrate.

Conifer woodlands and plantations also have many fungi including, of course, those associated with specific trees such as the yellow and brown brackets of **Dyers Mazegill**, *Phaeolus schweinitzii*, or the aptly named **Root Rot Fungus**, *Heterobasidion annosum*, which can cause serious

Birch Polypore

Porcelain fungus on slimy beech tuft

economic losses in commercial plantations – and can also grow on several species of trees.

A close look at old pine cones lying on the ground will often reveal a small rather unusual fungus growing out from between the scales of the cone. This is the **Ear Pick Fungus**, *Auriscalpium vulgare* which has a brown hairy kidney-shaped cap with spines, instead of gills, underneath, and a very hairy stem. It is a delight to be able to pick up the pine cone and have a close look (preferably with a hand lens) without having to disturb it, grovel on the knees or even get dirty hands.

Underneath all these trees, fungi proliferate too and they often have complex relationships with specific trees. Their extensive root systems are in the ground all the year round and these mycorrhiza (as they are called), which are often host specific, enable the tree to obtain nitrogen (principally from soil ammonia) and nitrates, and phosphorus (both organic and inorganic forms) from the fungi and for the fungal partner to obtain organic nutrients such as glucose and fructose from the tree. The partnership is mutually beneficial and nearly all species of tree are reliant on their fungal partners and do not thrive without them.

The **Toughshanks**, genus *Collybia*, with their very tough, unbreakable, fibrous stems, are one of the most important of the leaf decaying fungi. In every woodland you will see **Clustered Toughshank**, *Collybia Confluens*, **Spotted Toughshank**, *Collybia maculata*, **Russet Toughshank**, *Collybia dryophila*, and **Butter Cap**, *Collybia butyracea*, in varying degrees of profusion and sometimes forming 'fairy rings'. They are all shades of cream and brown and many merge well into the leaf litter, but without their help and the help of others like them, we would probably be unable to see much of the trees themselves because they would be deeply immersed in leaves! Fortunately where they flourish, their numbers are often startlingly enormous, certainly no foray in the woods is taken without seeing some or all of them.

Also present on every walk through the woods in our area, are fallen logs and branches that appear to be stained with a green ink. This staining is permanent and is caused by the growing mycelium of the **Green Cup fungus**, *Chlorociboria aeruginascens*. This infected wood was often used, particularly in Victorian times, in the manufacture of a decoration called Tunbridge Ware. The actual fruiting bodies of the fungi are not so often seen – but they are beautiful small green cups, very often hiding on the damper underside of the wood.

How lovely it is to see the colourful **Brittle Gills**, genus *Russula*, on the woodland floor with all their spectacular colours of pinks and reds, creams and yellows, purples and greens – truly wonderful 'roses of the woods' indeed, as they are sometimes called.

Their gills, usually white or cream, however are very brittle (hence their name) and easily shatter into pieces. Their lovely colours are water soluble, so after prodigious rain, they tend to become rather washed out. Some of them may have the colour of roses, but they certainly do not necessarily smell like them – such as the **Stinking Brittlegill**, *Russula foetens*, which has a very unpleasant burnt horn smell or the **Crab Brittlegill**, *Russula xerampelina*, which smells of rotting fish or crab!

In the space of only a few feet of the woodland floor, one may see the mauve/lilac of the **Purple Brittlegill**, *Russula atropurpurea*, the yellow of the **Ochre Brittlegill**, *Russula ochroleuca*, the dull green of the **Greencracked Brittlegill**, *Russula virescens*, and the pinky/red of the **Coral Brittlegill**, *Russula velenovskyi*. What a splendid sight!

Greencracked Brittlegill

Perhaps less spectacular in colour, but not necessarily in size, are the **Bolete** family of mushrooms which have sponge-like pores underneath their caps instead of gills. Some of them are edible, the most notable being the **Cep** or **Penny Bun**, *Boletus edulis*, and some of them can be brightly coloured, such as the **Yellow Bolete**, *Boletus junquilleus*, or the very poisonous red-pored **Satan's Bolete**, *Boletus santanas*. The New Forest is a good area for rare Boletes too, with a marvellous display some years at Pig Bush of the beautiful dusky pink tones of the cap of **Oldrose Bolete**, *Boletus rhodopurpureus*. It always gives a thrill of sheer excitement, to cut a red-pored specimen of **Scarletina Bolete**, *Boletus luridiformis* in half with a knife and see the almost instant change of the flesh from a dull yellow to a very vivid blue/black!

Parasitic Bolete

A rather strange member of the *Boletus* genus – the **Parasitic Bolete**, *Pseudoboletus parasiticus*, is parasitic on a fungus that looks like a Puffball, but it is in fact much harder and more solid and is an **Earthball**, *Scleroderma*, one of three varieties which are common in the Forest. Sometimes it is possible to come across an area where this rather rare fungus has infected many **Common Earthballs**, *Scleroderma citrina*. One can see several Bolete fruiting bodies surrounding, and attached to, the several rather squashed looking and eventually soft, Earthballs.

The genus *Cortinarius* the **Web Caps**, has a great many species in it, and they are well represented in our area. Many of them are rather dull brown in colour and most are difficult to identify accurately. It is almost impossible to identify the species in the field, but they all have a thin web-like veil, or cortina, when they are young, joining the edge of the cap to the stem and their rusty-coloured spores are usually evident as a light dusting of rust colour on the edge of the gills and the stem.

The **Bruising Webcap**, *Cortinarius purpurascens*, which is a

Common Earthball

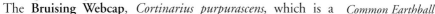

lovely lilac/purple coloured mushroom and the smaller **Blood Red Webcap**, *Cortinarius sanguineus*, with its stunning deep red cap, stem and gills, are probably the most beautiful in the genus and are certainly two of the easiest to identify in the field.

Nail fungus

If a brown, cream or orange coloured mushroom is found in, or near to, our woods, often with a funnel shaped cap, or at least with a depression in the centre, it may well be a *Lactarius* or **Milkcap**. These mushrooms are very well named, because they exude a 'milk' from the cap or stem, if they are broken or damaged. The exudation may be a clear colour, or white or orange, and it may even change its colour when exposed to the air. It also often tastes (just a fraction on the tip of the tongue is necessary) bitter, hot or mild to varying degrees and some of them also have a distinctive smell. All these features help with identification in the field. The **Coconut Milkcap**, *Lactarius glyciosmus*, has mild tasting milk which then becomes hot on the tongue, and smells distinctly of coconuts. The **Mild Milkcap**, *Lactarius cimicarius*, has mild tasting milk which then turns to bitter and smells of old rubber! The **Curry Milkcap**, *Lactarius camphoratus*, has mild watery milk but a strong smell of curry. The **Saffron Milkcap**, *Lactarius deliciosus*, has bright orange mild tasting milk and smells rather carroty or fruity and pleasant, and in addition it is very good to eat. Some people (as the name implies) think it is very delicious, in spite of rather unappetising green hues in the orange of the cap. It is especially sought after on the Continent.

Shaggy Inkcap

On the heathlands of our area the fungi specialists include various species of the **Pink Gills**, *Entolomas*, the *Galerinas*, the *Omphalinas* and some of the **Wax Caps**, *Hygrocybes*. They are often well represented if the conditions that they require are appropriate but with the exception of the Wax Caps perhaps they are among the least obvious and interesting of our fungi.

The dung from the free ranging ponies of the New Forest out on the open heathland, has a fascinating fungus, a national rarity which flourishes on New Forest pony dung and mycologists come miles to see it! It is the **Nail Fungus**, *Poronia punctata*, which looks somewhat similar to a nail and can only grow on dung that has passed through the digestive tract of an equine that exists on a poor nutritional diet that has a high fibre content. It can also be seen in our area of East Dorset – on Hartland Moor, where New Forest born ponies have been relocated and are now grazing the rough non fertilised grass areas.

Common Dung Roundhead

Dung from any mammal is a popular substrate for some fungi – including some of the short-lived genus of *Coprinus*, the **Ink Caps**, which are known for their habit of deliquescing or auto-digesting, and for some of the *Stropharia* genus, the **Roundheads**, such as the **Common Dung Roundhead**, *Strophia semiglobata*, and also the **Egghead Mottlegill**, *Panaeolus semiovatus*.

A small but interesting habitat in our area, is the sand dunes of Studland Bay and Shell Bay. It may seem rather an unlikely habitat for fungi but it is an area of specialised ones and is at present somewhat under recorded compared to the New Forest for instance. Seeing and recording is not easy because sand dunes have unique problems for fungi in that parts of them tend to be fairly mobile – so a fruiting body can be very obvious one day, but perhaps after wind and rain, it can be buried completely and may not reappear until the following year or so.

The 'yellow dunes' are unstable and constantly moving. They are usually only colonised by marram grass, *Ammophila* species, and the fungi that are specifically mycorrhizally associated with it, such as the **Agaric**, **Yellow Fieldcap**, *Bolbitius vitellinus*, *Inocybe serotina* and the **Dune Brittlestem**, *Psatherella ammophila*. The actual 'fixed dunes' have vegetation that depends on the pH (including calcium carbonate) content of the substrate. However the most important, certainly, as far as fungi are concerned, are the dune slacks, hollows and depressions with a high water table which are liable to flooding and where **Creeping Willow**, *Salix repens*, flourishes. *Geopora arenicaol* (a blackish coloured eggcup shape) and the rare *Microglossum olivaceum* (small blackish coloured fingers) and the **Fibre Caps**, genus *Inocybe*, which are rather dull coloured mushrooms, will often flourish here.

The most prolific genus of fungi in this unique habitat is probably the *Agaricus* with the sand dune specialist *Agaricus devoniensis* being the most common. It develops under the surface of the sand and emerges only when it expands as a newly formed mushroom.

Although the **Common Stinkhorn**, *Phallus impudicus*, with its white 'egg' has been found in the Studland area, the rare sandy soil specialist – the **Dune Stinkhorn** with its lovely pink coloured 'egg', has not yet been found or recorded and the unusual-looking **Stilt Puffball**, *Tulostroma mezanocyllum*, as yet also seems to be absent.

Bournemouth and the areas in and around the town, is fortunate in that it has many parks and gardens. Here the recent trend in gardening practice is to use wood chips as a weed suppressing mulch. This increasingly popular form of gardening and park management has given some species of fungi a new area to exploit. Whilst the frequently mown and fertilised manicured lawns are not very good hunting grounds for fungi the flowerbeds and shrubberies are very often the opposite.

Wood decaying fungi of many species have readily colonised this large exposure of decaying wood chips and mycologically many alien species to the United Kingdom are making an appearance.

For instance the **Redlead Roundhead**, *Strophia aurantiaca*, with its bright orange/red caps can often be seen in great profusion and even the rare **Devil's Fingers**, *Clathrus archeri*, looking like a red starfish with bright red arms may appear, both of these species originate from the Southern Hemisphere.

The lawns of our town parks and gardens, providing they have not been treated with chemicals to improve them or to kill fungi or moss, can be interesting and prolific places for grassland fungi to grow.

As in the grassland areas of the New Forest and the unimproved grassland fields of East Dorset including the military ranges where public access is limited, the **Wax Caps**, genus *Hygrocybes*, may abound in all their lovely colours of the rainbow, although, surprisingly enough, they actually originated as a woodland species. Even the rare **Pink Waxcap**, *Hygrocybe calyptriformis*, may be found in or near the woods in the short grass of the New Forest looking like a little pink ballerina dancing in the sward.

Members of the Puffball family are common here and can be an impressive sight if they are numerous. The **Giant Puffball**, *Clavatia gigantea*, is hard to miss, as it can easily grow to the size of a football. The smaller ones, such as **Meadow Puffballs**, *Vascellum pratense*, may look like a scattering of tennis balls in amongst the grass. Another species, the **Stump Puffball**, *Lycoperdon pyriforme*, is common, but it only grows on old decaying wood and tree stumps.

Notable features of open grassland, be it rough grazed fields of Dorset, smooth grass well-grazed plains of the New Forest or smart manicured lawns and parks of Bournemouth, are the very obvious fairy rings. These circular growth patterns may be caused by a variety of species of fungi and they can also occur spectacularly in woods. They were, in the past, linked to witchcraft, myths and folklore beliefs and they can indeed be very old and long lasting. As many gardeners may well be aware, they can be very difficult to eradicate from a 'well kept' lawn. The most common type in grassland is the **Fairy Ring Champignon**, *Marasmius oreades*, and also Puffballs; but in woodland some of the Agarics such as the Funnel Caps – **Trooping Funnel Cap**, *Clitocybe geotropa*, and **Clouded Funnel Cap**, *Clitocybe nebularis*, and the **Wood Blewit**, *Lepista nuda*, can sometimes make a very eyecatching show, as they encircle the trees.

Clouded Funnel Cap

There are really three kinds of Fairy Rings – the least conspicuous one being made by the true saprophytes, such as **Waxcaps**, *Hygrocybe*, confined to the upper layers of the soil only, but having no effect on the growth of the grass they can only be seen when the fruiting bodies appear. Another kind actually stimulate luxuriant grass growth and makes a lovely dark green circle but does no damage to it, and again is much more obvious when the fungi fruits. However the third type – the most often seen and so the best known, is the obvious circle caused by the **Fairy Ring**

Fairy Ring Champignon

Champignon, *Marasmius oreades*. No doubt, this is the one that was originally connected with mystery, magic and myths and is steeped in folklore. The circle itself is composed of three areas – one of lush grass from nitrogen being released from decaying mycelium, then a dead area where the mycelium is too dense for water to penetrate so that the grass dies or is stunted, then on the outer limit of the circle a lush green area of grass again where the fruit bodies appear and where the nitrogen is being actively released again into the soil.

All over our area where the grass has been allowed to go to seed, small, hard, black banana-shaped spikes may be sometimes seen protruding from the ovaries of the inflorescence of the grass. This is the **Ergot**, *Claviceps purpurea*, which is particularly common on **Purple Moor Grass**, *Molinia caerulea*, in the New Forest and on **Rye Grasses**, *Lolium*, and **Timothy** and **Cats' tails**, *Phleum*, in Dorset. There is a smaller, more specialised, variety on **Salt Marsh Grass**, *Spartina*, along our coast which has spores adapted to float in salt water. This is the fungus that was responsible for infecting rye (and sometimes wheat) when it contaminated the grain of the flour used in bread making in the Middle Ages. The disease that it caused was then known as St Anthony's Fire, because of the intense tingling and itching in the poor person's body – and even in the twentieth century there have been occasional outbreaks in Europe. It can cause gangrene in the bodies' extremities, fits and convulsions, hallucinations and even death. The Ergot itself, or sclerotia, which can easily be seen, appears in late Summer, in time for the harvest of grain for bread making! It produces conidiospores (asexual spores) which exude a sweet 'honey-dew' attractive to insects (especially flies) so they are then readily dispersed from one grass inflorescence to another. This Ergot then falls to the ground where it remains for the winter and some cold weather, and then in the Spring the fertile stage commences when it produces small 'drumstick-like' structures, which produces sexual spores that are dispersed by the wind.

Scarlet Caterpillarclub fungus

Comparatively frequently in our area it may be possible to see small bright orange club-shaped fingers peeping out of the sward, especially in grass of woodland glades. These are the fruiting bodies of an amazing fungus, called **Scarlet Caterpillarclub**, *Cordyceps militaris*, which grow from the buried dead bodies of larvae and pupae of moths and butterflies. The mycelium of the fungus actually develops and grows and eventually replaces the insides of the unfortunate doomed insect, and the fungal spores are produced on the club-part of the finger.

In the area covered by our book we have a good variety of both edible and poisonous fungi. Considered to be the best of the edible ones, are the **Cep** or **Penny Bun**, *Boletus edulis*, and the orange apricot-scented **Chanterelle**, *Cantharellus cibarius*, and the **Wood Hedgehog**, *Hydnum repandum*, which has white spines, instead of pores or gills, under the cap.

The poisonous ones are prominently represented by the *Amanita* genus – the **Death Cap**, *Amanita phalloides*, is probably the most deadly, with the **Panther Cap**, *Amanita*

Chanterelle Fungus

pantherina, coming a close second. Many of the Amanita are poisonous to a certain extent and are best avoided, although the well-known **Blusher**, *Amanita rubescens*, which has 'blushes' of pink and red on its cap and stem, especially when damaged, is considered to be edible if it is cooked, and is probably the most common one to be seen almost anywhere in our area.

It is of course, important to make a correct identification before eating anything and the fact that a fruiting body has been nibbled by rodents or slugs is absolutely no guide to edibility. For instance who would have believed that the foul smelling **Stinkhorn**, *Phallus impudicus*, that one can smell before seeing it, is actually very tasty eaten raw when in its infancy and in the form of an egg lying in the leaf litter. It is probably safe to say that nobody would attempt to try and eat a mushroom with bright sulphur-yellow cap, stem and gills with an exceedingly strong, unmistakable smell of coal-gas tar. This is a rather curious smell for any mushroom. It is called the **Sulphur Knight**, *Tricholoma sulphureum*, and in some years it can be very common indeed growing almost anywhere in our area.

Perhaps the blue/green **Aniseed Funnel**, *Clitocybe odora*, would be a more appealing morsel with its strong smell of aniseed, which is best used to flavour a dish.

The ubiquitous **Field Mushroom**, *Agaricus campestris*, still abounds in East Dorset pastures and New Forest lawns, although in the latter place a closer inspection may reveal the mushroom to be *Agaricus porphyrocephalus*. Some years the fruiting bodies mysteriously appear in more profusion than others, but an early start is the order of the day, if a reasonable collection of them is to be made – before other collectors, and the mushroom maggots, make their mark! The much larger **Horse Mushroom**, *Agaricus arvensis*, can sometimes be found and is usually big enough, with a cap measuring up to 15 cm, for all to see, especially when it is forming majestic 'fairy rings' in a pasture! The marginal habitat, where the pastures meets the woods, is favoured by **The Prince**, *Agaricus augustus*, and then under the trees themselves, may be the **Wood Mushroom**, *Agaricus silvicola*. Both these last named are, however, less common, and they both smell strongly of aniseed and are highly prized by collectors for the 'pot'.

Death Cap Fungus

Although there are many species of Truffle in Europe, there is only one species that is important in Great Britain and that is the **Summer Truffle**, *Tuber aestivum*. Unfortunately it is seldom found in our area, only appearing, albeit regularly, in a few places and often in the gardens of houses, preferring to live under beech on calcareous soils. One wonders how often it is overlooked, and just not recognised, or simply mistaken for a lump of soil. As the fruit body forms underground, its life cycle depends on it being dug up and eaten by a mammal or rodent, so that the spores inside the blackish brown globose structure may be dispersed.

The recent interest of some people in drugs and their effects on them, has made the properties of some hallucinogenic fungi rather popular amongst young people and students. Our area has its fair share of these fungi – the most notable probably being the tiny **Liberty Cap**, *Psilocybe semilanciata*, which grows in profusion in short

Panther Cap Fungus

grassland swards, or perhaps the bright red, white spotted **Fly Agaric**, *Amanita muscaria*, which has an association with birch trees and can grow to the size of a dinner plate. In the former the drug involved is Psilocybin and in the latter, the drug is Muscimol, and both are highly dangerous. The Fly Agaric, with its love of birch trees, has a short paragraph devoted to it in the first book about our area so it is very satisfactory to have it still flourishing abundantly, with its habitat still intact.

Since the last book on Bournemouth and the surrounding area, fungi have been recognised as having a kingdom of their own. They are undoubtedly beautiful to look at and have had a strange evolution on our earth where they may now be found anywhere and everywhere in the world today, including the fuel tanks of aeroplanes! They can form important partnerships with other organisms, such as algae and trees, can cause disease in ourselves and our food, can break down and recycle matter, and can help with our existence in many ways; pharmaceutical companies are prepared to spend huge amounts of money on research into them. Although our knowledge of fungi has increased dramatically in the last 100 years it is still a considerable way behind that of Botany.

All the fungi that were mentioned in the book written a century ago are still easy to see, and still flourish in the Bournemouth area, but there is now a significantly greater number of species. This is not necessarily because they did not exist 100 years ago, but probably because there are more people seeing and recording them. There is also a larger number of people collecting them to eat, often on a commercial basis, than ever before.

Fly Agaric

The names of the majority of the fungi in the first book may have changed in the intervening years and there are now, of course, many more English names evident.

It seems that in the later part of the last century, fungi may have become more important than a 'mushroom to eat' or a 'toadstool to kick' and that a significant proportion of our population is now fascinated by them.

4 Botany

Margaret Evelyn
Mike Downing

The area covered by this book (see Map on p. v) encompasses probably the largest range of botanical habitats in the country. With the exception of mountain and high moor habitats, all other UK habitat types are present somewhere in the area. The rapid urbanisation of the Bournemouth/Christchurch/Poole conurbation, plus the spread of smaller towns since 1914 and especially after the 1960s, have had a major impact on the botanical diversity. This has also led to the loss of significant areas of heath. *The Flora of Dorset* states that nationally there were 400 square kilometres of heathland in 1811 when the first accurate survey was made, with only 70 square kilometres surviving in 1990. The majority of the lowland heaths can be found in Cornwall, Devon, Dorset and Hampshire. Fortunately the creation of protected areas has helped to safeguard this botanical heritage. The most sensitive sites have been designated Sites of Special Scientific Interest (SSSI) or National Nature Reserves (NNR). Other sites have been taken over by the conservation organisations (e.g. National Trust, RSPB, Wildlife Trusts) or have become Local Nature Reserves. The New Forest has recently been designated a National Park. More significantly from a national point of view, the Dorset and Devon coast from South Haven (Poole Harbour) to Exmouth is now a World Heritage Site ('The Jurassic Coast').

Since the reforms of the Common Agricultural Policy in the late 1980s there has been improvement in the health and diversity of plants within the hedgerows and field margins. However, changes in that policy can quickly alter the balance. Co-ordinated management by the conservation organisations and Local Authorities has resulted in significant improvement of these botanical habitats. Climate change is the current issue that needs to be assessed for its implications for the future of all our botanical sites.

It is not our intention to catalogue here the multitude of species to be found within the district – they are comprehensively documented in the Dorset and Hampshire County Flora books. County Authorities have each established a database of all the botanical species found within their county and **vice-counties**. The following sections look at each of the habitats found within the area and attempt to give a view on the diversity of the species to be found, identifying those that are indicative of the habitat, those that are locally rare or have a special point of interest.

Drawing by Alison Legg.

Plantains

Two plants found frequently in our area are **Ribwort Plantain**, *Plantago lanceolata* which can be found in almost any patch of grass, in gardens or roadsides; the tiny flowers are dwarfed by the prominent stamens and **Buckshorn Plantain**, *Plantago coronopus*, which is also common in our area as it favours soil near the sea, although it can be found in sandy places inland.

Use the variation in the leafshapes as an easy key to identification, although the flowerheads are somewhat similar.

CALCAREOUS SOILS

Within the area covered by this book, there are three areas where the underlying geology of chalk or limestone has led to the development of calcareous soils. These soils are found in relatively small areas within our region, highlighted in Map 4.1.

Firstly, to the northwest of Bournemouth is an area of chalk downland. This forms part of the south-east dip slope of the large chalk escarpment comprising Cranborne Chase and the area north of the Stour valley extending from Blandford to Wimborne and Cranborne. Secondly, a narrow chalk ridge extends west to east across the Isle of Purbeck from north of Kimmeridge, passing through Corfe Castle, continuing to Ballard Down and ending at Old Harry Rocks. Thirdly, calcareous soils have also developed on the limestone areas of South Purbeck on the coast between Durlston Head and St Aldhelm's Head, extending in an east–west band inland to the north of Kimmeridge Bay. These soils include a number of soil types but all are generally thin, lacking in humus and contain much of the underlying rock fragments.

In all the above locations, natural 'unimproved' grassland is very restricted. This is the result of farming practices, in particular during the last 50 years. Extensive ploughing of chalk downland

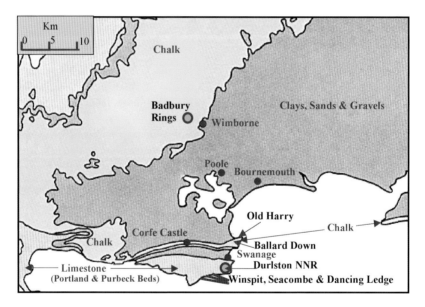

Map 4.1 Calcareous areas

Salad Burnet   *Lady's Bedstraw*   *Chalk Milkwort*

with the addition of chemical fertilisers, herbicides and pesticides, plus the compaction of soil by machinery has greatly reduced the diversity of grasses and herbs. Only on relatively undisturbed soils is the characteristic flora found. In effect this means that 'undisturbed' or 'unimproved' grassland is now mainly confined to ancient earthworks or steep slopes considered unsuitable for arable cultivation.

Horseshoe Vetch

Today these relatively small areas are still rich in flowering species and are monitored and recorded by both the national conservation bodies and local botanical groups. The Dorset Environmental Records Centre (DERC) database indicates that the total number of plants recorded across the three areas mentioned above is currently 590 of which 156 are common to all three. This compares with the BNSS 1914 Book Botany plant listing of 52 for these areas in total. This may be because of selection by the authors and also because of their limited access to the more remote areas. Equally it is not practical for us to list all 156 'common' species here.

The following list illustrates some of the diversity of these plants: **Squinancywort**, *Asperula cynanchica*, **Quaking Grass**, *Briza media*, **Musk Thistle**, *Carduus nutans*, **Dwarf Thistle**, *Cirsium acaule*, **Lady's Bedstraw**, *Galium verum*, **Horseshoe Vetch**, *Hippocrepis comosa*, **Birdsfoot Trefoil**, *Lotus corniculatus*, **Chalk Milkwort**, *Polygala calcarea*, **Salad Burnet**, *Sanguisorba minor*, **Wild Thyme**, *Thymus polytrichus*.

CHALK AREAS Badbury Rings

Situated on the dip slope of the chalk escarpment, is one of the most important sites for downland flora, Badbury Rings. This is located 5 km north-west of Wimborne on the B3082 (OS Ref: E118 ST 960 032)

Badbury Rings is an Iron Age Hill Fort, with surrounding fields and woodland. Originally part of the Bankes Estate of Kingston Lacy, it is now a scheduled Ancient Monument and has been managed by the National Trust since 1982. It is a

Badbury Rings looking NNE

striking example of the need to manage chalk grassland if the variety of plant species is to be maintained. During the years of neglect in the 1960s and 70s, nature was allowed to take its own course, resulting in the domination of the area by scrubland species (e.g. bramble, dog rose and field rose) to the detriment of the less robust plants and the consequential effect on the animal, bird, butterfly and insect populations. The National Trust undertook the mammoth task of returning the site to its former glory, a task completed in 1986 with the invaluable assistance of volunteers from The Prince of Wales Trust.

Based on the Estate Archives, the National Trust was able to understand and programme a land management scheme that would encourage and support the return of the plant species. However, one of the 'negative' consequences of the scrub clearance was the reduction of several insect, butterfly and moth species. The key to success is the grazing of the steep slopes of the Rings by sheep at appropriate times of the year. Similarly, cattle are allowed on the relatively level surrounding grassland. The level of grazing can be controlled ('light cropping' through to 'down to a stubble') such that, over a cycle of several years, conditions exist to suit a very large range of plant species. Now 20 years on we can once again enjoy the floral diversity of this location. The BNSS 1914 Book lists only a handful of plants specifically at Badbury Rings:

- Bastard-toadflax *Thesium humifusum* – still present
- Field Fleawort *Tephroseris integrifolia* – its presence was re-confirmed in 2003 when 2 plants were found and more recently in 2008
- Pheasant's Eye, *Adonis annua* – a weed of cultivation in a field adjacent to the Rings
- Fine-leaved Fumitory *Fumaria parviflora* – for both of these plants the last DERC current record is pre-1990 and both are now considered lost from these sites.

Pyramidal Orchid

DERC records currently indicate 215 plant species for the Rings and adjacent field margins. There is insufficient space to give a full account of all the species to be found here; the following illustrates the range and variety to be found progressively throughout the year.

In spring the steeper slopes slowly awaken with **Common Milkwort** *Polygala vulgaris* and **Chalk Milkwort**, *P. calcarea*, (not easy to differentiate), **Early Purple Orchid**, *Orchis mascula*, **Salad Burnet**, *Sanguisorba minor*, and **Twayblade**, *Listera ovata*; in the ditches can be found **Primrose**, *Primula vulgaris*, and **False Oxlip**, *Primula x polyantha,* (a hybrid of the Primrose and the abundant **Cowslip** *P. veris*). In the hedgerows **Blackthorn**, *Prunus spinosa*, and, slightly later, **Hawthorn**, *Crataegus monogyna*, are coming into bloom. As the season progresses, a succession of orchids appear. The **Common Spotted Orchid**, *Dactylorhiza fuchsii*, is widely distributed along the Rings; the **Pyramidal Orchid**, *Anacamptis pyramidalis*, and **Fragrant Orchid**, *Gymnadenia conopsea*, appear on the shorter turf; whilst the **Greater Butterfly Orchid**, *Platanthera chlorantha*, tends to favour the more sheltered ditch sides. The **Bee Orchid**, *Ophrys apifera*, occurs in small groups and the **Frog Orchid**, *Dactylorhiza viridis*, is very localised and difficult to spot. The diminutive **Autumn Lady's Tresses**, *Spiranthes spiralis*, appear towards the end of the summer.

Fragrant Orchid

Whilst the orchids are often the main attraction for visitors, there are many other interesting and readily identifiable plants, mostly on the Rings themselves, others in the fields or on road and track margins nearby:

Autumn Gentian, *Gentianella amarella*.
Goat's-Beard, *Tragopogon pratensis*.
Meadow Vetchling, *Lathyrus pratensis*.
Small Scabious, *Scabiosa columbaria*.
White Helleborine, *Cephalanthera damasonium*.
Eyebright, *Euphrasia officinalis agg.*

Autumn Lady's Tresses

Marjoram, *Origanum vulga*
Oxeye Daisy, *Leucanthemum vulgare.*
Small-flowered Sweetbriar *Rosa micr*
Wild Mignonette, *Reseda lutea.*

In addition, there are all the plants listed in the introduction to calcareous soils. We recorded 79 flowering species during our BNSS Field Meeting in June 2007.

Old Harry and Ballard Down

The second area of calcareous soils comprises the narrow chalk ridge extending west–east to Ballard Down and Old Harry Rocks.

White Helleborine

Dominated by the majestic chalk cliffs, rolling hills of rough grassland and panoramic views across Poole and Swanage Bays, the walk from the South Beach Car Park (OS Ref: OL15 SZ 037 825) at Studland along the Coastal Path to Old Harry, over Ballard Down and back down into the village is a botanical delight in early summer.

As with Badbury Rings, the area was part of the Bankes' Kingston Lacy Estate until passing to the National Trust. The coastal meadows were productive, ploughed fields until the late 1980s when the decision was taken to allow these meadows to revert to managed grassland. Now, remnants of the native arable plants, lost when chemicals were used on the land, are becoming re-established: **Corn Marigold**, *Chrysanthemum segetum*, **Field Pansy**, *Viola arvensis*, **Oxeye Daisy**, *Leucanthemum vulgare*, and **Yellow Rattle**, *Rhinanthus minor*. On Ballard Down the hedgerows separating the fields have been removed to return the downland to an open, exposed rounded ridge with marvellous views across Swanage Bay to the south and Poole Harbour to the north. Sheep and cattle are used as part of the land management programme. The top of the Down is, as yet, relatively sparse in flowering plants, dominated by **Tor Grass**, *Brachypodium rupestre*, and managed scrub such as **Hawthorn**, *Crataegus monogyna*, and **Gorse**, *Ulex europaeus*, with **Musk Thistle**, *Carduus nutans*, providing a splash of colour in summer.

Field Pansy

However it is along the cliff edge margin (following the Coastal Path), relatively untouched by the plough and in the adjacent field (now re-instated as a wild flower meadow) that the greatest diversity of plants can be found. It should be noted that the BNSS 1914 Book makes no reference to Old Harry or Ballard Down, but has a brief mention of Nine Barrow Down (further to the west towards Corfe Castle) where the rare **Nottingham Catchfly**, *Silene nutans*, was found and also a reference to the downs at Ulwell where the Glaucous Scotch Thistle, now named **Cotton Thistle**, *Onopordum acanthium*, was recorded.

Bee Orchid

A visitor to the cliff top near Old Harry can now find a colourful mix of plants including: **Rest-harrow**, *Ononis repens*, **Common and Greater Knapweed**, *Centaurea nigra* and *C. scabiosa*, **Common Centaury**, *Centaurium erythraea*, **Sea Beet**, *Beta vulgaris* ssp. *maritima*; **Horseshoe Vetch**, *Hippocrepis comosa*, **Kidney Vetch**, *Anthyllis vulneraria*, and **Wild Carrot**, *Daucus carota*.

Less prolific, but pleasing to find, is a small population of **Pyramidal Orchid**, *Anacamptis pyramidalis*, and the occasional **Bee Orchid**, *Ophrys apifera*.

The coastal path from Old Harry leads up and on to Ballard Down. The mix of plants slowly changes and becomes less diverse, however here one may find small clusters of **Yellow-wort**, *Blackstonia perfoliata*, **Common Rock-rose**, *Helianthemum nummularium* and **Tufted Vetch**, *Vicia cracca*.

The DERC records currently indicate 392 plant species at Old Harry and Ballard Down. During one of our BNSS Field Meetings in June 2007 (on a circular walk from Studland South Beach car park to Old Harry, on to Ballard Down and then down the north facing slope back into the village) we recorded 117 species in flower.

Common Centaury

Common Knapweed

Yellow-wort

Musk Thistle

LIMESTONE AREAS (Portland and Purbeck Beds)

South of the above chalk ridge and separated from it by the clay vale, lies the limestone plateau of South Purbeck. Soils are again thin and lime-rich and, although chemicals from the meadows that used to be arable fields have enriched some, there are areas relatively unimproved especially between Worth Matravers and Durlston Head. South of Worth Matravers are areas of medieval **strip lynchets** (a good example can be seen in the Seacombe valley) – indicating minimal disturbance in modern times. Along the coastal strip, stone quarries provide protected habitats and thin soils for the more delicate lime-loving species. Access to this area is limited. Car parking (with facilities) is available in the east at Durlston Country Park (OS Ref: OL15 SZ 033 774) and in the west at Worth Matravers Car Park (SY 974 776). A third access point between the above is at Spyway Barn NT Car Park (SY 998 777) but has no facilities and limited parking space. All these locations provide access to the Coastal Path. Note the paths down from Worth Matravers to either Seacombe or Winspit are steep in places and very rough. Similarly, the Coastal Path through Durlston Head Country Park is steep and rough in places, although the paths through meadows from the Information Centre are easy going.

Durlston Country Park NNR

Throughout spring and early summer, Durlston Country Park (managed by Dorset County Council) is a botanical haven. The meadows above the coastal area are actively managed (as at Badbury Rings) to provide conditions for a large range of species. Obtainable from the Visitor Centre is a checklist detailing over 350 species of wild flowers and their status within the park.

Wild Teasel

Grass Vetchling

Woolly Thistle

Walking through the inland meadows one may find many of the plants already mentioned in the chalk areas. Here is just a selection of others to whet your appetite: **Agrimony**, *Agrimonia eupatoria*, **Black Horehound**, *Ballota nigra*, **Field Madder**, *Sherardia arvensis*, **Marjoram** *Origanum vulgare*, **Meadow Vetchling**, *Lathyrus pratensis*, **Pale Flax**, *Linum bienne*, **Wild Parsnip** *Pastinaca sativa* and **Wild Teasel**, *Dipsacus fullonum*. A rarity is **Grass Vetchling**, *Lathyrus nissolia*.

Following the coastal path through the park one finds **Kidney Vetch**, *Anthyllis vulneraria*, **Sea Campion** *Silene uniflora*, **Thrift**, *Armeria maritima*, **Thyme-leaved**, **Sandwort** *Moehringia trinervia,* and isolated plants of the **Rock Samphire**, *Crithmum maritimum* and **Woolly Thistle**, *Cirsium eriophorum*. On the path between the Tilly Whim Caves and the Lighthouse can be found a large population of **Golden Samphire**, *Inula crithmoides*. Whilst the Golden Samphire is mentioned in the 1914 Book, very few other plants are noted for this area.

Dancing Ledge area

Spyway Barn provides relatively easy access down to Dancing Ledge. From there to Winspit in early spring the **Early Spider Orchid**, *Ophrys sphegodes* and **Green-winged Orchid**, *Anacamptis morio* can be found alongside the path in the short turf. The bright colours of the **Viper's Bugloss**, *Echium vulgare*, can be seen on the exposed rock platform at Dancing Ledge in early summer. You may also find the occasional plants of **Wild Clary**, *Salvia verbenaca* in the meadow side of the coastal path, and of **Yellow-wort**, *Blackstonia perfoliata*, and **Sea Campion**, *Silene uniflora*, on the cliff side in summer.

Sea Aster

Kidney Vetch

Early Spider Orchid

Wild Clary

Seacombe and Winspit area

Within the protection of cliffs and abandoned quarries at Winspit there are undisturbed niches for **Sea Aster**, *Aster tripolium*, **Golden Samphire**, *Inula crithmoides*, and **Rock Samphire**, *Crithmum maritimum*, **Danish and Common Scurvygrass**, *Cochlearia danica,* and *C. officinalis,* and **Early Spider Orchid**, *Ophrys sphegodes.*

DERC records currently indicate 463 plant species for the area between Durlston Head and St Aldhelm's Head. During one of our BNSS Field Meetings to Durlston Country Park in July 2007 we recorded 77 species in flower. An early meeting, walking from Winspit to Dancing Ledge, recorded only 15 flowering species in April 2006 (a very late spring!).

HEATHLANDS HABITAT

To recline on a stump of thorn . . . where the eye could reach nothing of the world outside the summits and shoulders of heathland which filled the whole circumference of its glance, and to know that everything around and underneath had been from prehistoric times as unaltered as the stars overhead, gave ballast to the mind adrift on change, and harassed by the irrepressible new, twilight combined with the scenery of [the] Heath to evolve a thing majestic without severity, impressive without showiness, emphatic in its admonitions, grand in its simplicity . . . for the storm was its lover and the wind its friend.

Return of the Native, THOMAS HARDY

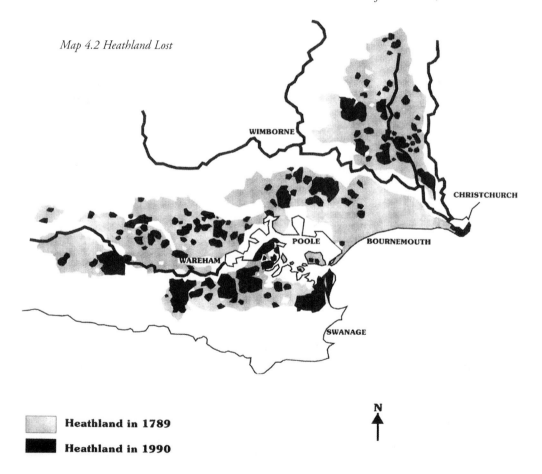

Map 4.2 Heathland Lost

WIMBORNE

CHRISTCHURCH

POOLE · BOURNEMOUTH

WAREHAM

SWANAGE

N

☐ **Heathland in 1789**

■ **Heathland in 1990**

In August, the lowland heaths are ablaze with colour. The purple and gold of the heather and gorse are simply stunning. Although we think of this landscape as natural, it is in fact manmade. The original wild wood was felled by early man. The soil, already of too poor a quality to grow crops, was further impoverished by the elements. Soon these areas could support little but heather. Resourcefully, the inhabitants used these apparently hopeless tracts for rough grazing. The heather was cut for animal bedding, and mature gorse stems were used as fuel. Silver birches provided materials for brooms, and roofs were thatched with heather. By these means the habitat was preserved as treeless areas of poor soil. Thus heathland, and the wildlife which relied on it, was maintained.

By the nineteenth century, such practices were dying out. The general urbanisation, led by the Industrial Revolution, meant that many deserted the land. Those that stayed lived in increasing poverty, especially when attempting to farm on poor soils.

In Talbot Village, such was their plight, that two local benefactors, the Misses Georgina and Charlotte Talbot took pity on them. Although they built a school and cottages, the records in St Mark's church show that shoes had to be found for some of the children, and sometimes food too.

Keen botanists will relish the challenge presented by heathland. What it lacks in diversity is compensated for by the hunt for such rarities as the Bog Orchid and the Marsh Gentian.

At the same time there is another more important reason for everyone interested in all branches of wildlife to keep the heaths to the forefront of the public consciousness. The urban pressures on this habitat are great, and any relaxation of the current protection would threaten this shrinking habitat with the danger of losing its unique flora and fauna. Motor cycling, vandalism and deliberate arson are constant threats. In recognition of this, local authorities in south-east Dorset have produced a planning framework to manage pressures on sensitive heathlands resulting from development. Residential development within 400 m of heaths is not allowed (with some exceptions) and mitigation fees apply in a zone stretching from 400 m to 5 km from heathland sites.

Tribute must be paid to enthusiastic local residents, such as the excellent Friends of Kinson Common. Similar groups have worked hard to maintain their local heath, and have made efforts to identify and record their botanical findings. As a result, these small areas are in surprisingly good shape, with a wide and fascinating collection of plants on site. Fire is an ever-present hazard, as is thoughtless motorcycling. Both of these occurrences, though still present, have been minimized through Urban Heath partnership wardening and education work and by sensitive policing and co-operation with schools and voluntary groups.

As well as being protected by law, the proximity to housing has had an unexpectedly beneficial effect. The thousands of residents whose homes back onto Canford Heath, for example, can hardly fail to notice the golden sheets of Bog Asphodel, or the purple haze of the Ling.

Local schools have done much to teach children about their surroundings, thus introducing a new generation to the glories of the local heaths.

The future certainly looks brighter than it did even twenty years ago, and one can only hope that continued appreciation for this nationally scarce environment will ensure its survival.

Ling with White Bell heather

It is also interesting to note that in spite of the fact that the area surrounding the BNSS was unspoiled heathland in the early years of the Society, very few field meetings were held there. In 1945, a group of botanists explored the Coy Pond and Bourne Valley areas, but little of note is recorded. Most of the 'excursions' were to the more exciting locations of chalk downland.

One wonders if wartime restrictions on travel and coastal defences were responsible for what seems to be an attempt to botanise in a place that was considered to be very much the poor relation of habitats. Such attitudes seem to typify the decline of lowland heath. Unlike the moors of the north, where grouse shooting ensured careful management, lowland heath apparently had little to offer. Thus the drift away from the heaths meant that the traditional management methods went as well.

The unproductive heathland through the first half of the twentieth century was often described as 'scrub', or 'wasteland'. It was no surprise, therefore, as Bournemouth and Poole grew apace, that these sadly neglected areas were seen as ideal land for building roads, factories and houses. By the time the value of this habitat became apparent, the large areas described in Hardy's novels were reduced to small fragments.

In the last two decades of the twentieth century, various organisations managed to halt the decline at the eleventh hour. EU regulations, the conferring of SSSI status by Natural England, local authorities and their countryside wardens, together with hard work by voluntary organisations such as the Dorset Wildlife Trust (DWT), Herpetological Conservation Trust (HCT) and the RSPB have combined to protect what is left of our wonderful heathlands.

For the purpose of this book, we are mainly dealing with the heathlands west of the Avon river. Although superficially similar, the New Forest heaths are slightly different because of the grazing and management methods over many years.

Dorset has one of the largest remaining areas of European lowland heath, some of it within the urban conurbation. Botanically, this is divided into two separate habitats: dry heath and wet and humid heath, and these are dealt with separately.

Dry Heath

The predominant botanical habitat in the Bournemouth area is dry acid heathland, where the natural nutrients have been washed away, resulting in a top layer of podsol.

'Podsol', or 'podzol', or 'spodosol', is a phenomenon that occurs worldwide. The basic process involves the leaching of nutrients from the top layer of soil, resulting in poor fertility. The word itself is descriptive : 'pod' and 'zola' are Russian for 'under' and 'ash', which perfectly evokes the whitish-grey so typical of this type of soil. Generally, podsols are the result of a combination of factors which occur naturally. However, in its European context it is distinctive in that it is largely formed as a result of human interference, as explained in the introduction. The porous nature of the poor quality soil means that rainwater passes straight through. The result is that any nutrients are washed away, and that the top soil is very dry. These conditions, coupled with the acidity of the soil, mean that the number of botanical species is restricted.

Ling, *Calluna vulgaris*, **Bell Heather**, *Erica cinerea*, and the three Gorses, **European Gorse**, *Ulex europaeus*, **Western Gorse**, *U. gallii*, and **Dwarf Gorse**, *U. minor*, dominate these areas.

Easily identified, the tall European gorse pervades the spring air with its smell of coconut. In the late summer and autumn, the keen botanist can spend many hours separating the Western and Dwarf Gorses. Normally a quick glance at a UK map would help, as in most cases there is an east–west divide, as can be guessed from the names. Central southern England, however is one of the few places where the species meet. As the two very similar species sometimes grow side by side, identification is a constant challenge.

Urban examples of dry heath include Canford Heath, Kinson Common, Turbary Common and Bourne Valley. Just outside the conurbation are Hurn and Avon Forests, Sopley Common and Upton Heath.

One of the largest areas in the country including dry heath is Purbeck. The huge tracts around Poole Harbour are relatively unaffected by urban pressures, and are heavily protected by law. However, this habitat is under continual pressure from increasing conifer afforestation.

Despite the very limited number of species, dry heath has one or two interesting curiosities. One of these is the **Common Dodder**, *Cuscuta epithymum*, whose delicate rusty strands may be spotted on the heather in summer. This strange plant has tiny tufts of creamy, honey-scented flowers. It is to be seen mainly on heather and gorse. It depends on haustoria, which are stem tips adapted to draw nutrients from the host plant.

Although dry heathland is generally of limited botanical interest, it is that very limitation which provides us with such dramatic swathes of purple and yellow in late summer.

Common Dodder

Careful searching among the vegetation in early summer may reveal the intense blue of the **Heath Milkwort**, *Veronica serpyllifolia*. In bare, shady patches one may come across the bluish purple of the **Heath Dog Violet**, *Viola canina*. Frothy white clumps of **Heath Bedstraw**, *Galium saxatile*, and the yellow stars of **Tormentil**, *Potentilla erecta,* can be found within gaps in early summer.

Wet Heath

Some of the impoverished heathland contains lens-shaped strata far below the topsoil. These areas of clay subsoil impede the drainage so characteristic of heathland. The resultant build up of moisture is responsible for wet, and the slightly less damp, humid heath. In these places, we see a greater variety of plants because of the increased water supply.

The Bell Heather and Ling give way to **Cross-leaved Heath**, *Erica tetralix*. Sphagnum mosses are intermixed with the insectivorous sundews. The **Round-leaved Sundew**, *Drosera rotundifolia* and the intermediate **Oblong-leaved Sundew**, *Drosera intermedia*, are found fairly easily, while the **Great Sundew**, *Drosera anglica* is something of a rarity. These plants supplement the meagre nitrogen supply they receive from the soil by catching tiny insects on the sticky glands of their leaves. The urban heaths of Bournemouth, such as Kinson and Turbary Commons have both of the former species, while the Great Sundew can be found on the Purbeck.

One can also be fortunate enough to find another insectivorous plant without going outside the Borough of Bournemouth. The **Pale Butterwort**, *Pinguicula lusitanica* is difficult to find, but this small attractive plant, with its delicate pale violet flowers, is present in at least one location in the Bournemouth area.

Further afield, on Purbeck, the bright yellow flowers of the **Bladderworts**, *Utricularia sp.* can

Round Leaved Sundew

Marsh Gentian

Oblong Leaved Sundew

Heath Spotted Orchid

Dorset Heath

Bog Orchid

Bog Asphodel

be found in ponds and wet heathy places. Also insectivorous, the bladders imbibe tiny creatures in pools of acid water.

One would have to visit the western margins of the area covered in order to see the beautiful upturned bells of the **Marsh Gentian**, *Gentiana pneumonanthe*, the silvery patches on the petals making the rich purple-blue appear even more intense. Its very particular requirements are mysterious, but it apparently favours damp, open heathland sites of the sort found on some of the Dorset heaths. It can be found on Slop Bog and DWT Nature Reserve Upton Heath.

The **Heath Spotted Orchid**, *Dactylorhiza maculata,* also grows extensively when conditions are right, preferring humid to wet heath. In similar sites one might find the attractive **Common Lousewort**, *Pedicularis sylvatica* together with the woody, aromatic **Sweet Gale** or **Bog Myrtle**, *Myrica gale*. This plant has male and female on separate plants, and the spicy scent pervades the spring marshes.

The damper heath is home also to three nationally rare plants. **Dorset Heath**, *Erica ciliaris,* is present on a few sites in the Purbeck area. Its vivid pink flowers in late summer look like a giant version of Cross-leaved Heath.

Possibly the **Bog Orchid**, *Hammarbya paludosa,* is not as rare as it would seem to be. The botanist who finds this plant will go home happy that he has found a 6 cm plant among tangles of robust grasses of a similar colour, in a bog.

Rarest of all is the **Heath Lobelia**, *Lobelia urens,* now sadly restricted to just one site in Dorset. As recently as 1956, the BNSS records reveal that 'large quantities' of this plant were found near Moreton station.

Not at all rare, and a joy to behold in many areas of Bournemouth and Poole, is the annual golden carpet of **Bog Asphodel**, *Narthecium ossifragum*. These delightful summer lilies thrive on the wet acid soil, and perform a great job in publicising the visual beauty of heathland. Such colourful displays are very effective as a way of convincing the public that urban heaths are to be valued for their scenic qualities.

Despite the best efforts of the authorities, this fragile habitat is under constant threat. Although stricter controls have been introduced recently, it is clear that the remaining heaths deserve the best protection we can give them.

———————oOo———————

Five Bournemouth Gems

Within the borough of Bournemouth, there are five open spaces, that are owned and managed by the council. Each one is ably assisted by an enthusiastic voluntary group. All are designated Local Nature Reserves (LNR). Some are formed from old commons, some have an agricultural history, and some have vestigial remnants of the heathland which covered so much of the land on which

Bournemouth stands. There is a great deal of botanical interest, with some rarities among the colourful Buttercups, Campions and Thistles. These areas have been much neglected in the past, but as a result of hard work by the wardens and volunteers, there are now five oases which are home to a variety of wildlife. They are tranquil places to visit for residents and visitors alike. It is inevitable that such places are under pressure when surrounded by an urban conurbation, but on the whole their beauty is respected and protected.

The five areas are: Turbary Common, Kinson Common, Redhill Common, Stour Valley and Millhams Mead. Details of the five Bournemouth Open Spaces can be found at: www.communigate.co.uk/dorset

Redhill Common SZ 088955

Thanks to the efforts of the Redhill Conservation Group, formed in 2002, this north Bournemouth oasis improves year by year in terms of interest and diversity. As is the case with many such sites in Bournemouth, its history is rather vague. It appears that there was once a scattering of cottages, with an alehouse and a bakery.

The common itself was formerly part of a north–south route between Poole Harbour and a ferry across the river Stour. Thus, although predominately heathland, the vestigial remains of cultivation give rise to some non-heathland plants. A special bonus is the creation by Bournemouth council of one of the wildflower meadows scattered around the Borough. Here one can see the red and yellow of **Common Poppy**, *Papaver rhoeas,* and **Corn Marigold**, *Chrysanthemum segetum,* set off by the blue of **Cornflower**, *Centurea cyanus,* and white of **Scentless Mayweed**, *Tripleurospermum inodorum.* All the usual heathland plants are here as well.

Turbary Common (both dry and wet heath) SZ 061948

(Friends of Turbary Common) Main entrance: Turbary Park Avenue. Other entrance: Downey Close. Notice boards at each of the entrances, with details of guided walks, etc.

This surprisingly peaceful area is a rectangle bounded by four busy roads. As well as being a LNR, the heathland section is a designated Site of Special Scientific Interest (SSSI), and contains a rare valley mire. This area, in particular, is of great botanical value. Exploration here requires wet weather footwear, and care should be taken to make sure that one does not stand on the very plant one has come to see. Management methods include grazing by several Exmoor ponies, aided by Shetland cattle in the winter.

Turbary Common has had several uses in the past, one of them being a municipal tip. As a consequence, many atypical plants appear. Examples are **Lesser Burdock**, *Arctium minus,* **Great Mullein**, *Verbascum thapsus,* a double form of **Creeping Cinquefoil**, *Potentilla reptans,* **Purple Toadflax**, *Linaria purpurea,* and **Creeping Jenny**, *Lysimachia nummularia.*

There is also the delicate blue of **Pale Flax**, *Linum bienne,* in early summer, and **Red Bartsia**, *Odontites vernus,* later on.

The dry banks of the heathland area are home to two of the common varieties of heather namely **Ling**, *Calluna vulgaris,* and **Bell Heather**, *Erica cinerea.* **Cross-leaved Heath**, *Erica tetralix,* favours the slightly damper conditions of the lower slopes.

It is here that a careful search should reveal the two species of Sundew present on the common, the **Round-leaved**, *Drosera rotundifolia,* and the **Oblong-leaved**, *D.intermedia.* The occasional insignificant white flower might be seen, but it is the glistening sticky drops on the red hairs which one notices first. This insectivorous plant relies on the insects thus trapped for its nutrition.

Great Mullein

Nearby, one might be fortunate enough to find the beautiful but diminutive **Pale Butterwort**, *Pinguicula lusitanica*. This plant, also insectivorous, is deceptively delicate in appearance. The slimy basal leaves, arranged in a star shape, are traps for unwary insects. The flower is pale violet with a yellow throat. It is only ever found on wet heaths such as this.

Much easier to find, especially in high summer, are the golden yellow spikes of **Bog Asphodel**, *Narthecium ossifragum*. The species name (*ossi* – bones, and *fragum* – broken) came about because in the past the plant was blamed for the lameness of farm animals which had been grazing in the area where the plant thrived. Eventually it was realised that the damaged feet and limbs were caused not by Bog Asphodel, but the dampness of the land which led to the lack of calcium in the grazing.

In the wettest part of the bog, one has to take care, as the tussocks are very wet and slippery. In early June one can be rewarded by the sight of the splendid **Early Marsh Orchids**, *Dactylorhiza incarnata*. These lovely flowers vary greatly in colour, ranging from pink through rose to deep purple.

Kinson Common (both dry and wet heath) access and parking next to Kinson cemetery

In spite of being surrounded by an intensely built-up urban area, Kinson Common is home to many interesting plants. It was scarcely mentioned in the 1914 book, possibly because it was then simply a part of a large tract of Dorset countryside of similar character.

Kinson's success botanically is due almost entirely to the efforts of the excellent Friends of Kinson Common. Together with the countryside wardens of Bournemouth Borough Council, the management work they have undertaken has resulted in a small area which is full of interest for the botanist.

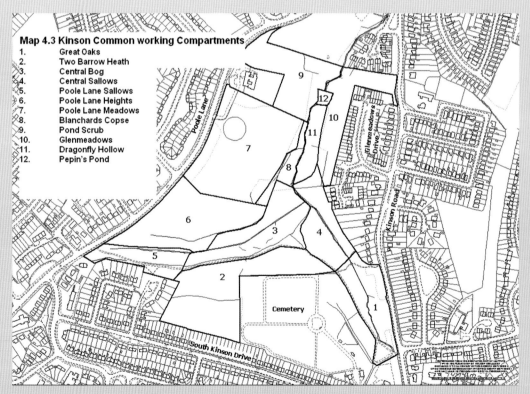

Map 4.3 Kinson Common working Compartments

1. Great Oaks
2. Two Barrow Heath
3. Central Bog
4. Central Sallows
5. Poole Lane Sallows
6. Poole Lane Heights
7. Poole Lane Meadows
8. Blanchards Copse
9. Pond Scrub
10. Glenmeadows
11. Dragonfly Hollow
12. Pepin's Pond

Map 4.3 Kinson Common working compartments

An extremely successful grazing scheme was set up in 2005. The four Shetland cattle have settled in happily, and they have had an important role in keeping down the coarse scrub which otherwise would threaten to obliterate the smaller plants.

The Common has a number of diverse habitats, which are given popular names for convenience. Poole Lane Heights and Two Barrow Heath consist mainly of dry heath. Among the dominant **Ling**, *Calluna vulgaris* and **Common Gorse**, *Ulex europaea*, can be found the tiny pink **Sand Spurrey**, *Spergularia rubra*, and the **Birdsfoot**, *Ornithopus perpusillus*, not to be confused with **Birdsfoot Trefoil**, *Lotus corniculatus*. Probably the richest area for notable species is the east–west Central Bog, which extends to Dragonfly Hollow and Pepin's Pond to the north. Here can be found two of the three native **Sundews**: the **Round-leaved**, *Drosera rotundifolia*, and the **Intermediate** *Drosera intermedia*. A more diligent search might reveal another insectivorous species, the **Pale Butterwort**, *Pinguicula lusitanica*.

Perhaps the best time to see the Common is early June. A stunning display of orchids in their hundreds greets the visitor. The **Heath Spotted** *Dactylorhiza maculata*, the **Early Marsh**, *D. incarnata* and the spectacularly tall **Southern Marsh**, *D. praetermissa* dominate the marshland. They are followed by the regal spires of **Yellow Loosestrife**, *Lysimachia vulgaris*, and the carpets of **Bog Asphodel**, *Narthecium ossifragum*.

The footpath in the Great Oaks compartment is of interest, as the drier banks provide habitat for Speedwells, Vetches and the creamy-yellow **Cowwheat**, *Melampyrum pratense*. Poole Lane Meadows is managed by traditional methods as a hay meadow. Plants of interest growing alongside the grasses include **Sheepsbit**, *Jasione montana*, **Devils Bit Scabious**, *Succisa pratensis*, **Meadow Thistle**, *Cirsium dissectum*, and **Greater Knapweed**, *Centaurea scabiosa*, along with **Pignut**, *Conopodium majus* and **Cuckoo Flower**, *Cardamine pratensis*.

Southern Marsh Orchid

One wonders what the Revd Linton, who surveyed the area exhaustively in the early 1900s, would have made of such a superbly maintained botanical oasis one hundred years later. Although several species have disappeared, others have appeared, and still more have increased in number. This is a delightful area whose survival should be supported wholeheartedly.

Millhams Mead SZ 063969

Again benefiting from the hard work of volunteers, namely the Millham Meaders, this footpath takes in a variety of habitats, including streamside vegetation, woodland and land reclaimed from a former rubbish tip. One of the main features of this route is the ancient Cudnell Wood. Here important oaks, some over 200 years old, are surrounded by **Wood Anemones**, *Anemone nemorosa*, and other spring flowers in the early part of the year. The BBC are currently working to improve this site for visitors.

Stour Valley Local Nature Reserve (LNR) SZ 096961

This area is part of the 23 mile long Stour Valley Way. The footpath links Christchurch and Sturminster Marshall. The Bournemouth section includes the ancient Throop Mill. By parking here, crossing the weir and following a clockwise route, one can enjoy a 2–3 mile flat walk, while passing a variety of attractive habitats, including meadows, riverside, farmland and woods.

As well as the colourful Foxgloves, Comfreys and Clovers, there are the lacy white clouds of **Cow Parsley**, *Anthriscus sylvestris*, and **Hemlock Water Dropwort**, *Oenanthe crocata*, edging the river. In the wet areas, yet another umbellifer, **Tubular Water Dropwort**, *Oenanthe fistulosa*, can be found among the wet grass.

The delicate spikes of **Water-Speedwell**, *Veronica anagallis-aquatica*, might be seen where the water flows slowly, while the handsome **Flowering Rush**, *Butomus umbellatus*, anchors itself to the debris in midstream.

In the quieter waters behind the weir the yellow of wild **Waterlilies**, *Nuphar lutea*, contrast with the intense blue of **Brooklime**, *Veronica beccabunga*.

A careful search at the field edges might reveal some interesting weeds of cultivation, such as Common Fumitory, Common Poppy and Scarlet Pimpernel.

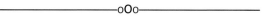

Ham Common Local Nature Reserve

This delightful area, with stunning views of Poole Harbour and its islands, is well worth a visit. Its LNR status is largely on account of its unspoilt heathland.

As well as the three main heathers, one can see **Round-leaved Sundew**, *Drosera rotundifolia*, and **Marsh Woundwort**, *Stachys palustris,* in the damper places. There are also several plants of **Yellow-wort**, *Blackstonia perfoliata*, a beautiful member of the Gentian Family, Gentianaceae, the diminutive **Yellow Centaury**, *Cicenda filiformis*, whose grey-green leaves completely encircle the stem, as its scientific name suggests.

The lake, whose colour changes from deep turquoise to a sinister dark grey, is lined with the remains of the clay which was once quarried in this area. The marshy edges are home to a rich variety of water plants, including **Common Water-plantain**, *Alisma plantago-aquatica,* **Marsh Marigold**, *Caltha palustris,* **Meadowsweet**, *Filipendula ulmaria* and the violet spikes of **Purple Loosestrife**, *Lythrum salicaria.*

The reserve is bordered by the 'storm shingle' beach that marks the seaward limit of the Reserve. Here are some interesting maritime plants, including **Sea Campion**, *Silene uniflora*, **Sand Couch**, *Elytrigia juncea* and **Sand Sedge**, *Carex arenaria.*

SMALL PLANTS OF COASTAL AREAS

Coastal habitats are characteristically bleak. The continual erosion by sea and winds results in poor soils with an element of salt in their makeup. At first glance, the more sheltered parts of this environment seem to be dominated by large, robust plants and colonising grasses such as **Marram**, *Ammophila arenaria,* and **Cord Grass**, *Spartina anglica.*

Closer examination, however, reveals a fascinating world of tiny plants. They are too small to be affected by rough winds, and, in particularly exposed locations, untroubled by competition from the larger plants. Grazing, as at Stanpit Marsh for example, together with nibbling by rabbits, go even further to control the coarser plants.

The following can be seen in our area, either close to the sea or in similar conditions not far away. **Mossy Stonecrop**, *Crassula tillaea*, is present on Coward's Marsh and other parts of our area. This tiny plant becomes easier to spot as the summer progresses, as the leaves become intensely red. Although declining nationally, we are lucky enough to have an increasing population locally, with the result that Dorset has become one of its main strongholds. It is almost exclusively near the coast, but it can also be found on bare, sandy soil slightly inland. **Sea Sandwort**, *Honckenya peploides,* is found occasionally in parts of Christchurch Harbour, and on sandy grass verges in Sandbanks. Sometimes the male and female flowers are on separate plants, which may account for its comparative rarity. Clues to identification are the greenish white flowers which are roughly equal in length to the **sepals** on the male, but much shorter on the female ones. The yellow-green leaves are arranged neatly, with geometric regularity.

Identifying the Sea-spurreys can be a problem. **Rock Sea-Spurrey**, *Spergularia rupicola* with its pink flowers is mainly found on the rocky coasts of Devon and Cornwall. However, there are several plants at Durlston Country Park near the disused quarry area. The very specificity of its habitat is helpful in distinguishing it from the **Greater Sea-Spurrey**, *Spergularia media*, and **Lesser Sea-Spurrey**, *S. marina*. *S. media* can be found in the drier parts of saltmarshes. The pale pink flowers have petals longer than sepals. This is the main factor in distinguishing it from the Lesser Sea-Spurrey, where the position is reversed. Both *S. media* and *S. marina* can be seen in our area in open spaces and along roadsides near to the sea in Poole and the Purbeck.

Lesser Sea-Spurrey

Sea Knotgrass, *Polygonum maritimum* is an extremely rare plant which is, none the less, present in our area. Its discovery in the Christchurch area shows how important it is to scrutinise every plant rather than assuming that it is of the common variety. At one stage its extinction in the UK was recorded, but diligent botanists found it in one site in the mid-1990s. It can be distinguished from the similar **Ray's Knotgrass**, *P. oxyspermum* by the woody stems and the down-turned margins of the leaves. **Sea Milkwort**, *Glaux maritima,* is not related to the other milkworts. This plant is a member of the primrose family, *Primulaceae*. Its apparently pink

Greater Sea-Spurrey

flowers at the base of the leaves are in fact sepals, while the true petals are absent. It can be seen in Christchurch Harbour and on the Purbeck coast. **Sea Campion**, *Silene uniflora,* has bladders similar to those of **Bladder Campion**, *Silene vulgaris*, but its shorter height enables it to contend with the buffeting of the strong winds of its coastal habitat. It is plentiful on our coast, with good sized colonies at Durlston. **Sea Bindweed**, *Calystegia soldanella*, is an attractive plant of sandy areas by the sea. The pink and white flowers are similar to those of **Field Bindweed**, *Convolvulus arvensis*, but the leaves have a uniquely rounded kidney shape, with the fleshiness associated with many maritime plants.

The Scurvy grasses, Brassicaceae family (formerly Cruciferae)

English Scurvy Grass, *Cochlearia anglica*. This crucifer has the larger flowers of the two species found in our area. The lower leaves taper gradually to the stem, and the whole plant has a much more robust look than the similar **Danish Scurvy Grass**, *C. danica*. The latter can be seen in the spring on the roadsides of dual carriageways, as well as the central reservations. Originally a coastal plant, winter road salting has afforded it a new inland habitat. As the saline spray is splashed onto the roadside, the slipstream from the traffic spreads the seeds far inland. As a result, this attractive blush-pink haze now embellishes most dual carriageways in the country.

The Pea Family, Fabaceae (formerly Leguminosae)

Clovers and other members of this family are to be found near the sea in our area.

One of the most satisfying experiences for the botanist is to find and identify some of the tiniest and least common members of this family. Although not strictly maritime plants, some of the most interesting clovers thrive in conditions that are never very far away from the sea, or else are replicated slightly inland. The dry, sandy soils so typical of the Bournemouth area are made additionally attractive to these plants by traditional grazing, as at Stanpit Marsh. Rabbits also help by nibbling the turf. These factors ensure that tall grasses and other vegetation do not compete with these special plants for space. One such site is the grassland surrounding Hurst Castle. **Rough Clover**, *Trifolium scabrum* was recorded here on a BNSS field trip in 2007. It can be distinguished from the very similar **Knotted Clover**, *T. striatum*, partly by its white flowers, and partly by the backward curving sepal teeth. **Clustered Clover**, *Trifolium glomeratum*, enjoys similar conditions. It merits the honour of a star in Blamey and Fitter, owing to its increasing rarity. The common name refers to the fact that the mauvish-pink flowers are embedded in the sepals, which spread in a star-like formation when in fruit. Among **vascular** plants in the UK, this phenomenon is unique, and is presumably a result of evolutionary pressures which we can only guess at. This fact alone makes it all the more sad that most of the thriving colonies in the Christchurch area were destroyed when a new housing estate was built. However, a few plants still remain, as well as those on the short turf at Hengistbury Head.

The well-named **Burrowing**, or **Subterranean Clover**, *T. subterraneum*, is an equally fascinating plant. Among the few fertile flowers are many sterile ones. These consist only of green sepals, encircling a small petalless space. When the fruits of the fertile heads are ripe, the stems which bear them recurve and bury the fruits into the ground. This plant is nationally scarce, but is present in several sites round Christchurch Harbour. Equally interesting is the **Suffocated Clover**, *T. suffocatum*. The green sepal teeth rise erectly above the tiny white flowers, while the sharply-serrated leaves stand proud of the whole. This tiny plant has been found on a new site in 1993 on Boscombe cliffs as well as Christchurch Harbour. It too demands short turf and sandy soil. Its appearance in Boscombe may well be thanks to more sensitive management of the cliff tops latterly.

Fenugreek, *T. ornithopodiodes,* can also be found on Boscombe cliffs. However, where similar conditions prevail, it can also be found inland. There is a good colony at Turbary Common, and sharp-eyed drivers can spot it on roundabouts, such as the one at the junction of Wallisdown Road and Ringwood Road. It bears a slight similarity to Burrowing Clover, although it can be distinguished by having hairless leaves and fewer flowers to each head.

The magnificent **Sea Pea**, *Lathyrus japonicus,* was present until recently on the shingle at Hurst Castle. In 2007 it was nowhere to be seen, being a victim of the summer storms the previous year. One can only hope that this handsome plant reappears. With its robust, fleshy leaves and stunning purple flowers, it stood resplendent among the stones. Its main stronghold in the UK is on the east coast, where it reputedly saved Suffolk villagers from famine in the seventeenth century. At the other end of the Fabaceae size scale is the **Tree Lupin**, *Lupinus arboreus.* Its scented yellow flowers are a familiar sight on the coastal areas of Boscombe and Southbourne. Introduced from California in 1793, it has taken well to the mild climate and sandy soil of the Bournemouth district. It self-seeds regularly, and helps to stabilise the dry sandy areas of the coast.

HURST CASTLE

This monument enjoys a unique position on the western Solent. Built by Henry VIII, it was one of a chain of such defences along the south coast. The causeway leading to the Castle is far from being an easy walk. The ferry from Keyhaven runs regularly in the summer months, and is strongly recommended.

It is of great botanical interest. It has a geological connection with the Isle of Wight, and is surrounded by a mixture of marsh, grassland and shingle. The mixture of habitats and freedom from disturbance has enabled a wide variety of plants to thrive. The following details some of the highlights, but even a short walk in the summer will reveal many more discoveries.

On the seaward side, the shingle is punctuated by the magnificent blue-green mounds of **Sea Kale**, *Crambe maritima*. Richard Mabey, in *Flora Britannica,* describes them as looking like, 'enormous sea urchins' from a distance, or a

Sea Kale

'rotund desert cactus'. At first glance, it looks very different from its crucifer relations of the family Brassicaceae (ex-Cruciferae). On closer examination, however, one can see clearly that the large, creamy white flowers are indeed in characteristic cross formation.

The plant has had a chequered history. The young shoots of Sea Kale became a desirable addition to the smart nineteenth-century dinner table, after its popularisation by the botanist William Curtis. The shingle in which the plants grow had the effect of blanching the growing tips in a way similar to that of celery. In the early twentieth century, Revd Keble Martin noticed its increasing scarcity, and it has declined gradually ever since. It is generally felt that loss of habitat is to blame for this, rather than solely as a result of uprooting.

It is easy to see that the present day garden cabbage has evolved from *C. maritima*, although the very tough outer leaves of the original would be unacceptable today as a vegetable.

Little Robin, *Geranium purpureum*, is one of the specialities of Hurst Castle. It is a true curiosity, being, as the name implies, closely related to **Herb Robert** (*G. robertianum*). It is so close, in fact, that it is thought by some to be a subspecies.

It is an extremely rare plant of seaside areas, with only a few sites, all in the south of England. Although it can grow taller than Herb Robert when conditions permit, it adopts a prostrate form on the shingle at Hurst Castle. It has yellow pollen, which distinguishes it from the orange of Herb Robert.

Yellow Horned Poppy, *Glaucium flavum*, the brilliant yellow flowers and silvery leaves of this plant make a stunning addition to the coastal shingle of Hurst Castle. The drama continues as the poppy goes to seed. The thin, curving capsules which give the plant its name can be up to 30 cm long. The stems contain a poisonous yellow latex, no doubt as a deterrent to grazing animals.

Yellow Horned Poppy

Samphires

There is a cliff, whose high and bending head
Looks fearfully in the confined deep:
Bring me but to the very brim of it, . . .
stand still. How fearful

And dizzy 'tis, to cast one's eyes so low!
The crows and choughs that wing the midway air
Show scarce so gross as beetles: half way down
Hangs one that gathers samphire, dreadful trade!

King Lear, Edgar to Gloucester. WILLIAM SHAKESPEARE

Rock Samphire

This section is devoted to three plants. They have two things in common. Firstly, they are all residents of the coastal habitats in our area. Secondly, they are all called 'samphire'. In all other respects, they differ from one another greatly. We have a supreme example here of the dangers that result from dependence on the common, rather than the scientific name of a plant.

Golden Samphire, *Inula crithmoides*, is a member of the daisy family (Asteraceae, formerly Compositae). It is our only native yellow daisy with fleshy leaves, which grow in linear formation up the stem. It is by no means common nationally, but can be found on the drier saltmarsh areas of Hurst Castle. **Rock Samphire**, *Crithmum maritimum*, this plant is the one referred to above, in

Shakespeare's *King Lear*. Often it is mistakenly thought that **Marsh Samphire**, *Salicornia europaea*, now known as Common Glasswort, is being spoken of, of which more below. *S. europaea* lives on saline mud, so no climbing is called for in its gathering, whereas *C. maritimum* clings to the sheerest of cliffs, thus indicating that this is the one of which Edgar speaks in the play. Rock Samphire is a handsome member of the umbellifer or carrot family, (Apiaceae, formerly Umbelliferae). It is a true seaside plant, whose robust leaves subdivide into fleshy linear lobes. Its smell when crushed, has been variously described as sulphurous, or redolent of furniture polish. Its name comes from the Greek word for barley: 'krithe', which the strongly ridged fruits were supposed to resemble. Rock Samphire has long been used as a pickle, and in the nineteenth century, four shillings would be paid for each bushel brought in from the south coast. The 'dreadful trade' referred to in *Lear*, gives one an idea of the dangers involved in making one's living this way. In our area, in spite of the fact that its habitat has been decimated over the years by coastal developments, it still hangs on in patches, such as the zigzags and promenades in Boscombe. It appears that the building stone used successfully replicates the cliffs that are its natural home.

Marsh Samphire or **Common Glasswort**, *Salicornia europaea agg*. I first came across this fascinating plant when it was served as an accompaniment to a fine salmon at my nephew's wedding. Its delicious taste explains why it is also known as 'sea asparagus'. Once again, the common name will mislead. It could not be more different from the previous two samphires. In appearance, the description by Jack Bishop of Blakeney, quoted in *Flora Britannica* cannot be bettered, comparing it to : '… a plump, jointed pipecleaner.' The stem is divided into segments. At the top of each is a pair of triangular lobes, each representing a **vestigial** leaf. The tiny petalless flowers are in groups of one to three in the axils of these lobes. A tiny single **anther** emerges in late summer from a central pore, although the **stigma** remains hidden. Toward the end of the year, the whole plant turns a rusty purple, giving a dramatic look to the muddy shore on which it lives.

Although the stronghold of Marsh Samphire is Norfolk, we are lucky enough to have a good colony on Stanpit Marsh in Christchurch. Picking by the general public is strongly discouraged elsewhere for obvious reasons, as with any wild plant. On this SSSI it is illegal. Those given permission to gather Samphire commercially nowadays always snip the tender shoots rather than uprooting the entire plant as in the past. Marsh Samphire is perfectly adapted to its muddy saltmarsh home. It contains sodium to prevent osmotic pressure by the seawater. Without this, the seawater would leach moisture from the plant, resulting in dehydration.

Salicornia aggregates are a very difficult group. The following species can be found in our area.

S.dolichostachya	Long-spiked Glasswort	*S. obscura*	Glaucous Glasswort
S. fragilis	Yellow Glasswort	*Sarcornia perennis*	Perennial Glasswort
S.nitens	Shiny Glasswort	*S.pusilla*	One-flowered Glasswort
S. ramosissima	Purple Glasswort		

All these plants have very slight differences, and further add to the confusion by hybridising readily.

In the past the sodium content of *S. europaea* enabled it to be used in the glass-making process. When dried and burnt, the ash could be mixed with limewater and then evaporated. The resultant crystals could be used to make a rough form of glass, hence the alternative common name **Glasswort**. Soap could be produced in the same way with the addition of animal fat. Unusually among maritime plants, *S. europaea* thrives better on newly created mud. In more stabilised areas, it has to compete with more robust perennials, and is less successful. Marsh Samphire's new popularity in the restaurant trade has helped to preserve the existing plants, and its habitat is increasing thanks to climate change. While sinking coastlines, especially in the east of England, submerge existing habitats, rising sea levels provide new ones.

BOSCOMBE CLIFFS WALK

W Bournemouth is fortunate in having extensive cliffs in a state far more natural than that of most seaside resorts. Since the local authorities have become more aware of the importance of this habitat, the area has seen the rapid colonisation by many interesting plants, with the accompanying insect, reptile and bird life.

The clifftops are mainly composed of the light, sandy soil which characterises the whole area. The added element of saltspray gives another dimension, providing conditions for a varied maritime flora.

The briefest of strolls, especially in early summer, will prove very rewarding. Boscombe cliffs are easily accessible by bus, and parking in nearby roads is easy. It is worthwhile to leave the paved footpaths and explore the areas covered by short turf.

Many of the tiny legumes are here. These are dealt with in more detail in the Fabaceae section, but the following are specialities to spot. The very small flowers of **Birdsfoot**, *Ornithopus perpusillus*, are present in large numbers. The leaves are distinctive, being minute versions of those of a vetch. Yet again, one should not be led astray by the English, or common name. The **Birdsfoot Trefoils**, although belonging to the same family, are of a completely different genus. One member of this group is **Hairy Birdsfoot Trefoil**, *Lotus subbiflorus*. Easily recognised because of its almost shaggy appearance, it is present in large numbers, especially near the entrance to the formal Boscombe Cliff Gardens.

Hairy Birdsfoot Trefoil

Careful searching on hands and knees is essential to find the minute **Slender Trefoil**, *Trifolium micranthum*. At first it might easily be mistaken for the more common **Lesser Yellow Trefoil**, *T. dubium*. Closer inspection will show that each flowerhead contains only 2–6 florets, rather than the 10–20 of *T. dubium*. Down the zigzags, and behind the wire fence, one should be able to see the delicate pink **Haresfoot Clover**, *T. arvense*. The flowerheads appear to be covered with soft pink fur, giving the plant its name.

Other members of the pea family one might find in this habitat are **Knotted and Burrowing Clovers**, *T. striatum* and *T. subterraneum*, and the more common **Black Medick**, *Medicago lupulina*.

If one searches carefully on the sandy soil, one should find the tiny **Parsley Piert**, *Aphanes arvensis*. This miniature version of the **Lady's Mantle** of gardens has distinctive foliage but the flowers are either petalless or completely hidden. Both this and the even smaller **Slender Parsley Piert**, *A. australis*, have been recorded in this area, and one would need a lens and a good flora to distinguish between the two. The fruits differ from each other in shape, and also in their relationship to the stipules.

Haresfoot Clover

Tree Mallow

Common Broomrape

Small Flowered Catchfly

At the other end of the size spectrum are two showy plants of the clifftop. The **Tree Mallow**, *Lavatera arborea*, was possibly introduced to the east of England originally, and was planted extensively on the coastal grassland sometime in the twentieth century. It is neither mentioned in the original BNSS book of 1914 by Revd Linton, nor in his books on the local flora which he researched together with F. Townsend. It is fairly clear, therefore, that *L. arborea* has been deliberately planted since in this situation. The plant can be distinguished from the **Common Mallow**, *Malva sylvestris,* by the deep purple centre of the flowers and greater height.

An equally handsome introduction is the **Tree Lupin**, *Lupinus arboreus.* Its creamy yellow, honey-scented flowers have long been a feature of the Bournemouth clifftop. However, the first record of its existence here was as recent as 1953, in spite of the fact that it was brought originally from California to this country as long ago as 1793. The **Tamarisk**, *Tamarix gallica*, too, is an introduction. Possibly the early founders of Bournemouth as a seaside resort thought that the sandy cliffs needed extra embellishment as well as stabilisation.

Native species can be equally attractive. Great swathes of **Thrift**, *Armeria maritima*, cover many parts of the clifftop with their neat pink flowers in tightly-packed heads. Taller, and also pink when in bud, is the **Wild Carrot**, *Daucus carota.* A member of the Apiaceae family (ex-Umbelliferae), the showy **umbels** turn white when in full bloom, with the exception of a single dark red central floret. This is not present in all plants, but one can soon be found after a quick search.

The curious and rather sinister looking members of the Broomrape family, Orobanche, should be found by looking carefully around the evergreen shrubs in the Cliff Gardens. This parasitic plant is devoid of green pigment, and the dead flowers frequently are still standing through the winter. It is very difficult to identify, as the host plant is sometimes several metres away. The one most often seen, however, is **Common Broomrape**, *O. mino*r.

Sometimes the cliffs present surprising plants. Occasionally a Pyramidal Orchid can be seen, and there are several thriving **Salad Burnet**, *Sanguisorba minor*, plants. Normally both of these plants require lime in the soil. One can only assume that something in the composition of the stone walls is to their liking.

One of the stars of this habitat is the **Small Flowered Catchfly**, *Silene gallica.* There are several patches of this plant, which is decreasing nationally. Linton and Townsend recorded it in several sites in the Bournemouth area in 1888, since when numbers have dwindled to this one remaining area. It is thriving on the clifftop at the moment, and one can only hope that this situation will continue.

———————————oOo———————————

STANPIT MARSH

W Stanpit Marsh stands at the confluence of the Stour and Avon river mouths. Its combination of fresh, brackish and salt water in the marshland results in a richly varied botanical habitat. It is traversed by many narrow channels, which are subject to tidal movements. The higher ground is sandy, and is grazed by ponies and rabbits. As a consequence, it has areas of closely cropped grassland in which small plants thrive. As the area is not farmed, the ecology is unaffected by artificial fertilisers and herbicides.

Below is a selection of the species found there. It is one of the most popular venues for all sections of the Society. It should be remembered that the following is simply a subjective choice, and a visit to the marsh on a self-guided search would be very rewarding.

Sea Lavender, *Limonium vulgare.* This member of the Thrift family, Plumbaginaceae, is not a true lavender, despite its wonderful lilac colour. The small flowers are crowded together very tightly, as are the plants. Together they make a dramatic splash of colour among the marsh grasses.

It appears in areas where the water is predominately salt. In the same habitat one might see the plantain-like spikes of **Marsh Arrow-grass**, *Triglochin palustris*, or the very similar **Sea Arrow-Grass**, *T. maritima*. A trace of purple on the tiny green flowers of *T. palustris* and the deeply furrowed leaves are the main keys to identifying it from *T. maritima*.

Also on the Marsh, is **Brookweed**, *Samolus valerandi*. At first glance one might think that it is a crucifer, but closer inspection reveals the five, rather than four, white petals. Surprisingly, it is a member of the Primrose family, Primulaceae. The flower stalks are bare but for the tiny green leaf-like bract attached to each one. The uncommon **Parsley Water-dropwort**, *Oenanthe lachenalii*, can be occasionally found in the Marsh, though in fresh rather than salt water. Although similar to the more familiar **Hemlock Water-dropwort**, *O. crocata*, it can be identified by the narrow bracts below the umbels and the two pinnate leaves.

A closely related member of Apiaceae and also found in the brackish water, is the **Wild Celery**, *Apium graveolens*. It can easily be identified by the characteristically celery smell when crushed. Wild Celery should not be confused with the **Celery-leaved Buttercup**, *Ranunculus sceleratus*, which occupies a similar habitat. If possible, one should look for a fruit. Once the petals have dropped off, the many achenes are attached to an unsually long, almost cylindrical head.

In the fresh water area, one can admire the beautiful **Flowering Rush**, *Butomus umbellatus*, in the mid to late summer months. It is the only British member of the family Butomaceae, and is not in fact a rush at all. The three dark sepals act as a foil to the paler pink petals, which are further highlighted by the thread-like veins. Another stunningly handsome plant of the Marsh is the silvery-grey **Marsh Mallow**, *Althaea officinalis*. This plant enjoys the brackish water habitat of Stanpit. Its delicate rose-coloured flowers immediately remind one of the sweets once produced by immersing its root in water. Sadly, its popularity for this purpose hastened its decline. Thousands of plants on the Thames estuary and elsewhere were dug up to create this treat. Those in Stanpit, however, are much loved and closely watched.

URBAN AND ALIEN PLANTS

The sound of a chain saw raises instant alarm in the British breast. Terms such as 'desecration', 'vandals masquerading as wildlife wardens', and 'ruination of our beautiful countryside' appear in the local press. Nowhere is this reaction more likely than in the case of *Rhododendron ponticum*. This plant loves Bournemouth as, much if not more than, the Pontic Alps in its native Turkey. It revels in the sandy soil and mild climate. In vain do the countryside wardens point out that these all-enveloping evergreens spell death to our ecology. For the sake of a few weeks of purple glory this inconvenient fact is ignored, and this relatively new visitor has suddenly become part of our heritage.

Its history is one which typifies alien plants in the Bournemouth area. In the years since the publication of the 1914 book, its progress from object of admiration to most disliked among botanists is one which it shares with many other aliens. In the original book, Sir Daniel Morris wrote of private woodlands in the Bournemouth area, . . . the first place must be given to Heron Court, the property of Lord Malmesbury . . . The splendid growth of the rhododendron is a marked feature of the district. Much has been learned in the intervening period, although sadly a large section of the population still share the view of Sir Daniel.

As environmental considerations became increasingly important after the Second World War, the plant rapidly fell out of favour. It was discovered that *R. ponticum* was an ecological disaster. It was host to neither birds nor insects. It marched aggressively across heathland, eliminating native flora, and was extremely difficult to eradicate. By the time local authorities and other agencies decided it was time to act, *R. ponticum* had swamped large areas of Brownsea Island, parts of Upton Heath, Ferndown, Hurn Forest and St Catherine's Hill, as well as a sizeable portion of the Poole to Christchurch coastal area. Perhaps no other plant is better suited to standing as a warning to anyone contemplating the introduction of non-native plants.

Not all aliens were brought over deliberately to enhance Victorian estates, as will be seen in succeeding sections. The 1914 book contains very few. **Alexanders**, *Smyrnium olusatrum*, still seen in Christchurch and elsewhere locally, is casually mentioned as an introduced potherb, but as it is of 'old standing', it hardly counts. There could be several reasons for these omissions.

Sadly gone is the **Sand Catchfly**, *Silene conica*, in sandy turf near Parkstone, and **Lamb's Succory**, *Arnoseris minima*, from both Iford bridge and Winton. Nor would one now find **Moonwort**, *Botrychium lunaria*, in Branksome Park.

What we have gained are **Hottentot Figs**, *Carpobrotus edulis*, **Butterfly Bush**, *Buddleia davidii*, **Himalayan Balsam**, *Impatiens glandulifera*, and many more. At first this may not seem to be a fair exchange. Local authorities have to spend thousands of pounds to control these newcomers, and the environmental impact on native flora and other wildlife can be severe.

It would be convenient to blame the Victorians for their irresponsible gathering of whatever took their fancy without a thought for the consequences. However, twenty-first-century lifestyle has much to answer for. The popularity of Spain as a holiday and second home destination must surely account for the recent presence of **Bilbao Fleabane**, *Conyza bilbaoana*. The low cost airlines who take us there, possibly several times a year, are among the factors which influence climate change.

The Bournemouth area, with its busy airport, international ferries and road network, combined with its balmy south-facing aspect, has to be the ideal setting for any imported seed, whether deliberate or not. Some of our most successful aliens might not have survived the British winters a hundred years ago, or at best be very poor specimens.

While fully in support of the control and attempted eradication of the most invasive aliens, however, it might seem sensible to accept the fact that they are here. Bearing in mind how closely linked these newcomers are to our daily lives, it would be foolish to ignore their presence. With the exception of a few well-known culprits, these plants are easily controlled and can live more harmoniously with native species than, say, brambles, ivy or gorse, all of which can spread aggressively.

The most successful alien plants are sometimes the only greenery in heavily built up urban areas, having as they do the most amazing ability to survive against all odds. Such situations offer little attraction to native plants, so in those circumstances the element of competition does not exist. One frequently hears naturalists bemoaning the absence of a true wilderness in the UK. Maybe the new wildernesses are not the carefully managed nature reserves, essential though they are, but instead we have disused coalyards, railway embankments and supermarket car parks. Such places have the added advantage of quite often being built on imported hardcore, which frequently contains soil and seeds from an area which is different geologically from the surroundings. Thus some exciting botanical finds will result. So what we have are plants springing up in inner city areas where previously there were simply bricks and concrete. It is not impossible that a strange plant appearing between kerb stones might lead to investigation and start a lifelong interest in botany.

The following sections deal with three notable aliens in some detail, together with others in brief. The list is by no means complete. I have concentrated on those which are particularly relevant, in that they are the ones most likely to be seen by visitors to Bournemouth, residents, or local gardeners.

Japanese Knotweed, *Fallopia japonica*. **Family Polygonaceae.** This sprawling thug has become public enemy number one in the public consciousness. It is, however, understandable to see why the Victorians made the monumental mistake of bringing it to this country. Its heart-shaped leaves and spiralling clusters of white flowers made a dramatic backdrop to the garden. The attractively rust-spotted stems, and an ability to send out lusty new shoots every spring was an added bonus. Although originally introduced from Japan as a dual purpose plant, partly for fodder, it was as a response to the fashion for the picturesque in garden design that it made its mark. As its aggressiveness became evident, the dense thickets were hacked down by teams of weary gardeners and thrown away.

It soon became clear that *F. japonica* does not take kindly to this treatment. Wherever the plant was thrown – woods, ditches, or, worst of all, streams and rivers – it regenerated and multiplied with gusto. On top of this, the original plant, far from being eradicated, grew afresh. The tiniest scrap of rhizome left behind produced a new plant.

The current scientific name of the family is well-chosen: *poly* (many), and *gonum* (jointed knee). It is unusual in that it is a single clone, and needs separate male and female plants to reproduce sexually. In the UK, we have female plants only. This does not seem to present a problem to Japanese Knotweed, achieving its great success rate due to spreading **rhizomes**. There is recent evidence, however, that it has hybridised with **Giant Knotweed**, *F. bohemica*, presenting the possibility of reproduction by seed. In the area covered by this book, Japanese Knotweed has been seen on many field meetings.

However, an interesting point of view has been put forward in a paper by David Pearman and Alex Lockton (BSBI 2002). They point out that it occurs in 236 2-km squares in the area out of a possible 739, thus giving the impression that it is a frequent pest. However, they then point out that it is very rare for it to occur in more than three sites in each 2-km square.

One of them is the triangular piece of land bordered by railway lines at Branksome. This area is used as a car park for employees at the Liverpool Victoria building – a typical site for this plant which could shade out the habitat of the rare Sand Lizard if left unchecked.

A programme of eradication is taking place. Although the thickets are spectacularly dense, the Knotweed has been controlled to some extent by the paved areas and the constant movement of cars. It co-exists with a wide range of interesting alien and native plants.

Pearman and Lockton compare situations such as this with bramble, ivy, gorse and nettle, which appear on every 2 km square and are hundreds of times more invasive. *F. japonica*, however, is undeniably a problem. The Japanese Knotweed Alliance was formed in 1999, comprising several large agencies including DEFRA, Network Rail and the Environment Agency.

The plant has a multitude of negative influences apart from its effect on the native flora. It blocks drains, undermines buildings and railway lines, and even makes parts of the country less attractive to tourists. The Bournemouth botanist cannot ignore it. The most vigilant will be looking out for hybrids and any illegal tipping of this aggressive plant. One might be tempted to infer, after reading of monsters such as Japanese Knotweed and Rhododendron, that all invasive plants eliminate the native flora by virtue of their superior size. It would, however, be a mistake to assume that size is everything.

New Zealand Pigmyweed, *Crassula helmsii*. The tiny Australian Stonecrop or New Zealand Pigmyweed, is every bit as dangerous.The plant has white or pink four-petalled flowers, with succulent pale green leaves, the whole giving a misleading impression of fragile delicacy. First sold as an oxygenating plant for aquaria in 1927, it became increasingly popular, and first appeared in the wild in 1956. What followed was a sadly familiar pattern. While some customers were innocently buying the stonecrop from garden centres, others, realising their mistake, were busily raking up huge bundles and dumping them in the wild. The plant thrived enthusiastically on damp ground, forming dense mats of vegetation. No area of fresh water was safe. Not only was the native flora destroyed, but also the dependent amphibians.

A pond dip survey in a SSSI in Worcestershire revealed that tadpoles of the **Great Crested Newt**, *Triturus cristatus*, had been adversely affected since *C. helmsii* was present. Despite there being five healthy adults, there were only two tadpoles. The **Lesser Spearwort**, *Ranunculus* *flammula*, which had been specially planted as host plants for the newts' eggs had disappeared. The lack of open water caused by the matted vegetation was also seen as a reason for the newts' decline.

In the area covered by this book, the New Forest has been very badly affected. Thousands of pounds have been spent on the plant's eradication, with only limited success. In other situations it blocks ditches, and can be a danger to animals who mistake the tangled mats for firm ground.

Mechanical control (i.e. pulling the weed out by its roots) is useless. Even the tiniest node will grow with renewed vigour. The only successful means of control is by using the glyphosate group of chemicals. The BSBI (Botanical Society of the British Isles) distribution map shows clearly the massive increase in our area from the late 1990s onwards.

Fleabanes. The story of **Canadian Fleabane**, *Conyza canadensis*, is a fascinating one which typifies many in our area. A member of the Asteraceae family (ex-Compositae), it is easily overlooked, with its almost colourless, brushlike flowerheads.

Originally from North America, its seed was reputedly brought into the UK as part of a herb stuffing inside the seventeenth-century version of an oven-ready bird. One wonders how tempting this dish was after a long sea voyage. Possibly the rancid smell was responsible for the whole thing being quickly thrown away. The seed, however, doggedly refused to waste this new opportunity, and finding the new conditions agreeable, promptly established itself.

The BSBI's excellent distribution maps record a very sparse population in the 1930s, mainly in the south. One feels that the botanists responsible for the 1914 book would have been quite excited by finding one of these plants. As with many aliens, its numbers increased gradually until the massive surge post 2000. Now any walk in the urban environment can reveal at least one of these plants, thriving as they do on tiny cracks in paving stones, kerbsides and walls. Its success must be in part due to its steely resistance to trampling and ability to survive with a minimal supply of food and water. It is tempting to be anthropomorphic, and think of *C. canadensis* as the streetwise rough sleeper among wild plants. The very short ray florets surrounding the four-lobed yellow disc florets give the whole the appearance of a small wiry brush. It is hardly eye-catching, but possibly this has something to do with its success.

It is not the remit of this chapter to look for theories, but simply to record what is there. However, the restriction of pesticide use by local authorities must be a factor in this plant's recent increase, together with more travelling by the general public.

Closely related to Canadian Fleabane is **Guernsey Fleabane**, *Conyza sumatrensis*. Unhelpfully named, this plant is from neither Sumatra nor Guernsey. A native of Chile, it can grow to a height of seven feet. It rarely reaches anything like this height, partly because it needs a tropical climate, and partly because its liking for patios and paving restricts its growth. It differs only slightly in appearance from *C. canadensis*, but the toothed, rather than simple lanceolate leaves, persist into the winter.

Although the BSBI distribution map shows an extremely sparse presence before 1969, the first official sighting was by the distinguished alien expert Brian Wurzell in 1984 during the massive upheaval and redevelopment of London's dockland. Possibly it might have been there for many years, presumably unwittingly imported with one of the cargoes when the docklands were in their heyday. Since 1984, the story is a familiar one, with a gradual increase towards the end of the twentieth century, and an almost total coverage of the

Guernsey Fleabane

UK post 2000. The central southern area with its mild climate, however, remains the most favoured site as with most other aliens.

Interestingly, the most recent advance of *C. sumatrensis* follows the M5 from Bristol to the Midlands. It would be a study in itself to give reasons for this, but there is evidence that winter gritting and salting helps to disperse seeds and establish habitats.

The third member of this genus to be found in the Bournemouth area is **Argentinian Fleabane**, *Conyza bonariensis*. From 1930–69 this plant was recorded in isolated spots around the Midlands, whereas in 2008 it is common in the area covered by this book. Its distinctive red-tipped **bracts** separate it from the previous two species, and make it simple to identify with a hand lens.

The most recent arrival is **Bilbao Fleabane**, *Conyza bilbaoana*. Presumably arriving from Spain, the BSBI records no presence in the UK before 1987. One is tempted to make a connection with the increase in Spanish holiday homes, holidays and cheap flights.

SOME ALIENS IN BRIEF

A thriving colony of **Pitcherplant**, *Sarracenia purpurea,* has been in the New Forest for some time. There are also several on the Ham Common LNR in Poole. This exotic and slightly sinister looking plant stands out among the native flora, and is not liked by wardens. At present, however, it does not seem to present any major problems.

Summer visitors to the Bournemouth beaches cannot fail to notice the glowing pink, yellow and purple of the **Hottentot Fig**, *Carpobrotus edulis* and *C.acinaformis*. Some efforts have been made to clear the huge mats of vegetation which swathe the cliffs like a brightly coloured blanket. This South African invader is a variety of *mesembryanthemum*. In Cornwall, the common name Sally-My-Handsome apparently is a corruption of this, although one needs to use one's imagination to see how this has come about!

Alongside, and rather less aggressively, grows the **Seaside Daisy**, *Erigeron glaucus*. Originally introduced to the Isle of Wight, these attractive plants are now well established on the Poole/Bournemouth cliffs. Their pale violet and gold flowers remind one of a common daisy in all but colour and size.

Riversides in central southern England which have managed to escape the all-enveloping Japanese Knotweed are most likely to have been invaded by one of the introduced balsams. The **North American Orange Balsam**, *Impatiens capensis*, with its colourful egg-yellow flowers splashed with scarlet, is attractive and easily containable. Examples can be seen in Christchurch, alongside the river Avon. Its seeds are catapulted into the water, and bob about like tiny boats. **Himalayan Balsam**, *Impatiens glandulifera*, however, is a different matter. It gives rise to a wide spectrum of reactions. The undoubtably beautiful blooms have many fans, but the plant is undeniably a

Pitcherplant

Hottentot Fig

Seaside Daisy

nuisance. It is an aggressive coloniser of damp ditches, and competes successfully with the more delicate native flora. There are many places to see it in the Bournemouth area, one being alongside Ivy Lane near Ringwood.

The magnificently statuesque **Giant Hogweed**, *Heracleum mantegazzianum*, also likes riversides. Introduced from the Caucasus in the early nineteenth century, it was a stately presence in large Victorian gardens. With the advent of suburbia, the three-metre high giant with its 5000 seeds became very unwelcome. From 1970 onwards, its unpopularity was further increased by the discovery that it could cause skin blisters. No one seems to know why this problem took so long to come to light, but it is partly because of this that it is now an offence to plant it in the wild.

The **Spanish Bluebell**, *Hyacinthoides hispanica*, has been given a fair amount of attention by the media. Every spring, purists anxiously check the bluebells in woods such as those at Pamphill and Breamore. They examine the anthers to see if there is any trace of the blue which is one of the distinguishing features of *H. hispanica*, rather than the cream of the English native Bluebell, *H. non-scriptus*. It hybridises readily, and most of the non-natives are crosses between the two.

The acid soils of the Bournemouth area provide a congenial home for **Shallon**, *Gaultheria shallon*. Originally planted as suitable cover for game on pheasant shoots, it has now become familiar in urban situations. The tough, matted shrubs form carpets at Hengistbury Head and Avon Forest Park to the detriment of other flora. It can even be seen alongside roads in central Bournemouth.

Some plants amaze us with their ability to survive on so little. *Buddleia davidii* needs only a crack in the pavement, or even a damaged brick on an old signal box. It was introduced from China in the 1890s, and has thrived ever since. Its purple honey-scented flowers are loved by late summer butterflies and other insects, so its establishment has to be seen as a positive one in an increasingly built up environment.

Neglected railway sidings, derelict coal yards and the like provide a happy home for this tough plant. Its habitat is often shared with another rugged alien: **Oxford Ragwort**, *Senecio squalidus*. This is the ultimate urban plant of the UK, in spite of its origins on the slopes of Mount Etna. First planted in the Oxford University Botanic Garden in the eighteenth century, its seeds, aided by their white silky parachutes, soon found homes in all parts of Oxford. The new railways helped further, and thousands of seeds travelled in the trains' slipstreams to all parts of the country. Railway embankments, however, remained the favourite resting place for *S. squalidus,* and the cheerful yellow flowers can be seen at most times of the year, offering minimal competition to the native **Common Ragwort**, *Senecio jacobaea*, a plant of farmland.

When the injured English soldiers were carried back from the Napoleonic wars to Thanet, the grass-filled palliasses on which they were laid were blood-stained, and quickly disposed of. One farmer, of a frugal nature, decided not to waste this unexpected bounty, and ploughed it into his land. The spring crop of an alien peppercress whitened the field with its flowers. This new plant became known as **Thanet** or **Hoary Cress**, *Lepidium draba*. It is another success story of urban situations, favouring similar habitats to the two previous plants. A large patch thrives on Turbary Common, a SSSI bordering the busy Wallisdown Road.

Another familiar plant which owes its success as a result of economy is **Annual Dogs' Mercury**, *Mercurialis annua*. In the 1880s, dockers at Watchet in Somerset used to sweep up leftover grain imported from Danzig, and take it home to feed their chickens. One Bob Williams decided to plant the seeds in his garden instead, and the resultant pale green plants were admired by all. When they spread through every vegetable patch in the village, enthusiasm waned considerably. Although Watchet is not in our area, the conditions here are particularly favourable for *M. annua*, with the milder climate and light sandy soil which it enjoys. Even the most conscientious gardener must be familiar with this plant, cropping up all the year round in patio cracks and kerbsides.

Also appearing regularly in less cared-for gardens are the **Gallant** and **Shaggy Soldiers**,

Galinsoga parviflora and *quadriradiata*. These dainty plants, looking rather like a nibbled daisy, escaped from Kew Gardens, and are originally from Peru. The common names are derived from the *galinsoga* of the scientific name.

Just in case the impression is given that urban plants are a new phenomenon, and usually a problem as well, it is worth noting that many once common garden and allotment 'weeds' have virtually disappeared. **Corn Marigold**, *Chrysanthemum segetum*, and **Weasel's Snout**, *Misopates orontium*, have not been made scarce by aggressive aliens, but as a result of the use of herbicides in adjoining fields.

SOME LOCAL WALKS

Within easy reach of Poole are several areas of interest:

W **Lytchett Bay**, between Hamworthy and Upton, is formed by one of the inlets that characterise Poole Harbour. A great deal of it is marshy, requiring waterproof footwear all the year round if one is to explore fully.

In mid and late summer, the low scrub is aglow with the purple of **Tufted Vetch**, *Vicia cracca*, **Sea Aster**, *Aster tripolium* and **Purple Loosestrife**, *Lythrum salicaria*. Earlier, there are **Ox-eye Daisy**, *Leucanthemum vulgare*, and the grey-green umbellifer, **Tubular Water-dropwort**, *Oenanthe fistulosa*.

W Close by is the delightful **Upton House Country Park**. This council-owned land is botanically attractive throughout the year. As well as the specimen trees and the colourful herbaceous borders, the area towards Holes Bay has been left in its natural state. Apart from careful management necessary to encourage the native flora, the plants are left undisturbed. Walking either towards the Holes Bay road (A350) or following the circular route southwards towards the railway line, one is certain to find much of interest.

Dog Violets, *Viola sp.*, **Herb Robert**, *Geranium robertianum*, **Ground Ivy**, *Glechoma hederacea* and **Greater Stitchwort**, *Stellaria holostea* edge the pathways in spring. Later on, **Red Bartsia**, *Odontites vernus*, **Great Willowherb**, *Epilobium hirsutum* and **Rosebay**, *Chamerion angustifolium* provide subtle variants of pink and purple.

In May, the Dorset Wildlife Trust's Nature Reserve at Corfe Mullen Meadow is not to be missed. This Waterloo Road site is one of the best for seeing great drifts of the beautiful **Green-winged Orchid**, *Orchis morio*. Here they contrast with the vivid blue of **Germander Speedwell**, *Veronica chamaedrys* and the gold and white of Buttercups and Greater Stitchwort.

W In complete contrast are the dramatic undulating contours of **Canford Heath**. Once threatened by encroaching urban development, this magnificent stretch of heathland is now protected by SSSI status. All three heathers are present here, and the predominating Ling is at its best in August, when the slopes are resplendent in hazy violet.

W Slightly further from Poole, but still within easy reach, is **Wareham Forest**. Although most of the Sika Trail comprises conifers, there are occasional clearings dominated by heather. There is an excellent opportunity in the Decoy Heath/Morden Bog area to see the nationally rare **Dorset Heath**, *Erica ciliaris*. Looking rather like an inflated version of **Cross-leaved Heath**, *E. tetralix*, the intense colour of the pink flowers stands out amid the surrounding vegetation.

W Also worth visiting is the RSPB Reserve at **Arne**. The coloured posts on the roadside are there to mark the stretches that are not to be cut in the early summer. This rich wayside flora, untypical of the surrounding heathland, is a result of the importation of lime as part of the road construction process. Among the plants are **Southern Marsh**, *Dactylorhiza praetermissa*, **Heath Spotted** and **Common Spotted Orchids**, *Dactylorhiza maculata* and *D. fuchsii*, as well as **Twayblade**, *Listera ovata*, **Yellow Rattle**, *Rhinanthus minor*, and **Fragrant Agrimony**, *Agrimonia procera*. There are also many sedges and grasses, and even **Royal Fern**, *Osmunda regalis*.

On the eastern side of the conurbation, there are three sites of particular interest to the botanist.

W **St Catherine's Hill**, just outside Christchurch, has a long history. It was used as a beacon for many centuries because of its superior height compared with the surrounding area. The hill, and neighbouring Town Common, is a good place to find many heathland plants. As well as the heathers, other lovers of sandy, acid soil are present here, such as **Sand Spurrey**, *Spergularia rubra,* **Heath Groundsel**, *Senecio sylvaticus* and **Devilsbit Scabious**, *Succisa pratensis.*

W On the other side of Dudmoor Farm Road lies **Coward's Marsh**. For many centuries it has provided grazing for animals owned by the Commoners of Christchurch. From 3 May to 15 February, they are entitled to graze up to six horses or twelve cows on the Marsh. The three-month close season enables the ground to recover, while the animals are moved to Millhams Mead. This ancient method of grazing is partially responsible for the botanical interest here. In late spring, Marsh Marigolds carpet the area with gold, followed shortly afterwards by Marsh Ragwort. Careful searching may be rewarded by the sight of Marsh Lousewort and the tiny, red-stemmed Mossy Stonecrop.

The star attraction, however, is the curious **Marsh Cinquefoil**, *Potentilla palustris.* Its appearance is evocative of an exotic alien, rather than a native plant. The dark russet sepals form a dramatic background to the much smaller purple petals and white stamens. This plant depends on very wet marshes. Modern agricultural drainage systems have been responsible for the loss of this specialised habitat, and consequently local sites for this lovely plant have decreased since the publication of the original book.

SANDBANKS AND LUSCOMBE VALLEY LNR

W Visits to these sites can be combined, being within reasonable walking distance of each other. Best seen in early summer, the short grass surrounding the large Sandbanks car park is home to many interesting small plants. A careful search should soon be rewarded with the sight of the bright red leaves of **Mossy Stonecrop**, *Crassula tillaea,* as well as some of the tiny clovers which need the kind of sandy, acid soil prevalent here. One of these is **Suffocated Clover**, *Trifolium suffocatum,* with its distinctive leaves held proud of the tiny white flowers, almost hidden by pale green sepals. Fragrant **Evening Primrose**, *Oenothera stricta,* is easily spotted among the sand dunes, together with **Sea Bindweed**, *Calystegia soldanella.* Luscombe Valley boasts several interesting sedges, including the unusual **Dotted Sedge**, *Carex punctata,* as well as **Narrow leaved Birdsfoot Trefoil**, *Lotus glaber.* At nearby Evening Hill, one might find the tiny **Slender Parsley Piert**, *Aphanes australis,* together with more small clovers.

NEW FOREST RARITIES – Bob Sharland

This western part of the New Forest has several interesting rarities. The beautiful **Bastard Balm**, *Melittis mellissophylum,* may be found after a search on the shady banks in the Wootton area. This large member of the nettle family reminds one slightly of the familiar White Deadnettle. However, it differs in its size, the presence of pink on the lower lip of the flower, its hairiness and its strongly aromatic smell. In the same part of the Forest one should look closely at the pathway and any other trodden ground. **Coral Necklace**, *Illecebrum verticillatum,* seems to thrive on well-used tracks and paths, sometimes spreading over ruts in cart tracks. This tiny but beautiful plant is sadly now confined to the New Forest and the westernmost tip of Cornwall. The flowers are small and white, but it is the red stems which give rise to its common name.

At nearby Wilverley Plain, one may be lucky enough to see the bluish purple of the **Field Gentian**, *Gentiana campestris*. There is considerable variation in colour on individual plants, some being so pale that they are difficult to see among the surrounding vegetation. Unusually for gentians, which generally prefer lime, they thrive in the New Forest soil. These plants are at their best in late summer and early autumn.

In the earlier part of the year, the same area is host to the **Lesser Butterfly Orchid**, *Platanthera bifolia*. One needs to look carefully among the bracken for these lovely plants, but the search is well worth while. It differs from the **Greater Butterfly Orchid**, *P. chlorantha,* in its smaller size, its stronger vanilla scent, and its spur, which is slightly straighter than the curved one of the Greater Butterfly. Closer inspection with a lens will show that in the latter the two pollen masses are pressed together in a parallel position, whereas in *P. bifolia* they are curved, forming an almost circular shape.

The Holmsley area is full of interest, especially in the areas close to the disused railway line. The sinister-looking alien **Pitcherplant**, *Sarracenia purpurea,* with its mottled purple-brownish flowers, is present here. Originally from North America, this insectivorous newcomer is very much at home in a New Forest bog. Fascinating as it is, there are concerns that it may have adverse effects on the local insect population, as well as the neighbouring flora.

Close by is one of the New Forest's stars, the **Native Gladiolus**, *Gladiolus illyricus.* This beautiful member of the iris family is now found only in the New Forest, and the numbers tend to fluctuate each year. Its intense pink-purple flowers are hard to see among the bracken, but finding it is a joy. Smaller than the garden version, this plant is worthy of all the protection we can give it.

One might be surprised to come across the small colony of **Bee Orchid**, *Ophrys apifera,* at Holmsley. They are normally associated with calcareous soils. However, there is a possibility that they were introduced when the railway line, now disused, was built with the aid of hardcore containing chalk.

At Boundway Hill, a short walk at the right time of year can lead one to another chalk-loving plant. The **Fragrant Orchid**, *Gymnadenia conopsea*, sub-species *borealis*, again, is a surprise presence, and is probably here as a result of railway or other building. In the same area is the majestic **Marsh Helleborine**, *Epipactis palustris*, with its frilly yellow-spotted lower petal and crimson stripes on the upper. One should search carefully among the many yellow flowers which carpet the open grassland at Boundway Hill in high summer. The reward may be the sight of the tiny **Yellow Centaury**, *Cicendia filiformis,* which is in fact a gentian. It is sometimes only 2 cm high, and as its petals open only in sunshine, it is very difficult to see.

The unusual arrangement of flowers on the stem of **Autumn Lady's Tresses**, *Spiranthes spiralis,* makes it easy to identify. It is one of our smallest orchids, and can be seen at Boundway Hill on the drier grassy and heathy areas. The fascinating spirals of blooms ascending the stem give rise to both its scientific and common names.

Near the Avon is the unusual **Rampion Bellflower**, *Campanula rapunculus,* with its pale blue flowers. Near the river at Ibsley, one can find the **Trifid Bur-marigold**, *Bidens tripartita*, and the closely-related **Nodding Bur-marigold**, *B. cernua.* Both are rayless yellow flowers of the daisy family and are found usually by fresh water, they make a handsome addition to the waterside scene in late summer.

Surprisingly far from the sea, the **Sea Storksbill**, *Erodium maritimum,* can be found by the sharp-eyed botanist at Blashford. Apart from its diminutive size, the fact that its petals drop very quickly does not help with the search. Also at Blashford, and much easier to see and identify, the handsome **Yellow Bartsia**, *Parentucellia viscosa,* can be found. A member of Scrophulariacea*e*, the Foxglove family, it has the two-lipped flower of the louseworts and cow wheats to whom it is related.

Going northwards towards Fordingbridge, it is worth looking for **Small Fleabane**, *Pulicaria vulgaris*. Despite its scientific name, it is a rare speciality of the New Forest, and is decreasing further. With smaller flowers than **Common Fleabane**, *P. dysenterica*, the ray florets are held erect, giving the compound head a cup-like appearance.

Further north still at Godshill, there is a small colony of **Pink Purslane**, *Claytonia sibirica*. This naturalised plant is successfully established nationally, but mainly in the Midlands and North. Its delicate pink flowers are an attractive addition to shady ponds and streamsides.

Just west of the New Forest boundary, the area around Damerham and Rockbourne is home to the beautiful **Golden Saxifrage**, *Chrysosplenium oppositifolium*. As its name implies, the leaves are in paired opposites and spring from a square stem. The petalless flowers are surrounded by lime-green sepals and bracts, surrounding the bright yellow anthers.

To the east, at Bramshaw, one might be lucky enough to find the sadly decreasing **Broad-leaved Helleborine**, *Epipactis hellebore*. A mere five plants were found in 2007, and one can only hope that its future is assured under National Park status.

Wootton, in the southern part of the Forest, is a good place to find the commoner New Forest plants. It is worth hunting in the damper areas for **Brookweed**, *Samolus valerandi*. This plant, with its white flowers, could be mistaken for a member of the Brassicaceae family. It is the five, rather than four, petals which help in identification.

The very rare **Hampshire Purslane**, *Ludwigia palustris*, has its main stronghold in the eastern part of the Forest, and therefore outside the area covered by this book. However, it is possible to find small colonies in the Puttles Bridge area. It is an exciting find, exclusive to the New Forest, making it a fitting climax to this section.

Pennyroyal, *Mentha pulegium*

One of the delights of late summer in the eastern New Forest, is the discovery of this small plant. By the end of September, there is little else in flower, but Pennyroyal is at its best. Looking rather like a small version of **Corn Mint**, *Mentha arvensis*, it can be additionally distinguished by its strongly-ridged sepal tube, with the two lower teeth longer and narrower than the three upper. The pale lilac coloured flowers are in whorls on the largely prostrate stem, and the whole plant is strongly aromatic.

Its rapid decline over the twentieth century throws up some interesting questions regarding habitat and the human impact on the countryside. In the early part of the century, village ponds and greens were seen simply as workplaces, where horses and carts rolled in and out, creating a network of muddy ruts. These conditions were perfect for Pennyroyal, as the plants increased and thrived under the combination of trampling and damp ground.

The post-war tendency to 'tidy up' such areas thus prompted the decline of this plant. Concreted pond margins, herbicide together with paved areas with seating and flowerbeds created an alien environment for it and other species. The few remaining patches where it is seen now are a mini-recreation of its original habitat, being mainly small damp ditches trodden frequently by ponies and cattle. The story of Pennyroyal is in itself a lesson in sensitive management.

TREES

W The Upper Gardens Bournemouth

Very near the hectic bustle of the Square in central Bournemouth is the War Memorial. This marks the start of the Tree Trail. By following the course of the Bourne upstream, one can see some splendid specimen trees in tranquil surroundings. Even a short walk will reveal much of interest.

The Victorian fashion for seaside resorts and their gardens, reflecting the new passion for health, recreation and the open air, was responsible for the establishment of the Upper Gardens.

Dawn Redwood   *Bournemouth Pine*   *Indian Bean Tree*

W and D Stewart of Ferndown nurseries supplied nearly 4,000 trees. Among them were current favourites of the time: Monkey Puzzle, Deodar Cedar and Silver Firs.

Among the magnificent evergreens are the **Monterey Pine**, *Pinus radiata*, the **Western Red Cedar**, *Thuja plicata* and the **Scots Pine**, *P. sylvestris*, familiar to visitors and residents alike.

Most majestic of all is the vast **Dawn Redwood**, *Metasequoia glyptostroboides*. It is deciduous, and in autumn is clothed in the most stunning shades of pink, yellow and orange. A native of China, it was thought to be extinct. It was re-discovered in 1941 by Mr T Kan, after which in 1948 it was introduced to the west. Fossils of *Metasequoia* have been found and identified. Further examination revealed that the opposite shoots distinguished it from the true redwoods (*sequoia*). This particular example has the largest diameter at chest height in Britain. The massive size of the divided trunk necessitates the use of a steel brace to prevent the whole tree from splitting. The brace is just visible from the ground, and the whole tree is monitored regularly by the woodland specialists employed by the local authority.

There is something of interest here throughout the year, but it is in spring and summer that the deciduous trees come into their own. The beautiful **Indian Bean Tree**, *Catalpa bignonioides*, with its huge purple and yellow spotted flowers, is unconnected with India, but named after the native Americans of the southern United States from where it was introduced. The long thin seed pods are an amazing sight, sometimes reaching 40 cm in length.

In contrast is the dainty **Paper Birch**, *Betula papyrifera*, with its fascinating white peeling bark, and fresh spring green foliage.

As well as the well-known **Copper Beech**, *Fagus sylvatica purpurea*, the Upper Gardens is home to an unusual sub-species, whose leaves turn deep purple rather than the familiar dark brown.

A series of interpretation panels are posted at intervals throughout the gardens. More information can be obtained from Bournemouth Borough Council.

———————————————oOo———————————————

The 'Bournemouth Pines'

Many visitors to Bournemouth, intent on an active holiday, are baffled by the unexplained drowsiness which overtakes them on arrival. One theory concerns the presence of the many pine trees in the town. Whether there is any truth in this theory or not, this belief has a long history, and probably is in part responsible for the creation of the town.

When Lewis Tregonwell had his house built on heathland at the mouth of the Bourne, in the early nineteenth century his main concern was for his wife's health. It was generally accepted by the Tregonwells, Dr Granville and his contemporaries, that the aroma from trees, particularly pines, had beneficial properties for those with chest complaints.

The **Scots Pine**, *Pinus sylvestris,* had long been extinct south of the Grampians. However, the 1914 book tells us that in 1776 it was re-introduced to the New Forest.

The gardens of Lord Malmesbury's Heron Court, both commemorated by local place names, were established with the help of Scots Pine seeds obtained directly from Scotland.

By the time of the Tregonwells' arrival, the pines had spread rapidly in the *sandy moors and commons* of Bournemouth. Formal planting began in 1900, so that by the time Sir Daniel Morris wrote his chapter on Woods and Forests in the original book of 1914, it caused him to note the rapid increase of this tree in the previous fifty years.

Chusan Palm

Gradually, from the beginning of the twentieth century, the Scots pine was supplanted by the more drought and salt resistant **Maritime Pine**, *P. pinaster.* This Mediterranean import thrived in the mild climate and sandy soil of the Bournemouth area. The Branksome Park Conservation Policy report of 1989 notes that the predominance of the Maritime Pine has given rise to its alternative name : the Bournemouth Pine.

The **Chusan Palm**, *Trachycarpus fortunei,* which tower above Bournemouth Square are also present in the Tropical Gardens of Alum Chine. With the increasing effect of climate change, it is possible that in the future these might become known as the 'Bournemouth Palms'.

———————————oOo———————————

The New Forest Trees – Background and History
The story of New Forest trees is the story of the New Forest itself. Although the area covered by this book is limited to the western fringe of the Forest, the following is true of the whole area, which is now a National Park. A stroll at any time of year brings the visitor face to face with some of the most magnificent trees in the UK.

The last thousand years, however, have seen many changing fortunes for this unique landscape. When William the Conqueror decided on this area as his private hunting ground, it was seen as a temporary solution to a problem. Since then, the Forest has survived through less happy times, until today's sensitive management by the Forestry Commission. Most of this long period has been dominated by the constant conflict between the Commoners and the Crown. The poor soil and the presence of deer meant that crop-growing was out of the question. Instead, the Commoners relied on their right to turn out their livestock into the open Forest. Competition for grazing was already beginning to be fierce. Temptation in the form of deer poaching was punishable by death.

By the fifteenth century, it became clear that some of the great oaks and beeches were a valuable source of house building material. Hunting was no longer seen as the main reason for the New Forest's existence. In order to protect this resource, the first Inclosure was created in 1483. Although the main reason for this action was to prevent damage by deer, it also meant that the grazing acreage for the Commoners' animals was reduced. More Inclosures followed when it became apparent that the felled trees were not being replaced, due to the fact that the young seedlings were being eaten by ponies and cattle. Much conflict between the Crown and the local inhabitants followed.

By the eighteenth century the New Forest was seen as an excellent source of timber for the country's warships. A major Naval shipyard was established at Bucklers Hard, near Beaulieu. As a result, the importance of protection and regeneration for oaks was further increased. The number of Inclosures increased, together with the inevitable hostility from the Commoners.

Until then the New Forest trees consisted solely of native varieties, mainly oak and beech.

The first introduction of conifers was in 1776, not as a source of timber, but simply as an added protection for oak saplings. Together with prickly shrubs such as hawthorn and holly, they were planted around the young oaks to ward off the deer. When the saplings were considered robust enough to withstand animal attacks, the pines and shrubs were pulled away and discarded. Thus the open space around the oak allowed it to grow freely. In time, the oaks themselves were thinned, encouraging the trees to spread horizontally.

The Navy required branches that were naturally bent in such a way that they could provide a strong basis for the hulls for their warships. By allowing the oaks maximum space, these requirements were fulfilled. By the time of the First and Second World Wars, these plantings had reached their full maturity. Both of these conflicts accounted for millions of **hoppus feet** of timber.

Mistakes were made. The urgency to produce timber quickly in the First World War meant that huge clearings were made to enable speedy dispatch of the felled trees. By the time of the Second World War, lessons had been learned, and a far more thoughtful approach meant that fifteen years later, most areas had recovered. The mixed plantations that one sees today are a result of the clear fellings of the First World War. The spaces between the remaining oaks were subsequently re-seeded with pines. Those that remain have been kept for their aesthetic and ornamental value.

Lawrence Cumberbatch was Deputy Surveyor from 1849–80. He instituted many more Inclosures, and in an effort to placate the Commoners, instigated the Deer Removal Act of 1851. Although many deer were taken, the Act was a failure. Enough survived to establish new herds, the descendants of which we see today. Cumberbatch decided that still more Inclosures were needed, however, and this time 10,000 acres more were enclosed.

By this time, good quality soil was in short supply. Only poor quality sandy areas remained. As a result, he re-introduced the Scots Pine, which so far had been used only as a shelter plant. This tree thrived in the unpromising conditions and rapidly became an important source of revenue. It was soon followed by the Douglas Fir, which enjoyed similar success. It grew with amazing speed and attained heights much greater than the surrounding trees.

David Wilberforce Young's time as Deputy Surveyor will mainly be remembered for his use of 'mother trees' in regeneration projects. By leaving mature pines at regular intervals, the resultant seedlings thrived in their shelter, with a fairly equal distribution throughout the area. However, a German bomb dropped on Bolderwood Grounds resulted in an exceptionally heavy crop of seedlings in the same spot.

Since the war, more hardwood trees, especially beech and birch have been planted, both as an economic resource, and for scenic purposes.

The Ornamental Drives

As the Victorian fashion for gothic and picturesque scenery grew, so did the desire for non-native conifers. The taller, darker and more impressive the tree, the more it gained in popularity.

Deputy Surveyor Cumberbatch was already planting large areas with native conifers such as the Scots Pine. However, these were purely as an economic resource, and not chosen for their scenic value. Realising the value of the Forest as an aesthetic attraction in itself, he responded by creating the two ornamental drives, namely Rhinefield and Bolderwood. The imported trees were selected on the grounds of size, shape and their potential for creating an atmosphere of drama.

Originally, Rhinefield Drive was a simple gravel track leading to Rhinefield House. This house was built in 1887 on the site of a series of earlier dwellings. Although the trees lining the drive were planted in 1859, it was only in 1938 that the track was upgraded to a metalled road and opened to the public. A fabulous collection of conifers can be seen here, including the massive

Wellingtonia, *Sequoiadendron giganteum,* and a huge variety of cedars, firs, pines and spruces. Several of these trees are the tallest examples of their species in the country.

The Bolderwood Arboretum offers a similarly bewildering variety of trees. Planted in 1860 on the site of an old manor house, the more unusual species, such as **Blue Gum**, *Eucalyptus sp.*, **Western Himalayan Spruce**, *Picea smithiana*, and **Chile Pine**, *Araucaria araucana*, reflect the Victorian desire for imported exotica.

The **Lawson Cypress**, *Chamaecyparis lawsoniana*, and the **Nootka Cypress**, *Xanthocyparis nootkatensis*, are very similar, both coming from North America. One of the main distinguishing features is the colour of the male flowers : red in the Lawson and yellow in the Nootka.

Coppicing and Pollarding

One of the New Forest Commoners' traditional rights was that of estover, the collection of fallen wood as fuel. Once this supply had been exhausted, it was customary to help things on their way by cutting off the ends of branches. The result was that in the following spring the wounded branch would produce a cluster of shoots, thus providing more wood. Soon this method became accepted as an appropriate form of management on deciduous trees. The word 'copse' or 'coppice' in many New Forest names commemorates the early use of this method.

Pollarding was an even more invasive practice. From the word 'poll', meaning head, it simply means that the tree is beheaded at a height of about two metres. A lower cut would leave the resultant branches prey to browsing animals. The practice was made illegal over 100 years ago, so that all old pollarded trees are at least that age. Although the Act was repealed in 1971, this form of management is gradually disappearing.

One of the most notable trees from the first period of pollarding is the **Knightwood Oak**, *Quercus robur*, at the south end of Bolderwood Drive. It is at least 300 years old, and is a majestic example of a successfully pollarded tree. A protective fence prevents damage from animals, and allows natural regeneration.

The nearby Monarch's Grove is where in 1979 eighteen oaks were planted, one for each monarch's visit throughout the life of this well-loved tree.

Knightwood Oak

Conjoined Oak with Beech

Invertebrates

Jonathan McGowan, Mike Skelton,
Brian Weekes

SPIDERS, ARACHNIDA

The Bournemouth and surrounding area boasts the most species of arachnids in the UK. The mixture of habitats and biodiversity of other invertebrates such as insects plays a key role. Although many species are now very rare or even extinct many species have just not been found and recorded for decades or more.

Arachnology is a very specialised subject as certain genera are difficult to identify in the field and need the aid of a microscope. The family Linyphiidae for example comprises hundreds of so called 'money spiders' which are very difficult, even as adults, to identify so we will only touch the surface with regard to one or two of these species. The specialist spiders are usually linked to the most biodiverse habitats such as heath or chalk grassland. One or two depend on sandy dunes, certain trees, bogs or houses. We have acquired several foreign species in the last hundred years.

The region is well known for its rare species but unfortunately since the first book, we have possibly lost several of the species listed there. We have also gained a few. Of course there are hundreds of species to be found in the region so I will only mention a few of the more common species or rare types and the types more likely to be encountered by people.

All spiders have venom glands (except one in the UK), but they are only dangerous to insect size animals, and a few have very potent venom, enough to cause health problems in humans. We have only a few in our region, but they are very unlikely to bite unless they are held or touched in such a way that they either fear for their lives or being hurt. Some have huge jaws and are aggressive. A long standing well known member of our society sipped his bedside glass of water to be bitten by a **Bark Sac Spider**, *Clubiona corticalis*, and he had a serious reaction. Several people have been bitten by members of the genus Steotoda which are related to the black widow or red-backed spider, They are extremely common in our houses but rarely bite people, so are not worth bothering about. They do more good in keeping down the numbers of clothes moths, beetles and flies. Our area of south Dorset and the New Forest is the most diverse in the whole of the UK for spider species. Some species are only found in our area away from the continent.

Spiders have been poorly understood in the past, and disliked by many, yet they are so important to us, as they consume so many household and garden pests. They are the most common food source for most of our small garden birds and even small mammals. They have rather complex lives and some groups vary considerably from one another. Much work needs to be done in regard to conservation of certain species and also much more recording.

Orb weavers, Araneidae

These are the species most likely to be observed, as they spin the typical hub-shaped web that we are familiar with. These species can be very large and indeed include some of our largest species as well as some of our rarest. These creatures have an annual life-cycle: eggs are laid during late summer by a very large fat female, which usually dies soon after or with the onset of cold weather. The eggs remain throughout the winter and hatch in late spring. The spiderlings disperse by 'ballooning', that is releasing strands of gossamer silk to be caught by a breeze which lifts the animal high into the air (in many cases into the upper atmosphere), but usually just for a few miles at low height. Spiders also use this method to anchor guide lines for the web.

Not all spiders spin webs as such, but all possess silk, which is used for a variety of functions. They are also venomous, but that varies considerably with species. The males of many spiders are much smaller than the females and certainly within this group they are not as big, or rounded and they have a short season.

Common Garden Spider or **Cross Spider**, *Araneus diadematus*. This is the most likely spider to be seen during late summer and autumn. Big and bold, it is common in all kinds of grassland and rough vegetation from heath, waterways and gardens, even in the towns.

Marbled Orb Weaver, *A.marmoreus*. Similar to the previous species but not as common and is usually found on the heathlands and damp areas around fields or rough grassland. It can be found in country villages but rarely in Bournemouth itself. It has a variation called *A. pyramidatus* which is yellow with a pyramid shape on its abdomen instead of the usual grey green reticulations with spots.

The **Four Spot Orb Weaver**, *A. quadratus*. Similar, but is usually orange brown with four distinct pale spots on its abdomen. It can be found in similar habits to the previous species. They have been found in the Bournemouth Central Pleasure Gardens when the grass has not been cut, but otherwise they are to be found on all the heathland sites.

A. angulatus is a rarity and can be found on the more remote heathland sites in the area. Studland, Godlingstone, Arne and Stoborough are the best places but it has been found on Brownsea and other heathland sites in very small numbers. They are the largest of the group and the webs can stretch for several metres.

Gibbaranea gibbosa is similar but smaller as an adult. Both species have two humps on the side of the front part of the abdomen. This species builds webs in trees especially conifers as opposed to the gorse bush habitat of the previous species.

Nuctenea species are within the same family and share similar characteristics.

N. cornuta is very common in the region along riverbanks, ponds and lakes in low vegetation, sometimes within Bournemouth and Poole. All major and minor water courses have them including the Bourne Stream. Variable colour, red, white or creamy brown with dark cross-bars divided by white lines.

Araneus angulatus

N. patagia is very similar but is uncommon. It can be found in Christchurch areas on heathland and town most frequent along the Avon, at Hengistbury and Stanpit.

Walnut orb weaver spider, *N. umbratica*. This is a flattened version of the previous two, but darker in markings, it has a small web and lives in fenceposts along the major rivers and farmland around the Stour valley. It can withstand much drier areas such as chalk downland. It is common around the Wimborne area.

Nuctenia sclopetaria. Generally a similar spider but larger and more velvety in appearance, living mainly on brick bridges over water. It can be found on most old river bridges in the area such as Christchurch and Iford. It is never found on vegetation.

Neoscona adiantum. A more linear marked species inhabiting natural grassland and can be found at Hengistbury, Martin Down and Badbury Rings.

Wasp Spider, *Argiope bruennichi*. A rather infamous newcomer to the area it is our largest orb weaver. Females can be over 20 mm in length, and are striped black, blue and yellow. A most striking creature of rough grassland and moorland it is a specialist in catching grasshoppers. Its web is usually close to the ground and small, but with a 'stablementum', a zig-zag structure to the bottom half of the central part of the web. The spider is native to southern Europe and appeared in Bournemouth after the 1930s, possibly arriving in Kent or Sussex originally. It is now very common everywhere in suitable habitat, such as the cliff tops, all the heathland sites and road verges. It is more apparent during August and early September.

Wasp Spider with Long-winged Conehead

Araniells cucurbitina. A small green spider very common in trees and bushes, especially pine trees. Can be found in its small orb web within the town gardens and on the pine trees. A similar but rare species inhabits the heathland at times.

Common Orb Weaver, *Meta segmentata*. A very common spider to be found anywhere in gardens, marshes and woodland. It has a diagnostic striated markings on abdomen. *M. merianae* is similar but less common. Darker in colour and preferring damper habitats.

Cave spider, *M. menardi*. Much larger than *M merianae*, females are among are the largest spiders we have. Dark with reddish patches. It only lives in dark cellars and caves as well as drains and tunnels. It is locally common.

Tetragnathinae is a family comprising three genus of small to largish elongated spiders with long legs and often long **chelicerae** in the males. They hang upside down under the small webs, often above water.

Tetragnatha extensa. Very common in meadows and rough grassland. It is brown and yellow striped.

T. striata is common in the region around waterside vegetation. *T. pinicola* is locally common in pine trees. It is small and pale coloured. *T. obtusa* is locally common and has a shorter abdomen than the other species and is smaller with more colour. It can be found on the heaths.

Uloborus plumipes. A non-native species usually found in the southern Mediterranean and Asia. It is small and angular looking with front legs looking as though they are finely feathered. It builds a small angular web and has recently colonised flower retailer's shops such as garden centres. It is most common among house orchids. It is the only spider to be found in Europe that does not have venom glands. Because of this inconvenience, it spends a lot of time wrapping its victim in silk. *U. walkenaerius* is similar in appearance but with small tufts of hairs sticking out of the abdomen. Very rare but could be on our heathlands.

Mangora acalypha. A tiny , but very common spider to be found all over the heaths on its orb web among the heather. It is dark with a few white speckles and stripes on the abdomen.

Zygiella x notata is very common in many habitats especially heathland. A small pale marked animal, with variety in shades of colour. *Z. stroemi* is much less common, to be found on tree trunks.

Hunting, Wolf spiders and Sheet Web spiders

Water spider, *Argyroneta aquatica*. This is the only spider in Europe to spin a silken bell under the water and fill it with air and remain in it and eat water creatures. A velvety grey spider when viewed out of water. Can be found on many heathland sites especially Town Common and Parley. Sometimes in slow flowing streams and drains.

Grass Funnel Weaver, *Agelana labyrinthica*. A very common spider on the heaths and can be found by noting the large sheet webs with tunnels radiating from the edges. It looks similar to a house spider. They are very abundant and live for more than a year.

Nursery web spider, *Pisaura mirabilis*. Essentially a hunting spider but the female makes a conspicuous nursery web in the top of grasses and guards her egg sac until birth. Quite large and strongly marked it is very abundant in all areas of grassland, even in the towns, parks and gardens.

Nursery Web Spider

Raft spider, *Dolomedes fimbriatus.* The raft spider is a well known species, being big and striking in appearance and locally common. It is perhaps Europe's largest spider and females can grow to 25 mm in length. They are usually dark with cream or yellow borders on their abdomen. Juveniles are olive green and brown. They live in swampland, ditches and other boggy areas mainly on heaths. Spiderlings first live up on the trees and descend as they get larger. The adult can walk on water and even submerge to escape danger or to catch tadpoles, tiny fish and amphibians. A much rarer species, *D. plantarius*, has not been recorded in the county but recent sightings will have to be confirmed.

Alopecosa fabrilis. This species is only found on dry heathland in Dorset and Surrey and is very rare. It can be found on Studland and Godlingstone heaths. The genus

Raft Spider

Alepecosa includes the real tarantula to be found in Alpine Europe, and is very similar to this species of which there are several in the area. They are not the bird eating spiders of tropical climates but we do have a mygalomorph spider which is related to those types and more closely related to trap door spiders.

Purseweb spider, *Atypus affinis*. The purseweb looks like a miniature bird eating spider. It has huge **chelicerae**, short hairy legs and moves with a slow gait. It is more common on chalk downland where it constructs its silken tube alongside the mounds of yellow meadow ants on which it feeds. Good places to find it are Ballard Down and Hambledon Hill. It can also be found on some heathland sites such as St Catherine's Hill.

The genus *Pardosa* contains some of the most common spiders. Hunting spiders, they can be found on a variety of habitats including woodland leaf litter, boggy heaths, gardens and hedgerows. Some are rare such as *P. agricola* which can only be found on shingle beaches or *P. purbeckensis* which lives on tidal mudflats such as Poole Harbour. A very common species *P. lugubris* can be found in thousands in woodlands.

Sheet Weavers, *Linyphiidae*. The family Linyphiidae, commonly known as Money Spiders, is very big and comprises over 620 species. Many are only 2 mm in length or less. They are the most abundant spiders, and possibly invertebrates, second to ants. In late summertime fields shimmer in the early morning with what looks like millions of strands of silk. They are a major food source for all kinds of insects and birds. These spiders are also high fliers. They have been found ballooning many miles up along with aphids and other light invertebrates. Larger members of the family such as *Linyphia triangularis*, female 6 mm, male 5 mm, make tatty sheet webs and hang underneath. They are very common in a variety of habitats.

Ladybird spider, *Eresus cinnabarinus (niger)*. The true heathland rarity is the very pretty ladybird spider. The male is dark with large blue or black occeli on its red abdomen with white banded legs. The female is much larger, but dark grey all over. The male looks the same until final moult. First described from Bournemouth airport area, Parley Heath, in 1816, up to 1906 only a handful of specimens had been found, with only one female. In 1979, two males were found and in 1980 the second female. Since then, there has been a successful introduction programme and now hundreds can be found farther out around the Wareham areas such as Bovington, Winfrith and Worgret heaths. A specimen has also been found within the Bournemouth area. It has possibly been overlooked due to its long duration in a drab colour. This is a protected species.

Woodlouse spider, *Dysdera crocata*. The woodlouse spider is very common in both rural and urban areas around stone walls and ivy. It has huge jaws to grab woodlouse with, it can bite human fingers too. It is a smooth reddish-pink in colour.

Segestria bavarica is local to our region and is largish, dark and smooth looking.

S.florentina is even larger and can be found in similar places in dry stone walls and buildings around Poole and possibly Christchurch.

Spitting spider, *Scytodes thoracica*. This is a recent colonist and is now cosmopolitan in its distribution. It lives in non-centrally heated houses in dark dampish places. As its name suggests it spits a sticky poisonous venom at its prey. With its stilt like legs, the carapace slopes up towards the rear end and the abdomen down.

Pholcus phalangoides. The common '**daddy long-legs**' of room corners which is common everywhere, and will be in your home.

Psilochorus simoni. This species is like a tiny version of 'daddy-long-legs' and is blue grey in colour. It is common in the Bournemouth area in cellars and damp dark places.

The genus *Steotoda* includes spiders that are related to the Black Widow and Red-backed Spider of Australia which are highly venomous. We have several species within our region, and one or two species have received a lot of undeserved attention recently due to their bites causing allergic reactions in people. They all have a light coloured border to the front of the abdomen, are basically shiny and look hairless.

False Widow Spider, *Steotoda nobilis*. This species is said to have come from the Canary Islands over a hundred years ago and has colonised many parts of southern Britain, especially the south coast. A medium sized shiny, hairless animal, dark brown or black, it likes to live indoors or in out-houses and is extremely common. One or two people have been bitten with severe consequences, but the spider is not at all aggressive, and people live with it in thousands of houses all across Bournemouth and Poole without any problems arising. Some people react badly when accidentally bitten as they squash it.

Rabbit-hutch Spider, *S. bipunctata*. A similar spider, native and common in and around houses or trees in warm places.

Dark Comb-footed Spider, *S. grossa*. A native spider, black, living in houses and out-buildings.

The House Spiders comprise several different species, and are renowned for their appearance in baths. They simply fall over the edge during their nocturnal wanderings and cannot get back out. Washing them down the plug hole will not help. They rarely bite and when they do it is harmless.

Cobweb Spider, *Tegenaria gigantea*. Possibly one of the commonest here, living in houses and out-buildings. Up to 18 mm body size but produces a small web.

T. saeva. Similar to the previous species, again 18mm body size. Inhabits the north and west of Britain as well as the south coast.

Cardinal Spider, *T. parietina*. This species seems to be much less common in Bournemouth. They are brown,

Cobweb Spider, Tegenaria gigantea

hairy, with long legs and although they build sheet webs, the males especially can be found running around the house. This species is possibly our largest spider with legs often attaining 65 mm in span with a body size of 20 mm. The name derives from the belief that Cardinal Wolsey was terrified of the spiders at Hampton Court.

T. domestica. The smallest of the four with a body size of 10 mm. It is cosmopolitan in its range and is common in the area. The spiderlings and juveniles of this species live outdoors.

Mouse Spider, *Herpyllus blackwalli.* A medium to large spider found in houses; it is similar in shape to house spiders but it has a silvery sheen all over. It prefers dryer habitats such as sheds and garages and has been observed feeding on already dead insects.

Crab Spiders. These are small hunting spiders that have the appearance of little crabs in the way they walk sideways with shortish back legs and longer front legs. They have large swollen abdomens.

Thomisus onustus. A beautiful coloured creature, usually pink in our region, as it lives mainly on heather flowers or other pink flowers such as thrift on the sea cliffs or orchids in meadows. It is nationally rare but here we have good populations of them, mainly on the heaths such as Parley, Turbary, Canford, Studland, Hartland and the Bournemouth sea cliffs. On mainland Europe it can be yellow, but here a yellow crab spider is certainly *Misumena vatia*, which can be white or a combination of colours and has a round abdomen as opposed to a triangular shaped one as in the previous species. We did have *Pistius truncatus*, but it has not been seen for over a hundred years, possibly extinct.

Thomisus onustus on Hottentot Fig

Xysticus is a genus comprising several common and uncommon crab spiders. They are smallish, dumpy, and generally light pinkish buff or dark brown, especially in the males.

Wandering Crab Spider, *Xysticus cristatus.* Light brown to brown with a patterned body. This is the most common of the Crab Spiders in the area.

X. audax. Similar in appearance but is less common and usually found on the heaths. *X. erraticus* is smaller and darker and even less common. *X. lanio* is a tree dweller and common in oak trees. *X. bifasciatus* is rare but has been found in our region on the heaths. It is slightly larger than the previous species.

Philodromodae. The *Philodromus* genus comprises several crab spiders with long legs.

Misumena vatia with Meadow Brown

House Crab Spider, *Philodromus dispar.* A common creature of trees such as oak and pine, and gardens, male is dark above and the female is paler.

P. aureolus. Common on bushes, trees and walls, sometimes accidently comes into houses. The male is dark with a shiny iridescence.

P. histrio is to be found on the heathland amongst heather.

Tibellus oblongus. A crab spider of the heaths and boggy woodland. It is a small, long-bodied spider that can be found on low trees especially birch, or on grasses. *T. maritimus.* Less common, it can be found in dunes such as Studland amongst the marram grass.

Jumping Spiders, Salticidae. Small or tiny, squarish, short-legged hunting spiders that seem to jump about around gardens or in the home during summertime. They like fences and walls. They have huge eyes and have exellent vision giving the appearance of being aware of their surroundings.

Zebra Spider, *Salticus scenicus.* A very abundant species with the colouring of a zebra. *S.*

cingulatus. Less common but can be found on heathland or built up areas around the heaths.

Sitticus pubescens. A rare species but can be found on the heaths around Bournemouth. *Evarcha arcuata* is to be found on heathland. *Evarcha falcata* can be found in the same types of places. *Phlegra faciata* has been found on Bournemouth cliff and Studland heath. It is rare in the UK.

Opiliones. Harvestmen are similar to spiders being arachnids, but they differ in not having silk-making glands, or venom, and they have simple one section bodies instead of head and abdomen and a single pair of eyes more reminiscent of scorpions.

Dicranopalpus ramosus is a newcomer to Britain from the continent and is common around Dorset. It is odd amongst the dozen or so other local species by having very long legs that are held horizontally out from its body, and enlarged pedipalps that look more like pincers.

Pseudoscorpionida. We have several species of Pseudoscorpions in the area. These are tiny scorpion-like animals that lack a telson (tail) along with the venomous apparatus, but they possess it in their claws. They are not often seen but may live in houses or leaf litter or moss. They are usually under five mm but a continental species is ten mm or more, and it has been said that they have been found along the Bournemouth railway line.

We may have a true scorpion in the area: *Euscorpius flavicaudis*, has been found in Kent and Sussex, and has been found in Bournemouth, but not confirmed. It is harmless to humans and usually found around seaports in dry stone walls.

Damselflies and Dragonflies, ODONATA

All species are short lived as winged adults and aquatic as larvae. Larvae spend various amounts of time in the water predating on many types of aquatic insects, other invertebrates and small vertebrates. With Dorset's southerly aspect and abundance of suitable habitats we have a rich dragonfly fauna. The variety of acid and chalk streams and general water bodies are ideal for many species, a number of which are more suited to mainland Europe, or even southern Europe. We have many nationally scarce species, especially in the New Forest and Purbeck. The acid heaths play a big part. Conservation bodies have been aware for a long time of the importance of preserving certain habitats and waterways hence the suitable local nature reserves. In many cases waterways have been constructed solely for species of Odonata.

When mating the male uses his claspers (situated at the tip of his abdomen) to grasp the female by the pronotum, situated just behind the head (damselflies), and by the head (dragonflies). The female then curves her abdomen forward to receive the sperm that the male has previously transferred to his accessory copulatory organ on the underside of his second abdominal segment. This is unique in the insect world. The damselflies spend a lot of time in this position and often the female submerges to lay her eggs with the male attached to and fertilising her.

It is often quite difficult to tell species apart, as colour varies considerably within species, especially in the females. A good field guide is helpful. Attention must be given to the small markings behind the head or on the abdomen in most species.

Damselflies

Banded Damoiselle, *Calopterix splendens*. This is a common, active insect of flowing unpolluted rivers with bank-side vegetation. It is very pretty and distinctive in colouration being metallic-blue in males with a dark blackish-blue patch on the wings. Females are metallic bright green without the wing patch. They flit about bankside vegetation and low across the water. Males hold territories and invite females by displaying. There are always more males than females so chases are very common between males. Parts of the River Stour have huge populations of these creatures.

Beautiful Damoiselle

Southern Damselfly

Blue Tailed Damselfly

Scarce Blue-tailed Damselfly, orange form

Beautiful Demoiselle, *Calopterix virgo.* Similar to the previous species but even more exotic looking, with brown wings on a golden-green female and dark blue wings on a blue-green male. Nationally rare they can be found around the New Forest's swift flowing small streams surrounded by woodland. They are not to be found in such abundance as the previous species.

Common blue, *Enallagma cyathigerum.* The male is a small, boldly marked blue and black insect. The female is brown, greenish or black. They are commonly seen in small groups over many types of water bodies.

Southern Damselfly, *Coenagrion mercuriale.* The southern damselfly is nationally rare, but can be found at the Dorset Wildlife Trust site as well as near Bournemouth Airport. It is also present in a few New Forest sites. A small delicate looking species identified by a mercury shaped mark to the front end of the abdomen. Males are blue with black blocks on the top of the abdomen, whilst the females vary from light blue to white then brown.

Blue tailed, *Ishnura elegans.* Common in southern England, and particularly so in our area. Not so particular in its pH requirements of water to breed in. Does not mind chalk streams, but less common in acid ones. The male is blue and black in colour, the female varies from light to dark brown. They can be found in most of our rivers, especially the Stour and Allen.

Scarce blue tailed, *Ishnura pumilio.* Very rare and only to be found in a few spots near Beaulieu in the New Forest. A very small delicate species largely dark in colour but with a distinctive blue end to its tail. There is some variation, especially in females, including an orange coloured form.

Azure, *Coenagrion puella.* The azure is similar to the Common Blue, but not as common. It can be confused with similar species but is more likely to wander away from water and across fields.

Azure Damselfly

Small Red Damselfly mating

Emerald Damselfly

Small Red, *Ceriagrion tenellum*. This species is rare and very small, only 31 mm long. The male's abdomen and legs are all red but the female is red and black. There are two rare variants where the female's abdomen is either all red or all black. It can be found in sheltered well vegetated bogs in the New Forest.

Large red, *Pyrrhosoma nymphula*. Larger at 36 mm this is a common and active damselfly. It is mainly red with thin black band. It can be found on all types of water both flowing and still and on stagnant ponds.

Red eyed, *Erythromma najas*. Widespread in the area but nationally uncommon. A distinctive small blue and dark brown damselfly with red eyes. They can be found around Dorset, the New Forest and other places around Bournemouth and Poole. Seen on many water body types but mainly ponds with floating vegetation.

Emerald, *Lestes sponsa*. A small, delicate slow-flying species, a light coloured metallic emerald-green with a blue tail end. It is common on the wet heaths. A similar species is the rare **Scarce emerald**, *Lestes dryas*, which may live in the area in several places but is generally overlooked.

Dragonflies

Southern Hawker, *Aeshna cyanea*. This is one of the so called hawker dragonflies and is green and blue in the male, and brown and bright green in the female, it is *c* 70 mm long. Common in still ponds and slow moving water ways.

Emperor, *Anax imperator*. The male is a big blue and green dragonfly 78 mm long with a dark broad line along the length of the abdomen, the female is darker.

Hairy Hawker, *Brackytron pratense*, is local in the south. It can be seen at Studland, Hengistbury Head and in the New Forest.

Migrant Hawker, *Aeshna mixta*. Every year, thousands of these blue beauties cross the Channel and in August can be seen virtually anywhere. But with climate change this species has managed to colonise the UK and now is an established breeding insect all over England. A similar migrant, the **Southern Migrant Hawker**, *A. affinis*, could become more common as a migrant in the future.

Brown Hawker, *Aeshna grandis*. The brown hawker is one of the larger hawkers at 73 mm long but is not common though it can be found along the Stour. It has golden-brown wings and a brown body.

Golden Ringed, *Cordulegaster boltonii*. A very impressive dragonfly with black and gold rings on the body. The male is 74 mm long and the female the longest british dragonfly at 84 mm. Although never abundant it is present in most areas of bog, slow moving waterways and ditches. It is widely distributed and can be found frequently in the New Forest bogs.

Common Darter, *Sympetrum striolatum*. The male of the species is a pinkish red-brown and the female a dark greyish-black. Darters are small to medium sized dragonflies that are very active and rest often on the ground or on rocks protruding from the water.

Golden Ringed Dragonfly

Scarce Chaser

Keeled Skimmer Dragonfly

Ruddy Darter, *Sympetrum sanguineum*. This species is smaller than the common darter at 34–36 mm but the male is a very vivid red. Common in acid bogs, good places to observe them are the RSPB Arne nature reserve and DWT reserve on Brownsea Island. It is also very common in the New Forest.

Black Darter, *S.danae*. The black darter is well known on the Hants and Dorset heathy bogs and also on Brownsea Island. It is a widespread, common and late emerging small dragonfly. Males are basically black and females are yellow and black.

Yellow Winged Darter, *S.flaveolum*. This is a rare migrant in late summer, but some records suggest that it is breeding in the area and is likely to become more common. Similar to the red darters, but the base of the wings has a yellow hue.

Broad Bodied Chaser, *Libellula depressa*. A striking dragonfly relatively common in the area around ponds.The male has a broad powder blue abdomen bordered by yellow half moons while the female abdomen is golden brown with the half moons.

Scarce Chaser, *L. fulva*. This species is nationally rare but can be found along the River Stour, and the Moors River. A good place to see it is in the Throop, Holdenhurst and Tricketts Cross areas. Males have a slim light blue body, females are orange and black.

Four Spotted Chaser, *L. quadrimaculata*. In this dragonfly both sexes are a yellowish brown. The leading edges of the wings have dark spots on them. Common on the heaths and other places with ponds or bogs.

Downy Emerald, *Cordulia aenea*. A medium sized metallic-green dragonfly with a hairy abdomen. Although not common it can be seen around sheltered ponds in the area.

Brilliant Emerald, *Somatochlora metallica*. This is a very vivid green species with distinctive apple-green eyes. It is rare but can be found in Dorset and the New Forest at sandy lakes and ponds.

Black tailed Skimmer, *Orthetrum cancellatum*. A common widespread species 44–49 mm long. Light blue in the male, darkening towards the tail, yellowish-brown in the female with dark lines along the body. Found near open water with bare onshore patches.

Keeled Skimmer, *Orthetrum coerulescens*. This is far less common, but can be found in the New Forest in wet areas. Similar in appearance to the previous species, 40–44 mm long with a pronounced keel on the abdomen.

Bugs, HEMIPTERA

Bugs or (true) bugs lack jaws but possess sucking mouth parts for plant juice abstraction or consuming other invertebrates.

Brassica Bug, *Eurydema oleracea*. Common on wild beets and rocket they are small and rounded with red, yellow or white blotches on the black body. They can be found on the Bournemouth cliff tops. These pretty little bugs are becoming less common due to the cutting of clifftop vegetation in Bournemouth.

Ornate Brassica Bug

Ornate Brassica bug, *Eurydema ornatum*. This is a continental species recently found in Dorset and on the Boscombe cliff top. Usually vivid red and black.

Dock Bug, *Coreus marginatus*. These are brown and angular and many can be seen together on docks. They are common in parks and improved meadows. Kings Park and the cliff tops are good places to look for them.

Blue Bug, *Zicronia caerulea*. The blue bug is a small, metallic dark blue predatory insect. It is uncommon in the region, but can be found on the chalk downs such as Ballard and Martin Downs, and also Badbury Rings.

Dock Shield Bug

Sloe Bug

Mirid Bug

Assassin Bugs: Heath Assassin Bug, *Coranus subapterus*. This bug is predatory on spiders and other insects. It also stridulates when handled. A reddish brown tree dwelling bug.

Two other species of predatory bugs inhabit the region.

Marsh Damsel Bug, *Nabis (Dolichonabis) limbatus*. This predatory creature lives in the damp heaths or grassland feeding on other insects and spiders. It has a broad body and short wings.

Common Damsel Bug, *Nabis rugosus*. This species is common in a variety of habitats and is likely to be seen in gardens. A light brown colour it also feeds on insects and spiders.

Gorse Shieldbug, *Piezodorus lituratus*. Common on the heaths and cliff tops not only on gorse but on the *Genisteae* family. It is yellow green and about 13 mm long.

Forest Bug, *Pentatoma rufipes*. This is a large 14 mm bug, brown with square shoulders. As the name suggests it can be found in trees especially sallow and other deciduous trees such as oak and alder. It lives on the sap with the adults being in part predarory.

Sloe Bug, *Dolycoris baccarum*. The Sloe Bug can be found on a variety of vegetation not just sloe. It is *c* 5 mm long and usually purple-pink, its long hairs give rise to the alternative name of Hairy Bug.

Bishops Mitre, *Aelia acuminata*. This is a bug of unimproved grasslands. It can be found at Hengistbury, Badbury, Troublefield, and other flower-rich and damp woodland meadows. Adults overwinter and feed in the spring on grasses. The distinctive pointed head and ridges give it its name.

Common Tortoise Bug, *Eurygaster testudinaria*. This species feeds on rushes and sedges and can be found frequently in damp meadows, but never in abundance.

Mirid bugs. Dozens of species of these small but colourful bugs are to be found on grasses and other flowers. They are more elongated than shield bugs and much smaller. We have many rare or uncommon species in our area. Whether predatory or vegetarian they are mainly associated with flower rich meadows.

Ground bugs are similar, but dark and remain on the ground.

Giant pond skaters, *Aquarius najas*, can be seen in New Forest streams, and the **Common Pond Skaters**, *Gerris lacustris*, can be found on almost any kind of water, especially still, and even in drinking troughs for livestock. They are good flyers, like **water boatmen** (backswimmer), *Notonecta glauca,* and **water beetles** (*dystica sp.*) *Eurygaster*, and can see the reflection of water from a great height. They feed on small insects and spiders that fall into the water.

Water scorpion, *Nepa cinerea*. This species can be found in stagnant non-acid ponds. It looks like a flattened scorpion but has a long breathing tube at the end of its abdomen.

Grasshoppers, Locusts and Crickets, ORTHOPTERA, M Skelton

That the orthoptera were not included in the 1914 *A Natural History of the Bournemouth District*, in spite of the fact that our area supports a greater diversity of species than anywhere else in

Britain, is witness to the neglect these insects have suffered until recently. Lately, though, climate change and the resulting often dramatic changes in the distribution of some species have focussed more attention on this fascinating order. The reasons for the relative richness of our orthopterous fauna lie in the presence locally of a good diversity of semi-natural habitats and a climate characterised by high insolation on the coast and generally warm summers. Among the more important habitat types are hard and soft cliffs, salt-marsh, calcareous grassland, wet and dry heathland, dry acid grassland, unmown and only lightly grazed moist grassland in river valleys. It is worth remarking that some of the afforested heathlands, such as Hurn Forest, support a notably diverse fauna, often superior to some of the more highly esteemed heaths. In many ways the orthoptera might be regarded as the awkward squad by conservationists, because many species thrive in scrub or other coarse vegetation, and may be intolerant of mowing or anything more than light grazing of grassland. In order to maintain populations at a healthy level, it is desirable that management of nature reserves and other conservation areas should be carried out in such a way that some coarse herbage and long grass is available throughout the year.

Bush-crickets, *Tettigoniidae*. **Sickle-bearing Bush-cricket**, *Phaneroptera falcata*. The first and so far only record of this species from our area was of a single specimen found in a garden at New Milton in September 2006. The species has been extending its range northwards on the continent, and its arrival in this country was anticipated. An established colony was found near Hastings, also in 2006, but so far no colony has been located in our area. Green with long wings. The song is not easily heard, but the insects often betray their presence by taking to the wing when disturbed.

Speckled Bush-cricket, *Leptophyes punctatissima*. One of our commonest bush-crickets, this species is often present in urban and rural gardens as well as hedgerows and woodland edges. A flightless species, bright green with dark red speckles on the body it has very long legs. It is generally absent from heathland and, more surprisingly, from most of the Purbeck coast. The song is scarcely audible to the human ear, but the use of bat-detectors by orthopterists has given us a better idea of its distribution.

Oak Bush-cricket, *Meconema thalassinum*. This nocturnal and arboreal species tends to be overlooked, but is probably common in most parts of our area, both urban and rural, except open treeless heathland. It readily flies to light and often enters houses. They do not stridulate, but males produce sound by drumming against a leaf with a hind leg. Mention should be made here of a related, but flightless, species *Meconema meridionale,* which has been found in various parts of the country in the last few years. It was probably inadvertently imported from Italy on shrubs or young trees. It may well be seen in our area before long.

Long-winged Cone-head, *Conocephalus discolor*. This species was unknown in Great Britain until it was discovered in 1931 at Chale in the Isle of Wight. From 1945 onwards it was found at a number of sites on or near the coast in Sussex. The first records from our area were in 1953 at Anvil Point and 1955 at Chapman's Pool, Purbeck. After the hot summers of 1975 and 1976 it began to spread dramatically, so that it is now one of the commonest bush-crickets in our area and over much of southern England. The first record from Bournemouth was from Honeycombe Chine, Boscombe in 1977. It occurs in ungrazed or lightly grazed grassland, both wet and dry. The song is a continuous reeling, which has been likened to a very distant Great-green Bush-cricket. A bat-detector assists greatly in locating the adults.

Short-winged Cone-head, *Conocephalus dorsalis*. Once the commoner of the two cone-heads, this species is now much the more local, being restricted to wetter habitats such as coastal salt-marshes, and rushy meadows in the flood plains of rivers. It also occurs locally in some of the bogs on the Purbeck heaths, but not apparently in New Forest bogs. Although this species has been expanding its range in many parts of the country, there has been no sign of increase in our area. The very high frequency song consists of a reeling similar to the preceding species alternating every few seconds with a slower ticking. Bat detectors recommended.

Short-winged Cone-head   *Large Cone-head*   *Great-green Bush-cricket*

Large Cone-head, *Ruspolia nitidula*. Like *Phaneroptera falcata* this fine species is a recent arrival from the continent, where it has been moving north lately. Three males were found on two of the Isles of Scilly in 2003, and a specimen was discovered at the foot of Canford Cliffs in 2005 and again in 2006, suggesting successful local breeding for the first time anywhere in Britain. It is possible that it may have arrived in our area at the same time as the Scilly specimens, but was overlooked. A large bright green species with a conical head. Although the song is very loud and resonant, it is produced only during the hours of darkness. On the continent it is said to favour damp grasslands dominated by **Purple Moor grass**, *Molinia caerulea.*

Great-green Bush-cricket, *Tettigonia viridissima*. This spectacular insect is common in Purbeck among scrub and other coarse herbage, though generally absent from typical heathland and rare north of Wareham. In Bournemouth and Christchurch it is common locally in the lower Stour and Avon valleys, and at Hengistbury Head. Absent from the New Forest. Large, 40–55 mm, leaf green coloured with a brown stripe down its back. The loud rattling song, heard mainly from the late afternoon onwards, is a characteristic sound of warm summer evenings and well into the night, especially near the coast.

Wart-biter, *Decticus verrucivorus*. This extremely rare species used to occur at Godwinscroft near Bransgore in the early nineteenth century, and two single specimens were found in the New Forest, also in the nineteenth century. In Purbeck it was first reported from near Corfe Castle in 1923. Since then its appearance has been somewhat sporadic, in various places around Stoborough and Slepe Heaths. In spite of its inhabiting a National Nature Reserve, numbers have dwindled in recent years and it may now be extinct in our area. However, it has been lost sight of more than once before, so we may hope for a rediscovery. A large dark green species. The song, produced in warm sunshine, starts as a slow ticking, gradually accelerating to a continuous chirping lasting several minutes.

The English name of this species derives from the old Swedish practice of allowing the cricket to bite warts from the skin. The scientific name *verrucivorus* derives from the Latin, *verruca* meaning 'wart' and *vorous* 'to devour'.

Grey Bush-cricket, *Platycleis albopunctata*. In Great Britain this thermophilous (warmth loving) species is seldom found more than a few hundred metres from the sea. It is common on the Purbeck coast eastwards to Ballard Point, and also along the whole length of Ballard Down. It just persists in sub-optimal habitat west of the Ulwell gap. In Bournemouth it is only found east of Boscombe pier, but quite common on the Boscombe and Southbourne overcliff and at Hengistbury Head, where it has spread to new areas since 2004. It also occurs in lesser numbers from Friars Cliff to Milford on Sea, but is absent from salt-marshes. In 1998 a strong colony was discovered on a brown-field site at Ringwood, nearly 14 kilometres from the coast, by far the most inland locality known. It thrived there until the site was re-developed, but is now extinct in this location. It is a small, 20–28 mm greyish brown species.

Bog Bush-cricket, *Metrioptera brachyptera.* Not strictly confined to bogs, this species is generally common on remaining heathlands and in plantations on heathland, where it can be found in humid and moderately dry heath as well as in stands of **Purple Moon Grass**, *Molinia caerulea.* In Bournemouth it occurs on Turbary and Kinson Commons, but is absent from Hengistbury Head, where it is replaced by the previous species. Green and/or brown with a bright green underside, 11–20 mm long with short wings. The songs of both these species are similar, a series of chirps repeated at rapid intervals; this species has a faster rhythm than the Grey Bush-cricket at any given temperature.

Grey Bush-cricket

Roesel's Bush-cricket, *Metrioptera roeselii.* This normally brachypterous, (short winged), species used to be almost confined to brackish grasslands around estuaries until, in the 1970s, the Thames estuary colonies underwent a population explosion, leading to a rapid expansion into London and beyond. It finally reached our area in 2005, when large numbers of macropterous (large winged) specimens were found in many places in south-west. Hampshire and south-east. Dorset. An isolated colony has long existed at Needs Ore, but it is believed that the dispersing macropters originated from mid Hampshire, where numbers had increased explosively in the previous two or three years. In 2006 it was found that many colonies had been established in our area, in Bournemouth chiefly in the Stour valley. Management of grassland by mowing in late summer generally prevents this species from establishing, as the eggs are laid in the stems of grasses and other vegetation. Generally brown and yellow but sometimes tinged with green, 13–26 mm long. The fairly loud song consists of a continuous high-pitched buzzing.

Roesel's Bush-cricket

Dark Bush-cricket, *Pholidoptera griseoaptera.* Generally absent from heathland, this otherwise common species is often plentiful among brambles and other coarse herbage in hedgerows, woodland and neglected corners. In Bournemouth it is more or less confined to the Stour valley and Hengistbury Head. virtually wingless it is dark brown with a yellow underside, 11–21 mm long. The loud song is a harsh chirp repeated regularly. Sometimes males will produce a longer chirp in the presence of rivals.

Mole-crickets, Gryllolapidae

Mole-cricket, *Gryllotalpa gryllotalpa.* Writing in 1965 Ragge describes the meadows by the lower reaches of the Hampshire Avon as one of the few remaining localities in the British Isles for the Mole-cricket. Matters have deteriorated since then, and it is now uncertain whether the species still occurs in our area. A specimen was unearthed at Wareham in 1991, which gives hope that it may yet survive there. There is also a credible sighting from Corfe Common in the 1990s. A determined search in the lower Avon valley, by means of visits to likely habitats on warm evenings from April to June, when the males stridulate, offers the best chance of success. Somewhere like Coward's Marsh, with its transition from low lying riverside meadows to slightly drier sandy conditions on the edge of Town Common, seems quite promising. A large, 35-46 mm species, chestnut colour with strong forelegs for digging.

Crickets, Gryllidae

Wood-cricket, *Nemobius sylvestris.* The New Forest is certainly the main stronghold of this species in Britain, where it is often plentiful in the wooded parts. A small 7–12 mm dark brown wingless cricket. The rather quiet churring song is usually produced by a chorus of males, and will be familiar to anyone visiting the Forest from July onwards. The species is now also well established west of the Avon in the southern half of Ringwood Forest, on Avon Heath and nearby. It has not yet colonised Hurn Forest, but is present at Burton Common and reaches Christchurch at Nea Meadow.

Field-cricket, *Gryllus campestris.* This species had declined to such an extent that it was only known from a single site in West Sussex. It formerly occurred in the New Forest, and it is understood that under the terms of a species recovery programme introductions were to be attempted there. However, all is shrouded in secrecy, so we do not know whether these have met with any success. Grigg Lane in Brockenhurst may recall a distant memory of this cricket. The loud song may still be heard ringing out over flowery meadows in many parts of Europe. A shiny black cricket with a large head and a yellow base to the forewings.

House-cricket, *Acheta domesticus.* There have been very few reports of this species recently, mostly of singletons heard out of doors in the summer, which may be escapees from stock held as live food for captive reptiles. Normally the species is found in centrally heated buildings, and formerly also outdoors on rubbish tips. Greyish brown with dark bars on the head it is 17–20 mm long.

Grasshoppers, Acrididae

Large Marsh Grasshopper, *Stethophyma grossum.* This impressive insect, the largest of our grasshoppers, is characteristic of quaking bogs, both large and small, in the New Forest, which is its headquarters, and on the Purbeck heaths, such as Hartland and Stoborough. Because of declines and extinctions elsewhere, it is possibly now confined to our area in Britain. The males produce a ticking sound by kicking with a hind leg against the wing-tip. They readily take to the wing when disturbed. yellowish-green to olive-brown coloration, 21–36 mm long with the female larger than the male.

Common Green Grasshopper, *Omocestus viridulus.* The most cold-tolerant of our grass-hoppers, this species occurs most commonly in moist permanent grassland. It may be declining in southern England in response to climate change. However, it is still fairly common in Purbeck in the absence of the Woodland Grasshopper. On the Purbeck Hills it is found on the northern slope and high up on the south side, but not on the hotter lower slopes. It is very local north of Bournemouth and Poole, where it may be in competition with its close relative the Woodland Grasshopper. In the New Forest it is mainly seen among tall grass in the inclosures. The quite loud song starts quietly and reaches a peak of loudness after about five seconds and continues for several more seconds at maximum loudness. A green or green and browm, the female can be in part purple, 14–23 mm long.

Woodland Grasshopper, *Omocestus rufipes.* A close relative of the previous species, but with a preference for warmer and drier places, it has probably benefited from afforestation of heathlands. It is frequent in Hurn, Ringwood and Wareham Forests, where it is usually commoner than the Common Green Grasshopper. The New

Large Marsh Grasshopper

Forest has long been a stronghold for the species. There have been only sporadic reports from Purbeck, sometimes of only single specimens. In Bournemouth it has recently colonised Hengistbury Head and Boscombe Chine. The song resembles that of the previous species, but is quieter and shorter in duration, usually lasting less than ten seconds. Darkish grey-brown, 12–20 mm long.

Stripe-winged Grasshopper, *Stenobothrus lineatus*. This handsome grasshopper is found in fairly short dry turf on both calcareous and acid soils. In Purbeck it is sometimes numerous on the Purbeck Hills and the coastal limestone at Durlston. It has also been found on dry grassland around Stoborough Heath and near Middlebere. Elsewhere strong colonies have been found on fire-breaks in Hurn and Wareham Forests, and on golf courses, such as Queen's Park Bournemouth, Corfe Hills and Knighton Heath. It has recently colonised Barton Common. Absent from the New Forest. A brightly coloured species it is green and brown with red on the abdomen, 15–23 mm long.

Stripe-winged Grasshopper

The song is unique among European orthoptera, consisting of a high-pitched wheezy buzz, fluctuating in loudness and lasting more than ten seconds.

Mottled Grasshopper, *Myrmeleotettix maculatus*. The smallest grasshopper of our area, this species is also one of the most variable in colour and pattern of markings, twelve variations have been recorded. In its natural habitat of sparsely vegetated dry sandy heathland it is

Mottled Grasshopper

astonishingly well camouflaged. It is often the first species to re-colonise recently burned heaths, when some individuals can be almost entirely black. One of its most interesting features is the elaborate courtship display of the males in which the body sways and the clubbed antennae are flung backwards. A detailed description is given in Ragge (1965). The ordinary song consists of a rapidly produced series of chirps, quiet at first and becoming louder, lasting ten seconds or so. Generally distributed on dry heathland and in forestry rides. Present in small numbers at Hengistbury Head.

Heath Grasshopper, *Chorthippus vagans*. This species was first suspected to be resident in Britain in 1922 when a specimen was noticed in a collection in the Natural History Museum labelled 'New Forest', but it was not till 1933 that it was finally recognised in the field, at Studland Heath. It now seems that the range of this rare species falls entirely within our area. It still occurs on some of the best heaths in Purbeck, though perhaps not as plentifully as in the past, and is very rare at Arne. To the north of Wareham it can be seen in Wareham Forest and on Decoy and Gore Heaths. A string of colonies extends from Town Common, Sopley Common, through Hurn Forest, Avon Heath and in Ringwood Forest as far north

Heath Grasshopper

Common Field Grasshopper   *Lesser Marsh Grasshopper*   *Meadow Grasshopper*

as Boveridge Heath. In the New Forest it is confined to a small area to the west and south-west of Burley. It is unique among the British grasshoppers in being able to live in dry heathland that is entirely devoid of grass, so long as there is a good supply of **Gorse**, *Ulex,* present, on the spines and flowers of which it feeds. All three gorses can be utilised in this way. The species is, therefore, never found in pure stands of heather. Heather fires are not necessarily harmful to this species, which seems to do better on rather disturbed or regenerating heathland. Although the last DWT record is for 1984 it is believed that a colony survives in the small isolated urban heathland at Alder Hills in spite of frequent arson attacks. A dark, greyish-brown grasshopper, 13–21 mm long.

Common Field Grasshopper, *Chorthippus brunneus.* This very common grasshopper of dry grassland is found throughout our area, even in towns where it is often present in gardens on not too well manicured lawns. It is the only grasshopper on most of the Bournemouth cliffs, but is relatively scarce in the New Forest, where it is most often found on roadsides. Another very variable species, the rare green form has been seen occasionally on the Boscombe overcliff. The song is a series of quick, urgent sounding chirps. Two or more males will often reply to each other in rapid succession, which is regarded as a rivalry song. Generally brownish with striped and mottled forms, 15–25 mm long.

Lesser Marsh Grasshopper, *Chorthippus albomarginatus.* This species is characteristic of the drier parts of salt-marshes and moist, but not very wet grassland in the flood-plains of rivers, especially, but not exclusively, near the coast. It appears to favour places that are liable to inundation in the winter, but are sometimes quite dry in the summer, and so it may be found in the company of most other species from time to time, except the Large Marsh Grasshopper. In recent years it has been noted as far north as Breamore in the Avon valley, and as far inland as Cowgrove in the Stour Valley. It is common in many places near the Moors River and its tributaries, at Hengistbury Head, and between Lymington and Milford on Sea. Straw-brown or light green in colour, 13–23 mm long. The song resembles a slower, more laid back version of that of the previous species.

Meadow Grasshopper, *Chorthippus parallelus.* The commonest grasshopper in the general countryside, it is often abundant in a wide range of grassland types, from downland to bogs. It is, however, sometimes absent or rare in places subject to occasional inundation by the sea, unlike the previous species. The song is a rather scratchy burst of stridulation lasting from one to three seconds according to temperature. It is the one species likely to be heard on dull days. Both sexes are normally flightless, but occasionally a macropterous form occurs, which can fly well. It is interesting that it is absent from Brownsea Island. Generally green in colouring but frequently with brown wings and occasionally all brown, 10–23 mm long.

Ground-hoppers, *Tetrigidae.* The three British species all occur in our area. Ground-hoppers are inconspicuous small grasshopper-like insects usually living on bare ground in damp places. They have an unusual ability to swim well, even underwater. They do not stridulate.

Slender Ground-hopper, *Tetrix subulata*. A 9–14 mm long greyish brown insect with long wings. This species is mostly to be found in damp places in the vicinity of ponds and riversides, where it lives primarily on mosses growing on bare ground. It avoids acid conditions, and in the New Forest it appears to be confined to disused marl pits at Crockford Bridge and Marlborough Deeps, though possibly overlooked elsewhere on the Headon beds.

Cepero's Ground-hopper, *Tetrix ceperoi*. Unlike *T. subulata* this species often occurs in extremely acid conditions, such as bare peat and ditches near the Soldiers Road by Hartland Moor. The two species are difficult to separate, but this species is usually a little smaller, and more graceful in general appearance. For more detailed descriptions readers are referred to the literature cited at the end of this article. Strong colonies exist on wet undercliffs, such as at Barton on Sea, and it has recently been seen around a Natterjack pond at Hengistbury Head.

Common Ground-hopper, *Tetrix undulata*. Easily the commonest of our ground-hoppers, it is not so strictly confined to wet habitats, but may even be found on chalk downland so long as some moss is present. More robust tham the previous two species, with short wings.

Cockroaches, DICTYOPTERA

We have two native Cockroaches in the region. Both live in sandy dry districts such as heathland. They are small and generally stay outdoors. They run very fast and also fly, They are rare in the UK. We can boast two of over a dozen similar European species. They can be found under debris, rubbish, wood and especially on flowers, especially Ragwort, or on surfaces of fences, bus shelters etc. They are mainly nocturnal. Bournemouth cliff top is an ideal place to find them.

Dusky Cockroach, *Ectobius lapponicus*. This native species is a greyish-brown and rounded with dark spot on its head. 7–11 mm long.

Tawny Cockroach, *Ectobius pallidus*. This native species is more common and larger. It is long and uniformly tawny colour. It can be found on all heaths and other dry areas, even in the centre of Bournemouth in gardens.

Butterflies, LEPIDOPTERA

The history of butterflies in Bournemouth and the surrounding areas in the last 100 years is similar to their history in the whole of the United Kingdom. This is a steady decline, punctuated in recent years, by frantic efforts to halt this decline – normally, without much success.

The headlong development of Bournemouth, plus, to a lesser extent, that of Poole and Christchurch has reduced the amount of land that is suitable to the often specific needs of these insects in the various stages of their development.

As described in the section on wildlife conservation (Chapter 7) the fragmentation of the Dorset heather has resulted in the decimation of heather specialists such as the **Silver-studded**

Peacock Butterfly

Tortoiseshell Butterfly

Red Admiral Butterfly

Blue, *Plebejus argus*, and **Grayling**, *Hipparchia semele*. These are now only found in those fragments of heath that are covered by support groups, such as Kinson Common and Turbary Common, or larger self-supporting areas, such as Canford Heath, Parley Common, Upton Heath and Sopley Common. In these latter cases, they are all outside the Bournemouth boundaries and suffer quite badly from vandalism e.g. arson and motorcycling.

The current state of butterflies in Dorset is well known, thanks to the development of transect walking over the past 30 years. Transect walking involves walking a set route (the transect) through a selected piece of land once a week from the beginning of April until the end of September. The route is chosen to cover as many different habitats as possible within the area which is also chosen to provide a good coverage of the butterflies to be found in the location. A transect is walked at a steady pace and should take no more than 1–2 hours. The transect is further broken down into sectors and all butterflies that are seen in an imaginary box, 5 metres on either side of the walker and 5 metres in front are counted. Limits are set on the weather conditions under which a transect can be walked.

This method enables the annual distribution of butterflies to be determined and, if the transect is walked for several years, the annual changes in butterfly numbers can also be calculated, which, in turn, can provide information on the success, or otherwise, of any management plans.

Transect walking in Dorset has shown that the numbers of butterflies are declining throughout the whole county, Bournemouth included. The reasons for this are discussed under the section on wildlife conservation and, since butterflies are included by the Government as an indicator of the status of the health of the environment, this must be viewed with some apprehension.

Several species are under no threat but these are mainly country-wide species, e.g. **Small Tortoiseshell**, *Aglais urtica*, **Peacock**, *Inachis io* and **Large White**, *Pieris brassicae*. There are also several regular migrants, which fall into this category, although their annual numbers depend on factors occurring in their home habitats, normally North Africa (**Red Admiral**, *Vanessa atalanta*; **Clouded Yellow**, *Colias proceus* and **Painted Lady**, *Vanessa cardui*). In these cases, butterfly numbers can vary enormously from single figures to thousands.

All species to a greater or lesser extent are affected by the weather and the last two to three years (2006–08) have been extremely difficult for butterflies. A poor summer means that breeding is not very successful, while a poor winter means that mortality rates during overwintering are high. Several of these in succession have a dreadful effect on butterfly populations. It is to be hoped that future years provide better summers and more suitable winters to enable butterfly numbers to pick up.

The possible changes due to climate change are a mixed blessing for butterflies. Some species are at the northernmost part of their range, e.g. the **Lulworth Skipper**, which is limited to south-facing slopes of the Purbeck. It is at present holding its own and doing reasonably well. With increased summer temperatures, it could be expected to increase its range, assuming its habitat is not compromised. Increasing temperature is also thought to be the cause of the Red Admiral now overwintering in the county and it can be seen on the wing on every day of the year. The Clouded Yellow has also been noted as overwintering as a caterpillar on Southbourne cliffs for several years now and must be considered as an all-year resident.

Threats to other species come from a rather unexpected source. The **Small Tortoiseshell** has suffered a catastrophic reduction in numbers, due, it is thought, to the arrival in this country of a tiny parasitic fly probably helped by climate change.

A further surprise is the arrival in this country of the **Geranium Bronze**, *Cacyreus marshalli*, which has arrived from

Marsh Fritillary

South Africa where it is a pest on geraniums and pelargoniums. It is believed that this butterfly was accidentally imported with imported plants into Majorca and has since spread into most of mainland Europe.

It is impossible to quantify the number of species becoming extinct in the Bournemouth area because of the lack of historical recording but it is reasonable to assume that changes in the surrounding areas of Dorset mirror the changes within Bournemouth.

Common Blue Female

This will mean that the famous Bloxworth (or Dorset) Blue described by W E Kirby in *Butterflies and Moths*, among others, is no longer a resident – if it ever was one. This butterfly is, in fact, the **Long-tailed Blue**, *Lampides boeticus*, which is now only an irregular migrant, although fairly common on the continent. Butterfly lists from long out-of-date publications are not a good method of determining which species have become extinct over the years. Using the Kirby book as a source, we can see that some 14 or 15 species are extinct but as some have a very dubious claim to residency in the first place, these lists must be treated with caution.

A further loss, and in this case more significant, is the **Marsh Fritillary**, *Euphydrias aurinia*, which has vanished from several sites near Bournemouth. Its name is somewhat misleading as it is found both in marshy areas and chalk

Common Blue Male

downlands since its food plant is **Devil's bit Scabious**, *Succinia pratensis*. Its loss in marshy areas is probably due to drainage schemes and urban development. A successful colony was discovered in the early 1990s at Purewell Meadows in Christchurch, a few years after the Purewell Cross Road was built. This road appeared to bisect the colony and is thought to be the major cause in the colony's extinction. Marsh Fritillaries are quite capable of recolonising suitable sites from up to 10 kilometres distance but channelling the River Stour probably destroyed any local sites and the butterfly is now limited to sites in West and North Dorset. It is fair to note, however, that the Marsh Fritillary is an endangered species throughout the United Kingdom and Europe and not just Dorset.

Other butterflies threatened with extinction in Dorset are the Pearl-bordered and Small Pearl-bordered Fritillaries, although they are unlikely to have been seen in the Bournemouth area. These butterflies depend on the correct woodland management, which has, often, not been forthcoming in recent years.

Concentrating on possible extinctions and the possible effects of climate change, bad or otherwise, keeps us from realising that Dorset is one of the most fortunate of counties in terms of resident species and that Bournemouth, in spite of its increasing urbanisation, is home to about 30 species. The rise of wildlife support groups, be they well-organised, like the Dorset Wildlife Trust or the Dorset Branch of Butterfly Conservation, or, ad hoc like most of the Friends groups, is helping to ensure that this number does not decline in the coming years and who knows may, in fact, increase.

These latter groups are a common feature of urban areas. They are formed from members of the local community concerned about the possible loss, from whatever source, of their local green spaces. This leads them, amongst other things, to record the state of wildlife in their locality. These records should then be transferred to their county environmental recording centre. In many cases, they are not and this could cause problems when considering applications for development of a particular site since up-to-date information is not readily available. Sedentary butterfly species, such as **Common Blue**, *Polyommatus icarus*, are particularly sensitive to disruption and do not easily transfer colonies, or re-establish them. It is, therefore, incumbent upon those with the interests of butterflies and their habitats at heart to ensure that the locations of all our butterflies are known and that these locations are kept as secure as possible.

BUTTERFLY WATCHING IN THE BOURNEMOUTH AREA

Anybody who wishes to watch butterflies, anywhere in the United Kingdom and not just in the Bournemouth area, should invest in a good field guide of which there are many. One of the best is that published by Philip's and written by Dr Jeremy Thomas, one of the great names in entomology.

Silver-studded Blue Butterfly

After this, it is important to know where to look for them. Within Bournemouth itself, most local nature reserves will hold the common species, such as the three Whites, the various Nymphalids, a number of Browns and at least two Blues and two skippers. Through the year, this could yield up to 20 species. Sites such as Kinson Common, Turbary Common, Upton Heath, Sopley Common and other heathland areas should also hold reasonable numbers of heathland specialists e.g. Silver-studded Blue and Grayling.

To see the full range of species in the Bournemouth area requires venturing further afield. One of the best sites to visit is Ballard Down high above Swanage, which will yield **Adonis Blue**, *Polyommatus bellargus,* and **Brown Argus**, *Aricia agestis,* as well as the more common **Green Hairstreak**, *Callophrys rubi.* A visit at the end of May with sun shining provides an excellent reason to study butterflies.

Adonis Blue Butterfly

Another excellent site is Martin Down, on the Dorset/Hampshire/Wiltshire border. All the chalk downland species can be seen here as well as the **Small Blue**, *Cupido minimus,* and **Chalkhill Blue**, *Polyommatus coridon.* **Dingy** and **Grizzled Skippers** should also be seen.

Lydlinch and associated areas (Deadmoor Common, Rooksmoor and Alners Gorse) will provide sightings of **Marsh Fritillary**, *E. aurinia* and **Silver-washed Fritillary**, *Argynnis pahia.* This area is noted as a stronghold of the *valezina* form of the Silver-washed Fritillary.

Green Hairstreak

Chalkhill Blue Butterfly

Silver-washed Fritillary

The Purbeck sites of Durlston and Tyneham should also be searched for the **Lulworth Skipper**, *T. acteon.*

To ensure that the watcher is kept up-to-date with butterfly sightings and events, the website of the Dorset branch of Butterfly Conservation is essential – www.dorsetbutterflies.com

This site will enable anybody interested in butterflies to find out what is on the wing and where to see it. It will also allow any sightings to be recorded. This point is very important since updated records are vital to a study of the fate of butterflies, which are one of the Government's environmental indicators.

Moths, LEPIDOPTERA J McGowan

There are hundreds of moth species within our area, so one can only remark on the most often encountered or some of the rarer or existing species. Many are migrants and show up at various times of year from the continent, others are resident, some are regional and a few are to be found only in a few locations. There are micro-moths and macro-moths. The micro-moths are often very tiny and too many to mention, but some of them are very rare and specialist feeders. The larger moths are perhaps more easy to recognise, especially the renowned hawkmoths. Most of them are nocturnal in their habits, this includes the larvae, but many of the most colourful are day flying.

Hawk Moths

Lime Hawk, *Mimas tiliae.*This moth is common in Bournemouth as there are many lime trees in which the larvae feed, and the fat larvae are often encountered when they descend from the trees to pupate in the ground in late August and September. With a scalloped forewing, the pinkish and green colouring and its up to 70 mm wingspan it is a very recognisable creature.

Poplar Hawk, *Laothoe populi.* Quite common as a larvae on black and lombardy poplars, especially the latter within Bournemouth and Christchurch. The town parks have a few and the larvae are often to be found in September when they descend from the trees to pupate.

A large scalloped winged, latticed grey colour with russet flushes at hind wing base, up to 90 mm wingspan.

Elephant Hawk, *Deilephila elpenor.* The elephant hawk is most striking in colour, being a bright rosy pink or crimson, with kaki banding on wings and abdomen. Common yet not often seen unless caught in moth traps. The larval host plant is common willowherb or fuchsias if living in urban gardens. The larvae can be brown or green and with prominent eye spots on front of head. They are designed to look like snakes and not only fool the bird predators but sometimes humans as well. Pupae overwinter and adult emerges in May. Wingspan up to 60 mm.

Small Elephant Hawk, *Deilephila porcellus.* Much smaller than the elephant hawk and less common. It has similar colouration but more gaudy, and feeds mainly on bedstraws. Can be found

Lime Hawk Moth Larva

Elephant Hawk Moth

Small Elephant Hawk Moth Larva

on the chalk grasslands inland and along the coast. Wingspan up to 45 mm.

Convolvulus Hawk, *Agrius convolvuli*. This is an uncommon moth. It is a migrant and is our largest moth with a wingspan up to 120 mm, its larvae feed on bindweeds.It pupates and emerges the same year, like other migrant hawk moths. The adult feeds on various deep nectar flowers with its long proboscis. Has been found within Bournemouth gardens and along the sea cliffs.

Deaths head Hawk, *Acherontia atropos*. This is the most famous of the tribe, and is a most massive moth with a wing span up to 130 mm Yellow and brown with bluish tints with the distinctive skull shaped mark on its thorax it is unmistakable. It feeds as larvae on members of the nightshade family such as potatoes in gardens or fields. It has been found on Bournemouth cliffs feeding on related plants.

Pine Hawk, *Hyloicus pinastri*. Perhaps the second most common of the sphinx moths in the region as the larvae feed on various pine trees which Bournemouth is renowned for. The colourful green and yellow striped caterpillars are often found at the end of summer and piles of droppings can be found under trees overhanging walkways in parks or roadsides. The moth itself is a rather uniform grey. It over winters as a pupa and is also migratory.

Hummingbird Hawk, *Macroglossum stellatarum*. This moth has been of much interest lately, as it was rather uncommon, but now very common. It is a migrant, day flying medium sized creature which is similar in appearance to its name sake, and many people are fooled. The adult sucks nectar from flowers with its long proboscis, the larvae feed on bedstraws in flower rich

Hummingbird Hawk Moth Larva

meadows and metamorphosis is complete within the year. The moths can now often survive warmer winters to continue an early brood in springtime.

Broad bordered Bee Hawk, *Hemaris fuciformis*. Found in flowery places especially in sheltered forest areas. It is day flying and resembles a large bumble bee, but flies very fast taking nectar from various low growing flowers. The larval host plant is honeysuckle.

Narrow bordered Bee Hawk, *Hemaris tityus*. This is smaller and even more bee like with a short dumpy body. Frequents marshy and damp environments.

Striped Hawk, *Hyles livornica*. A migrant that has been found within the region in recent years. It is pretty to view with white stripes on a grey-brown body, its larvae feed on bedstraw.

Bedstraw Hawk, *Hyles galii*. A similar moth to the previous one which is found more and more often in the county, but still a rarity. The caterpillar is an attractive dark green or brown with yellow spots.

Emperor Moth, *Pavonia pavonia*. The emperor is common on the heathland areas where the larvae feed mainly on heather, but also on bramble and sallow or other trees. The females are large and bulky like a typical silk moth, being members of the *Saturniidae* family. They hang around near their silken cocoon awaiting the males, of which sometimes there are hundreds flying around the heaths at dusk searching out the females pheromone. Studland and Godlingstone heaths are places to look for them at dusk in early summer.

Goat Moth, *Cossus cossus*. A large (up to 9 mm) bulky greyish mottled moth quite common in the area. The larvae spend years munching through the living and dead tissue of various deciduous trees, especially willows and poplars before they pupate.

Gypsy Moth, *Lymantria dispar*. This moth was once extinct in Britain, it was a serious pest to deciduous trees. More common on the continent, but has made a sudden tiny re-appearance within the Bournemouth area. The white female is larger than the dark male and is a poor flyer.

Vapourer, *Orgyia antiqua*. As an adult the moth is not particularly remarkable in appearance, but the larvae is most pretty; colourful, extremely hairy with appendages at the front end, and tussocks along the back, it can be found on a variety of low growing shrubs and fruit trees. The male is a day flyer but the female is virtually wingless.

Pale Tussock, *Calliteara pudibunda*. A creamy coloured large moth, both it and the larva are hairy. Its beautiful yellow or green tufted larvae can be found when searching for a pupation site after leaving the host trees, usually sallow in the New Forest or other more rural areas.

Fox, *Macrothylacia rubi*. Not often found as an adult which is large and tawny coloured, the male flying in the day and the female at night. The larvae are always to be seen around the heathland areas trundling along footpaths and roadsides. It is very big, finger size, dark very hairy, and soft to the touch. It needs its fur coat as it feeds through the early winter on grasses and continues in spring. Can be found within urban areas but mainly the heaths.

Lackey, *Malacosoma neustria*. Often seen as a caterpillar on various trees within the urban areas. It has various blue, white and red stripes along its brown length like pyjamas. They can defoliate fruit trees. the moth is a drab brown colour.

Fox Moth larva

Small Eggar, *Eriogaster lanestris*. This smallish (up to 40 mm) brown moth is uncommon due to lack of its hedgerow habitat. Seen in areas of mainly chalk downland on blackthorn and hawthorn. The caterpillars live in communal silken tents and are bluish striped. They can be found at Martin Down nature reserve and other areas in Cranborne Chase.

Oak Eggar, *Lasiocampa quercus*. The oak eggar does not feed on oak but is so called because of the acorn-like shape of its cocoon. The adult male flies during the day but the female

Small Eggar Larva

is nocturnal. The caterpillar is colourful, with quite short hair. Less common than the small eggar and in mainly chalk areas.

Speckled Footman, *Coscinia cribraria*. These can be found in East Dorset and the New Forest as well as on some sites in the Purbeck. A mainly crème colour with red and black small dots. Very rare. Found on Parley common in the 1990s.

Silvery Y, *Autographa gamma*. This greyish moth with a 35–40 mm wingspan is extremely common as a migrant, varying in numbers each year, day flying and nectaring at any flowers they are a very common sight in town and country. There are several similar species.

Clearwing Moths. There are several species of small moths that mimic wasps . The wings are clear often with markings on them, and the larvae bore through trees, or shrubs.

Currant Clearwing, *Synanthedon tipuliformis*. This is the most common clearwing in the area, the larvae can be seen often in gardens feeding on cultivated and wild red currants. The adult is small at up to 20 mm wingspan.

Red Belted Clearwing, *S.myopaeformis*. A rare species only found in southern England, the larvae live in fruit trees such as apple and pear. The adult wingspan can be 26 mm and it has a red band on the body.

Large Red Belted, *S. culiciformis*. This species feeds on birch and alder. They can be found in New Forest heaths. The adult is very similar to the red belted but slightly larger.

Six Spot Burnet Moth, *Zygaena filipendulae*. A very common day flying moth which is one of our most colourful species with its red spotted wings. It can be found in all the natural flowery places and areas where its larvae's food plant, birds foot trefoil, can be found. The larval cocoons can be found as angular structures adhered to grass stems. In some places such as Martin Down nature reserve or Badbury Rings, the numbers of these moths are amazing as they flit from one flower to the next of scabious and knapweed.

Five Spot Burnet, *Zygaena trifolii*. This is earlier to emerge than the six spot and can be found in damp flower rich meadows. Not very common and declining in area. It was once found around the site of Bournemouth hospital and the golf course. It is smaller than the six spot with a wingspan of up to 33 mm.

Common Forester, *Adscita statices*. A lovely green moth uncommon with the larvae feeding on sorrels. It can be found in unimproved flower-rich pastures such as Martin Down.

Cistus Forester, *A.geryon*. This is a smaller and much less common moth. It can also be found in similar places to the common forester, mainly chalk downland. The larvae feed on common rock rose.

Scarce Forester, *A. globulariae*. Similar again to the above but even more rare. It is slightly larger at 30 mm wingspan. the larvae feed on knapweeds.

Mother Shipton, *Callistege mi*. So named because the markings on its fore wings resemble the face of an old hag or witch. A day flying moth it is found in unimproved grassy areas such as Hengistbury Head, Badbury Rings and Martin Down. The larvae feed mainly on clovers.

Large Red-belted Clearwing

Cinnabar Moths

New Forest Burnet, *Zygaena viciae argyllensis* var. *ytenensis*. This five spot moth used to be found in a particular location in the New Forest coastline but is now believed to be extinct.

Scarlet Tiger, *Callimorpha dominula*. An uncommon moth in the area, it can be found almost anywhere, but especially on the Bournemouth cliff tops. It is a most striking large moth (55 mm wingspan), day flying in warm sunshine. The wings have white markings.

Cream Spot Tiger, *Arctia villica*. A most striking large and colourful moth. It can be found on the chalk downs and surrounding areas. The larvae are brown and hairy, they feed on grasses.

Cinnabar Moth, *Tyria jacobaeae*. A very colourful and poisonous day flying moth of dry rough grasslands where its foodplant ragwort grows. It is crimson and dark green black. Its caterpillars are yellow and black rings.

Gentian Plume Moth, *Stenoptilia graphodactyla*. A small pretty greyish moth that has only been found on our heaths in the region. Sites include Ferndown and Ringwood as well as Beaulieu and Lyndhurst areas.

Heath Bagworm, *Pachythelia villosella*. This is one of the small moths in which the caterpillar trundles around in a sleeping bag made up of collected debris such as stones, twigs leaves or frass (droppings). It eats heather. The male is a small grey day flyer but the female is wingless.

This particular species is only found on the southern heaths around Bournemouth, Christchurch and the New Forest.

Micro moths are usually very small to minute moths of many species. There are really too many to mention. Many are not seen by the casual observer, but some are, especially the swarming **Long**

Horn Moths such as *Adela reaurella*. A dainty metallic bottle green species with very long antennae. The male flies up and drops down repeatedly, like several other similar species. The larvae eat dead leaves on the ground.

Nemorphora degeerella is golden with a yellow stripe on its wings. Both species can be seen in many natural woodlands in the area, especially oak. They can be seen on the clifftops and Kings Park in the borough during May. They are diurnal.

Flies, DIPTERA

Hoverflies, *Syrphidae*. A number of these bee and wasp-mimicking insects are to be found across the region. Hoverflies are not as active and do not seem' busy'. They are so named for their ability to hover in one position for long periods of time. There are many species most of which have a predatory larval existence, either on plants, trees or in water. Others live in wood or animal dung. Some are vegetarian. All adults feed on nectar from plants such as umbellifers (hogweed, carrots, parsleys) as well as ivy.

Drone Fly, *Eristalis tenax*. This 10–12 mm fly resembles a honey bee and is very common.

Pied Hoverfly, *Scaeva pyrastri*. A large fly with pairs of white bars on its body. It is very common and the summer numbers are enhanced by continental influxes.

Banded Hoverfly, *Volucella zonaria*. A large and impressive fly with an orange-brown body with black bars. It is a hornet mimic and is rare outside our area. It can be found in Bournemouth in shady places in gardens. Its larvae live within the nests of wasps eating their grubs.

Other members of the same genus resemble bumble bees. They live in the underground nests and eat the developing grubs.

Chrysotoxum bicintum. Black with two yellow stripes. A nationally rare fly but can be found around Kingston Lacey and Ballard Down and also around the Bournemouth district.

C.octomaculatum. A striking fly with a yellow body with a series of black bars. It is an endangered species and only known from our local heathlands and Sussex.

Ferndinandea ruficornis. Only survives in the New Forest, in association with goat moths, or at least the sap oozed from the borings of larvae in the trees.

Brachyopa bicolor. This species is only known from the New Forest and may similarly require a special habitat such as old trees with sap flows caused by boring larvae.

Caliprobola speciosa. Another extreme rarity with only one place of existence outside Windsor Great Park and that is of course the New Forest. The larvae feed in rotting beech tree roots to the further detriment of the roots.

There are a few other very rare hoverflies only known from the New Forest and other old woodlands.

Conops quadrifasciatus has a long black and yellow striped body and visits flowers in natural places. Its larvae develop in underground bees' nests.

Fungus Gnats

There are hundreds of small flies of which many are classed as gnats, and with them, many are fungus gnats, the larvae of which can be found inside mushrooms(for those of you that eat the many types of wild fungi). Some feed in decaying wood in close association with the mycelium of certain fungus.

Neoempheria lineola has only been found at Brockenhurst and Denny Wood, feeding in decaying wood.

Lacewings, NEUROPTERA

There are many species of Lacewing, several of which are rare.

Giant Lacewing, *Osmylus fulvicephalus*. This is the biggest Lacewing in the UK and can be found in the New Forest; it is about 2.5 cm long, mottled-brown and lives along the small shallow streams. Adults can be found resting under bridges.

Common Lacewing, *Chrysopa perla*. One of several similar species. Small, emerald green in colour. The larvae feed on aphids in deciduous woodland and gardens.

True Flies

Stiletto Fly, *Thereva annulata*. A small but silver-white insect showing distinctive red eyes. It is to be found on Studland Heath on the sand dunes.

Bee Flies, of which we have three species are small, dumpy, very fast-flying nectar-sipping flies with a very long rostrum always out. They make a high pitched whine as they hover in front of flowers such as primroses. Usually seen in the springtime, they are rare but can be found around Wareham Forest and Purbeck.

Mottled Bee-Fly, *Thyridanthrax fenestratus*. 7–9 mm with black blotched wings and body. A rare endangered species but found on heathland in the district such as Town Common near Christchurch.

With so many flies, one can only note a few special species.

Robber flies are big, hairy predators of the air, and one or two are very rare. *Asilius crabroniformis*. It is like a small dragonfly when sighted, being large and half yellow; it takes other flies, grasshoppers and spiders and sucks them dry. The larvae feed on the droppings of herbivores that have fed on natural unimproved pastures. Places to see them are the Forestry Commission site at Crabfield, by Bournemouth Airport, and DWT reserve at Powerstock Common in the west of the county, but also on a few other sites near Bere Regis, heathland around Wareham Forest and parts of the New Forest lawns .

Smaller species within the same family are commonplace, such as *Laphria marginata*, which is common on the heaths and *Pamponerus germanicus*, both of which are brownish and less hairy.

Machimus atricapillus. This Robber Fly can be found at Kingston Lacy and Badbury areas, also in Cranborne Chase and the Purbeck hills. A 14–18 mm long dark brown species.

Horseflies are well-noted within the region mainly because they following and bite people as well as the normal large mammal prey.

Cleg-fly, *Haematopota pluvialis*. The most common, especially in the New Forest, it is small and sneaks up on people without a sound, always approaching from behind.

Giant Horsefly, *Tabanus sudeticus*. Our largest horsefly, up to 3 cm long. It usually feeds on cattle and horses but does attack people. Two other similar, smaller but rarer species can be found in Purbeck.

Splayed Deerfly, *Chrysops caecutiens*, is to be found on the heaths. A dark angular-looking insect 8–10 mm long with beautiful multi-coloured eyes. *C. relictus* is similar but has a lighter coloured abdomen.

C.sepulcralis is only known from a few sites on Purbeck, Ferndown and from the New Forest.

Crane Flies, Tipulidae

Common Crane Fly, *Tipula paludosa*. Found everywhere around grassland especially cut lawns. The larvae are known as 'leather jackets' and eat the roots of grass. The adults, up to 25 mm long, emerge 'en masse' after pupation in the autumn causing the well known plagues.

Giant Crane Fly, *Tipula maxima*. Huge in comparison with mottled wings and a span of up to seven cm. Found in small numbers in damp natural meadows.

Limonia bezzii. Only known from Dorset, Chesil Beach and Poole Harbour where it lives in association with inter-tidal zones of brackish water.

A number of midges occur, and some of them bite mammals for their blood including man. Many belong to the black fly tribe, *Simulium sp*. and the **Blandford Fly**, *Simulium posticatum*, is the most famous. They are notorious for their nasty painful bite with large swellings. The larvae live in rivers such as the Stour and its tributaries, and an extermination programme has been mostly successful, yet could be harmful to other insects.

Wasps, HYMENOPTERA

Social Wasps. Colonies are an annual occurance with hibernating fertile queens forming new colonies in early summertime. The colony enlarges and by autumn the wasps become noticeable as they number thousands and hunt for other insects such as aphids, caterpillars, flies as well as fermenting fruit. They are all passive towards humans unless threatened. They play a very important role in keeping down the numbers of other insects and are the gardener's friend. They should not be destroyed even if in attics of houses. They will only sting if they feel threatened, or something is destroying the nest. The pesticides used for the destruction of wasps are far more lethal and spread into the environment. Unlike bees, wasp stings do not have barbs and are less toxic, but each wasp can sting a multiple of times. All social wasps are also important pollinators of flowers.

Hornet, *Vespa crabro.* Common all around the district, but not as much as the smaller social wasps. Nesting in tree holes and sometimes in houses such as in chimneys, they are very large and predatory on other insects. They have become more common in the last twenty years and sometimes occur within Bournemouth and Poole. A colony was present in Boscombe some years ago. Hengistbury has them and of course the New Forest has countless colonies as does Purbeck and all areas of deciduous woodland especially oak. These wasps are docile and rarely attack people, they are harder to annoy than common wasps.

Media Wasp, *Dolicovespula media.* Larger than the common wasp, this is a newcomer from the continent. It builds its large paper nests in trees, it is more docile than the smaller common species.

Several species of smaller common wasps can be found in the area. They are of the Vespula genus. They are all similar in size and looks but facial markings are different. A good key is vital to identify these similar looking species.

German Wasp, *Vespula germanica.* A typical yellow and black wasp which nests underground or in a hole in a tree. The hole will be increased in size to accommodate the nest. Common throughout the UK.

Norwegian Wasp, *V. (Dolichovespula) norwegica.* This species is of similar appearance but builds its small nest among twigs. Again common throughout the UK.

Common Wasp, *V. vulgaris.* The well known wasp, very common all over the area. The most common type likely to nest within human dwellings.

Red Wasp, *V. rufa.* Named for the russet colouration around the segments of the upper abdomen. This species has a parasitic species, Cuckoo wasp, *V. austriaca.*

Sand Wasps:

Purbeck Mason Wasp, *Pseudepipona herrichii.* A small attractive red, black and yellow wasp that makes it s nest in bare clayey heathland. The only place it is known from is the Purbeck Heaths. Present at Godlingstone and Studland.

Bee Wolf, *Philanthus triangulum.* This species is an impressive black and yellow, occasionally all yellow, large slender wasp. It predates on honey bees, paralyses them and stores them in a tunnel in sandy ground. It lays one egg in the bee's body for the developing larvae. It was once very rare, now more common especially locally. Colonies can be very large with hundreds of little holes peppering sandy paths. The best place to see them is Hartland Moor, or Bournemouth cliffs and Hengistbury Head.

Hunter Wasps:

Spider Wasp, *Ammophila sabulosa.* This insect hunts caterpillars of mainly noctuid moths. It is about an inch long, black with a long red abdomen. They rush around the ground, and bury

Ruby-tailed Wasp   *Sabre Wasp*   *Ophion luteus*

their quarries in dug out tunnels where they lay an egg on the paralysed larvae which supplies the food source. Common on the heaths and cliffs.

Ruby-tailed Wasp, *Chrysis ignita*. A beautiful metallic green-blue with a red abdomen. It parasitises Mason Bees. There are a few similar species. It can be found on umbellifer flowers or investigating old wood, such as fence posts.

Ichneumon Wasps:

Sabre Wasp, *Rhyssa persuasoria*. A very large and long impressive parasite of the larvae of the Greater Horntail Sawfly, Urocerus gigas, which in itself is also impressive. It feeds in the stumps of conifers. Both are not common but can be found around the heaths and within Bournemouth and Christchurch areas.

Ophion luteus. A yellow or orange long-legged and long-bodied, 20 mm wasp. It is parasitic on moth caterpillars. It is common throughout the region.

Velvet Ant, *Mutilla europaea*. A large shiny black ant-like wasp that parasitises bumblebees. It is frequent on heathlands.

Bees, Apidae

Social bees:

Honey Bee. *Apis malifera*. The Honey Bee is still a wild bee in the area despite the dwindling colonies due to the viroa mite infestations. Less common than it used to be, it is still a very important pollenator of flowers, especially heather and trees. Many apiarists have gone out of business but in our area things are not as bad as in other parts of the UK.

Bumblebees

It has been noted that many species of bee have been declining at an alarming rate for the last decade with some of our most common types now under extreme pressure. It is believed that many factors contribute to this alarming trend. They include a lack of flower rich meadows, flowers flowering at unusual times possibly due to extreme weather conditions, wet and milder winters and the constant use of fungicides and herbicides.

A bumble bee may seem obvious to the casual observer, but things are not that straight forward as there are true **bumble bees**, *Bombus*, and **cuckoo bumble bees** sub-genus, *Psithyrus*. They may all look similar, with the different sexes of the same species looking different. Cuckoo bees do not carry pollen baskets, and have sparse covering of hair. They live in the nests of true bumble bees. They are not enemies as such but there may be a symbiotic relationship. They are fed by the true species and also will attack them. They do not possess a worker cast like their hosts. We have six species of cuckoo bumble bees in the UK.

We have 25 species of true bumble bee in the UK. We have possibly lost two species, yet gained at least one. Six throughout Britain, six in the south and another five rare or uncommon.

Fertile queens hibernate over winter to found new spring colonies like social wasps, but differing in that bumble bees will emerge on mild winter days and collect pollen.

They make small nests, or cells within a small area underground or in walls or other tight spaces often in old bird or mammal nests.

Large Earth Bumblebee, *Bombus terrestris*. A large black bee with yellow bands on its body and a yellow or white tail. The most common European bumblebee.

Small Garden Bumblebee, *B. hortorum*. A large bee with yellow and white bands on a black thorax. A very common species.

Common Carder Bumblebee, *B. pascuorum*. A common species with a ginger coloured thorax.

Early Bumblebee, *B. pratorum*. A small bee with a black body with yellow hair on the thorax particularly in the male. The tail is a light orange.

Red-tailed Bumblebee, *B. Lapidarius*. A short tongued bee, black with an auburn-red tail. Common all over the area it nests below ground.

White-tailed Bumblebee, *B. lucorum*. A dark body with yellow bands and as the name suggests a white tail. It is one of our most common bees and the population is stable at moment.

Shrill Carder Bee, *B. sylvarum*. A southern species mainly grey-green with a black band on its thorax. Formerly seen in the area, now decreasing nationally.

Brown Banded Carder Bee, *B. humulis*. Tawny coloured with a brown band on the upper abdomen. A southern species and local, it was in decline over the last few decades but is on the increase again.

Short Haired Bumblebee, *B. subterraneus*. Was a southern species and in our area, is now believed to be extinct.

White-tailed Bumblebee

Red Shanked Bumblebee, *B. ruderarius*. Similar in appearance to *B. Lapidarius* it is locally widespread but declining.

Heath Bumblebee, *B. jonellus*. A small bee with two yellow stripes on the thorax and a white tail. Often seen on heaths and moorland it is a local species although recently in decline.

Moss Carder Bumblebee, *B. muscorum*. A species predominantly of coastal areas. A light reddish-brown body it is rare and declining in the area.

Cullem's Bumblebee, *B. cullumanus*. A limestone and chalk specialist, once occurred in the Purbeck, possibly now extinct.

Tree Bumblebee, *B. hypnorum*. A new UK species, ginger thorax and black abdomen with a white tail. It has been found in the New Forest and Dorset since 2001.

Solitary Bees. These are small to medium sized bees that often nest in colonies but not in a built shared nest. They either dig holes in sandy ground, or make use of other insect holes or gaps in wood to fill with cell material for their larvae to live in. They are mainly vegetarian and gain safety in numbers by building burrows next to each other. Sometimes hundreds or even thousands of individuals may be nesting in a sandy bank or pathway. There will also be other parasitic bees and wasps using them. Sometimes there can be up to five different species of wasps parasitic on each other. On big wasps there may be small wasps and on them even smaller ones.

There are always huge numbers of these species and so they are a very important food source for birds and reptiles. They are harmless to man. Many of these belong to the genus of *Andrena*, many of which are rare or very rare, although some are very common.

Tawny Mining Bee, *Andrena fulva*. Very common and very obvious. It is a shiny, hairy, golden orange-brown and nests in sandy pathways or lawns, creating a little volcano like mound.

Early Mining Bee, *A .haemorhoa*. A common species, 10–12 mm long that is half black and half red, it lives on various plants.

A. cineria. A rare species which resembles a black and white bumblebee. It can be found at Badbury Rings and other flower-rich places.

Colletes succinctus. This species nests in colonies and can be seen swarming in May or June along the Bournemouth cliff tops. It generally feeds on heather.

Red Mason Bee, *Osmia rufa*. 6–11 mm, it nests in pre-existing holes in walls on buildings and is common anywhere in the towns.

Megachile maritima. This is one of the leaf-cutter bees. They cut out neat little circles from rose bushes and other plants to roll up and take into their nests.

Six-banded Nomad Bee, *Nomada fulvicornis*. Breeds in the nests of Andrena species and is pretty to look at; 11 mm long. A very common species.

Cuckoo Bees

Barbut's Cuckoo Bee, *B.barbutellus*. A common bee with a white tail, cuckoo of *B. hortorum*.

Red Mason Bee

Red Tailed Cuckoo Bee, *B. rupestris*. One of the largest species of bee with a tail to match its common name. In the past a rare species but it is becoming more common, cuckoo of *B. lapidarius*.

Gypsy Cuckoo Bee, *B. bohemicus*. A very common species, yellow patches above white tail. Cuckoo of *B. lucorum*.

Forest Cuckoo Bumblebee, *B.sylvestris*. common in the area it is a parasite on *B. pratorum*. It has a dark body and a white tail.

Ants, Formicidae

There are many species of true ants in the region, many of which are heathland specialists. There are some chalk downland specialists, and others are just grass pasture specialists. There are too many species to mention them all, but again our area hosts a wealth of very rare species. Ants are social insects like social bees and wasps, and have a worker caste and one or two queens with seasonal male emergences like the bees and wasps, these create swarming in the mid summer time. They often have stings, but more often biting jaws that give out formic acid, that can be painful to humans. Only a few species such as **Red Ants**, *Myrmica rubra,* are renowned for this.

The common **Black Garden Ant**, *Lasius niger*, doesn't bite or sting, and is very important in the garden taking many pests. Unfortunately too many people are quick to poison both them and the environment with nasty cruel chemicals. They are also known for their milking of aphids for honey-dew. Many other invertebrates rely on ants for protection. Some of our blue butterflies such as the rare Adonis and Large blue need the **Yellow Meadow Ant**, *Lasius flavus*. These ants make the conspicuous little mounds all over grasses meadows especially on chalk downland. The New Forest lawns are also good places to find them. There are several similar species that like either dry, humid or damp positions.

We have at least two non-native species now in the UK, and although rare in our area, may become more common, at least in warm houses or greenhouses. The **Pharaoh's Ant**, *Monomorium pharaonis*, is African in origin and is a pest as it lives indoors at the moment as it is too cool out doors. This may change.

Southern Wood Ant, *Formica rufa*. A reddish coloured species found all over heathland sites in the area. It is a nationally common species in dry heath or forest areas especially pine forests. They are renowned for their large conspicuous mounds of pine needles, and thousands of individual workers either massing in the spring, or marching in long lines in a similar fashion to Army ants. Some mounds can reach four feet in height and five or six feet across. They are harmless and do not sting, but they can squirt formic acid if picked up. They are very placid and hard to upset.

There are one or two very similar species.

Black Backed Meadow Ant, *Formica pratensis*. Darker than the other *Formica* species this dry heathland ant can be found at one or two sites on the Bournemouth cliff tops. There has been a colony at Boscombe chine for many years, but is now under threat due to a new building development project that has blocked sunlight onto the cliff side, and overgrown alien vegetation. These wood ants do not normally make visible mounds like the common variety, but keep underground. The species is possibly due for extinction unless the local authorities take a stance to protect it.

Slave Making Ant, *Formica sanguinea.* As the name implies these large ants raid the nests of other ants and make the workers slaves. It is a nationally scarce insect but can be found on our heathlands, especially Parley Heath and a few New Forest sites.

Narrow Headed Ant, *Formica exsecta.* A medium-sized red and brown aggressive ant. Formerly found in Bournemouth and Poole, it may still be around on the cliffs or heathland but is nationally very rare.

Black Bog Ant, *Formica candida (transkaucasica)*, is very rare and only survives in the New Forest and Wareham heaths. It can be found at Matley Bog, Ridley Bog, Hartland Moor and the DWT reserve at Upton Heath. It is shiny black and builds conical mounds in purple moor grass clumps.

Beetles, COLEOPTERA

Beetles are a continuing study for many recorders and enthusiasts as the population is vast and often changing. They are the most numerous of the fauna with regard to species. It is not possible to name all of the varieties, but I will note the most common as well as the rarest and well known representatives of the area or special species. Beetles are under recorded, at least fifty four species of beetle had become extinct before 1900. Since then we may have lost a dozen more, and one fifth of all beetle species are classed as rare or endangered. The most famous must be the **Stag Beetle**, *Lucanus cervus.* This species was mentioned in the first book, it may have been more common in those days. One of the largest flying beetles in Europe it is a very distinctive creature of large proportions. The male has modified jaws which resemble the antlers of deer and used for the same reasons, to fight off rivals during the mating season. The larvae spend up to seven years slowly munching through rotting timber, mainly oak, and the adults finally emerge in May and June to fly at dusk. They were formerly widely distributed across southern England, now confined to the home counties, but with small colonies in the Midlands. The stronghold is now London, Bournemouth and Poole. It is now rare in the New Forest despite an abundance of decaying timber. It certainly seems to be more common in towns,

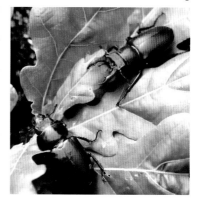

Stag Beetles, male and female

perhaps due to lack of predators and competition from the many other wood-boring species as well as a warmer environment. Much conservation effort is being applied to them by educating the public, putting buckets of earth and dead wood into the ground in known habitats and by saving old timber. In some well known haunts, magpies gather in large flocks and pick them off as they fly in the late evening.

Longhorns family, *Cerambycidae.* Other notable beetles are of the longhorn family, which comprises dozens of genera and around sixty to eighty species, some of which are very rare, and even endangered. Others are very common, local to the southern counties or locally common to heaths or woodland.

Sawyer Beetle, *Prionus coriarius.* A very large beetle which in some ways resembles a stag beetle, certainly in size and colouration. It is somewhat squat in appearance with short antenna, the larvae develop in deciduous trees, mainly oak. It is quite rare in the UK, and is one of Europe's largest beetles. It has been found on Parley Heath and parts of the New Forest.

The **Dusky Longhorn Beetle**, *Arhopalus rusticus.* Another large longhorn species but slimmer than the previous species, it is a rarity that has recently been found in the New Forest (author), it spends its larval form in damaged conifers.

Rhagium mordax. A common and much smaller species, larvae develop in deciduous trees and adults take flower pollen especially from umbellifers, it is very similar to *Rhagium bifasciatum* which is similar sized but larvae develop in conifers, both species can be found within the area. There are a few similar species which require a good beetle guide to identify them.

Musk Beetle, *Aromia moschata.* This is one of the prettiest of the family, being often metallic-blue or green, and quite large, up to 35 mm in length. It develops in willows and can be seen on umbellifer flowers, as can most species of longhorns. It is scarce in the UK but can be found along the Stour Valley and at Hengistbury Head. Its main haunt is East Anglia.

The *Strangalia* genus comprises many species of which over a dozen can be found within the area. Some common and pretty looking species such as *S. quadrimaculata*, *S. maculata* and *S. quadrifasciata* look similar with black and yellow stripes mimicking wasps, and the **Wasp Beetle**, *Clytus arietis,* which develops in beech is very common.

Anaglyptus mysticus, is small but pretty looking being grey and red-brown, it develops in beech and robinia but is not very common.

Longhorn Beetle, Strangalia quadrimaculata

Pogonocherus species of which two rare, tiny species occur around the New Forest and have been found in urban areas of Bournemouth develop in fallen twigs. *Agapanthia villosoviridescens* can be found on natural flower rich grasslands and develops in thistles and hogweeds.

Leaf beetles, Chrysomelidae

These beetles are often abundant with a shiny metallic, round appearance. They are slow moving seen on herbaceous plants and flowers.

Cryptocephalus species are small and mainly green, they can be found on hawkweed flowers. *Chrysolina polita*, is bicoloured and can be found on members of the mint family. *C. menthrasti*, also on mint is a uniform green.

Bloody Nosed Beetle, *Timarcha goettingensis.* This beetle is so known for its habit of releasing an orange red liquid on to one's hand as a defence mechanism when picked up. It is large, robust and slow walking, looking as though it is made from shiny black plastic. It lives on natural grasslands and the metallic green larvae eat bedstraws. A much smaller species, like a miniature version, is also quite common often in the same areas. Hengistbury Head, Badbury Rings, Martin Down and other chalk grasslands are some typical habitats.

There are so many species of beetles especially the Leaf Beetles that one can only cover a small number of them. Ground Beetles are an even larger category with far too many to list them all.

Ground Beetles, Carabidae

The Carabidae are the typical, generally black beetle uncovered when old logs are rolled over.

A small member of this genus is *Carabus nitens* which is rare nationally, but can be found on Studland Heath, and is metallic green and copper.

The New Forest oak woods may still have the large and bright green and blue *Calosoma inquisitor*, which is a predator of caterpillars in the tree canopy, but is very rare or may be extinct.

Ground Beetle, *Drypta dentata*, is only to be found on coastal silt on Brownsea Island. A few other very rare species occur in the county, but out of the region. *Acupalpus elegans* is a tiny coppery member which only lives in the Barton cliffs.

Tiger Beetles, Cicindelidae

Green Tiger Beetle, *Cicindela campestris*. As its name suggests is very abundant in open sandy districts, sometimes fields, but especially heathlands, and can be found on almost all fragments of such lands within the area. Some areas are better than others, especially if they are south facing with open areas such as paths, where the larvae live in small scooped out pits and lie in wait for ants and spiders that fall in. The adults are keen, strong flyers and often there are many present in a small area. They are predatory with very large jaws for tackling any similar sized invertebrates. The Bournemouth cliffs are an excellent place to find them.

Green Tiger Beetle

    Heath Tiger Beetle, *Cicindela. sylvatica*. A similar but much rarer species which can only be found in a few heathland sites in the district, especially Studland and Godlingstone. They have a preference for coastal heaths and sand dunes. The beetle is purplish black instead of metallic green and has a rather matt finish to it. Slightly larger than *C. campestris*, but otherwise similar it has been found on Sopley Common, DWT Reserve and Canford Heath.

    Cicindela hybrida, is similar but smaller and coppery brown. It is even rarer than *C sylvatica* but may occur in the same habitat.

    Cliff Tiger Beetle, *Cicindela germanica*. This species did exist within the district, possibly on the Bournemouth cliffs, and was seen prior to 1879. It is much smaller than the previous species and may be overlooked. It is still frequent on the Isle of Wight.

    Paromalus.parallelepipedus. A small black bark beetle only known from the New Forest (Brockenhurst) and possibly Kent.

    Chafers and Dung Beetles, *Scarabaeidae*. These are often abundant and obvious beetles especially the chafers of which we have half a dozen common types within the area, as well as some local rarities.

    May Bug, *Melontha melontha*. The most well known of this group and often called the cockchafer. Its larvae feed on the roots of various plants, as do all the species. It is large and robust, flying on warm evenings to eat leaves or pollen and is attracted to light.

    Summer Chafer, *Amphimallon solstitiale*. A similar but smaller type it develops in natural grasslands and appears around the summer solstice.

    Garden Chafer, *Phyllopertha horticola*. Smaller again but with green head and often occurs in gardens and likes rose bushes as does the **Rose Chafer**, *Cetonia aurata*, which is a lovely green all over, with tiny white markings on the wing cases.

    Euchlora dubia can be found on Bournemouth cliffs as it likes sandy areas, it is quite large with green and chestnut markings.

Glow-worms, Lampyridae

The UK has just two species of these beetles. We do not have any of the firefly species that mainland Europe had.

Glow-worm eating snail

Common Glow-worm, *Lampyris noctiluca.* The most likely species to be encountered although it is not now common. Living in natural grasslands, meadows and heathland, most of its habitats have disappeared. It is still to be found on chalk downland and some heathlands, and sometimes in other natural grassy areas . The New Forest has certain areas where they are still quite common as does east Dorset including Town Common, Parley Heath, Avon Park and even the Bournemouth East Cliff. The chalk areas are richer mainly because their food source snails, are more abundant. The larvae are flattened and armoured although looking soft, dark and with a pinkish border. Both sexes have lighting ability, but female larvae stay in a similar looking state while the male metamorphoses into a nocturnally flying winged beetle, and is attracted by the female's green glow. Badbury Rings, Martin Down and Hambledon Hill are probably the best areas to see them. June and July being the best time.

Lesser Glow-worm, *Phosphaenus hemipterus.* This species is extremely rare but may occur in Purbeck near Worth Matravers.

Dung Beetles, Scarabaeoidea

The most numerous and noticeable of this family are the large, dark metallic Dor and Minotaur Beetles that inhabit the dry heaths and meadows.

Minotaur Beetle, *Typhaeus typhoeus.* These are active throughout the year and are seen more during the winter months when vegetation is reduced. They are square shaped, the male having three horns on its head. They make burrows in the sand and bury one or two faecal pellets, usually from deer or rabbits.

Dor Beetle, *Geotrupes stercorarius.* Less common it uses the same kind of habitat, but also farmland and forests. There are two other similar species in our area, good guide books must be consulted for identification. *Geotrupes vernalis* has smooth elytra and is more blue than black, it is quite common around the Poole and Bournemouth heaths during the summertime.

Minotaur Beetles

There are a number of tiny scarab type species that inhabit the area. They are easily overlooked but are worth finding. *Onthophagus nuchicornis* lives in cow dung, its rarer counterpart, *O. nutans*, has not been noted since 1900. Other members of the family also have not been recorded since the same time. *Aphodius niger* is only known from the Brockenhurst area and lives around muddy pools frequented by cattle and horses. They may also live in the Burley and Bransgore areas.

Another small member is *Trox perlatus,* found around the Purbeck coast in animal debris and in nests of birds of prey on the continent.

Horned Dung Beetle, *Copris lunaris.* The largest and also most rare species of the Dung Beetle tribe. Although once found at numerous sites of natural grazed land, they could be extinct, although possibly I may have seen one at Martin Down nature reserve in June 2005.

Dor Beetles

Hister quadrimaculatus. A small coastal dung beetle that is very rare in UK. There are only records from the south coast including Dorset.

Water beetles, Dytiscidae

Water beetles are perhaps the most under recorded because of the problem studying them. Both adult and larval stages are aquatic, and predatory. Whilst some are just slightly larger than a pin head, others are nearly the size of a golf ball.

Great Diving Beetle and Wood Ants

Great Diving Beetle, *Dystiscus marginalis* is around five centimetres in length. Dark blue black with a distinctive yellow collar around the whole body, the male has smooth **elytra** whilst the female has many grooved elytra.

Helophorus laticollis. A small water beetle of heathland open pools in the New Forest. A threatened species.

Agabus brunneus. A diving beetle of shallow and possibly intermittent streams. Only in the New Forest and Wiltshire in small numbers. A threatened species.

6 Ornithology

Rosemary Broadey
Wendy Crossby

This is a poem written by one of our members after an ornithology field trip in 1991. We feel that it is an excellent description of a successful trip.

In ninety one on the fifth of September
At Keyhaven Marshes, do you remember?
George led us out – a full score and some more;
Some of us had never been there before.

With the cooling breeze from the Solent Way
The elements promised the perfect day;
Spirits were high as Lettice, with 'scope,
Strode seawards with anticipation and hope.
A little too noisy, the company follows,
Up there on the wires a party of swallows.

A greenfinch or two and some linnets flew by.
"Oh, they're only starlings" George said, with a sigh.
Black tailed godwits far out on the west
Were holding a party or taking a rest.

A wheatear and friend obligingly sat
On top of two posts, quite unaware that
We were ogling them and observing their features,
Black cheeks with white eyestripe and breasts like ripe peaches.

Curlew sandpipers were there in profusion;
Red shank and green shank forgave our intrusion.
Ringed plover and cormorant both caught our gaze
And an odd oystercatcher that looked in a daze.

Whimbrel and curlew appeared at some time,
Rock pipit, grey plover – and they'll never rhyme.
Sand martins darted, some more mallards stare;
Black headed gulls and a heron out there,
Two common scoter appeared to be flagging,
Whilst great crested grebe carried on their head wagging.

Yellow wagtails were communing with horses,
Whilst seabirds abundant sang out their remorses.
We packed up our' scopes and returned to our books,
As we said our good-byes to a field full of rooks.

Keyhaven Marshes JESSICA HOLDING

THE 1914 BOOK

This brief outline is intended to establish the base line from which this chapter was developed. It may also encourage people to read the original work, which contains much of interest and relevance to the modern naturalist.

The author, W Parkinson Curtis, was writing in his mid thirties and already referring to twenty-five years' collecting. It is assumed, from the general gist of other remarks, that it was birds' eggs that were being collected. E Harker Curtis, W Ps brother, collaborated in the work. There are also references to Mr Hart of Christchurch who was a very fine taxidermist. For example, One of the few specimens of Hooded Merganser was procured at Christchurch and is now in Mr Hart's beautiful collection.

This chapter opens with a very short description of the area, before launching into a genus by genus description of the occurrence and breeding status of the characteristic resident and migrant birds of the area. Many remarks are as pertinent today as they were in 1914. Surprises include the **Magpie**, *Pica pica,* described as a disappearing species, and the **Hoopoe**, *Upupa epops,* entry. This regular visitor was breeding throughout the area. Today it is a scarce Passage Migrant, mainly seen in the Spring. At the time the **Gadwall**, *Anas strepera*, was an irregular winter visitor, and the sea ducks – **Tufted Duck**, *Aythya fuligula*, **Scaup**, *A. marila*, and **Golden-eye**, *Bucephala clangula* – kept to deep water. The **Turtle Dove**, *Streptopelia turtur*,was a regular summer visitor and bred in some numbers. The authors despaired of 'Poole Nightingales', which, in their experience, usually turned out to be **Black-caps**, *Sylvia atricapilla*. Then as now, the bird preferred the clay-loam and chalk areas.

There are interesting observations about the freely occurring **Nightjar**, *Caprimulgus europaeus*. In the experience of the Curtis brothers this ground nesting bird varies its egg colouration with habitat – cloudy on heath, small spots on sand and large blotches in woods.

There is a discussion about the persistent return of Marsh Terns to an area which was then free of the swamps in which the bird breeds. They conclude that the bird's homing instinct was impelling it to return to the old place.

There are sad comments about birds of prey and Owls. Accipiters were struggling to maintain themselves against the relentless persecution of the gamekeepers, while the Owls' worst enemy was the selfish sportsman. It was not surprising to read that **Scoters**, *Melanitta nigra,* are very gun-shy and rarely enter harbours.

This then is the platform on which the current work is built. Nothing can replace the pleasure to be found in the original pages. Copies of the 1914 edition are available to members in the Society's library.

TWENTIETH-CENTURY ORNITHOLOGY AT BNSS

In the 1914 book the authors of the Bird Life chapter were usefully able to publish remarks about the characteristic resident and migrant birds of our area. Today such information can more readily, accurately and immediately be obtained from the County Avifaunas, County bird reports, location reports and the Web. Fuller references to these will appear at the end of this chapter.

Nevertheless the BNSS records and collections available to the present authors contain much of interest to the twenty-first century birder.

The Proceedings of the Society have been published annually from 1909, with wartime interruptions. Our Sessions run from 1 October until the following 30 September. Direct references to birds begin in Volume XX (1927–28 Session), where they form a sub-section of the Report of the Zoological Section. This was compiled from reports submitted by Members to the Revd F C R Jourdain, Chairman of the Section. From 1932 onwards these Summaries include comprehensive lists of the arrival dates of breeding migrants. This arrangement continued fairly regularly under a succession of Chairmen until, in the 1955/56 Session, they were discontinued due to the availability of comprehensive County Lists in the Library.

Presence Lists – results of observations made on Field Meetings have also been available to us. Field Meetings have always been an important part of the Society's life. In the early days, they took the form of General Summer Excursions, with little reference to Ornithology. This may have been due only to a lack of observation equipment, since a Paper on 'The Swifts' read to the Society by Aubrey Edwards in December 1912, testifies to interest in Ornithology. By 1940 the Zoological & Botany Sections were undertaking 25 such joint excursions annually. A visit to Stanpit Marsh on 17 April 1948 is an early example of a dedicated Ornithology excursion. But it was 1956 before winter Field Meetings began.

In 1944 a British Museum Committee was planning post-war Nature Reserves. The BNSS Council submitted proposals for the reservation of Stanpit Marshes and South Haven. The Society's interest in the fledgling Stanpit Marsh Reserve is reflected in a series of Field Meetings culminating in eight visits made during 1966/67 session. Species lists include **Spoonbill**, *Platalea* *leucorodia,* **Wryneck,** *Jynx torquilla,* and **Richard's Pipit,** *Anthus richardi,* (1964/65), and a flock of 38 Redwing, *Turdus iliacus,* in January 1966.

Other extramural activities include our participation in the Wildfowl Counts run annually by the Wildfowl Trust at Slimbridge. Members covered the Poole Harbour shore from the Haven to Rockley Point in January 1969. In the same year we began a three-year commitment to the British Trust for Ornithology's Atlas Scheme. We surveyed bird life in a 10 km square comprising the eastern part of Bournemouth, Christchurch, Hurn and Bransgore. Special Field Meetings were devoted to the project.

Volume LI (1960/61) refers to Organised Field Meetings at approximately fortnightly intervals, while welcoming new members possessing binoculars to the group. Vol LII (1961/62) has a tantalising reference to the Group Diary of the Field Meetings having again been carefully kept throughout the year. The following year we read that this Diary would be available occasionally at Headquarters. It has not been located during our present investigations. Ornithology first appears as a named sub-section of Zoology in Vol LV (1964/65), while lists of the Field Meeting locations are published from the mid 1960s.

The weather and its effect on bird life is an ongoing topic of report. The very wet winter of 1960/61 flooded the meadows in the Avon Valley resulting in huge flocks of wildfowl. For example we read of 70 **Shoveler,** *Anas clypeata,* and 60 **Pintail Ducks,** *A. acuta.* The opening months of 1963 were marked by below zero temperatures and a blanket of snow. The deaths of birds during this period were later investigated by the Ministry of Agriculture, and reported in Volume LV. 100 **Curlew,** *Numenius arquata,* and **Redwing,** *T. iliacus* were found to be emaciated as a result of a very small intake of food during the days of continuous frost. Conversely, **Starlings,** *Sturnus vulgaris,* who were largely dependant on man for food, were found to be of normal weight. Their deaths followed a night of severe frost, and were due to a lack of water and severe chilling.

Birding interests have been served in-house too. In 1942 a 'British Birds' reading circle was inaugurated. The magazine was founded by Harry Forbes Witherby of Burley, a close associate of the Revd Jourdain, and a luminary in Ornithological circles. Monthly parts of the periodical were studied, bound at year-ends, and presented to the Society Library.

In 1946/47 the Collection of Ornithological Lantern Slides was rebound and catalogued. Interest in the Glass Slides has been rejuvenated recently. Two broken projectors were piratized, to construct one working model. The vintage slides are being used again to illustrate modern presentations.

The Collections hold over three hundred stuffed birds, cases of bird eggs, nests, trays of skins and boxes of skulls. These collections are the result of practical investigations in the days before photography and modern observation equipment brought the living birds close. W Parkinson Curtis, FES, spoke to the Society about Order and Method in forming Collections (p 71, Vol 4, 1911/12). His contention was that the practical ornithologist, in his efforts to confirm the accuracy of observations, was making the local avian lists read like a catalogue of slaughter. During the first half of the twentieth century shootin' and stuffin' gradually declined, but **Oology** continued until after the Second World War.

White's Thrush

Contributions continue to arrive, as they have done down the years. Additions have included a 1946 gift of birds by Lord Malmesbury, President of the Society in the 1916/17 Session, and Member from 1930 until his death 20 years later. The gem of this collection was the **White's Thrush**, *Turdus dauma aureus,* shot on the Malmesbury Estate on 24 January 1828. A magnificent stuffed **Osprey**, *Pandion haliaetus,* that dominates the Museum Room, is part of the same collection, and dates from January 1832.

Osprey

Another important Collection was donated by H Gifford of Blandford in 1974. This consists of three cabinets of bird eggs, collected by the donor's late uncle, W J A Ashford, during the period 1890–1970. Known as The Ashford Collection, cabinet A1 holds eggs from Dorset only, while the eggs in cabinets A2 and A3 came from the rest of the British Isles.

The 1970/71 list of acquisitions includes nests of a blackbird and long-tailed tit. In 2004/05 the Society accepted two Egg Collector's boxes, each containing trays of labelled eggs, and of implements necessary to the 1940s oologist.

This has necessarily been a brief resumé of Twentieth Century Ornithology at BNSS. Present-day members have the additional benefit of observing living birds from the comfort of the Museum Room. Here they can watch the nesting exploits of blue tits via a nest-cam and colour monitor system.

It is important to point out that egg collecting and shooting of birds for study is not carried out today by members of the Society; with modern technology these methods are no longer necessary. However the collections have considerable scientific value and it would be an act of vandalism to dispose of them.

ORNITHOLOGY PERSONALITIES 1914 TO 1940

During this period Ornithology, in common with the other natural sciences, was the preserve of those with free time and spare financial resources to devote to their pursuit. Bournemouth was the hub of a road and rail network that allowed such people easy access to its varied surrounding countryside. Thus Bournemouth Natural Science Society (BNSS) attracted Members of National and International repute.

Francis G Penrose MD, FRCP, FZS, MBOU. Early retirement from medical practice in 1905, gave him leisure for study of wildlife and photography. He was Chairman of the Zoological Section from 1915, and served as President for two successive years from 1921.

The Conservation of Wild Life from both the world wide and local points of view, formed the subject of his two Presidential Addresses. He chided the **plumassiers** for encouraging the cruelty with which plumes were collected to decorate fashionable hats. The Importation of Plumage Bill soon arrived on the Statute Book. His local discussion examined the conditions that affected the birds in our area. The works and employments of man were found to be adverse to wild birds. He argued for greater protection of birds through the provision of Sanctuaries, coupled with education of the public. All this in 1921/2 !! He bequeathed his fine collection of British Birds in 36 cases to the Society.

Revd Francis C R Jourdain (1865–1940) was another enthusiast. A noted oologist, leading authority on the breeding biology of **Palaearctic** birds, and the initiator of the Hampshire Field Club's annual Bird Reports, he still found time for BNSS activities.

President in 1933–34, and Chairman of Zoology from 1931, his local *Observations of Birds and Arrivals of Migrants* appeared in the Proceedings for 12 seasons. His Presidential Address examined Ornithology in England over some 15 or 16 hundred years. He regretted that much historic knowledge of birds had come by way of their use as food. Arguing against this stupid spring shooting and trapping, his was a strong voice for conservation in the early 1930s.

W Parkinson Curtis FZS, FRES, FRHS, was the co-author with his brother, Eustace Harker Curtis, of the Bird Life Chapter in our 1914 book. On his death in 1968, the Society lost the last of its Founder Members.

Despite the wide knowledge of local birds displayed in Bird Life, his main interest was entomology of which he was a noted authority.

B J Ringrose of Harbridge, joined the Society in 1936. He is known as the keeper of meticulous bird diaries for the period 1922–39. His observations of New Forest birds were later discovered in the attic of a previous home. His name appears in lists of contributors to our Bird Notes from 1936.

The period 1940 to 2000

The Society's post Second World War revival of interest in ornithology as wartime restrictions were lifted, was led by:

Mrs Helen Winifred Boyd Watt, FZS., MBOU. (1878–1968). Our first Lady President in 1949–50, and Chairman of the Zoology Section from 1941–52. Mrs Boyd Watt developed her interest in natural history, and particularly ornithology, as a member of the Selbourne Society in the early 1900s. In 1950 her great organizational skills allowed her to arrange and Chair a capacity Lecture by Peter Scott of the Severn Wildfowl Trust at the Winter Gardens.

Christine H Popham. Bird Report Editor and official keeper of ornithology records (1941–52). Her reports contain fascinating details: for example in 1952 we read of a Pintail Duck, ringed in Newfoundland, being shot in Christchurch Harbour 10 days later. On 16 May of the same year a pair of **Spoonbills**, *Platalea leucorodia*, were seen on Stanpit Marshes.

Miss K Gorringe succeeded her in the 1952/3 Session, and the following year standardised the order of records to comply with the British Ornithologists' Listing, referred to as 'Wetmore order'.

Mr H V Harris began 11 years of service in 1955/6. He organised bi-monthly Field Meetings and in-house lectures, but discontinued the practice of printing bird lists as 'comprehensive County Lists' were now available for both Hampshire and Dorset. The lists were replaced in the *Proceedings* by short articles about items of particular ornithological interest. Thus we read of the inauguration of winter field meetings in 1956/7, and of **Great Crested Grebe**, *Podiceps cristatus*, nesting within 8 miles of Bournemouth in the same session. The following spring a total of ten young were reared on various pools.

Mrs L M Maddox took up the baton (or should I say binoculars!) in January 1968. Her enthusiastic and knowledgeable Chairmanship was to last for 25 years, and is still recalled fondly in the Society. On her death in 1998/9 she characteristically remembered the Society in her Will.

Phillip Powell (1992–93) was succeeded by **Robert B Reid**. His Chairmanship of the Ornithology Section continued into the twenty-first century.

Thus, seven remarkable people orchestrated the Society's Ornithological interest over a 60-year period.

ENVIRONMENT AND CHANGES TO BIRD POPULATIONS

Both in the original book and the Proceedings of the BNSS many factors affecting the range and numbers of birds are mentioned. These include the attitudes of people to the bird population, changes in the environment and climatic changes. These factors have contributed to varying levels of particular bird populations, the total decline of some species and the increase or arrival of new breeding species to the area.

The attitude of the public has been influenced by the trends and fashions of the day. It was a normal Victorian pastime to kill birds for sport and also for the feathers which were used for millinery purposes. At this time bird feathers were also imported on a large scale to facilitate this purpose. Brightly coloured birds, such as the Pheasants and Kingfishers as well as birds with long feathers such as the Little Egret and Grey Heron were among some of the popular species. Indeed Barn Owl and Tern feathers were also used.

In 1869 the Association for the Protection of Seabirds was formed to stop the shooting of Gulls and in 1891 the RSPB was formed to counter the trade in Grebe fur. Ladies were advised to choose flowers not feathers for their decorations. In 1933 the Protection of Birds Act was passed due to concern for the trade in and the taking of wild birds for aviculture. The twentieth century saw the transformation of interest in birds into a leisure pursuit and this has enabled species to thrive and indeed in some cases increase in population.

Environmental change has had a big impact on many of our birds. For example the following land use changes have meant loss of habitat and nest sites: abandonment of pastoral agriculture to cereal monoculture, housing, industry and road building due to the ever growing human population. Adaptation to the changing environment has caused changes in bird behaviour. It is not unusual to see Kestrels hunting on the banks of a motorway or to see them nesting on large road signs. Urbanization of some birds of prey, such as Peregrine Falcons, is becoming a common sight in our cities and industrial areas. This mainly because of a plentiful food source such as pigeons.

Birds are regularly used as indicators of climate change. The State of the UK Birds 2004 Report published by Natural England highlighted many climatic reasons for changing bird population. It is believed that wading birds have shifted their wintering distribution from the warmer west to the colder east and there is an upturn in Song Thrushes and Tree Sparrows in response to the milder winters. Breeding ranges for some birds such as the Dartford Warbler, the Woodlark and the Little Ringed Plover are spreading northwards. The Dartford Warbler was a victim of the very bad winters of 1962/63. Their numbers dropped and didn't recover significantly until the late 1960s. They have become a common sight on the heath lands in Dorset and the New Forest.

There appears to be a tendency for birds to nest earlier and migratory birds to arrive sooner possibly all linked to climate change. The warmer summer temperatures will be bringing new birds to colonise in the UK. Some species tipped for the future are Black Kite, Cattle Egret and the Great Reed Warbler. Little Egrets have become a familiar sight in our area since the 1990s and are indeed breeding here. Unfortunately birds like the Spotted Flycatcher are in decline. This could be due to food loss. With spring becoming warmer, caterpillars on which the birds feed will hatch earlier and therefore leave the birds without a food source in the breeding season. In this area we have seen a decline in the presence of Woodlark and Stone Curlew. Both these species used to breed in the area. This could be explained by the change of land usage rather than climate change.

In the struggle for survival the Accipiters (Hawks, Buzzards, Eagles and Kites) have come through some difficult times. In the original book it mentions that the Peregrine hangs in the cliffs; the Montagu's Harrier ekes out a precarious existence; the Sparrow-hawk and Kestrel struggle to maintain themselves against the relentless persecution of the Gamekeepers. The remainder of this splendid group are no sooner seen than destroyed. This is a situation that has happily improved. The Victorian's egg-collecting and game shooting helped to reduce the numbers of these birds. Game rearing in the nineteenth century to facilitate the sport increased the persecution of the birds by the Game Keepers.

During both World Wars the level of persecution reduced and the bird population increased. The introduction of DDT into major agricultural use after the war indirectly poisoned the birds through their food supply. By 1960 the Sparrow-hawk was virtually extinct in Britain. From the beginning of the 1970s there was a more stringent control of the use of organic chemicals in farming which allowed the bird numbers to increase. According to the Society records in this area the Montagu's Harrier was frequently seen during the 1930s and 1940s. Since then we have two sightings in 1974 and 1986. The Common Buzzard was seen regularly in the early years and then interestingly no records of their presence until 1974. Since then the records show their numbers increasing and sightings of the bird are common throughout the region.

BIRD WATCHING SITES

This favoured piece of both Hampshire and of Dorset is a birder's paradise. The Hampshire Avifauna lists 364 resident or visiting species, while George Green states that 405 (the list stands at 412 as from 2 October 2008) species or 72 per cent of the British List have been recorded in Dorset. All of these birds will not have been seen in our area, nevertheless we do watch an impressive variety in our many local habitats. The coastline runs eastward from Durlston to Lymington, including estuaries, headlands, coastal marshes, spits and cliffs. The Avon valley, bordered by flood plain meadows, and enriched ornithologically by flooded gravel pits, dissects the area from south to north. The New Forest, Hampshire's brightest gem, is included, while Chalk Downland forms the northern boundary. Can any other small area hold so many diverse habitats each attractive to its specialists as well as commoner species? Our Field Meetings tour around the area, and occasionally visit neighbouring locations such as Portland to our west, Titchfield Haven to the east and Porton Down to the north.

In winter we look for flocks of waders and wildfowl. These can be discovered in great numbers in Poole and Christchurch harbours, or from the section of the South Coast footpath that runs from Lymington to Milford on Sea. During a December 2005 excursion here, 60 different species were ticked. These included **Avocet**, *Recurvirostra avosetta,* which we also see on Brownsea Island. The three hours before high tide tend to give the best views, with the birds feeding busily on the rapidly disappearing mud flats.

The Avon Valley's flooded water meadows and gravel pits are another excellent location for winter duck and goose flocks. Blashford Lakes Wildlife Reserve (www.hwt.org.uk) now has five Hides giving views over Ibsley Water and Ivy Lake. On 17 January 2008 we saw 45 different species here including **Ruddy Duck**, *Casarca ferrugine,* **Black-necked Grebe**, *Podiceps nigricollis,* and an over-wintering **Bittern**, *Botaurus stellaris.* The reserve also has a Woodland Hide from which we have enjoyed views of **Brambling**, *Fringilla montifringilla,* **Siskin**, *Carduelis spines,* and **Redpoll**, *C. caber.*

Another popular winter excursion finds us on an RSPB BirdBoat from Poole Harbour. Some trips explore the Harbour, others include time on Brownsea Island. Here we have seen 1000+ **Avocet**, *Recurvirostra avosetta,* in their second most important wintering site in Britain. Poole Harbour also holds the largest population in Britain of wintering **Red–breasted Merganser**, *Mergus serrator,* outside Scotland.

As spring approaches and the winter visitors leave, we turn our attention to nesting birds and returning migrants. Beaulieu Heath is home to nesting waders, such as the **Curlew**, *Numenius arquata,* and **Redshank**, *Tringa totanus.* Both are ground nesters, so it is very important to observe the notices that ask walkers to stay on the paths and keep dogs on the lead. At this location we have also watched hawking **Hobbys**, *Falco subbuteo,* and nesting **Redstart**, *Phoenicurus phoenicurus.* There is a frequent train to Beaulieu Station, giving easy access to all.

Hirundines usually return to known nesting places. So we can look for **Sand Martin**, *Riparia riparia,* in the cliffs at Hengistbury Head and the **House Martin** at, say, Hoburne Farm Estate. Both **House Martins**, *Delichon urbicum,* and **Barn Swallows**, *Hirundo rustica,* can reliably be seen

Sand Martin   Goldcrest   Chiffchaff

flying high above the chalk Downs that surround Swanage Bay. During the winter of 2007/8 a nesting bank for **Sand Martins**, *R.riparia,* was constructed at Ibsley Water, and occupied the following spring.

Martin Down, in the north, is a good spot to listen for **Nightingales**, *Luscinia megarhynchos,*as they sing from scrubby bushes to compete for territory. The more males present – the more song! This also used to be the place where we saw **Stone Curlew**, *Burhinus oedicemus,* but not in recent years. Garston Wood Nature Reserve is nearby. In this woodland area, we have found **Chiffchaff**, *Phylloscopus collybita*, **Goldcrest**, *Regulus regulus,* **Nuthatch**, *Sitta europaea*, and **Bullfinch**, *Pyrrhula pyrrhula*, among commoner woodland species.

Another rewarding early summer walk takes us to Talbot Heath. Here, on 9 June 2005, we watched a Dartford Warbler feeding two fledglings in the shelter of a gorse bush. We have seen these little signature warblers of our heathlands at Middlebere, Studland and Godshill. They also frequent the gorse at Normandy Marsh, and are often accompanied by Stonechat.

A mini cruise is a popular summer evening ornithological excursion. The Dorset Belles boats can be boarded at Bournemouth or Swanage Piers – we have done both. As the boat cruises past the cliffs of Durlston Head you can see and hear nesting **Guillemots**, *Uria aalge*, **Razorbills**, *Alca torda,* and **Puffin**, *Fratercula arctica*. The Guillemots can also be seen via cameras in the Visitor Centre at Durlston County Park, yet another great place where we see birds.

In late summer many birds are moulting after the rigours of parenthood. They hide away and are hard to see. This is a good time to visit places like Stanpit Marsh to look for returning waders. Our September 2007 visit yielded 33 species, including **Whimbrel**, *Numenius phaeopus,* and a group of **Sandwich Terns**, *Sterna sandvicensis.* Whimbrel are passage migrants, and can be seen at Stanpit in April and May too. Memorably, we watched a Warden count 1048 **Black-tailed Godwit**, *Limosa limosa,* at Arne RSPB reserve in September 2004.

December may well find the group at Moors Valley Country Park. In 2007 we saw a flock of about 250 **Lapwing**, *Vanellus vanellus* there, as well as **Woodpeckers**, **Nuthatch**, *Sitta europaea,* and **Treecreeper**, *Certhia familiaris.* Excellent views of an over-wintering **Chiffchaff**, *Phylloscopus collybita,* brought the day's total to 40 species. Then there was the bonus of a hot drink and mince pies in the Visitor Centre to round off another year's birding.

Greater Spotted Woodpecker

SUMMER MIGRANTS

In the nineteen thirties the Chairman of the ornithology section, the Revd Jourdain, had a large team of observers reporting to him. For example, in 1938 he acknowledged contributions from two-dozen Members. He collated their data and published it annually in Proceedings under the titles Observations on Birds in the Bournemouth District, and Arrival of Migrants.

His death, and the Second World War brought these arrangements to a halt. They were restarted in 1948 and continued until 1954 when restrictions in the size (due to increasing costs) of Proceedings, together with the availability of comprehensive County Lists for both Hampshire and Dorset, made them redundant.

In 2008 the Members were invited to record their first sightings of several species for comparison with this historical data. Selected extracts from this data follow.

In all cases, the scarcity of our data makes it impossible to extrapolate trends although there appears to be no significant change in arrival dates over the years.

Common Cuckoo, *Cuculus canorus*

Arrival dates for cuckoo

Years for which BNSS holds data

Our first observations of the Cuckoo lie around 10 April, with very much later observation dates in both 1930 (26) and 1947 (27), and one very early observation on 27 March 1938. Our modern date of 10 April 2008 falls neatly into the historical pattern.

Cuckoo eggs have been found in the nests of over 50 different British birds. The Society's Glass Slides Collection holds pictures of **Meadow Pipit**, *Anthus pretences,* **Dunnock**, *Prunella modularis,* **Robin**, *Erithacus rubecula,* and **Sedge Warbler**, *Acrocephalus schoenobaenus* nests being parasitized by the Cuckoo.

Other comments of interest from Proceedings tell us that in 1931, Cuckoo eggs were found in the nests of both **Dartford Warbler**, *Sylvia undata,* and **Blackcap**, *S. atricapilla.* The former held four eggs of the fosterer,

Cuckoo

while the latter held two eggs. The Dartford Warbler was said to be one of the rarest fosterers of Cuckoo in the British Isles (BNSS *Proceedings* p 43, Vol XXIII).

Two years later a **Pied Wagtail**, *Motacilla alba yarrellii* nest at Ferndown was reported to hold two Cuckoo eggs laid by two different hens. In 1939 a pure white, fully fledged young bird was picked up on the road at Sway. Unable, or unwilling to feed, it died, and is now in the British Museum. In 1948 a member reported that near Picket Post a cuckoo flew in front of his car for about 400 yards, while the car was travelling at 50–60 mph.

Nightjar, *Caprimulgus europaeus*

A summer migrant to southern Britain from Africa. They appear around April and mainly home in on the lowland heaths, but also open parkland and other scrubby sites. Mostly to be found on the dry heath of Hampshire and Dorset. A nocturnal bird similar in build to a large swift, but flying low and slower, hawking for moths, mosquitos and other flying insects, it has a small beak, but a very large gape. It is cryptically coloured to imitate tree bark or leaves. Its call is a long drawn out warble that seems to alter in loudness and direction due

Nightjar

to the bird turning its head at intervals. It is similar to the 'churring' of certain cricket species. Its display flight is a series of warbles and chirps accompanied by wing clapping. On warm summer nights the nightjar seems to take control of the local heaths, and is popular for bird watchers.

The pair make a depression on the bare heath ground and lay two eggs. The birds, the eggs and then the chicks are well camouflaged but are very vulnerable to destruction or disturbance. The nightjar occurs on all the local larger remaining blocks of heath. The best way to observe it is sit in a car, windows open and listen and watch the skyline. Studland and Godlingstone Heaths and Hartland Moor are good watching places.

Hirundines and Swifts

The arrival of the Hirundines, namely **Sand Martin**, *Riparia riparia,* **Swallow**, *Hirundo rustica,* and **House Martin**, *Delichon urbicum,* is keenly anticipated. 'One Swallow does not a summer make', reflects the March arrival of a few early swallows. It is not until the main influx from Africa occurs some weeks later that the warmer weather sets in. Our earliest arrival date for Swallows is 26 March in 1938, the latest, 21 April in 1954.

Swallow

Sand Martins are usually the first of the hirundines to arrive from mid-March. The earliest BNSS record is 23 March in 1936, the latest, 24 April 1949 – nearly a month later. A few February arrivals are on record with 25 February 2000 and 27 February 1990 being the earliest observations in Dorset and Hampshire respectively. Field Meetings to Hengistbury Head still enjoy the sight of a nesting colony in the sandy cliffs, and of feeding birds swooping over the big pond on Warren Hill.

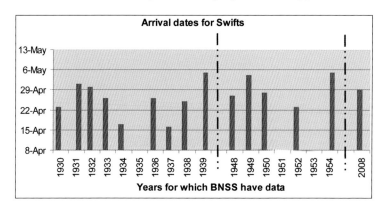

House Martins begin to arrive, according to our records, in the second week of April, they will return to traditional nesting areas, so long as there is a ready supply of mud with which to build and repair their under-eaves homes. A July 1979 survey of Dorset found 97 per cent of the County's 6,717 nests were within 1 km of water. (p 206 Prendergast & Boys 1983).

The **Swift**, *Apus apus,* belongs to a different family, but its aerial life style is so similar to that of the Hirundines, that the species have converged in many ways. All are insect eaters and may be seen hawking for prey over reservoirs and marshes. In early May 2008, flocks of 100 Swallows, 200 House Martins and 400 Sand Martins were to be seen over Ibsley Water, Blashford Lakes.

This Chart illustrates the data that we hold about the earliest reported sighting of Swifts by BNSS Members. The earliest date was 16 April 1937, the latest 6 May, in 1954, a difference of three weeks. Our 2008 date of 29 April, falls in the later half of this period.

In periods of cold, wet weather young Swifts go into a state of suspended animation as their food supply dries up. In hot weather the parent birds fly at great altitude seeking the insect swarms on which they feed.

Nightingale, *Luscinia megarhyncos*

BNSS holds thirteen years of data for this species. Its arrival has been noted during the last three weeks of April in all but three years. The earliest April date was the 10th in 1933. The latest of the May observations was on 10 May 1938, nearly a month later. In both 1948 and 2008 the bird was first reported on 1 May. With so little data it is impossible to extrapolate a trend. That the earliest observation of arrival was twenty days prior to our 2008 date, must be viewed as nothing more than coincidence.

The Nightingale is at the western edge of its range in Dorset. It prefers areas of open scrub and will move on when the scrub becomes too mature. Thus it is known for short term occupation of sites. Over the years BNSS field meetings to Verne Ditch near Martin Down, have been productive. One area has been dubbed 'Berkeley Square' because the bird has frequently been heard singing in this patch of scrubland. 2008's successful foray found the bird in a new, less dense area of scrub.

The male Nightingale arrives from its winter quarters in tropical West Africa, and sings to set up territory and to attract the female bird who arrives a fortnight or so later. Thus the most songs are heard where several males are in competition for territory or mates. In 1949 BNSS records report a 'plentiful' number of nightingales in Bransgore and neighbourhood. A 1979–81 census of a 54 ha sample of Martin Down found 14 males or pairs, which translates to a density of 26 per square kilometre. (Prendergast & Boys p 31). Clearly the birds have been more common in our area in some past seasons than they are today, when we count ourselves fortunate to have heard one singing male.

Despite their name, the birds do sing in the daytime during their six-week song period. At

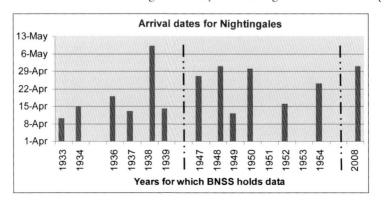

night their beautiful varied song has little other choral competition. Why do they sing at night? One hypothesis is that the male is trying to entice a mate down from her nocturnal migration flight. Plausible as this sounds, it does not explain why the night song continues well into the breeding season.

Warblers

This is a huge group; *The Hamlyn Guide to Birds of Britain and Europe* lists fifty species. All belong to the Order of Passerines, whose members have perching feet with three forward pointing toes and one backwards. Warblers are sub divided into genera, of which examples follow.

Acrocephalus Warblers (9 species). *Acrocephalus* means 'pointed-headed' and refers to the characteristic head shape. Of the nine species in the genus, Reed and Sedge Warblers are most common in our area. As their name suggests they live in reeds and swamps. Their loud, repetitive song can be heard from deep in the vegetation. In common with other warblers they migrate by night.

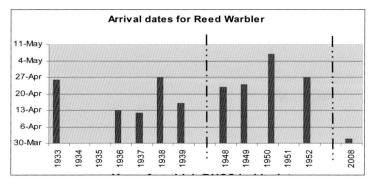

The BNSS data illustrated above shows that they have been first observed during April in all but one year, 1950. The 2008 data recorded their arrival on 1 April, ten days earlier than other figures.

Sylvia Warblers (15 species). *Sylvia* meaning 'the woodland (bird)'.

Whitethroat, *Sylvia communis*. This bird breeds in scrub and bushy areas. Look for it particularly at Martin Down, Garston Wood, Winspit and Hengistbury Head. Its scratchy song is delivered from a perch with head thrown back to give great views of its white throat. Occasionally it flies up a few metres to perform its chattering song flight.

In our experience the bird typically arrives during the middle two weeks of April.

Blackcap, *Sylvia atricapilla*. An easy bird to identify, the male's cap is black, the female's reddish-brown. This bird is a breeding summer visitor, migrant and winter visitor. It is such a common winter visitor to urban gardens that it is impossible to say when returning birds first arrive.

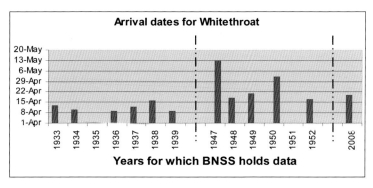

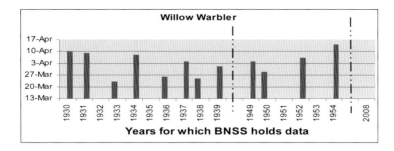

Phylloscopus Warblers (11 species). *Phylloscopus* means 'leaf-explorer' with reference to the bird's habit of exploring leaves for insects. Most warblers are insectivorous. This is a genus of small birds, greenish above and yellowish white below, giving excellent camouflage in vegetation.

In our experience **Willow Warblers**, *P. trochilus*, arrive during the last week of March and first two weeks of April.

The **Chiffchaff**, *P. collybita*, is another member of this genus. His onomatopoeic song repeats his name at speed, and is often delivered from the top of a tall tree. The Willow Warbler's song, in contrast, slows as it drops down the scale, and typically comes from the heart of a pussy willow tree.

Chiffchaffs begin arriving in early March, but a number remain to overwinter in our area. A December 2007 Field Meeting to Moors Valley Country Park enjoyed excellent views of one such bird on the winter-bare shrubs.

Furthermore, two Warblers are breeding residents in this area, namely, Cetti's Warbler, *Cettia cetti*, and the Dartford Warbler, *Sylvia undata*.

Cetti's Warbler, *Cettia cetti*. Named after the Italian Jesuit zoologist, Francois Cetti (1726–80), this bird has been recorded in our area since the 1970s, when its range expanded from south and west Europe. In the 1980s it became established as a scarce breeding resident, which is its current status. It favours dense low vegetation in marshes and reed beds. Here it skulks, occasionally giving voice to an explosive alarm call, or singing from deep in the cover. This 14 cm long, reddish-brown bird with its broad, rounded tail and white **supercilium**, is rarely seen. Hengistbury Head is a reliable place to hear it in 'our patch'.

Dartford Warbler, *Sylvia undata*. First recorded in 1733 on a site near Dartford in Kent, the bird was to be found on heathland almost anywhere south of the Thames until the 1940s.

The Bournemouth/Poole conurbation retains remnant pockets of once vast tracts of Dorset heathland. Successful management by the local authorities and other agencies has optimised the value of these precious areas to wildlife. Talbot Heath is one such small haven. Here the **amber listed** Dartford Warbler lives. At the time of writing (2008), three breeding pairs have been recorded.

Cetti's Warbler

Dartford Warbler

The sedentary Dartford Warbler does not migrate from Britain as do many other wholly insectivorous warblers. Skulking deep in the cover of gorse and heather, it manages to find a subsistence diet of heathland spiders and hibernating insects on which to survive all but the severest winters.

The birds are thought to pair for life, and are easiest to see in April, when the cock emerges from cover to perform a brief lively display flight. Being on site at the start of the breeding season, allows them to make an early start to nesting. This may be the secret of their ability to recover numbers after a serious crash.

BNSS records illustrate these facts. This species is recorded at Keyhaven, Godshill, Arne, Talbot Heath, Ham Common and other like areas of gorse and heather. In *Proceedings* (Vols XXV and XXVI) we read of a two-year drought in 1933/34, which resulted in 120 fires in the New Forest. Numbers of Dartfords were decimated then, and again, in the severe winter of 1962/3.

Today our milder climate is favouring the Dartford Warbler. The biggest danger to the species may well be the fragmentation of the heaths that are its only source of food and cover.

Both warblers are listed in Schedule 1 – Part I of the Wildlife and Countryside Act 1981, and under its provisions are protected by special penalties at all times.

PASSAGE MIGRANTS

These birds can be seen in our area when they make refuelling stopovers during their migration journeys. Some stay for a time, but rarely breed in the area. The following selection is largely governed by a relevance to the Society. Thus, it may have been sighted by Members – usually on a Field Meeting – or a specimen may be present in our Collections.

Garganey, *Anas querquedula*. Parkinson Curtis reported that the Garganey Teal only occurs as a casual on upward and downward migration in the spring and autumn (p 228). Birds were observed by Society members on five occasions up to 1950, but have not been recorded in our Field Records since. Single birds were seen, usually in March, April or May. In March 1937 we read of three birds on Avon Beach and, most unusually, of three or four pairs breeding on a ten mile stretch of the River Avon in the spring of 1937. Prendergast & Boys (p 157) also report very occasional breeding, while the Dorset Bird Report 2006, observes the 'apparent wintering' (p 27) of one bird on the River Stour. The drake's chirping courtship call has earned it the country name of the 'cricket teal'. His courtship display with head thrown right back is similar to that of the **Goldeneye**, *Bucephala clangula*.

Garganey

Spoonbill, *Platalea leucorodia*. This large white heron-like bird with spoon-shaped, yellow tipped bill, is not mentioned by the Curtises in 1914. However, Prendergast & Boys (1983) found that it is an almost annual visitor to Poole and Christchurch Harbours in small numbers. Dorset Bird Report 2006 (p 54) found the birds

Spoonbills

present in the county in every month. A flock of 17 at Bestwall far exceeded their 2001 record of 12 birds at Christchurch Harbour.

The Society holds records of one Spoonbill at Beaulieu in April 1936 and one in Christchurch Harbour on 17 March 1938. At the end of September in that same year, two immatures with black on their **primaries** stayed in the harbour for 16 days. Two sightings in the 1940s, are followed by the appearance of two birds at Stanpit Marshes on 16 May 1952 and again on 28 October 1959. Two more records in the mid 1960s complete our twentieth-century sightings.

Since the turn of the century this species, in our experience, is becoming a regular visitor to Poole Harbour and Arne RSPB Reserve. In March 2007 a group of seven was observed from a birdhide at Arne. In the autumn of 2008 eighteen birds were seen at the same location. This appears to be a species that is moving north from its usual territory in Holland. There was a 26 bird peak count 2007/8 on Brownsea.

Osprey, *Pandion haliaetus*. W P Curtis (p 287) observed that *Accipiters* are no sooner seen than destroyed, but did not refer to the Osprey, only member of the *Pandionidae* family.

Osprey were ruthlessly persecuted by gamekeepers who considered that the Fish Hawk's diet brought it into competition with their sportsmen employers. The *Shooting Journals* of the 2nd Earl of Malmesbury of Heron Court, Hurn speak of a 'fine specimen' being shot at Avon Cottage on 29 September, 1822. This is almost certainly the magnificent work of taxidermy that was given to the Society with other birds, by a later Lord Malmesbury in 1946. It has pride of place in the Museum Room. As a result of this persecution and the enthusiastic activities of egg collectors, Osprey were absent from Great Britain as a breeding species in the first half of the twentieth century. Nowadays they have returned to the Scottish highlands – notably at Loch Garten.

In the local area we see them as still scarce, but increasing, migrants on their spring and autumn passages from and to their winter quarters in tropical Africa and southern Asia.

Two early records from our *Proceedings* speak of an Osprey being seen at Ibsley on 12 April 1952 by three observers and, in August 1953, of a bird (almost certainly an Osprey) seizing fish in its talons in Poole Harbour. A fishing Osprey was seen at Holes Bay, Poole in the autumn of 2008. Ospreys are annually seen in autumn in Christchurch and Poole Harbours (4 seen together at Middlebere 2008) and almost annually at Blashford Lakes.

Golden Plover, *Pluvialis apricarius*. In 1914 the Golden Plover was an almost certain winter visitor. By 1983 large winter flocks were turning up in consistent localities that included Horton.

Society records for September 1954 speak of a flock of about 50 at Lower Kingston, Ringwood. This was considered to be an unusually early date for the district.

Recent records tell of a flock of 100+ being seen in October 1999, March 2003, and March 2006 at Keyhaven, still a reliable location. On the later dates the weather was cold, with a stiff east wind. Such conditions favour the arrival of many waders.

Whimbrel, *Numenius phaeopus*. The Whimbrel is a smaller version of the more familiar, **Curlew**, *N. arquata*. A combination of distinctive striped crown; shorter, less curved bill; and quicker wing-beats identifies this passage migrant. The Whimbrel was reported to be *a regular May and August visitor* in 1914. In 1983 we read of parties being far more numerous in the spring than autumn. In the 1970s large spring eastwards movements at Arne culminated in a passage of 3,360 in 1977. (P&B p 182.)

BNSS records the birds at Stanpit Marshes in August 1952, throughout April and May 1953, and again in May 1954. Nowadays we still expect to see them around Christchurch Harbour. A party of three were observed flying south over Martin Down in July 2008.

Hoopoe, *Upupa epops*. This exotic bird has black and white barring on wings and tail, pink-brown plumage and a black tipped crest. Two specimens can be seen at the Society. One was shot on the Malmesbury Estate, Dudsbury in 1892, the other was collected some 25 years earlier.

W P Curtis stated that the bird occurred regularly in the area, and that *we have authentic evidence of its breeding within the last two or three years in the western part.* In 1983 Prendergast & Boys (p 203) found this scarce bird turning up throughout the year, with most records in the spring.

The Dorset Bird Club wears the Hoopoe on its logo. They found 2006 to be a very good year with up to 20 Spring birds and a few in October. These numbers refer to the whole of Dorset, but some occurrences were in our area, including three April and May sightings in Christchurch Harbour.

BNSS records April sightings in 1952 at Hengistbury Head and Wick. A report in the Bournemouth Echo 21/4/52 may have been of

Hoopoe

the same bird. In April 1954 one was seen at Studland, while another was present in gardens at Hightown, Ringwood, for a week from 29 September the same year. It was feeding on mown grass. (*Proceedings* Vol XLIV p 36).

Recent records do not include Hoopoes, but as with sightings of any species, luck plays a large part in what you see on the day, when Field Meeting dates have to be programmed well in advance.

Wryneck, *Jynx torquilla*. The Wryneck is commoner in the eastern part than the western, but is steadily decreasing from some unknown cause (W P Curtis 1914).

Britain's only brown woodpecker is so named because of its ability to twist its head right round on its neck. In 1983 Prendergast & Boys noted that since 1950 the bird's status had become that of a scarce but regular autumn passage migrant. The 2006 Dorset Bird Report concurs.

BNSS holds a record of a bird feeding in a garden at Carbery Avenue, Southbourne on 21 and 22 August 1954. Eight other records place

Wryneck

the bird at Bournemouth, Burley, Parkstone, Stanpit Marsh and Throop on subsequent dates in April or May.

Northern Wheatear, *Oenanthe oenanthe*. In Victorian England this sparrow sized, white-rumped bird was considered a delicacy. Many were trapped for the table as they rested on the south coast on their way to breeding grounds further north. In Derbyshire, for example, they nest in crevices of dry-stone walls. Breeding still occurs occasionally in the New Forest area though numbers have decreased in recent years and no breeding occurred in 2006. In Dorset they still occasionally breed on the Isle of Purbeck and Portland.

W P Curtis does not mention the species, but in 1983 it was considered to be a common and conspicuous passage migrant (Prendergast & Boys p 213), with springtime day totals in excess of 100 at Hengistbury Head.

The bird appears frequently in BNSS records. For example, there were March arrivals at Stanpit and Highcliffe in 1952. The earliest date in 1954 was 11 March at Picket Post, while three birds were seen at Hengistbury Head in September. In recent years we have observed Wheatears at Christchurch, Lymington and Swanage.

WINTER VISITORS

As outlined in the section on bird watching sites, both Dorset and Hampshire see the arrival of many winter visitors. The coastline in particular is a magnet for wintering geese and wildfowl and often rarities to our country have been seen in this area.

We can only mention a few in this book but using a reputable bird guide will help in the identification of other winter visitor birds.

Bewick's Swan, *Cygnus columbianus.* One of the special winter visitors is the Bewick's Swan. These can be seen wintering in the Avon Valley near Ibsley Bridge in Hampshire. They were first recorded here by the BNSS in the winter of 1958/9 and have returned after a break in the 1990s when no birds appeared. They peaked in the late 1980s.

Bewick's Swans are smaller than Mute or Whooper Swans and usually arrive in mid-October after their breeding season in Siberia. They are normally associated with the Wetland Centre in Slimbridge, Gloucestershire and the studies made by Sir Peter Scott. So we feel very privileged to see them in our area.

Bewick's Swan

Their name was given to them by the scientist William Yarrell in 1830 to honour the memory of Thomas Bewick. Thomas Bewick, 1753–1828, was an ornithologist, bird illustrator and wood-engraver. He illustrated two volumes of the *The History of British Birds, Land Birds* 1797 and *Water Birds* 1804, with Ralph Beilby. He left a great legacy in both his engravings and sketches.

Brent Goose, *Branta bernicla.* Of Geese we have no breeding species, but all the British listed species occur occasionally, the Brent alone being a regular visitor. This is the opening sentence of the Anseriformes section of the 1914 book.

The Brent Goose is still a regular winter visitor to our area. Records of the Society show it to be in the area annually from the early seventies, prior to that it was a frequent but not so common winter visitor. It is a slim-bodied dark goose with a small white crescent on the side of the upper neck. It arrives in late September and leaves for the breeding season in the Arctic in March. There has been a considerable increase of Brent Geese wintering in this country. Growth in numbers is due to two factors. The major change is in feeding habits. They largely fed on salt marshes but, with the depletion of these areas, they have adapted to grazing on arable fields. The second factor has been the 1954 Protection of Birds Act; this has reduced the number of birds hunted in this country. Brent Geese can be seen at many areas in the locality such as Poole Harbour, Keyhaven and Pennington Marshes and Blashford Lakes, Ringwood. It is very rare to see them inland away from the coast.

Northern Pintail, *Anas acuta.* In the 1914 book the Pintail was described as a winter visitor only and not common. This duck is slightly bigger than a mallard but with a long neck and small head. The ducks fly with curved back pointing wings and a tapering tail, making this the best way to distinguish them from other ducks in the UK. It has been called the 'greyhound' among ducks.

According to the RSPB website, the pintail is a 'quarry' species. This means that it can be legally shot in winter, but – unlike in parts of Europe – this does not appear to happen now in the UK. However BNSS records for December 1952 show that one was shot in Christchurch Harbour which had been ringed 10 days earlier in Newfoundland. Sightings of these ducks have occured annually since the early seventies and some are now thought to breed in the area particularly in

Poole Harbour. The only recorded breeding in Poole was a pair that raised 3 young in 1983, and there is a single record for Hampshire at Farlington Marsh where a pair summered also in 1983.

Avocet, *Recurvirostra avosetta.* The Avocet is a very distinctive black and white wader with a long up-curved beak. Most people will recognize it as the emblem of the Royal Society for the Protection for Birds. It disappeared in the nineteenth century because of loss of habitat and egg collectors. The first breeding record was in East Anglia in 1941. Subsequent increase of population makes it one of the most successful protection projects. The Avocet is

Avocet

listed on Schedule 1 of the Wildlife and Countryside Act 1981 which affords it special protection at all times. It is one of the few species that have true internal migration, breeding in East Anglia and wintering in the South West of the country. There is now an established wintering flock in Poole Harbour. A number of ringed recoveries have been shown to come from Holland and there have been records from France. Numbers have risen dramatically during the 1990s to reach a Dorset county record of 870 in December 1998 rising to 1387 in February 2006. Poole Harbour is the second most important site for Avocets in the British Isles.

In the 1914 book the bird warranted a mention of 4 words – The Avocet also occurs! Records of the Society show many sightings of the birds in the early 1930s, a total absence during the 1950s and 1960s, a slight peak in the early 1970s, then a drop, but a continual rise from 1987 to the present day.

Little Egret, *Egretta garzetta.* This is one bird that is not mentioned in the 1914 book because it is only in the last twenty years that the Little Egret has gone from a rare migrant to being locally numerous. It is a medium sized white heron, slim, elegant with black legs and bill. There is some increase in autumn numbers due to post breeding dispersal from the close continent. The Little Egret first bred on Brownsea Island in 1996. Now we can expect to see them all along our coastal district and also inland on lakes and river margins. A colony can also be seen roosting in the trees on Hengistbury Head. Records from the Society show a marked increase of sightings in the last ten years.

Little Egret

Siskin, *Carduelis spinus.* Once described as a winter visitant and one of the rarest of our Finches by Mansell-Pleydell it is now more regular in our area.

The Siskin is a very small neat bird that can often be seen feeding in alders and birch trees. A visit to Blashford Lakes, near Ringwood, Moors Valley Park or Kingston Common is often productive in spotting this colourful bird. The Siskin breeds in the forest zone from

Siskin

Scandinavia eastwards across Northern Asia. From 1950 it has increased in many parts of England. The first proven breeding record in the New Forest was of 1 pair in 1953; increasing to 10 pairs by 1960 (Cohen 1963) and then becoming quite common by 1987.

Redwing, *Turdus iliacus.* The Redwing is the smallest true thrush. It has a creamy stripe above the eye and, as its name implies, orange-red flank patches that make it so distinctive. These migrants usually arrive late September to early October.

The Redwing has been reported with flocks of up to 500 birds. In fact much larger flocks occur in periods of severe cold. In January 1963 several thousand birds were seen in our area because of the exceptional bad weather conditions further north.

During the winter months Redwings are seen frequently on our field meetings mainly in fields and woodland edges.

Fieldfare, *Turdus pilaris.* Like the Redwing the Fieldfare belongs to the thrush family. It is larger than the Song Thrush but smaller than the Mistle Thrush. It has a red-brown back with a grey crown, breast heavily spotted with a rusty-yellow tinge. Its migration pattern is similar to the Redwing. Since the 1970s the average date of the first arrivals has gradually become later possibly due to the increase of temperature in the south. Again, like the Redwing, periods of cold bring increased numbers to the area and cold springs often keep the birds in the area for longer.

Owls, *Striges*

An Extract from *Bird Life*,(1914) by W Parkinson Curtis, FES, and E Harker Curtis.

We may record that the senseless persecution to which they were formerly subjected by game preservers is beginning to wane, as their economic importance is now better understood; but they still suffer acutely from the selfishness of many sportsmen. The Brown Owl occurs in every wood, the Long-eared Owl in the fir-woods, and nearly every isolated clump of firs that occurs on the outliers of the Reading Beds in the chalk area shelters a pair. The Barn Owl is not uncommon, and seems to have a partiality for the old quarries in Purbeck; but this useful bird is quite insufficiently protected. The Little Owl occurs as a migrant and also as an escapee. Specimens have passed through our hands shot as Partridges. The Scops Owl (Kelsall) gives two records within the area – Holmsley and Wilverley, New Forest. W.P.Curtis heard a strange Owl in Queen's Bower and fetched a gentleman acquainted with Scops in its proper habitat. This gentleman identified the note as that of Scops. It was heard every night in August for a fortnight, and seemed particularly partial to one very large, partly hollow oak tree.

RAPTORS

The situation regarding birds of prey at the beginning of the twentieth century was very different from that at the beginning of the twenty-first.

Game-keeping had a knock-on effect on the health and numbers of carnivores, both mammal and avian. The elimination of any predator was classed as rightful, and bounties were placed on the heads of any predatory species, regardless of whether it was rare or common. Falcons and hawks in particular were targeted without mercy. Species became very rare or extinct. Gamekeepers and land owners had no pity or knowledge of how the cycles of life turned and how an imbalance of predators would have a causative effect on the health of the whole ecological system. Although we claim to live in more enlightened times, many birds of prey are illegally killed every year, even in our area.

Birds were shot, poisoned or trapped. The carnage had a long lasting legacy that is starting to change. During the 1950s and 1960s pesticides also took their toll in preventing certain birds from breeding properly. Egg collecting from the rarer species also played a part. Now certain species are returning, either involuntarily or with the aid of reintroduction programmes by conservation bodies. The resident species such as falcons, buzzards and owls have slowly become more numerous but other larger birds have needed a helping hand, and still do. Some have not yet returned, but hopefully will in the future.

RESIDENTS

Northern Goshawk, *Accipiter gentilis* Renowned for its predation on game birds, it was heavily persecuted almost to extinction. Now the species has re-colonised our area partly due to conservation efforts. Successful breeding has only been proved twice in Dorset during the period 1990–96 although several breeding pairs have been seen in the New Forest.

Sparrowhawk

Eurasian Sparrowhawk, *Accipiter nisus.* The population declined during the 1960s and 1970s. Now quite common, they can be seen within the urban sprawl, hunting during the day but mainly at dusk. The hen takes domestic and wood pigeon, the smaller 'musket' (male) takes members of the thrush family or smaller birds.

Common Buzzard, *Buteo buteo.* The buzzard was very scarce in the early part of the century, and then decreased even further. Numbers rocketed in the 1980s, and reached record levels in the 1990s. Nowadays it is by far the most common bird after the Tawny owl.

It can be seen in and around Bournemouth and Poole. There are nests in Queens Park, and Redhill, and at another site in Poole. In towns the birds can be seen hunting squirrels and rats and even eating carrion from the road, or parks. Rural areas are overflowing with Common buzzards. Here they eat mainly Wood Pigeon (which they often feed to the young), worms, which can make up a large part of the winter diet, rabbits, voles, mice and rats, which have had huge increases over the last decade.

Common Kestrel, *Falco tinnunculus.* It was always present and probably not considered so much of a threat to game as larger birds of prey. Nationally it is thought to have decreased slightly in recent years. It is common and widespread around heathland, rough meadows, and roadside verges. It can be seen vole and lizard hunting in any suitable rough field and woodland area, and around Bournemouth cliffs.

Peregrine Falcon, *Falco peregrinus.* A winter visitor and increasing breeding species in our area. BNSS records sporadic sightings through the last century. Now we see the bird regularly at Swanage, Durlston, Christchurch and Keyhaven.

They are mainly wild birds but a few captive birds of hybrid status may have been released or escaped. Hybrids would be with lanner, saker or gyr falcons.

The most recent figure available for Dorset is 25 pairs which raised 32 young in 2006. Breeding birds use coastal sites. Inland, electricity pylons were used until the removal of the caps, which formed a nesting platform.

Barn Owl, *Tyto alba.* Nationally they are in decline and are on the Amber list. Changes in farming practice such as leaving rough field margins and set aside land, conservation campaigns, and the provision of nest boxes have all helped.

Never common, they are specialist feeders and require field voles for their chicks. Out of the nesting season they adapt somewhat to pursue different species, but only in long grass or reed bed habitats.

The Stour and Avon valleys have good numbers and of course in more rural locations they can be found wherever there is suitable habitat. Birds do however enter the towns. Talbot Heath, Turbary Common, Boscombe cliff passage (most probably post juvenile dispersal), Kings Park, are just some of the seemingly unlikely places where they have been observed.

Little Owl, *Athene noctua.* This species used to be quite common in farmland, but over recent years has become absent from many parts of our area. This may be due to competition from other, now more successful, species, especially the Barn Owl and the Buzzard. A non-native species, it was introduced to this country in the nineteenth century, its population derives from owls released in 1888. The Little Owl was not classed as a pest so has not been subjected to persecution.

Tawny Owl, *Strix aluco.* The Tawny Owl is our most common raptor, medium sized with a large rounded head and reddish brown in colour it is mainly resident with pairs keeping the same territory. In some wooded areas there can be as many as ten birds per square kilometre, depending on under-storey and rodent abundance, but they do not always just eat mice or voles. Opportunistic hunters, they will take wildfowl, reptiles, songbirds, squirrels, rats, caterpillars and beetles. They have also been recorded taking fish. The New Forest possibly has the largest concentrations of Tawny owls in the area.

Tawny Owl

Long-eared Owl, *Asio otus.* This is mainly a winter visitor, and overlooked due to its nocturnal habits. The Hampshire breeding population may be as low as 10–20 pairs. In Dorset there have been no recent breeding records just a handful of records of migrant birds.

Short-eared Owl, *Asio flammeus.* A common winter visitor, and maybe growing in numbers. It is medium sized and has wings which are very long, narrow and rather pointed. On Martin Green's farm near Wimborne St Giles, there were at least nine birds in a small area about three years ago. Other farmland areas also have visiting populations with reports from mid and east Dorset.

Eurasian Eagle Owl, *Bubo bubo.* This huge bird was probably a native, but for unknown reasons disappeared long ago. There is not much reference to it in historical times. However, it has made its own way back, helped along by escaped captive birds. Recent research has proven that the bird can fly considerable distances and migrates. The English Channel would pose no problem to it and it can also live on the European continent. There have been no formally reported sightings of European Eagle Owl in Dorset or in Hampshire although sightings may have been made of a few birds in the area, towards north Dorset, and at least one may have been seen in Wareham forest. The world's largest owl, it should not be confused with any of the many other species of eagle owls, some of which are commonly kept in captivity. The bird eats rabbits, foxes, hares and wildfowl and any other medium to large bird, even other raptors such as buzzards, which puts it at the top of the bird food chain. The species will become more common if it is not molested.

MIGRANTS

European Honey-buzzard, *Pernis apivorus.* A rare passage migrant. There were just seven known breeding pairs in Hampshire 2006, and only one pair in Dorset in 2006.

Black Kite, *Milvus migrans.* Rare passage migrant occurring in May–June in Dorset, where there are 19 records involving 20 individuals between 1980 and 2002. In Hampshire, between 1980 and 1993, there are 11 records of this species mostly from coastal locations. They do not stay long, but one or two birds can be seen between March and June anywhere in the region. Earmarked as a possible future breeding colonist, they have been seen around Purbeck and Bournemouth heaths.

Red Kite, *Milvus milvus.* A scarce but increasing visitor to both Hampshire and Dorset three pairs have been proved to be breeding in the northern Hampshire region. It is believed they are from the expanding introduction scheme that has been going on over several years in the Chilterns. Wandering young birds from this scheme are being recorded with increasing regularity in the area during the non-breeding period.

White-tailed Eagle, *Haliaeetus albicilla.* Also known as the Sea Eagle, the last record for Dorset was a probable on 14 November 1941 at Eggardon (Green). In Hampshire an immature at Somerley Park 6 January 1947 (Cohen) until last year 2007 when a Finnish ringed individual frequented the area around the Hants/Wilts border near Shipton Bellinger.

Marsh Harrier, *Circus aeruginosus.* A past breeding species which bred last in Poole Harbour in 1962, but is now re-assigned as a passage and wintering visitor. One or two are often seen in winter around the reed beds of Poole Harbour and associating farmland. They are often recorded on passage along the coastal area from Portland to Keyhaven and occasionally inland.

Hen Harrier, *Circus cyaneus.* A non breeder in this area but a passage migrant, and winter visitor often seen around Poole and Christchurch Harbours as well as the New Forest. They roost at Poole.

Montagu's Harrier, *Circus pygargus.* A rare species with just one or two breeding sites in the area which have yearly breeding birds. It is uncertain whether they are still in the Wimborne St Giles area.

Rough legged Buzzard, *Buteo lagopus.* There was a winter visiting bird every year for over twenty years that could be seen around Corfe Castle and Creech. Norden Woods was its main dwelling place. It has not been seen since 2004. Otherwise a rare bird in Britain, possibly overlooked due to its similarity to other buzzards.

Osprey, *Pandion haliaetus.* This is a passage migrant travelling to northern England and mainly Scotland. Birds can be seen in both spring and autumn around all of the harbours and waterways within the area, especially Poole. Also breeds in Rutland and Wales.

Red-footed Falcon, *Falco vespertinus.* There have only been 29 records in Dorset from 1854 to 1997. A rare spring migrant that may be seen along the cliffs of Bournemouth and Purbeck, feeding on sand martins or

Red-footed Falcon

swallows. There is a stuffed specimen in the BNSS museum collections that was taken locally.

Merlin, *Falco columbarius.* A winter visitor, many are seen around farmland, especially flat arable fields which have populations of wintering thrushes and pipits. The New Forest moors and the Ringwood area are good places to see them.

Hobby, *Falco subbuteo.* A summer visitor and common breeding falcon, especially on heaths and in the New Forest, where there were a possible 30 territories in 2006.

Hobby

7 Zoology

Jonathan McGowan

There has been constant climatic change over the last several million years, with warm and cold periods alternating: ice age glacial periods, interglacial periods and 'mini ice ages'. This has had many effects on our wild life. At the moment the earth is probably starting to shift into another period of change. Whether it is a warming period or a cooling period, or one preceding the other, it will have significant consequences for the environment.

The changes in the natural history of the Bournemouth district since the early 1900s are immense. At the moment in our area we seem to be gaining species of animals and plants more suited to a warmer environment. Our average temperature in the UK has risen by perhaps one degree in two decades. This means that we can and do have temperatures much higher at the top end. This also means that animals and plants that tolerate higher temperatures have a better chance of thriving.

Over the last twenty years we have seen an influx of continental species edging their way in a northwards direction. The south coast, being warmer and nearer to the continent, seems to be at the forefront of colonising species, especially if the animals can fly, travel with man, or swim the ocean.

For many centuries, a variety of animals and plants have been at the most northerly point of their range here on the south coast. Now they are moving northwards and other species are moving up from the continent taking full advantage of their natural instinct to colonise. The most obvious are the plants then the insects, followed by other invertebrates. Birds have been the most adept, as they are long lived and can move around easily, and can always retreat south if they need to. Other species that had once colonised for small periods of time have disappeared altogether or sporadically re-colonise again and again.

Many of the invertebrates that are now to be found within our area, can be attributed to man's travelling habits. Insects, arthropods, arachnids, bacteria and disease follow us about, making changes. If a new plant species, for example, colonises an area, a moth that feeds on it may do so also, together with its parasite and the parasite's parasite. Then a species of spider or wasp may move in to fill the evacuated ecological niche.

Other species such as arachnids or cockroaches hide in our luggage and stow away in other places. Many species have become truly cosmopolitan.

All these changes affect us in our region. In other respects, we have lost many species due to elimination, purposefully or not. We like to change our culinary habits, and by farming non-native, or once native, species we have changed the nature of waterways, woodlands and farmland. This of course has a knock-on effect. Changing farming practices have had some of the biggest effects particularly with the use of organophosphates and chlorides and with pesticides and herbicides. Many other chemicals and metals we humans use, either in our food, industry or as household cleaning products have deleterious effects.

All in all though, the Bournemouth district can boast fewer changes for the worse than for the good, as far as biodiversity is concerned.

WILDLIFE CONSERVATION IN BOURNEMOUTH — Brian Weekes

Urban conservation

Conservation of wildlife in Bournemouth played second fiddle to the development of the town during the first part of the twentieth century with the inclusion of Kinson and other areas into the borough. It was further compromised due to the need to accommodate the rubbish produced by these changes, which, in turn, meant that several green sites in Bournemouth were used as rubbish tips, notably, Millhams Mead in Kinson and Iford Meadows, and, to a lesser extent, Kinson and Turbary Commons. The situation was compounded by various realignments of the River Stour, producing the odd result that part of Christchurch lies on what is now the Bournemouth side of the river. It is now recognised that these sites include some of the last remnants of the original countryside, especially heathland, and should be preserved before the whole of Bournemouth becomes completely built over.

Pressures on wildlife

Indifference to the fate of wildlife in Bournemouth was probably the main factor in the decline of wildlife in the early part of the twentieth century but this has been replaced by two other factors, described below, which are now being addressed by a variety of initiatives.

Development

The open nature of Bournemouth, exemplified by the Upper Gardens, is one of the major attractions of the town and this attraction produces demand for development on the available space and hence, increases pressures on the wildlife within Bournemouth. Further pressure arises out of the current practice of converting houses and their back gardens into housing developments. Research by Kevin Gaston at Sheffield University has shown that back gardens are a major wildlife habitat in urban areas and should be preserved as far as possible. Due to the restricted size of the town, there appears no easy solution to these problems.

The attractions of the town have also meant that it is a desired destination for tourists, a market that is also targeted by the Council and local businesses. This has further increased the pressures on wildlife and their habitats, for example, at Hengistbury Head. This has meant that free access to the whole of the Head is restricted to ensure the conservation of the wildlife on the Head and the habitat.

These two factors have led to the rapid expansion of the town over the last fifty years and the current pressures from government to expand the housing stock will make the situation worse.

This rapid expansion of Bournemouth has meant that the original heathland that covered the countryside from Poole to Christchurch has been reduced to a few remnants within the borough, such as Kinson and Turbary Commons and Hengistbury Head. The surrounding areas have not been exempt from this reduction although the surviving spaces are somewhat larger, e.g. Upton Heath, Canford Heath and Sopley Common.

These changes have, in turn, resulted in specialist heath species, such as **Silver-studded Blue**, *Plebejus argus*, and **Grayling**, *Hipparchia semele*, butterflies, **Emperor moth**, *Saturnia pavonia*, **Sand Lizards**, *Lacerta agilis*, **Nightjar**, *Caprimulgus europaeus*, and **Dartford Warbler**, *Sylvia undata*, being confined to small areas of heath and thus being vulnerable to extinction if habitat pressures increase. Records exist of the presence of Silver-studded Blue, Grayling and Sand Lizard on Turbary Common and elsewhere in the borough but recording is not regular enough to determine if the populations can be considered of stable sizes, especially as vandalism is one of the major threats to these sites.

Wildlife Trusts

In the 1960s and 1970s DWT focussed its work on the acquisition and management of nature reserves. Since then, DWTs work has broadened to include land management and conservation advice, including the identification of Sites of Nature Conservation Interest across the county and conurbation, and working with Local Authorities to protect habitats and species through the planning system. In recent years, DWT has recognised the role it can play in raising awareness of wildlife and the contribution it makes to quality of life. With Heritage Lottery Funding, DWT has been able to set up a new and inclusive urban programme and greatly developed its role in the urban area.

Community Support Groups

Support groups can be council or community led. Whatever the source of motivation for the group, it is made up of concerned local residents who do not wish to see their local green space vanish. This has led to many groups being formed across the conurbation who are making a considerable difference to their sites. Typical examples of success can be seen at Kinson Common, Turbary Common, Stour Valley and Millhams Mead.

Recent research, however, has highlighted the problem of identifying the effect of the groups on the biodiversity of their sites. Groups have concentrated, mainly, on ensuring that sites are kept clear of vandalism and litter and that information is available to local residents. While this is good practice and essential for the wellbeing of the sites, lack of experts in fauna and flora identification has led to patchy recording of species, which is exacerbated by the fact that not all records made are centrally stored for analysis for example at the Dorset Environmental Records Centre (DERC). This shortfall is now being addressed by initiatives being developed by the BBC, Dorset Wildlife Trust, DERC, Bournemouth University, Butterfly Conservation and Bournemouth Natural Science Society through 'Bournemouth 2026'.

Statutory and other designations

One method of helping to maintain wildlife sites and their habitats and wildlife is the use of statutory designations for them. Nationally, there are a plethora of them but, locally, the main ones are Special Site of Scientific Interest (SSSI), Site of Nature Conservation Interest (SNCI) and Local Nature Reserve (LNR). These designations can give statutory or advisory protection to a site and serve to highlight the importance of that site to wildlife. Within the conurbation, there are several such sites, for example, Turbary Common and Kinson Common (SSSI) and Redhill Common and Iford Meadows (LNR). A further SSSI extending that covering the Bournemouth Cliffs is in the process of being set up. Protection can be further enhanced by the use of the Green Flag Award scheme, although this is mainly orientated towards municipal park schemes.

Whichever way one looks at wildlife conservation in Bournemouth and the surrounding areas, the picture is not all doom and gloom but neither is it rosy. Considerable energy and vigilance is required to ensure that those wildlife spaces still extant will be saved for the next 100 years. While wildlife trusts and other organisations can provide the conduit for wildlife conservation, it is up to the residents of the conurbation to provide the urge to conserve, rather as the collecting stalwarts of the nineteenth century provided the urge to increase our knowledge of nature.

FRESH WATER FISHES

The region has several good rivers within it, each with a common natural history. The Stour, running through the entire length of Dorset after leaving its Wiltshire source, meanders along a sixty-mile course through the countryside before meeting its sister river the Avon near

Christchurch harbour. The Avon starts as a chalk stream, also in Wiltshire, and remains shallow and fast for most of its length. The Stour in contrast is a slow, deep, often murky river as it flows along its clay bed after leaving the chalk in the downs, although its tributaries the Allen, the Crane and the Moors rivers are chalk born.

The chalk streams are shallow and fast providing an ideal habitat for salmonids, the salmon and trout. The most famous of these is of course the **Atlantic salmon**, *Salmo salar*. This species has suffered a massive reduction during the last hundred years, mainly due to over fishing and silt build-up along the gravel breeding areas. Pollutants have also taken their toll.

Recently conservation efforts have striven to reintroduce salmon to some areas, although with limited success. The Stour has only small numbers travelling upstream to breed and only a few succeed. There are additional fish released into the river in their juvenile forms.

The Avon has larger numbers entering to breed, and the Frome and Piddle that flow into Poole harbour also have varying amounts. Various agencies are monitoring their progress. Poaching remains a big problem, depleting already dwindling stocks.

The other well known member of this genus is the **Trout**, *Salmo trutta*. It has two forms, the resident type and the sea going type. The resident type is a small fish, *S. trutta fario*, rarely exceeding five pounds in weight and usually under two. The **Sea trout**, *S. trutta trutta*, grows much larger than the river type which is marked in olive green with red spots. It does not have so many juvenile forms as does the salmon and is a great indicator of stream health as it feeds mainly on the typical aquatic invertebrates such as stone, may, alder, needle and caddis flies which abound under and on the surface of clean water. The sea-going variety, which may have been the original type, comes up-river to breed in the winter or early spring like the salmon, entering the rivers after spending a long time at sea. All salmonids feed on small vertebrates such as fish, as well as any kind of invertebrates.

Grayling, *Thymallus thymallus*. This beautiful looking fish is said to smell like thyme, hence its name, but is certainly the most colourful of the salmon family. Its purplish-blue forms seen feeding on the bottom of the Frome and Piddle and also the Allen make one marvel at its beauty. A rather delicate sensitive animal it is also a good indicator of river health. This species does not grow as large as its cousins, and a fish of five pounds is exceptional. It is only to be found in the small chalk streams together with the brown trout.

Grayling

Rainbow trout, *Salmo gairdneri*. This species is American in origin and has escaped from trout farms. Mainly a fish of slower waters it does better in lakes rather than the small rivers. It is a distinctly larger trout, easy to breed and farm and is our most common species reared for the table. With the large number of trout farms in the region, some of which are fed by the Avon and Stour, many have escaped especially during river floods. The fish is capable of growing to ten pounds or

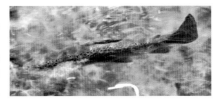

Brown Trout

more in weight, but not as large as the salmon. Fortunately, it does not breed in our rivers.

Perch, *Perca fluviatilis*. A handsome green and black striped small shoaling predator with red fins, and a large spiked dorsal fin. The Stour and its tributaries are well known for this sporty little fish, feeding mainly on small fish, but as with most species of fish, it will eat any invertebrate and small vertebrate. Relatively common in all the medium and larger waterways.

Pike, *Esox lucius*. This is the ultimate predator of the rivers, being streamlined and capable of overpowering anything it can fit in its mouth from fish to birds, it can grow to very big proportions. The Stour is well known for its large sized pike and specimens of thirty pounds have been caught in the past. A very common fish that when small can live together with others of the same species, but as it matures will need its own space. It is thought of as a pest by fisheries but of course it is natural and provides good sport for the angler. Size is determined by the size of waterbody in which it lives. All species of fish naturally colonise ponds and lakes by local flooding or being carried on the bodies of water birds such as ducks and moorhens. Pike often turn up in fish ponds due to this method.

Eel, *Anguilla anguilla.* This is surely the most complex and misunderstood of all our fishes for many reasons. Firstly it has a bizarre life history. The eggs are laid in the Sargasso Sea in the Gulf of Mexico and take around three years to reach our estuaries travelling on the Gulf Stream currents and passing through various larval stages during which they do not feed. When they reach our shores in their millions, as elvers, the ones destined to be females continue migration up the rivers into fresh water where they may remain for many years, called yellow eels, feeding on invertebrates and some small vertebrates such as amphibians and fish, along with worms, snails and carrion, whilst the males stay in the estuaries or open sea and are called silver eels. These are much smaller than the freshwater animals. The fish has the ability to breathe out of water and can migrate across land to ponds and ditches. All of our local waterways have ample amounts of eels but numbers are reduced due to over collection of elvers in the estuaries. A staple food source for many wild mammals and birds and, of course, other fish.

Chub, *Leuciscus cephalus.* This is one of the 'bright fish' family, which includes half of all freshwater fishes.because they are basically silver-scaled. Chub are medium sized averaging three pounds in weight, but can be up to eight. They like the slower, deeper regions of the Stour, Avon, and the Frome inhabiting small areas of waterway, on the edge of the fast current where there is calm and often shade by the way of overhanging trees. A very strong fish with golden tint and orangey fins is common, those in our area tend to be smaller than those in the north of the region. Two similar looking species are the **Dace**, *L. leuciscus*, and the **Roach**, *Rutilus rutilus*. The roach is similar to the chub in habits but forms larger shoals and has a more angular shaped body, smaller mouth with bright red fins and rarely exceeds two and a half pounds in weight. The former is small without the red fins and prefers the shallower and faster currents. Both species are common in all our waterways. The lower reaches of the Stour at Christchurch and its man-made tributaries create ideal breeding nurseries.

Gudgeon, *Gobio gobio.* A small, common bottom dwelling species of muddy and gravelly rivers preferring some current. It is similar to the barbel types in that it has feeling barbs around its mouth. Often heavily marked in brown or greyish silver, of up to twenty cm in length. The Stour and its tributaries have very healthy populations.

Minnow, *Phoxinus phoxinus.* This is possibly our most well known freshwater fish, as it is the most visible and the one that we all caught as children. They form large shoals especially when they are fry or half grown and can be seen in the warm shallow pools and ruts on the water's edge in summertime. The most common of all our fish, and one of the smallest up to ten cm in length. The males in June turn multi-coloured in their breeding condition.

Three spined stickleback, *Gasterosteus aculeatus.* This is our smallest fish being only five or six cm, it lives in all slower and shallower areas of rivers and neighbouring ponds within the floodplain, it is common in the Bourne stream. It does not require as much oxygen as other species and is warm water tolerant. It can usually be found living among algae in which the male builds a nest. It has three dorsal spines and mature males have a bright red belly. It has no scales but bony plates. It is also salt water tolerant to some extent, but not as much as its relative the **Nine spined stickleback**, *Pungitius pungitius* which lives in Christchurch and Poole harbours.

Bullhead or millers thumb, *Cottus gobio.* This is a small distinctive bottom dwelling, flattened fish with a large broad head. Up to twenty cm in length it lives under stones in faster flowing water such as the Avon, as well as stretches of the Stour, Frome and Moors rivers. It is very common and can be found alongside the **Stone loach**, *Neomacheilus barbatulus*, with its longer thinner body. Both species tend to be nocturnal leaving their rocks to rummage along the bottom for small insect larvae and molluscs.

Petromyzontidae. The lampreys are very odd fish. They are the most primitive vertebrates known and some zoologists refuse to class them as fishes. They have no jaws, the mouth being a circular sucking device lined with sharp horny teeth. They have weakly developed fins very unlike those of true fishes, and the skeleton is cartilaginous. They have seven holes along the side of the head leading to primitive gill chambers. The larvae filter algae and bacteria from the water and mud, but as adults they suck blood from other fish and eat carrion.

Brook lamprey, *Lampetra planeri*. This is a small species which is non migratory like the other members of the genus. This species does not attack other fish as food, but only eats during its larval period, feeding on tiny invertebrates. They mature within a year and then die. They can be found in the Moors, Stour and Frome rivers, as well as a few brooks and streams that feed from the main rivers.

Tench, *Tinca tinca*. Not native to UK but introduced into lakes for sport fishing. Some may have found their way into the Stour. A thick bodied carp-like fish of green or bronze colouration with distinctive red eyes about 30 cm in length. It originates from south east Europe, and Baltic regions.

Carp, *Cyprinus carpio*. Originally an Asiatic fish it was soon distributed around the world, mainly as a food source but later as a decorative fish being bred in all manner of forms. Indeed our common goldfish is just a small carp. For many years it has been used by man. It inhabits slow moving or still waters, often muddy, with dense vegetation. In UK waters we have at least two forms, the common and the mirror(which has enlarged body scales). Both can be found in the Stour and the

Common Carp River Avon

Avon, but particularly the Stour although not common. They can be seen from various river bridges such as Christchurch and Throop. Carp have the potential to grow very large, with a massive thick body. They can grow to over 13 kg in weight, but in our rivers, usually under ten.

Common bream, *Abramis brama*. An eastern European fish of the Danube region and Caspian Sea areas it was introduced to British waters for coarse fishing purposes. A medium-sized angular, bronze-coloured fish forming large shoals in rivers such as the Stour. A good place to watch them is Throop footbridge just under the weir. Also stocked into fishing lakes with many escapees forming shoals in the rivers.

Barbel, *Barbus barbus*. This is a native fish of south eastern England, but has been introduced to the Stour and Avon. A medium to large fish of up to 4.5 kg in weight. A bottom feeder similar to the gudgeon, but looking like the chub in appearance. Likes clean faster moving waters with slow deeper pools. Not very common in the region.

Flounder, *Platichthys flesus*. A marine and estuary fish that is able to live in fresh water with minimal salt content. It can be found in the lower reaches of the Stour as far up as Iford and the Frome well away from Poole Harbour. It has also been found in the Bourne Stream, and other small streams in Swanage as well as the Corfe River. The two harbours of Christchurch and Poole are certainly the best places to find it especially Poole where fisherman take many every year from the quiet bays. The flounder rarely enters the open sea. It is a flat fish of small to medium size and is sought after for its flesh.

Thick lipped grey mullet, *Chelon labrosus*. This is a marine fish, but is often to be found in estuaries and harbours during the summer months. Here it enters the Stour and can be found just north of Bournemouth and Christchurch. Many can be seen under Iford bridge at low tide where they are sometimes trapped. They like to feed on the algae and fly larvae in the muddy bottoms. A large fish often reaching over 2 kg in weight and 45 cm or more in length. They have large pale mouths hence the name of thick lipped grey mullet. They are not easy to catch with rod and line, despite the large numbers of them. Christchurch Harbour is often full of them in the summer and they can be seen basking in the shallows in calm water. Can also be seen around the pier pillars as they circle them grazing on algae.

REPTILES AND AMPHIBIANS

The changes to our herpetofauna have not been too drastic in the last hundred years with regard to the survival of the species themselves, as we have only three native lizards and three snakes, together with three newts, two toads and one frog – at least that is the accepted view. Since the last publication we can add a new-found species of snake as native, and possibly two species of frog. We can also add two new species of lizard which may be native or alien. If alien, we are unsure of when they were introduced.

Obviously newts, being semi-aquatic, are prone to local extinction as land is drained and housing developments or agriculture take over. Bournemouth and district is very much in the forefront of research, since having so much heathland and other types of prime habitats we can boast all native species of reptile and most amphibians. In fact Dorset and Hampshire heaths contain perhaps ninety percent of sand lizards and smooth snakes in the UK. Conservation here is important because both species require heathland for their survival in Britain, where they are at their most northerly point of distribution. Higher temperatures on the continent allow them to live in a variety of different habitats, but in this country they need lowland heath particularly, as it is warmer and dryer than any other habitat.

Common Lizard, *Lacerta vivipera*. The common lizard is the most northerly distributed of lizards and needs cooler climates, so much so that parts of France are becoming too warm for it with the advance of climate change. Even the warm Bournemouth sea cliffs may be too warm for it to flourish, as numbers seem to be diminishing with no apparent cause. But the two so-called aliens are doing very well, which does suggest that they enjoy a more Mediterranean-style environment, along with various species of plants and insects. The Bournemouth area sea-cliffs have their own micro-climate, different from the rest of Britain with the possible exception of a few blocks of heathland. The common lizard was once well known throughout the district and its basic distribution has not changed much, since it is hardy, hibernating and live-bearing (an adaptation to cool climates). It has the ability to live in a variety of habitats, even in urban gardens and parklands, and it is not a specialist as far as feeding and breeding are concerned. However, the heaths do hold the largest concentrations. It is a small species, rarely attaining a length of more than twenty cm and is mottled in various shades of brown with spotting and horizontal stripes. **Melanic** specimens occur occasionally.

Slow worm, *Anguis fragilis*. This was once thought to be a snake; even today people confuse it with the smooth snake locally and the adder and grass snake nationally. It shows typical lizard traits such as moveable eyelids, a short tongue and smooth scales, and the skeleton reveals vestigial leg bones. It also lacks the muscle structure of snakes and is a slow mover, hence its name. It was once more common

Slow worm and Smooth Snake

in this region than it is today, as it favours dryer habitats, particularly heathland, but it can also be found in suburban parks and gardens. It lives a subterranean existence and is a live bearer, like the common lizard. It also lives in similar habitats, but may be found in so-called 'improved' or unnatural grasslands, and in manure or compost heaps. It feeds on molluscs and other soil invertebrates, so it should not have as many problems as other reptiles. Nevertheless it is on the decrease. Domestic cats, the tidying

Sand Lizard

up of gardens and ignorant killings are to blame. The reptile can live for up to fifty-eight years in captivity, whereas the common lizard probably only lives for up to ten years in the wild. The slow worm can reach a length of forty centimetres but is usually shorter. The females are bigger and usually have a central dark line dorsally. The males are uniform in colour and larger headed, sometimes with blue spotting on the front part of the body. These were thought of as a separate sub-species at the time of the last publication, but that is not the case.

Sand lizard, *Lacerta agilis*. This is a rare species, only inhabiting the dry heathland. In former times it may not have needed the heath, as it does not on the continent. As it requires sand to lay its eggs in it is most often found on the sandy heaths, mainly in southern England but also in Merseyside which is cooler. There are also old records from Wales and Gloucester, Devon and Cornwall; east towards London, some still survive in Surrey. Dorset certainly has the largest concentrations. The sand lizard is much larger than the common lizard and robust, with large, distinct **ocelli**, especially in adults. The male has green sides and is splendid to see from April to June. In our locality it can be found on all surviving patches of heathland except for King's and Queen's Parks in Bournemouth. The clifftop holds small colonies and there are other small inbred colonies in other little blocks of heath. They are abundant, as they should be, on the larger areas of heath.

Like the common lizard the sand lizard feeds on invertebrates of many forms: insects, spiders, centipedes, ants and larvae of butterflies and moths, as well as grasshoppers and crickets, bugs and flies.

Because of their national rarity sand lizards are protected by law, but the heathland habitat is more prone to destruction, which is the main reason for the species' decline. With climate change the species' habits may change, and some may start to colonise dry areas away from heathland, as they do in Europe. The common lizard, on the other hand, may find it too warm in southern England; it may be that Bournemouth clifftops, in becoming too warm, are causing the demise of the species, or it may be attributed to the fact that they have two other species to compete with.

Common wall lizard, *Podarcus muralis*. It is believed that this slim, very active and agile species was not native to the British Isles. This may be true, although it may have occurred here thousands of years ago, along with the Western green lizard. It has not adapted to hibernation, so in the past it has not been suited to our environment, although now, with climate change, it is doing much better with stable colonies on the south coast. Bournemouth clifftops can boast the largest naturalised colonies in Britain outside the Channel Islands, and they are not only thriving, but perhaps

Common Wall Lizard

forcing the common lizard to have smaller colonies, which is natural in northern Europe. In Britain they have no other species to compete with. As its name suggests the common wall lizard likes to be active on vertical surfaces and will hunt there or on the ground for the same sorts of invertebrates as the other species described. They are egg layers, may have up to three broods per year, and the young grow rapidly. The males can be very territorial. The wall lizard is larger than the common lizard but they can easily be mistaken for each other. The females especially look similar to common lizards, but have slimmer profiles and small reticulated patterns on the sides, with a very long tail. The mature males here in Bournemouth are very colourful, being green- or yellow-backed with small blue scales along the sides of the belly. There is much variation and there may be two or more sub-species or variants present. This anomaly seems to be mainly in the Boscombe area, but the green individuals are also along the Poole chines. It is not known where they came from, but the pet trade is most likely. They were present at Bourne Bottom in 1978 and one was collected, mistaken for a sand lizard, bottled in formaldehyde and presented to our Society along with sand lizards collected at the same site. I noticed the difference in 2004 whilst doing routine checks. At the moment the species has a limited distribution with other colonies in Purbeck and Portland. But this is sure to change in the future.

Western green lizard, *Lacerta bilineata*. This is not thought of as a native, but it did live here thousands of years ago. It occurs in the Channel Islands and northern France. There have been a number of introductions since the early eighteen hundreds, but most have failed or lasted only for a decade or so. However, there are many records of the species having been found in a wild state in various parts of southern England, especially Poole and Wareham. These observations were made by naturalists familiar with both the

Western Green Lizard

green lizard and the sand lizard. *Our Reptiles*, 1865, by M C Cooke probably contains the most important information about whether or not *Lacerta bilineata* is native.

It is now here on Bournemouth cliffs, and has been for longer than people would think. I was possibly one of the first people to find the species, a sub-adult female in 1999 at Portman Ravine in Boscombe. although I had a record from the same place from 1991, when a member of my family had found a dead, all-green very large animal on the steps there. It had gone by the time I could get there. There are reports from beach-hut owners of big green lizards being seen, but they may have thought that they were sand lizards. The odd thing is, there have not been sand lizards in this part of Bournemouth for at least thirty years and there are no positive reports of them before that. The reason is unclear, but could it be because green lizards were present? Although that is unlikely, the western green lizards are now firmly established and are doing well. They are spreading, but only slowly, since severe weather conditions seem to set them back, but generally, owing to climate change, they are thriving. They are almost identical with their European counterparts, being very large, around thirty cm or even up to forty, two thirds being tail. They are basically twice the size of sand lizards, but they tend to vary. The smaller adults also tend to be more colourful with males having vivid blue heads or throats. The larger ones have white throats similar to the **Eastern green lizard**, *Lacerta triliniata*. This is probably just a colour morph rather than the possible introduction of the eastern species, but that cannot be ruled out: females and young sometimes have three or five stripes as the name suggests, and these animals seemed to perish when we had a cold and prolonged winter.

Whatever the exact genetic makeup of these animals, they certainly show up more variation than other colonies in Europe, and they are wonderful to see, bringing in naturalists and herpetologists from far and wide. I have watched them closely for years and have seen no aggression to other species of lizard, or even much to their own species. They seem to be almost totally insectivorous, with occasional blackberry eating.

Snakes, Serpentes

We have only three native species of snake in Britain. All of them occur in the Bournemouth area.

Smooth Snake, *Coronella austriaca*. As recently as 1858 this was regarded as a new species, having once been thought to be a variation of the adder. It was here in Bournemouth, mainly due to the building of the town, on the heathland where they were found in abundance, that opinion first changed. It has been found that they occur on other southern heathlands as well, for example in Surrey, while in Hampshire they occur in the New Forest. It was first thought that they are linked to their main food source, the sand lizard, but it is now known that they eat other reptiles including

Smooth Snake

other snakes and small rodents, so are not just heathland specialists. Like adders and unlike the grass snake they give live birth. Yet they are little observed because they live under thick heather and moss layers, burrowing with their slightly flattened head and smooth body (from which they are named). They do not have keeled scales like other snakes, so they feel silky to the touch. They can be found under refuges such as sheets of corrugated iron or wood.

They are a small species, rarely exceeding sixty-five cm and generally slim in appearance unlike most vipers, although they resemble both adders and grass snakes in having dark spots and stripes. However, they lack the zig-zag patterning of the adder but have a similar deep triangular mark on the head. Comparison with the adder shows the obvious differences. The smooth snake has round eye pupils (unlike the adder's elliptical pupils) and has no venom glands. It is more prone to biting when handled. Mating occurs in autumn or spring, and small striped replicas of the adults are born in September. Like the sand lizard the smooth snake is given full protection and our heaths are renowned for these two species.

Grass Snake, *Natrix natrix*. This is our largest snake. It can attain lengths of two metres, albeit rarely: they are more likely to be about 1.2 m. The females are larger than the males. Grass snakes are easily identified by the conspicuous yellow and black collar just behind the head. Generally they are olive green or brown with darker vertical stripes along the sides, but colour can vary with bluish and pinkish and even cream specimens occurring. Some could be local variations, once thought of as subspecies. They prefer a watery habitat, like many other species of water-snake, and usually hunt amphibians and fish, occasionally taking baby birds and small mammals. When captured they release the contents of their **cloaca**, thus giving off a foul

Grass Snake

smell. If that fails, they may sham dead, rolling on their backs, opening mouths and rolling the tongue out. Generally they disappear fast at the first sight of an animal or human.

They are common in this region as we have many rivers and waterways, farmyards and heath. They lay eggs in decomposing vegetable or manure heaps. The lack of the latter is the main reason why they are not as frequent as they used to be, especially in suburban areas, since not so many people have compost heaps these days. There is a very high mortality rate among eggs and young, unlike the adder.

Adder, *Vipera berus.* This is a true viper adapted to live in cool conditions, widely distributed in the northern hemisphere way up into the Arctic circle, where they tend to be darker, giving them an ability to absorb more warmth. As the name suggests they give live birth, usually in August or September. The snakes often hibernate in traditional underground sites and emerge early in spring, males before females, as with most of our reptiles. This is so that the males can have a head start with their sperm production, ready for the competition when the females emerge and (in the case of lizards) to stake claim to a territory. The adult male adders often embark in ritualistic fighting over females where they intertwine themselves as most snakes do when fighting. The snakes are rather short, have small tails, especially the females, and typically have a dorsal patterning of zig-zag markings (darker in the males) on a light background, with a prominent v-shaped marking on the head. The eyes have elliptical pupils with a red iris. Black forms occur locally.

Adder

The snakes often hiss a warning to animals or humans at their approach and are less inclined to flee than the grass snake. They have the back-up of possessing venom, which can be as lethal as venom from other species of vipers, depending on amounts injected and the person's or animal's tolerance. For the small mammals, which it is designed to kill, there is no escape from a swift heat-seeking strike. The animal's dying path is tracked by a scent-seeking device in the adder's head. Generally the snakes are docile and reluctant to bite as they need the venom for its proper purpose.

Adders are widely distributed in the UK and can be found all over Dorset and the New Forest, mainly on heathland and on woodland edges in the proximity of bracken, bramble or gorse (where they are often in abundance). Young animals are usually brick red as are some adults, with much variation throughout the district. Although adders are protected as are all our reptiles, people still have an ignorant fear of them and many are beaten to death. Like all reptiles, they can only regulate their body temperature to a small degree and can easily overheat, so they avoid being out during very hot sunshine. At ground level, especially in the dry places where our reptiles bask, the ground temperature can be a dozen degrees higher than the surrounding air above it. Basically, though, reptiles need warmth to activate them, unlike the amphibians which can tolerate and be active in temperatures near to freezing

Amphibia

Common frog, *Rana temporia.* This can tolerate broad temperature variations and is widely distributed across Britain. It is common in our area, although less so than formerly, due to a number of factors: the filling in of a number of ponds in the name of health and safety, land drainage, poisons entering the water supply from household detergents and chemicals, industrial chemicals and waste or farming poisons such as organophosphates and chlorides. Pesticides and herbicides all play a sad part in the demise of a very sensitive and finely-tuned amphibious group and indeed such a group acts as an environmental indicator. Many diseases are picked up by amphibians, and frogs suffer most because they directly absorb the water which they touch: they cannot afford to dry out and must be damp at all times. Toads are different, as are newts to some extent. All amphibia need to breed in water; the larval form needs to metamorphose in water, eating both plant and animal matter.

Common Frog

Common frogs are quite large (but not as large as common toads on average) yet smaller than the edible or pool frogs of which we have none in this area. Colours can be extremely variable. Inbreeding diversifies the colour, but may result in their all looking similar, and suffering birth defects and other problems. Generally the common frog is an olive-green or brown, with yellowish or pinkish areas, with or without darker spots and leg banding.

Adults at three years old return to the pond of their infancy and males call with one inflated throat sac, not through sacs on both sides as with other species. The call is a soft purring staccato belching. Spawn is laid in gelatinous lumps early in the year corresponding with the phase of the moon, peaking at the full. The frogs can breed in January through to March. They feed on all manner of invertebrates and some small vertebrates. There are many colonies in the region with perhaps more in urban areas because of garden ponds and less predation.

Toads

Natterjack Toad, *Epidatea calamita*. This small native toad has been reintroduced to at least two sites after a long period of absence . It was formally abundant around Hengistbury Head, and also Poole Harbour, as mentioned in the 1914 publication. The re-introduction to Hengistbury and Stanpit Marsh have been a great success, along with the construction of special shallow pools which warm up quickly, attracting certain algae and small crustaceans on which the tadpoles feed. The adults arrive

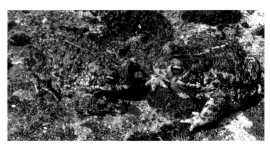

Natterjack Toad

later than those of the **Common toad**, *Bufo bufo*, in the spring, at the breeding sites in April or May or in both months giving a double brood. However unlike the Common toad, these smaller animals stay around the ponds at night and call. The sound is loud and carries long distances. In the daytime they dig out a short burrow in the sand and remain there. They are distinguished from their larger cousins by a distinctive thin yellow line running along the middle of the back, and reddish or yellowish and green warts. These nationally scarce animals are protected by law.

Common toad, *Bufo bufo*. Far more common it can be

Common Toad

found anywhere in our region. But it is not as common as it used to be in rural areas. Again it is the urban pond that has kept the species strong in the region. Suburban lakes and large ponds are better than small bodies of water, but it does sometimes breed directly in the River Stour. Nocturnal, like all of our amphibians, it can live in very dry habitats without the need of water, unlike frogs, that need to be moist. This animal can be found slowly milling around town centre roads and parkland snaffling up anything it can overpower. Both species of toad lay their spawn in long ribbons rather than a solid mass like frogs.

Newts, Pleurodelinae

There are three native species in the British Isles and all within our region.

Great crested or Warty Newt, *Triturus* (formerly *Molge*) *cristatus*. Nationally scarce and protected by law. It is widely distributed on mainland Europe and Asia, not universally as the older book states. This may be because there are many other similar species which were not differentiated until later on. In Britain its stronghold is the South east, where there is lots more water. In our area it is pretty rare now, with colonies just off the map and a few within. Britain's largest newt is very diagnostic, with its black warty skin and orange or yellow belly. In the breeding season in early summer, it sports a colourful crest as do our other species of newt.

Common or Smooth newt, *Triturus vulgaris*. Not as common as its name suggests yet it is the most common of all our species. The Bournemouth area is acid heath and is not to the animal's liking, but in outer areas it is more common. In the built up towns, again due to man it is more common often being present in most garden ponds, sometimes along with the **Palmate newt**, *Triturus helveticus*, to which there is a great similarity. The adult breeding males of both species sport a crest but the Palmate has a long filament at the tail tip along with dark heavily webbed hind feet. The latter of the species seem to be more common than they once were, but both species seem to be doing well. They all breed in large or small bodies of still water, often semi-stagnant, females laying one egg at a time wrapped around plant leaves or fronds. Adults and juveniles enter land to hibernate in late summer and dry up to a small extent living under damp logs or stones etc.

MAMMALS

The majority of wild animals in the UK had no protection in the past unless species were classed as game or for hunting, shooting or fishing. Game rearing was rife throughout the district, and all birds of prey and carnivores were classed as vermin to be shot on sight, trapped or poisoned. This had a huge impact on our countryside. Changing farming practices, such as the invention of pesticides and herbicides, from the 1920s onwards had dire effects. It was not until the conservation-orientated 1960s that new legislation began to be written regarding the protection of Britain's wildlife, most notably the Wildlife and Countryside Act, 1981. I shall start with the smallest species of natives and compare them with the original publication, add any new species, then work my way up through the rodents, insectivores then small carnivores to the larger herbivores to new species of carnivores.

Insectivora

Starting with insectivores, we have three species of shrew, the same as the rest of mainland Britain. They are the **Common shrew**, *Sorex araneus*, **Pygmy shrew**, *Sorex minutus,* and **Water shrew**, *Neomys fodiens*. All are very small, active and voracious predators, usually of small invertebrates, but occasionally of rodents and other insectivores including members of their own species. They have a very fast metabolism and need to eat almost constantly, only sleeping for up to an hour at a time. They are creatures of varying habitats, especially where there is much cover, and are found in woodland, hedgerows, heathland and marsh, including the sea shore. They do not climb, but can be found inside hollow trees, as well as in rocky, mossy areas. They have minute eyes that are not visible, but a very sensitive large snout and whiskers. They are armed with an array of sharp primitive-style teeth tipped with red pigment. Of the three species which can be found in the district, the water shrew is the least common as many waterways and meadows have been drained. It not only hunts in the water, but around water and under the surface. Its tail is slightly wider and more furry than the other two species, and it has dark blackish fur, which is often white around the ears. The common shrew is smaller with a three-shaded fur pattern, a dark top, lighter sides and with a grey underside. The pygmy shrew is much smaller, often only reaching five or six cm. The common shrew is usually about eight cm. Not a great deal of research has been done on them, especially regarding their numbers, as they are easily overlooked, but they can readily be trapped, and this has provided the Mammals Trust with vital information. All the shrew species still seem to be common in most habitats, though the pygmy shrew has a preference for denser cover and so is possibly less common in open heathland alongside the larger common shrew. Shrews also feature greatly in the diet of raptors, but not in the diet of mammals as they are distasteful to them. Reptiles also feed on them.

Moles, of which we have just one species, *Talpa europaea,* are not as common as they used to be with the opening up of fields, more intensive farming and with their status of having been considered a pest for hundreds of years. Much larger than shrews, moles average 15 cm long with huge modified front limbs for digging, to enable them to live a subterranean life feeding on earthworms, and heaping dug out soil onto the surface. Usually dark blackish-grey, they can be apricot, silver, yellowish or piebald. Generally, they are still common in the region, even in the Bournemouth urban areas. They are not persecuted as much as they were, so are now holding their own. They can be found in most types of habitat including heathland, although they are much more common on the improved meadows and parklands and the natural unimproved grasslands, except for hard chalk.

The other ground dwelling insectivore is the **Hedgehog**, *Erinaceus europaeus*. Quite large, reaching about 30 cm in length, it is rather robust. It has modified hair to form spines for its protection as it is not the fastest of creatures, and is relatively weak except when it rolls up into a ball. Its main diet is molluscs and earth worms, but it will also eat soft fruit and carrion. It has never been persecuted to the extent of moles or small carnivores but was misunderstood and killed by gamekeepers as it is fond of eggs; it was also eaten by some people. Hedgehogs have always been abundant after the heathland was cleared, and were probably most common during the second half of the twentieth century, when game rearing started to wane and road traffic was not too great. Additionally, the general public fed them as they looked on them as their favourite mammal. These days they are endangered mainly because of the build-up of roads and also from their habit of entering wood and leaf piles that are subsequently burned. They also take in toxins such as slug pellets as their favoured foods are molluscs, and they are victims of chemicals and waste materials. In the Bournemouth area hedgehogs are disappearing at an alarming rate. In country towns, though, they are holding on and large country villages are probably their best strongholds.

Chiroptera

The other group of insectivorous mammals are the bats. We may have seventeen or more species, bearing in mind that bats fly and are not restrained in their movements like other mammals. Some species have been known to cross the English Channel. We have gained at least two new species since the last publication, and may have lost one species. There is much conservation effort regarding all species of bats in the UK, and they are all protected by law under the Wildlife and Species we know about: **Greater horseshoe**, *Rhinolophus ferrumequinum*, very rare, restricted to south west England occuring in the Stour Valley and Purbeck. **Lesser horseshoe**, *R. hipposideros*, very rare restricted to western England. **Daubentons**, *Myotis daubentoni*, relatively common near water. **Brandts**, *Myotis brandtii*, **Whiskered**, *Myotis mystacinus*, common in the area. **Natterer's**, *Myotis nattereri*, **Bechstein's**, *Myotis bechsteini*, very rare. **Mouse eared**, *Myotis myotis*, very rare, may be extinct, but overlooked. **Noctule**, *Nyctalus noctula*, common. **Leisler's**, *Nyctalus leisleri*, uncommon. **Common pipistrelle**, *Pipistrellus pipistrellus*, very common throughout. **Nathussius's pipistrelle**, *Pipistrellus nathusii*, **Soprano pipistrelle**, *Pipistrellus pygmaeus*, **Barbastelle**, *Barbastella barbastellus*, rare. **Common or Brown long eared**, *Plecotus auritus*, quite common. **Grey long eared**, *Plecotus austriacus*, rare. **Serotine**, *Eptisicus serotinus*, very common throughout.

Leisler's Bat

Bats are easily overlooked due to their nocturnal habits and hidden roosts. All British recorded species can be found within our region, perhaps even the mouse eared bat, as this area was its only known haunt outside Sussex. It was known at the beginning of the twentieth century but was very rare. Various naturalists remember seeing these huge animals with their slow low flight patterns around the Purbeck. I used to see them just north of Blandford. Unfortunately, as they are already thought of as extinct, the conservation bodies are not searching for any remaining animals.

All bats are protected by law. Even disturbing their roosts knowingly is an offence. Any planning for home renovation, demolition, roof or loft installations, or cavity wall insulation, and any tree work, especially large or dead trees, should be checked out by the local bat group or Natural England.

Bats are totally harmless to man and the home; they are long-lived mammals and we need them to eat the hundreds of tonnes of mosquitoes and midges and other insects. Bournemouth has large amounts of **Serotine bats**, *Eptisicus serotinus*, in and around the town, as well as the common pipestrelle. Noctules can be found around the larger parks; lieslers used to have a roost near Boscombe East, but the roadside tree was felled and the animals which used to hunt in King's Park are now gone. One could see them, at least forty at a time, catching **Summer chafers**, *Amphimallon solstitialis*, as they emerged from the ground on the football pitch.

We also have small numbers of Brown long eared, and even the rare *Barbastelle* has been found. The more bat boxes that are used in public and private premises, the better chance these animals will have.

Rodentia

Our only native rodents are the following: **Wood mouse**, *Apodemus sylvaticus*. Very common in all areas, especially woodland and in the Bournemouth, Poole, Christchurch conurbations themselves. **Yellow necked mouse**, *Apodemus flavicolis*. Larger than the previous species, not known of before the 1950s, likes woodland and is arboreal. Not particularly common in our area, but does seem to be present in the larger blocks of mixed woodland. **Harvest mouse**, *Micromys minutus*. Our smallest rodent, it is easily overlooked. Mainly countryside dwelling in woodlands, damp meadows, heathland and farmland. Builds a small round nest in the tops of grasses including cereal crops. **Hazel dormouse**, *Muscardinus avellanarius*. Widely distributed in the area, mainly in rural areas of differing habitats but mainly old mixed woodlands, especially hazel coppices. Presumed rare up until the 1990's when surveys carried out would suggest that it is not as rare as once thought, but quite adaptable to various habitats as long as they contain seed or berry producing plants, and a wealth of invertebrates. **Bank vole**, *Clethrionomys glariolus*. Common on grassy slopes and banks, sea cliffs and riverbanks. Also common in woodlands in the area. **Field or short tailed vole**, *Microtus agrestis*. Common in long grass and rough areas of fields and hedgerows, roadside verges and banks, and in parkland in town and countryside. **Northern water vole**, *Avicola terrestris*. Once very common along the Stour and its tributaries, now rare due mainly to changes in farming practices, chemical run-offs, pollution and disturbance. Also made rarer to a minor extent by the spread of American mink into its habitat. **Common vole**, *Microtus arvalis*. Not in the area.

Red squirrel, *Sciurus vulgaris*. In the area, the only places where it exists are the Poole Harbour islands, where periodic introductions of unrelated animals from Scandinavia prevent their disappearance. The Isle of Wight has natural populations, and no grey squirrels. The greys are partly responsible for Red squirrel demise due to passed on viral infections. **European beaver**, *Castor fiber*. Not in the area, exterminated by the thirteenth century. New reintroductin not carried out in our area.

Long standing non-natives are: **Brown rat**, *Rattus norvegicus*. Eastern Asian origin, worldwide distribution. Common in Britain for over 600 years. Very common all over our area, town and countryside. Has been encouraged by farming and game rearing and also from our wasteful habits. An extremely adaptable and intelligent animal some 25cm long plus its tail. Not as responsible for damage or disease as people would suggest, considering the vast number of them, especially in the built up areas. They are an important food source for many carnivorous animals and birds of prey. In the early book, it states that crowds of them at Kimmeridge Bay live on the seaweed. In my opinion, they are more likely to be foraging for shellfish, as they still do today and other flotsam and jetsam. **Black rat**, *Rattus rattus*. Their origin is southern Asia, they migrated to various European areas and southern Britain. Now replaced by previous species. May still exist in our area on the coast. **House mouse**, *Mus musculus*. Generally dark brown and 10 cm long with a similar length tail. Of Asian origin, spread over 100 years ago. Worldwide distribution. Common all over our area, but not as much as it used to be. In Bournemouth, the wood mouse is more common in houses.

Recent non-natives are: **American grey squirrel**, *Sciurus carolinensis*. Common all over southern and central England, very common in our area.

Lagomorpha

Brown Hare, *Lepus europaeus*. Often thought as a non-native, the brown hare was certainly an important food item for the Romans. It is an animal of open areas rather than thick forest. Being a long distance sprinter, it does not live in burrows like rabbits, but above ground, and the young or leverets are kept in a form, a shallow depression in the grass. It is much larger than the rabbit, with longer black tipped ears and much longer legs. The hare can trot, unlike the rabbit. In our area it is not as common as it used to be, but in some rural areas to the north and east it is not uncommon. It can still be found on the edges of Bournemouth around Throop and Holdenhurst and the airport, though with the ever growing recreational areas, it is dwindling.

Rabbit, *Oryctolagus cuniculus*. Thought to have been introduced during the twelfth century, this animal has became a very important food source for humans as well as other wild animals and although the introduced disease myxomatosis almost wiped them out during the 1960s, they have conquered it and only suffer periodic bouts of the disease. The more stressed the colonies, the more likely they are to suffer, with appallingly cruel consequences. Some immunity prevails. Still very common in our areas, but colonies never seem to reach the huge numbers of previous times.

Carnivora

Many of our predatory mammals were persecuted to such an extent during the eighteenth and nineteenth centuries that some species were totally wiped out. Mainly in the interests of game rearing, but also from simple ignorance and greed, carnivores were felt to have no place within our countryside. These animals were branded as 'pests' to be eliminated on sight. Since the 1960s due to the conservation laws and new and better ideas, some have legal protection, some do not. Some have made a come back, either on their own, or by having had a helping hand from conservation-orientated organisations.

Native carnivores

Red fox, *Vulpes vulpes*. Very common, more so in the urban environment than the countryside in many areas. It is still heavily persecuted in the countryside, by gamekeepers and farmers alike; also by the hunting and shooting fraternity, as a target or as a pest. It is of course not a 'pest', and without them the rodent and rabbit populations would be out of control. Urban foxes are generally a new phenomenon. The opportunistic animals have taken advantage of our dirty habits and clean our towns of rubbish and rats.

Unfortunately the sarcoptic mite-caused disease 'mange' has taken its toll and has wiped out vast numbers of town foxes. Even Bournemouth and Poole have had great problems as the milder and wetter weather has contributed to it.

Northern lynx, *Felis lynx*. This animal was thought to have been eradicated from Britain four hundred years ago, yet it may have survived in small numbers in the Scottish highlands. The animal was due for official reintroduction, but it seems as though it has already had a helping hand unofficially. There have been many reports in southern England since the year 2000. Some in our own area, and sightings by myself and other credible witnesses (see pp 00).

Grey seal, *Halichoerus grypus*. Also known as the Atlantic grey seal, it is the larger of the two species to be found around Britain's coastline, and can be occasionally found in our area. It does not breed here, and may be encountered along the Purbeck coast, usually as solitary individuals. They have been seen around Kimmeridge and Chapmans pool. The animal breeds to the west of us. **Common or harbour seal**, *Phoca vitulina*. This animal is smaller than the grey seal, and

Common Seal

has a shorter snout. As its other name suggests, it is common in harbours and estuaries, and can be seen in the rivers at times. The odd one or two have been seen in Christchurch harbour as well as Poole, and have been found in the Stour at Iford and Tuckton. It does not breed here, but more to the east.

Eurasian otter, *Lutra lutra*. The otter was common during the early part of the last century, but it was heavily persecuted along with all other types of predators, and was almost eradicated in southern England. In the south west it hung on, if only due to the remoteness of some of Devon's waterways and coastline. Otter hound hunts were employed all over the country, and Dorset and Hampshire were no exception. By the 1960s, otters were extremely rare in both counties, but did survive in places. With conservation and reintroduction programmes for the River Stour during the 1980s, a healthy population was established by the 1990s and now otters are common again throughout the region. They are territorial animals, often holding sway to up to a dozen miles of river or stream, which they guard and anoint with scats on the river banks. The males wander widely at times, as do the dispersing young which often brings them into contact with motor vehicles. The otter is not just a fish eater, although best adapted to fish, but also eats crustaceans, especially in the marine habitat. They will also take water voles, rats, frogs, snakes and some waterfowl. Most southern otters live on inland rivers, but some do spend time at the coast, and both Poole and Christchurch harbours have animals using them at most times. All the smaller

Dorset rivers have stretches incorporated in the ranges of some animals, especially males which have larger territories. They may use them as corridors, and even tiny field drains and ditches are used. The comeback of the otter is one of our most successful and well deserved conservation projects.

Badger, *Meles mele*. The badger has always been quite common in the west country, and Dorset has always had large colonies. Unfortunately this animal suffers more persecution today than it did in former times due to misunderstanding and politics. In spite of much persecution and many hundreds of road deaths every year, its numbers actually rise due to its social existence. The badger relies on a certain type of structured family life within its colony and if that breaks down it causes havoc, and more animals will breed. It is a complex interaction which is worthy of more study. Badgers probably pose very little risk in spreading bovine tuberculosis, and possibly the problem lies with farming methods and the damp weather in the west of England. Cattle can actually pass it to badgers, the animals directly feed in the manure rich pastures for worms and directly take in cattle faeces, saliva, and spores in the soil.

The area in which badgers now live has expanded to include heathland, towns and railway embankments, but the traditional habitat of hillsides still remain its principal domain. Whilst many large setts on farmland have been destroyed, others have cropped up in other areas. Some areas, where there is much persecution, mainly from baiters and the farming community, are devoid of setts. However, on the whole they are far more common now, due to the Wildlife and Countryside Act, damper summers and milder winters. Old setts may have consisted of hundreds of entrances of which maybe less than a third were in use at once, but these large setts are now gone, and lots of little setts are now the norm.

Their main food is earthworms, but all invertebrates, plant bulbs and corms, as well as small mammals such as mice, voles and young rabbits are consumed.

Western polecat, *Mustela putorius*. Or foul marten, or chicken cat, the common name being derived from *poulet chat*, was another victim of our ignorance, being eradicated from most of Britain, only to be found in mid Wales and perhaps some areas in Scotland. Its habits of living close to man in farmland and river valleys put it at the top of the 'wanted' list. A carnivore adapted to hunting on the land, marshland or riverbank, it will take any manner of bird, mammal or amphibian it can overpower. The male has a head and body *c*.38 cm long and a 14 cm tail. It is not equipped to hunt in water as the mink does, but can take fish, and there is an overlap with the mink, to which it is closely related, in its habitat and food preferences. These days polecats mainly eat rabbits and

Polecat

rats, but also game birds and waterfowl. The animal is back in our area after a long absence, and is now common in most of Dorset, Hampshire and Wiltshire, especially in the river valleys. It has spread from the west country down from Gloucestershire, and may have been helped along by the many lost domestic **Ferrets**, which are mainly descendants of the eastern variety *Mustela eversmanii*. Many hybrids are found, but the western genes seem to be dominant, with dark pelaged animals seeming to override the lighter forms. Can be found throughout the county, even on the edge of Bournemouth and Poole. Unfortunately this animal is very prone to road deaths which constantly hold back its true potential.

American mink, *Mustela lutriola*. Much bad press has given this poor creature an undeserved reputation. It is a shame, as this animal is not much different from the stoat or polecat in its hunting and general habits. It is adapted to a semi-aquatic existence so fits in between the otter and the polecat, taking all the same species as them, including water voles. Water voles had not adapted to avoid mink attacks, so were hit hard at a time when their numbers were down because of pollutants in the waterways. Many animals and birds prey on water voles to a greater extent than mink, so mink can hardly be totally blamed. Mink were used as fur-bearing animals during the 1950s and 1960s and escaped, finding a vacant niche which they exploited. During the 1980s mink reached high populations everywhere including the River Stour. Water voles were also very common, and did not seem to be under great pressure from the predator. Mink have large territories and only number a few animals within an area of waterway, yet voles can number hundreds with typical rodent-style birth rates. Herons actually take more voles than mink do, and voles are the better swimmers and divers. However, eradication programmes have been going on for some time, and to date have halved the numbers. This, along with competition from both polecats and otters, has made them uncommon in many areas, and possibly eliminated. Europe has its own species of mink, which is very similar, but very rare. It may have lived in Britain when we were joined to Europe. The American mink is the same size as the western polecat, often a little smaller and of slightly lighter build.

Stoat, *Mustela erminea*. Fortunately this animal never suffered the decrease rate that its fellows did, and although heavily persecuted, its predatory inclinations were not thought as serious, preying mainly on rabbits and rats, but also game birds. These small animals, up to 30 cm long including the tail, were slaughtered in their millions, but did not have such an impact in non-game rearing areas. The animal is fast and hard to see. An extremely agile creature it can climb, swim, and run faster than a rabbit. It has been seen in the middle of Bournemouth and on the cliffs.

Weasel, *Mustela nivalis*. Being smaller than the stoat, the little weasel is even more likely to escape the gun and trap; it is helped by not being considered much threat to man's livestock. Widely distributed across Britain, it is adaptable, feeding mainly on small rodents and birds, especially mice and voles. It is adapted to enter the tunnels of these creatures, having short legs and a long body. Less agile than the stoat, it has a short tail rather than the long and bushy black-tipped tail of the former. It is more likely to inhabit suburban districts than other mustelids as long as there is sufficient cover, especially in the form of dry stone walls. Durlston Park is a good place to see them. It is much less common than it used to be, even in typical country areas of dry walled field systems, possibly due to the use of rodenticides and the drop in small farmland bird numbers. They also feed on rabbits, especially the young. The male of the species being much larger than the female is more likely to cope.

Wild Boar, *Sus scrofa*. Was eradicated a few hundred years ago, yet has made a comeback thanks to modern farming and our taste for a more natural tasting pork. The 1990s saw an increase in boar farming. Up to 180 cm long and 90 cm at the shoulder, many escaped and started free-living herds in Kent, Sussex, Devon, Dorset and Wiltshire. Still in relatively small numbers, they are often seen in our area as lone boars who have taken off from their herds near Dorchester or Cranborne Chase. One roamed through Town Common in 2004, Martin Down in 2006, and rumour says that a small herd lives in the Bransgore/Ripley area. There are mixed feelings regarding their unofficial reintroduction, but as a native their reintroduction was at least due for debate, although perhaps not in these areas. They do plough up a lot of land, but in natural forest they can only benefit the biodiversity. They are shy and non-aggressive, and will expand their range.

NATIVE CARNIVORES NO LONGER WITH US

Brown bear, *Ursus arctos*. Eradicated in Britain by the 1500s. No introductions as yet, but there is new debate on reintroducing it along with other former native mammals. It was rarely kept in captivity by private collectors and there are no reports of escaped animals in the UK.

Grey wolf, *Canis lupus*. Eradicated by the thirteenth century, no official introductions as yet, but much debate regarding the possibility in Scotland. Unofficial reports of wolves crop up from time to time, with one or two in our area. It is possible that one or two escapees from zoos or private collections have crossed our area, but that seems to be all.

Wild cat, *Felis sylvestris*. Was once common all over Britain and Ireland, then confined to Scotland, but may have survived in remote parts of south west England. There have been genuine reports from the neighbouring county of Devon (on Dartmoor, dead specimens as road victims have been officially recognised), as well as reports from Somerset and Dorset. This animal is widely kept in captivity and maybe some escapees have helped any relict wild populations.

Pine marten (mustela), *Martes martes*. It was once believed that we had two species of marten in Britain. This could have been possible, as there are two in Western Europe, with the **Beach marten**, *Martes foina*, mainly restricted to the Mediterranian and eastern areas, although in more recent times it has spread up through France and Belgium, maybe recolonising lost ground. The pine marten was always an animal of more northern areas, not being found in the more dry or arid regions. Britain was ideally suited to the pine marten, but not unsuitable for the other, yet southern England may have once had them, more likely before the last ice age. Yet there seemed to be a distinction between two types of marten here. It may have been simply area variation, which is common in martens. Also marten species can and do readily interbreed especially where different species overlap.

Again this animal was persecuted as a pest, but more importantly as a fur bearer, and was soon eradicated from most of Britain, yet it survived in remote areas of Scotland, and small areas of Wales. It hung on in Dorset to the 1920s in Cranborne Chase and may well have survived up until now. There were certainly animals observed at the end of the twentieth century in this area, but whether they were relicts or escapees from the pet trade, we do not know.

The marten is a wonderfully adapted carnivore, to an arboreal lifestyle, climbing and leaping from trees in pursuit of mammal or bird prey. Also likes fruit and insects.

There is hot debate whether or not it should be reintroduced, but as a native it surely should never have been eradicated in the first place, and it plays a vital role within the ecosystem, as all native animal and plant species do. It is slow to re-colonise areas, as it does not like crossing open ground, especially in built up areas, unlike the foul marten or polecat .

DEER, *Cervidae*

There has been much change in the variety of species and distribution of mammals, large and small, throughout the UK, and of course it affects our area, with certain species being directly involved. The main changes concern herbivores, especially deer and to a lesser extent carnivores.

In the UK, we have had only three native species of deer since the last glacial stage: Red Deer, Fallow Deer, and the Roe.

Terminology for male and female are as follows: Muntjack, Chinese Water, Roe and Fallow, are Buck and Doe respectively. Red and Sika Deer are stag and hind.

Deer grow deciduous growths of bone called antlers, which are used for display, fighting, and territorial marking. They grow as mineral rich cartilage under a blood vessel rich, velvet-like skin which is rubbed off when the antler growth is complete and the bone hardens. Antlers start off small and grow more complex with maturity, before 'going back' at old age. A pointing system operates to award commendable heads of all deer species.

Red Deer

The stags of the three larger species wallow in dug out mud pools and fray vegetation with antlers. Tree scoring is rife. Roe and Sika do the most damage. Roe to small saplings, conifers or hazel with territorial markings and Sika to larger trees with deep scoring. Red deer and Fallow ring-bark small and large trees to shed velvet or during aggressive displaying.

Fallow Deer White Buck

Fallow deer, *Dama dama*. The fallow may have become extinct many thousands of years ago, only to be re-introduced, possibly by the Normans. They were kept mainly as food in the royal forests of Blackmore and the New Forest, and later on hunting estates. They then became feral, and now live wild in the UK. In Hampshire they inhabit the New Forest as the most common species of deer; in Dorset they are widespread but localised. There are only a few known documented herds in the Cranborne Chase area, such as in Martin Down nature reserve and in an area near Wareham. There are other small roaming herds but no one knows where they originated. The Cranborne herd is thought to have been derived from the Forest of Blackmore herds in medieval times.

There are small numbers dotted around Purbeck and around the Wimborne area. The herds move about so could be found almost anywhere within the region, often mixing with the introduced sika deer.

Sika Deer, *Cervus japonicus*. The Japanese Sika were introduced to Brownsea Island around 1900. Being expert swimmers they made a bid for freedom during their first night: some were captured at a later date, but the majority survived to form a herd in Poole Harbour, and then spread to neighbouring areas. The areas of boggy heathland, river valleys, floodplains and forest were ideal, and before long Dorset had the biggest free-living herds of sika in the UK. Hyde House also had a herd along with other species of deer. These sika, a different race, escaped *c.*1920 and mingled with the original Brownsea Island herd to create a special variation, although diluted.

Sika Deer Stag

The Brownsea strain used to be far more numerous; it is seen to be different from the New Forest herds that originated from Beaulieu Abbey. As yet they have not merged, for the huge urban area of Bournemouth, Poole and Wimborne is too formidable a barrier for them to cross, while the New Forest herds are kept behind the south side of the Bournemouth–Southampton railway line. Similar in size to fallow deer, yet shorter and stockier, the sika are easy to tell apart especially if the stags are in antler, as they are more reminiscent of red deer to which they are related, and with which they can hybridise in Scotland and Europe. We do not have the same problem here: they cannot hybridise with fallow as they are a completely different species. The fallow bucks are longer in the body and have larger palmated antlers. The two also have different vocalisations and rutting habits and live in slightly differing habitats. Whilst the fallow are the most common species in the New Forest woodlands, the sika are the dominant species of the Dorset heathlands, especially around Poole Harbour and Wareham forest. They are common as far as Dorchester, so their distribution takes up the whole area of the map west of a line drawn directly north–south from

Upton. The herds comprise several thousand animals, and are growing all the time, despite heavy control by official management and poaching. Road casualties and predation by carnivores also take their toll. A medium to large deer, their summer coat is foxy-red back on grey brown with varying amounts of light spotting. Winter colour is grey or dark brown with no spots. White animals are common, as are very dark ones. Stags sport a shallow mane with long neck hair with very thick fat laden neck skin. A diagnostic sika trait is an oval light patch just below the rear of the hind knee, and a heart shaped target(hind area around the tail). The Sika of the New Forest are renowned for their larger antlers, and often have more than four points (tines) per antler; also varying colour morphs are far less common. They have been subject to much study by the British Deer Society as well as by Bournemouth University, which proved via modern genetics that there has been no hybridisation with the local red deer.

Red deer, *Cervus elaphus.* The red deer on the other hand has had a rather turbulent history, as it almost became extinct at least twice in the last four hundred years, and has had to be restocked with park specimens from Warnham, from Surrey and with continental animals from France.

At that time the forest was larger and there was no obvious dividing line between it and what is now the Bournemouth and Christchurch area, as it was all heath and forest and the deer would have easily colonised these areas. There were still wild red deer around Poole harbour during the early nineteenth century, and some say they survived into the twentieth. Maybe a few were around between the wars, but any animals observed after then may have originated from Charborough Park, which lies between Wimborne and Bere Regis. Even so, some red deer still manage to be seen

Red Deer Stag

occasionally around the county. The New Forest herds were saved again from extinction during the 1960's, but have not done as well as expected, possibly due to the forest being opened up to recreational pursuits and dog walking. Much disturbance has played its part in their decline and today it is worse than ever, with people viewing them at the time of rut. Today they only number a few hundred and although the Forestry Commission do their best to preserve them, there may be not much of a future for them.

Red Deer are large to very big, especially older stags which have very large dark coloured complex antlers at the crown (top). They do not vary much in pelage colour throughout the year and are generally a reddish-brown, but stronger in summer and autumn. They form large herds of separate summer stags and hinds , autumn rutting stags lone off, gain weight and fight for harems of hinds. Their call is a cow like bellow deepening with age to a lion like roar.

The only consistent wild herds are in the New forest and they are small and local. Occasional wanders may be found elsewhere outside Bournemouth or purbeck. Park herds occur in several places.

Roe deer, *Capriolus capriolus.* There are numerous roe in the New Forest, and although they originated from the area, they were hunted nearly to extinction. Any that remained were affected by the Deer Removal Act, 1851, which was associated with the growing of timber, and enclosing areas. The roe made a comeback from Dorset into the Forest after the Second World War. Roe were eradicated from most of England by the end of the eighteenth century, but may have held on in Dorset as well as west Sussex. They are not a herd deer but live in small groups of three to five on average, and they are loners for large periods of their lives. They are much smaller than other deer and spend a lot more time in thick cover, so could easily be overlooked especially in Dorset's hilly wooded landscapes. They are different from the larger deer in that, instead of growing their antlers during the summertime, they do it in the winter. The antlers of roe buck show great variation and are typical to certain areas.

The Earl of Dorchester had animals introduced to the Charborough Park near Wimborne around 1900. They were of various origins, Scottish, Dutch and maybe French, even some from Sussex perhaps. Some were of the Siberian species, which is a much larger animal with large antlers. For a while they may have interbred with some of the common roe, but were hunted out of existence within twenty years.

Roe Deer Buck (moulting)

Some of the antlers from Dorset look exactly like the prehistoric shaped antlers found in Neolithic graves. This could be evidence that the Dorset Roe never became extinct, but held on in certain remote areas. Today, the Roe can be found all across the region, and in large numbers, on all the heathland areas and farmland, even close to built up areas. Roe have even invaded our towns, and can be seen in Wimborne, Ferndown, Bournemouth and Poole, as well as Christchurch suburbs.

Roe are all too often victims of their own success and fall foul of motor traffic, dogs and poachers. They do have predators though, as native and non-native large cats now breed in the UK and in our area, a natural balance should start to become apparent.

A small to medium species, summer pelage is a rich red brown, winter coat is grey brown. Often sports light bib of varying whiteness. More common in areas of large woodlands and inter-connected meadows or serial crops. Can be found in suburban areas. A Bucks mature antler has three tines, and are much smaller than the larger deer species. They also grow and shed the antlers at different times. Antler growth prevails throughout the winter months after November casting, and fully grown and harden by May. Because Roe antlers grow during winter, this increases risk of deformities due to frost bite, wire fences, or hormonal deficiency. Leg or testicular injuries cause problems. Due to these factors, roe exhibit the most diverse of all deer antler types which are highly collectable. Roe does also benefit from delayed implantation of the fertilised blastocyst. Mating may occur from July onwards, yet the egg will not start to develop until later so that all kids are born late April or May.

Muntjack. Originally there were two species of these small deer that escaped from captivity. Most of them from Woburn park in Bedfordshire. **Chinese muntjack,** *Muntiacus reevesi,* A very small deer, fox size with dainty little feet showing tiny hoof prints of only 2–3 cm in length. The Buck has tiny antlers up to 6 cm in length, with a small branch point at front. Short haired, reddish-brown with a short flicking tail, the deer sculks in thick vegetation. They possess small tusks in the way of canine teeth. They are one of the many species of musk deer, also called barking deer, and their sound can be mistaken for a dog.

In our area, they have only just managed to colonise the area west of the New Forest, around Poole and north to Wimborne, from the Ferndown areas of heathland. Matchams, Avon valley Ringwood and of course the forest itself which has larger numbers, not like the midland populations. Its small size and sculking habits enable it to pass through town gardens unobserved.

LARGE CATS

There have been reports of alleged large cats across the UK for several decades at least. In fact they go back hundreds of years, but within the last forty years, they have been continuous. The Romans were first to import exotic animals and much later, in the early nineteenth century, circuses and travelling menageries abounded with no rules or regulations. Large cats were especially adept at escaping and when they did, they were rarely recaptured. Over a hundred or so years of cat keeping, especially the exotic 'big cats', many escapees have easily eked out a living in our green and pleasant land that is teeming with wild and domestic animals. As the number of escaped commonly kept species such as puma and leopard increased, viable breeding occurred. There may have been hybridisation taking place, but we do not know for sure with this topic still under-researched. What we do know is that genuine leopard and puma do live and breed in our countryside and have done for many generations.

Hundreds of people have kept large cats in captivity since the 1950s. American air bases often had pumas as mascots; in the 1960s it was fashionable for celebrities to have them; in the 1970s it was fashionable for the drugs and arms barons to keep black panthers and a whole host of in-between cats were kept by zoos, wildlife parks or just in small private collections. In 1976 the Dangerous Wild Animals Act came into force which meant stiffer penalties for inadequate pens or housing and high-priced licencing and also involved keepers being vetted. This was obviously good, but many keepers decided to free their animals. Some have openly admitted to doing so. This may be one of many reasons why we now have escaped and freed cats living alongside all the other non-native animals in the UK.

Non-natives

Jaguar, *Panthera ounce*. These cats were hard to obtain but a small number of collectors kept them during the 1970s. The black or melanistic colours were preferred as was the leopard, which is why so many of the big cats seen are black. There may have been some escapees but it is not known if enough have been able to breed. The animal looks similar in appearance to the leopard, so it cannot be ruled out.

Puma, *Felis concolor*. Reports of these animals in the New Forest go back to the 1920s at least. They were few and far between then, now they have been seen on a regular basis since the 1960s as reports gathered momentum, similar to the Dartmoor and Exmoor 'beasts', but since 2000, there are many reports each year. With so much natural prey in the form of deer, rabbits, rats, fish and birds the Forest is ideal for them. In Dorset, reports go back to the 1970s, but perhaps the gap would suggest un-colonised territory with surplus animals from either Dartmoor, Surrey and Sussex. Puma have been breeding in the county at least since the early 1980s with my own sighting near Cranborne Chase of three cubs in 1984. Since then I have seen cubs in Purbeck once. These animals have large areas to beat, so they can appear and disappear every month or so depending on whether they are male, juvenile or a mother with cubs. They may come in and out of our area.

Common leopard, *Panthera pardus*. The common leopard was a pre ice age native of the UK and was once common all across the old world, making it the most successful of the large cats along with the puma of the Americas. Although we did have a puma-like animal far back in the continent's history, the nearest species is the cheetah or golden cat. The leopard lived in the UK when we were joined to mainland Europe but there is no real reason why a cold-acclimatised race could not have lived on into modern times. The species has many variants or even subspecies and is the most adaptable large cat on earth. Its ancestors in the new world became the jaguar, its ancestors in high cold climes became the snow leopard. It is truly a remarkable animal, and is more adapted to cooler temperatures. That is why it is doing so well here in the UK. It is our most common large cat to date, and in our area we can boast possibly the highest density anywhere in the UK. There are hundreds of reports each year from Purbeck and the New Forest, of big black, long slinky, shiny cats with long tails curled up at the ends. From hair I have analysed along with kill remains, droppings, cacheing in trees, footprints and my own sightings of the animals several times – including cubs twice in the area it would seem that they are certainly *Panthera pardus* and they are breeding and doing well, keeping down the huge numbers of wild deer as well as rabbits and foxes, wild fowl and the few farm animals.

Northern lynx, *Felis lynx*. Reports are mainly in west Dorset and Somerset, but Cranborne

Chase has had sightings since 2005 and I have gathered evidence from around Martin Down. In the New Forest, there are more sightings by keepers and foresters. Hair and faeces have been collected by myself and others. I have had a sighting in Oxlease Woods near Lyndhurst. Reports come closer to home with lynx-like animals seen just outside Bournemouth and Ringwood, but these animals seemed to be half tame and did not behave in a true wild manner so may result from a non-official release programme, which has been suspected since 2000, in the South West regions and in Scotland.

Lynx Footprint

Also believed to exist in a wild state are: **Ocelot**, *Felis pardalis*, a small to medium heavily marked cat. **Asian Golden Cat**, *Felis temminckii*, uniform to spotted, small to medium sized. **Jungle Cat**, *Felis chaus*, a small sized short tailed greyish cat with stripes. **Asian Leopard Cat**, *Felis bengalensis*, a small sized heavily spotted cat. The last two species have been designer bred with domestic cats, so hybrids occur.

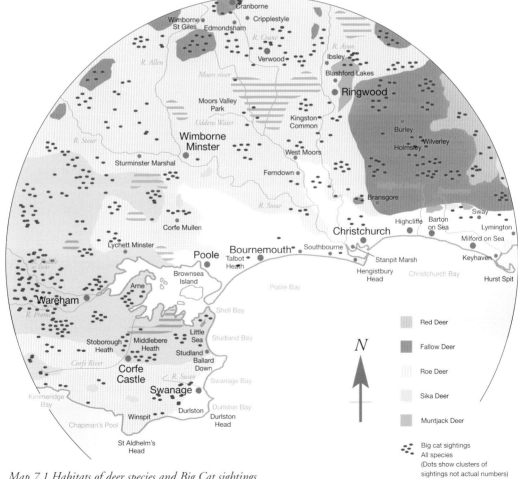

Map 7.1 Habitats of deer species and Big Cat sightings

8 Marine

Mary Thornton & Jonathan McGowan

From the sandstones and clays of Hengistbury Head to the chalk stacks of Old Harry there is the wide sandy beach of Bournemouth Bay, supporting a limited fauna and flora but dominated by **Man**, *Homo sapiens,* following a plethora of pleasure pursuits. Round the corner from Durlston Head and travelling westwards is a wonderful profusion and diversity of rocky habitats supporting a wide variety of marine fauna and flora. This is where the first UK underwater nature trail was established at Worbarrow Tout. From the Kimmeridge Ledges and on land westwards to Lyme Regis are a multitude of fossils and dinosaur footprints which have led to the recognition of the Triassic/Jurassic/Cretaceous coastline as worthy of World Heritage Status. The narrow entrance to Poole Harbour

Kimmeridge Bay Underwater ledges

belies the one hundred miles of harbour coastline where competing demands of man and his activities fight against the quiet and undisturbed requirements of the wildlife on nature reserves. Wild flowers, rare insects, natural amphibians, flocks of resident and migrating birds and even large mammals are all to be found in the southern reaches of the land adjacent to Poole Harbour. Their proximity to such a large conurbation of human residency is to be marvelled at and the competing demands of all are held in balance only through a variety of cooperating public bodies.

UNDERWATER AT KIMMERIDGE

A first glance underwater reveals a gently swaying mass of coloured seaweeds; browns, red and green with an occasional bright iridescent gleam of turquoise. Cruising as a snorkeller, one can see Anemones with their tentacles wafting in the swell trapping passing food, Hermit Crabs running after prey or the beautiful **Velvet Swimming Crab**, *Necora puber*, looking for shelter. In slightly deeper water it is common to see a **Ballan Wrasse**, *Labrus bergylta,* snoozing amongst the seaweeds or glimpse a darting blenny as it moves from one hideout to another.

Ballan Wrasse

Bladder wrack

Green Lettuce

Coral Weed

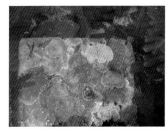

Lithothamnion and Lithophyllum
spp

Laminaria hyperborea

As an air-breathing human walking across the beach at low tide, one first spies the Brown Wracks, which are all able to withstand varying degrees of desiccation. As the tide recedes the temperature can vary from 28/30°C on a hot summer's afternoon to −3/− 4°C on a freezing winter morning. **Channelled Wrack**, *Pelvetia canaliculata,* is the brown seaweed at the top of the beach, and is able to withstand up to ten hours of dry fronds: **Spiral Wrack**, *Fucus spiralis,* **Bladder Wrack**, *F. vesiculosus* and **Toothed Wrack**, *F. serratus,* the larger brown seaweeds are found further down the shore as one moves towards the sea. Interspersed amongst the browns are the **Green Lettuce**, *Ulva lactuca,* the long cords of **Thongweed**, *Himanthalia elongata,* and a host of different red algae. In winter the purply brown fronds of **Purple Laver**, *Porphyra umbilicalis,* can be spied drying on exposed rocks close to the high tide mark, favoured by some to be picked and made into a gelatinous mush with oats as laverbread for breakfast. The abundant slightly gritty branching fronds of **Coral Weed**, *Corallina officinalis* and the pretty red *Polysiphonia lanosa* are abundant at all times of the year. Attached to the rock and looking like pink rock or pink paint are the calcareous flat thalli of *Lithothamnion* and *Lithophyllum.*

Further in to deeper water and only somewhat visible at low tide are the huge fronds of **Kelp** or **Oarweed**, *Laminaria digitata,* and **Tangle** or **Cuvie**, *L. hyperborea,* with an occasional long ruffled plume of **Sugar Kelp**, *L. saccharina.* These are all big flat brown fronds holding onto the rock by large holdfasts which can look like the branching roots of overland plants. Locally known as Furbelows with a great bulbous hollow holdfast is the *Saccorhiza polychides.* The iridescent turquoise seaweed is **Rainbow Wrack**, *Cystoseira tamariscifolia,* a dull brown out of water but not to be missed underwater.

Only to be seen in summer are the beautiful brown fans of the **Peacock Fan**, *Padina pavonica,* interspersed with the fat thick green fingers of **Green Sea Fingers**, *Codium fragile subsp tomentosoides,* an introduced Pacific species. The native species *C. tomentosum* which seems to have been largely displaced by the above can be found under Hen Cliff.

Also in deeper water are the long whip-like strands of **Sea Lace**, *Chorda filum.*

One of the first things to be seen on the beach as the tide recedes are small red brown blobs of jelly, these are the **Beadlet Anemone**, *Actinia aquina,* which curls up with a tiny amount of water

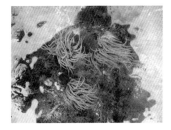

Snakelocks anemone

Beadlet anemone

Green Sea Fingers

Dogwhelk

Star Sea Squirts

Sea Slugs

inside to last while the tide is out. Also to be seen are the pink tipped green of the **Snakelocks Anemone**, *Anemonia viridis*, a slightly more aggressive anemone, which feels sticky to the touch. Hiding in the sand at the bottom of a rockpool will be the shy **Daisy Anemone**, *Cereus pedunculatus*, which closes up as soon as disturbed.

At Kimmeridge there are at least 100 species of alga, some always present others more sparse and occasional in their appearance, as Kimmeridge is halfway up the English Channel some western clean water species can survive here.

Limpets, Winkles, Dog Whelks can all be seen on the midshore rocks. In the rockpools tiny fish and shrimps can be found. Very sharp eyes might see a tiny spidery Brittle Star, or very occasionally a Starfish. The most common little fishes trapped in rockpools as the tide recedes are Blennies and Gobies. Crabs are a good place for the beginner naturalist to start differentiating between species. At least five species of crab will be observable to the most untrained eye, including the Broad-clawed Porcelain Crab, the Velvet Swimming Crab, the Edible Crab and the Hairy Crab. The distinctive pointed carapace of a small, elongated crab is really the shell of a **Squat Lobster**, *Galathea intermedia*, The majority of the tiny crabs and larger adults are the **Common Crab**, *Carcinus maenas,* and the **Hermit Crabs**, *Pagurus bernhardus,* often handled by youngsters in the summer as the first introduction to marine life. The Hermit Crabs are soft bodied and will inhabit an empty snail shell, most commonly those of the **Periwinkle**, *Littorina spp* or **Dogwhelk**, *Nucella lapillus*.

For the conchologist the seashore is a treasure trove with a multitude of pretty shells to look for. At least four different species of Periwinkle can be found, including the pretty coloured **Flat Periwinkle**, *L. obtusata*, the rough to the touch explaining its name, **Rough Periwinkle**, *L. saxatilis*, the small tiny grey **Melaraphe**, *L. neritoides* found only up in the splash zone and the larger fat grey **Edible Periwinkle**, *L. littorea*. The **Common limpet**, *Patella vulgata*, adheres closely to the rock by suction of its muscular foot, and even if it roams will return home to its patch where it can ensure a tight fit. Sometimes one can see radial scratch marks on the rock close by where the radula or scraping mouth parts of the limpet have grazed on the slimy layer of algae attached to the rock.

The first rule of the naturalist is to put back any plant, animal or habitat where it is found. On turning over a rock it is common to find patches of beige or orange or even blue. On inspection these are found to be **Star Sea Squirts**, *Botryllus schlosseri*, a colonial **tunicate** which is flattened against the rock. They are characterised by two vents, one taking water in and the other expelling water after the animal has sifted the water for particles of food.

The insignificant patches of brown and occasionally yellow/orange are Sponges or Bryozoans, also colonial animals which live by siphoning sea water. A more unusual find might be the **Common Sea Slug**, *Aeolidia papillosa*, which is able to nip off the darting stinging cells and tentacles from an anemone and ingest them and then grow them out of its own skin, thereby conveying protection to itself and looking as if it is inhabiting a fur coat. A very rare find and hard

Broad Clawed Porcelain Crab

Common Blenny

Tompot Blenny

to spot would be the 0.5–1.0 cm long **Sea Slug** called *Aeolidiella alderi* which has a characteristic white ruff around its neck.

All the star sea squirts and sponges are sessile. Darting across one's vision in a rockpool might be the small grey sometimes sandy-coloured laterally flattened Gammarid Shrimps. They swim on their sides in jerky pincer movements. The larger transparent grey forms of the **Common shrimp** are *Crangon crangon*, recognisable by long wiry antennae.

A rare species of **Snapping Prawn**, *Alpheus macrocheles,* can be found here, looking orange-red like a small two-inch lobster with huge pincers which when disturbed can snap its claws. Somehow their pincer is adapted to produce a burst of pressure which can be heard as a snap to the human ear but which is used to stun its prey.

Further out in deeper water and always covered by the tide one might see the **Spiny Squat Lobster**, *Galathea squamifera,* with its abdomen tucked tightly underneath but only 5–6 cm long. The **Edible Lobster**, *Homarus gammarus,* 23 cm minimum to land when caught, is a blue purple colour in the water and hides under rocks or in crevices. The **Edible Crab**, *Cancer pagurus,* is a beautiful purple with pink round the edges of its carapace. Much smaller and a sandy brown colour is the **Broad Clawed Porcelain Crab**, *Porcellana platycheles.* This crab is covered with a mass of tiny hairs looking like a furry swimmer. The keen eyed observer will soon find a number of different species of crab, varying between green, brown and purple, sized anything from minute to 18 cm across. In the more undisturbed parts of the sandy bottom there are Fan Worms.

Sometimes a tiny fish will be trapped in a rockpool as the tide goes out and this might be one of the blennies, a **Common Blenny**, *Lipophrys pholis*, or **Tompot Blenny**, *Parablennius gattorugine.* Generally common blenny colouration is greenish and the rock goby brownish. The **Rock Goby**, *Gobius paganellus*, can be dark black especially when guarding eggs.

A more adventurous swimmer and diver going into deeper water will be sure to see shoals of Sand Eels, tiny fish being hunted by the larger species of Pollock, Grey Mullet, maybe even a Sea Bass. There are numerous species of ray in the southern waters off Dorset namely the **Blonde**, **Spotted** and **Thornback**,

Rock Goby

Pouting and Pollock

Raja clavata, their egg sacs known as mermaids' purses can be found when walking the strand line at the top of the beach.

An observant diver might see Squid free-swimming in the water and sticking out from under a rock the nose of a Conger Eel. As the water warms up in spring and summer and there are masses of eggs, gametes and young of both plant and animal life swilling about in the water, this brings the heavy feeders such as Mackerel seeking food. They in turn draw larger mammals such as the Bottlenose Dolphin and Seals.

MARINE FISHES

The English Channel is semi-sheltered being a smaller body of water compared to the Atlantic side of the UK or the North Sea, consequently a slightly different fauna can be expected. Our area is just south west of the main body of Britain so we have a westerly influence, although our tides are easterly born. We are mainly influenced by Atlantic animals, and of course the Gulf Stream has great importance. Varying habitats are a feature of the region, ranging from sandy shores to deep-water rocky reefs to muddy harbours and weedy estuaries, thus providing a very diverse ecology. Being so close to the Mediterranean we are also influenced by that sea and some of its life forms. With changing weather patterns and slightly warmer waters we are acquiring many species of fish and other fauna not found here in the recent past.

The main areas of Poole Bay are sandy, with shallow silty areas of harbour on both sides. Very small amounts of rock exist, but large areas of gravel or shingle occur off shore, and around the harbour mouths. Sandy shores are home to both bottom-dwelling and surface-feeding species many of which are nomadic, travel seasonably or with the currents. Various ship wrecks offshore provide a form of midway haven for both resident and nomadic species. There is much change between the summer and winter species.

Flatfish

Flounder, *Platichthys flesus.* Mentioned in freshwater fishes, the flounder is a harbour species, rarely living in the open sea, but happy to live in the harbour mouth with its muddy bottom. Often moving around areas, this is the most common flatfish in the region. It is a dull blotched brown without red spotting like the plaice and ovoid in shape with a white underside.

Dab, *Limanda limanda.* Very similar to the flounder, this fish does inhabit the deeper offshore waters especially in winter, it has more rough scales on the upper edge and more cryptic markings. It can be seen around Hurst Spit and Hengistbury, and all along the Barton and Highcliffe areas.

Plaice, *Pleuronectes platessa.* A similar species to the two previous, but will grow larger and is characterised by the large red, orange or blue spots on its surface. Plaice live in deeper waters during the winter, as do most of our resident species. Very much over-fished, numbers have depleted drastically, although in our area numbers are still apparently reasonable, with several sheltered areas acting as a buffer zone from trawlers.

Sole, *Solea sp.* The three species are not thought to be common in Poole Bay, but off Lymington there are larger numbers as the east of the Channel and North Sea is their favoured area. The sole is a chunky but elongate fish inhabiting the sandy bottom.

Turbot, *Psetta maxima.* This is a large rounded flatfish, mottled brown on top and weighing up to 14 kg offshore. They are common in the bay often very close inshore, particularly during late summer and autumn; they can be caught on rod and line from the Bournemouth piers up to seven kgs in weight. Larger specimens of 14 or more kilogrammes in weight can be caught offshore. Its cousin the **Brill**, *Scophthalmus rhombus,* is very similar with knobbles behind its gills and lives alongside the Turbot; they may hybridise.

Other distinct forms of flattened fish are of course the Rays of the order *Rajiformes,* which unlike the previous *Osteichtyes* or bony fishes, have skeletons made of cartilage like the sharks, class *Chondrichthyes*. The egg cases of the Ray are known as mermaid's purses and are similar to those of small sharks.

Thornback Ray, *Raja clavata*. Common in the Poole Bay and around the area, a large species, as all the rays are, capable of reaching up to 13 kg. Triangular in shape with modified wing-like fins and shark-like gills and long tails. The thornback breeds in the bay and during summer many tiny individuals can be seen or caught by anglers along Boscombe and Southbourne beaches, Studland bay is a good area. Rays are basically nocturnal and especially this species. It has thorny spines along its spine and tail.

Undulate Ray, *Raja undulata*, **Small Eyed Ray**, *Raja microcellata,* and **Blond Ray**, *Raja brachyura,* are beautifully marked animals all of which live in the bay but mainly offshore, often entering shallower water by night.

Common skate, *Raja batis (Dipturis batis)*. These are far less common but can be seen off Bournemouth, even from the pier in springtime. Two huge, doorsized specimens slowly cruised under Boscombe pier during the late 1990s.

These species depend a lot on **Sandeels**, *Ammodytes tobianas,* (**lesser**) and *Hyperoplus lanceolatus* (**greater**) as do most other sea fish and of course sea birds. These fish shoal en masse and bury themselves in the sand. They can be seen on calm days hugging the shore line swimming under piers or even near the beach, the smaller ones hug the edges more closely. Being the bottom of the food chain, they are followed by nomadic surface-feeding species such as **Mackerel**, *Scomber scombrus*, which also shoal en masse and in calm water come into the bay to feed, generally at two distinct times, early morning and evening. They sweep in with the tides and can be seen sometimes from Bournemouth beach. The temperature of the fish is warmer than the surrounding water and they feel warm to the touch. They need to be warm blooded as they are very fast swimmers always on the move. Mackerel are members of the Tunny family, Scombridae, which all share this similarity. They all also have some dark red flesh more similar to that of mammals or birds, and higher in proteins and oils. These in turn bring along other predators such as bottlenose dolphins and harbour porpoises and a few gannets.

Bass, *Dicentrarchus labrax*. Bass feed on mackerel and other fish, inshore bass will feed on shellfish, crabs, marine worms and small fish. They patrol in large groups as young but in smaller assemblies as they mature. Sadly we rarely find fish larger than 2.5 kg in weight in the area although they are capable of reaching 9 kg. Commercial fisheries have been to blame for that. We do have a Bass nursery area in Poole Harbour where one cannot fish for them; this is vital for annual restocking.

Garfish, *Belone belone*. A summer-arriving species along with the mackerel, being **pelagic** feeders. They have long bodies and a long tooth filled beak and are renowned for their bright green coloured bones. They can be seen from the piers leaping in calm waters or even from the beaches when sand eels are abundant.

Gurnard, *Triglidae*, are fish of the sea bed especially sandy bottoms and Poole Bay has three species living in it, **Tub gurnard**, *Trigla lucerna*, **Grey gurnard**, *Eutrigla gurnadus* and **Red gurnard**, *Aspitrigla cuculus.*

These large headed fish have large pectoral fins often vividly coloured with modified spines, three on each side, that act like legs. They trundle around on the sea floor stirring the sediment with the spines and eating small fish, worms and crustaceans.

Weever Fish, *Trachinus draco* (**greater**), *Echiichthys vipera* (**lesser**). These are two well known small fishes that inhabit the sandy shallows. They are renowned for their very toxic venom which is delivered by way of a spine on the dorsal fin when trodden on. The animal looks like a Goby and buries itself in the sand to trap its prey, shrimps and small fish. Bathers must beware as its sting is extremely painful and dangerous. The **lesser**, only 10 cm long, is more common on our shoreline, the **greater**, up to 1 kg is more southerly and requires deeper water. If stung professional advice should be sought.

Cod Family, **Gadidae**. These are fish of deeper more rocky areas of the Heritage Coast between Swanage and the Kimmeridge Ledges which are well known for their large specimens of the following species: **Cod**, *Gadus morhua*, **Pollack**, *Pollachius pollachius*, **Coalfish**, *Pollachius virens*. All three also inhabit shipwrecks further out and are capable of growing to respectable weights of over 13 kg.

Haddock, *Melanogrammus aeglefinus*, is very much over-fished like the cod and big shoals are constantly targeted by commercial fishers. **Hake**, *Merluccius merluccius*, like the cod is over fished, and in big risk of becoming extinct in the near future. **Ling**, *Molva molva*, is a large elongated pollack type fish of deep rocky outcrops. **Whiting**, *Merlangius merlangus*, is an inshore fish preferring muddy or gravel sea floors that are not deep. **Bib** or **Pouting**, *Trisopterus luscus*, a small fish 25–30 cm long preferring sand and rocky floors, forms shoals.

Conger eel, *Conger conger*. Also in these rocky areas of the Heritage Coast the conger can grow to nearly 45 kg in weight and is targeted along with the *Gadidae* family by sports fishermen who supply much of the known information. The conger is very different from the river eel, the silver version can be found in the area, and has different habits. Small juveniles can be encountered in Poole Bay, sheltering in rocks and crevices during the day and hunting fish, crustaceans and cephalopods at night.

Horse Mackerel or **Scad**, *Trachurus trachurus*. Similar to the roving common type but plain silver with a black blotch behind the gill and spines along its flanks. It is a resident of piers and rocky areas. One of the more recent colonizers of warmer waters it has become very numerous in the last two decades; not targeted by British commercial fishing its numbers are stable. It can be seen around the piers at night.

The mackerel family, Scombridae, includes the Tuna fish. Very rarely do we have records of them in our area, but a **Bluefin Tunny**, *Thunnus thynnus*, was caught locally some time ago although they are not common here and are a deeper water fish.

Brown triggerfish, *Balistes carolinensis* (now *capriscus*). These are now commonplace, shoaling around Poole Bay and around all the piers including Swanage. They have long faces with small eyes and small mouths lined with hard plate-like teeth for crunching up corals, shellfish and crustaceans.

Black sea bream, *Spondyliosoma cantharus*. A pretty little rounded fish and is common throughout the region along with the **Red sea bream**, *Pagellus bogaraveo*. *Spondyliosoma cantharus* migrates in early summer from the Mediterranean.

Blennies, *Lipophrys pholis*, and **Gobies**, *Gobius sp.*, are common little fishes of rocky shorelines some of which live in rock pools. They are the most likely small fish to be encountered anywhere along the Heritage Coast. They are bottom dwelling and can breathe out of water for a short time. They have huge jaws and large facial muscles, with very sharp plate-like teeth. They eat shellfish and crustaceans.

Dragonet, *Callionymus lyra*. Similar to weever fishes and gobies but more elongated with a very long upright dorsal fin in the male. It is a **benthic** fish.

Monkfish or **Angelshark**, *Squatina squatina*. This fish is somewhere in between a shark and a ray, and comes inshore for the summer. It is caught as a by-product commercially, yet only a small part of the fish can be eaten. This fishing is threatening the population causing the monkfish to be declared extinct form North Sea and extremely uncommon elsewhere.

The **Anglerfish**, *Lophius piscatorius*. Also sometimes called a monkfish, is common as a cryptically marked, flattened fish of sandy bottoms. It lures other fish by waving a tentacle-like appendage above its head to mimic worms. It has a huge head and mouth and can engulf large marine animals.

Wrasse

Some of the most colourful of our rock dwelling fish are Wrasse, *Labridae*. There are half a dozen species but mainly three in our area.

The Ballan, *Labrus bergylta*. This is the most common and is a chunky animal of subtle browns, greens, blues and reds with speckles. It has a habit of hanging in the water around sea weeds and rocks waiting for prawns, shrimps and crabs.

Corkwing, *Crenilabrus melops*. Smaller with a dark spot near its tail and is westerly distributed, just reaching into our region.

Cuckoo Wrasse, *Labrus mixtus*. This beautiful fish can be electric blue, but is not common here although it can be found around Purbeck, usually in deeper water but common around patch reefs in Poole Harbour.

Corkwing Wrasse

Pipefish, *Syngnathidae*

These are related to sea horses and we have six within our region.

Great Pipefish, *Sygnathus acus*. This is the largest and is common around our sandy shores. It is long and thin and its body does not have scales but a number of bony ridges. It has the typical long jawless snout of sea horses and lives on tiny planktonic creatures. The male is responsible for the development of the young which it keeps in a stomach pouch. Pipefish are dependant on eelgrass beds, in which they disguise themselves. They are sometimes washed ashore along Bournemouth beach during storms.

Sharks, *Chondrichtyes* (cartilaginous fish)

There are up to twenty species of shark that inhabit waters around the UK. As many of them are southerly distributed and are pelagic, we get most of them in our area. Not all sharks are swimmers of open water, but are bottom dwelling like the rays, and many species are small.

Dogfish, Lesser Spotted, *Scyliorhinus canicula*. One of our smallest sharks (around 60 cm long) and very common, it is called rock salmon in the food trade. It has eye lids and can close its eyes. Its skin, like all sharks is made up not of scales, but tiny hooks and has been used as a sand paper alternative or as shagreen as a decorative covering for little boxes and sword handles. Dogfish have a light base colour with many minute dark spots. They like an open, sandy or gravel bottom so are common in Poole Bay and all along the south coast near the shore. Their egg cases are commonly found along the beaches after storms, especially between Bournemouth pier and Southbourne.

The Greater Spotted, **Nursehound** or **Bull Huss**, *Scyliorbinus stellaris*. Very similar to the dogfish but grows larger and prefers rocky areas of seabed with more weed. It is very common around Purbeck.

Smooth hound, *Mustelus mustelus*. This species is viviparous, has no spots and grows larger than the two previous species living further out in deeper water but along the sandy parts of the bay, whilst the **Starry Smoothhound**, *M. asterius*, has a sprinkling of white dots along body. This one lays eggs.

Spurdog, *Squalus acanthias*. A common shoaling species, used commercially as rock eel. It has a venomous spine by the dorsal fin. It is blue grey in colour with large white spots on top.

Tope, *Galeorhinus galeus*. This is larger than the previous species and is more typically shark-like in its appearance and is not strictly a bottom dweller. It also grows much larger, up to 2 m in length. A graceful sensitive animal much sought after by anglers unfortunately. It is still common though, but mainly in western southern England, so it is not very common along our stretch of coastline. Very occasionally they can be seen from Bournemouth or Boscombe piers in very hot weather following horse mackerel or small flatfish towards the shore.

Blue shark, *Prionace glauca*. A very fast and graceful animal often referred to as the greyhound of the sea. It is a summer visitor from warmer waters and follows the mackerel and sardines. Preferring the deeper water off shore it only enters the shallow waters of Poole Bay or the Solent in very warm weather. It grows to 7 m long and is steel blue in colour.

Porbeagle, *Lamna nasus*. A fish of cooler waters and lives in the Northern Atlantic. They follow the mackerel and herring or live as a territorial fish feeding on pollock and similar cod-like fish off Purbeck. They have large eyes for murky water living and are nocturnal feeders. They average 2 m in length but are very deep in the body.

Mako, *Isurus oxirinchus*. A large and fast-swimming pelagic shark, migrating to the Northern Atlantic in summer. It is rarely encountered in Poole Bay or Purbeck except in the deeper waters offshore. It is similar in size and appearance to previous species.

Both the two mackerel sharks bear live young.

Thresher sharks, *Alopias vulpinus*. They may be seen in Poole Bay but rarely, or off Purbeck following mackerel, they have huge long tail fins.

Basking sharks, *Cetorhinus maximus*. They can be seen in our region, but rarely. They have been seen after weeks of calm seas around the end of May or the beginning of June in Studland Bay and further round in Poole Bay and towards the Isle of Wight. This fish is huge and feeds only on plankton.

POOLE HARBOUR

Poole Harbour represents in microcosm coastal zone issues of the developed world. Contrasting and conflicting pressures on the harbour are startling. The harbour entrance is 370 m wide, separating the south west unspoilt protected natural environment and reserves of considerable importance, the Studland National Trust nature reserve, from a residential centre on the north east where property competes in world-wide league tables of real estate values.

Poole Harbour is a huge lowland estuary covering 3,600 hectares with one hundred miles of inland coastline. Because of the double high tide only 22 per cent of water is flushed at neap tides and 45 per cent at spring high tides. But a large area of 80 per cent is in the intertidal zone. Where freshwater enters at the eastern end by the rivers Piddle and Frome there is less salinity in contrast to the western end of the Harbour at Haven Channel.

THE 'DOUBLE TIDES' BY H. ST. BARBE (from 1914 book)

The contour of the Hampshire and adjoining coasts, with their numerous large and ramifying inlets of the sea, flanked by the lozenge-shaped mass of the Isle of Wight, gives rise to a peculiar natural phenomenon which can be observed any day in Bournemouth Bay, though more distinctly in the Solent and in Poole Harbour. This is known as the 'double tides' and its chief feature as the 'second high-water'. The ordinary rhythmic ebb and flow of the tides is subject along these coasts to a remarkable and constant variation. High-water occurs at its normal time; but after the ebb has commenced its fall is arrested and the tide again rises, usually to a greater height than before, and the whole of the ebb is thereafter carried out in a necessarily much restricted period.

A brief account, which must not be taken to be exhaustive, may serve to give some grasp of this local feature. It must first be understood that currents set up by the rising or falling tide near an indented coast-line are not uniform in strength or direction. It is not at all unusual to observe two currents, referable to one and the same cause, flowing in diametrically opposite directions in close proximity with no intervening spit or shoal.

The Channel flood sets in from the westward and makes high tide progressively towards the east. Its progress eastward is gradually arrested by its meeting with a *previous* flood tide which has worked down the North Sea and through the Straits of Dover. The position of the 'node' or meeting and parting places of these tides varies throughout the lunar month and according to the direction of the wind, but may be placed generally off Bexhill, on the Sussex coast.

Before the high tide has reached its maximum in this direction the ebb has run out to the westward and low tide is advancing rapidly up the Channel, so that a stage is reached when high and low tide points approach within forty to fifty miles of each other. The tide will be high at St. Catherine's Point and low at Portland Bill. About midway between these places, therefore, there occurs a 'node' of a second order, a *fulcrum* as it were, and it is evident that an unstable condition of things is set up, giving rise to great stresses.

One result of this is the *sucking out* of a westward going current in the Solent and past the Needles, earlier than the turning of the main Channel tide off-shore. This is the first ebb along this coast.

Before this Solent ebb has commenced, the flood tide eastward through the Solent has combined with the flood tide working round outside the Isle of Wight, and penned up the tide in all the great harbours from Southampton to Chichester, along with their not inconsiderable supplies of river water.

The pressure continues until relief is obtained by the falling away of the main tide outside the Isle of Wight and westward. The first effect is the escape westward by the Solent of all the pent-up flood in Portsmouth and Southampton and the adjoining part of the Solent. This *heap* of water then follows the first ebb westward, and causes a *second* rise of tide along the whole coast. As the normal high and low tides proceed progressively eastward whilst this false tide runs in the opposite direction, the interval between the two high tides becomes longer as the effect is traced westward. At Lymington it is less than two hours, at Christchurch two and a half, and at Poole three and a half hours. The influence is still felt in decreasing amount as far west as in Weymouth Bay. Here the slight rise is felt so long after high water as to coincide with the following low water, and it conse¬quently creates a double or divided *low* tide, known as the Guider.

The effects are enhanced and complicated in Bournemouth and Poole Bay by the westerly-going ebb-stream in the Channel. This, after rounding St. Catherine's Point, sets in a north-westerly direction along the Island coast and past the Needles, and being confined to some extent by the reefs at Peverel Point and Durlston Head, off Swanage, tends again to raise the water in Poole Bay. The results at Poole become very complicated. At one period of the tide it is possible to see a strong indrift on one side of the narrow entrance to the harbour and an equally strong outrush on the other. At Bournemouth the double tide may be converted into a simple prolongation of the high tide for as much as four hours, the succeeding ebb being all accomplished in the remaining two hours of its allotted period. At full and new moon, and for a day or two following, this often results in holding a brimming tide along Bournemouth beach during the whole of the morning and midday hours.

John Humphreys and Vincent May writing in *The Ecology of Poole Harbour* (2005) have collated a scholarly work incorporating a number of research projects. The interested naturalist is advised to read directly from this work for the scientific detail. A longboat dating from the Iron Age, now in Poole Museum shows the harbour has long been used as a trading port. The old town of Poole was built on the trading of cod from fisheries off Newfoundland reaching a peak of trading in the 1800s. Consequently new and alien species of flora and fauna have arrived on hulls, in ship ballast and in emptying of tanks, and this has resulted in a rise and fall of invading species. There are extensive mud and sandflats fringed by reedbeds and saltmarshes in a wide variety of habitats within the harbour. Sublittorally there are extensive **Eelgrass beds**, *Zostera spp*, while the saltmarsh is dominated by **Cordgrass**, *Spartina anglica*.

These mudflats provide an important feeding ground for migrating birds and resident populations of rare birds. Because of its international importance as a feeding ground this area has, since 1999, been classified as a Special Protection Area under the European Union Birds Directive. The double high tide means that the filter feeding mud dwelling invertebrates have a longer time to feed contributing to a diverse group of waders and fish stocks.

The arrival of *Spartina anglica* early in the twentieth century has at times altered the shape of the shoreline and the flow of water in the harbour.

The particular tidal regime in Poole Harbour has contributed to three distinct zones of saltmarsh. The lowest zone is composed mainly of the nodular fronds of **Samphire**, *Salicornia spp*, which are a succulent green, turning red in autumn, mixed with *Spartina anglica*. The **Grass**, *Festuca rubra*, and **Reeds**, *Juncus gerardii*, and *J.maritimus*, together with the previous pioneer vegetation make up the middle zone. The highest zone is a richly diverse flora including the fleshy silvery white thin leaves of **Sea Purslane**, *Halimione portulacoides*, common salt marsh grass and maritime **Sea Plantain**, *Plantago maritime*. Where there is a build up of mud and sediment inshore are species of sea aster, sea lavender creeping bent grass, slender spike rush, and sea purslane.

P Drynda from Swansea university carried out several underwater surveys in 1999. His diving assessments produced a species inventory of 68 seaweeds, 159 invertebrates and 32 fish found in Poole Harbour. The most significant feature were large forests of *Sabella pavonina*, a **Peacock Fan Worm**. The worm lives in a tube and displays a daisy like fan of tentacles. The tentacles filter food from the water and the whole head can be retracted back into the tube when disturbed. The peacock fan worm can survive in channels where tides are strong or where less fierce. The tubes can be up to 30-40 cm long, but with half the tube buried in the sediment. Sediment can settle within these forests making mudbanks up to 0.5 m thick. **Red seaweeds** and the **Sponge**, *Halichondria bowerbanki*, or clusters of **Sea Squirt**, *Ascidiella aspersa*, colonise the emergent parts of the worm tubes. These forests also host multitudes of subsidiary seaweeds, invertebrates and fish.

The native **Oyster**, *Ostrea edulis*, once farmed extensively in Roman times has been out competed by the **Slipper Limpet**, *Crepidula fornicata*. This invasive species was originally brought in accidentally as ballast with Pacific oysters from America and now forms extensive beds of widespread occurrence. Stacks of 7–10 individuals thick, grow in huge clusters on all types of substrate. Where *Crepidula fornicata* stacks are abundant, few other bivalves can live amongst them. It is thought that the pseudofaeces of the slipper limpet blanket an area making it inhospitable to other species.

In 1800s there were extensive farmed oyster beds of *Ostrea edulis*, the **Native Oyster**. To preserve stocks the tradition then was to leave a nucleus of harvested stock from open coastal waters within channels of the harbour to help natural regeneration. Sadly overfishing, the presence of slipper limpet and disease outbreaks have all contributed to the decline of the natural oyster. The sulphur sponge and tubeworm can burrow into shells of the native oyster, and barnacles, keel worms and seasquirts can all use the living and dead shells as a habitat.

There are a few beds of the **Pacific Oyster**, *Crassostrea gigas*, still farmed in the harbour. Sometimes individuals can suffer from a thickening of the shell resulting from pollution by antifouling paint.

The **Manila Clam**, *Tapes philippinarum*, also a non native species has become naturalised in

Poole Harbour and has been shown to provide a good food source for oystercatchers.

Another invasive species which has been noted are the fronds of **Wireweed**, *Sargassum muticum.* Sometimes these long brown fronds with masses of air bladders which aid buoyancy circulate in the channels moving with the tide. They can reproduce either sexually or vegetatively giving rise to dense mats very quickly.

Across the harbour from a south west to northeast direction is a gradient of increasingly large sediment. This could be due to wave sorting or deposition of silt at the eastern end from river inflows. The burrows of the **Common Eel**, *Anguilla anguilla*, can be found here in the soft mud. Other silt tolerant species are the **Sponges**, *Cliona celata*, *Haliclona oculata* and *Suberites massa*, and the **Korean Sea Squirt**, *Styela clava*,

A large brown seaweed **Wakame**, *Undaria pinnatifida*, originally from the north east pacific, arrived in the Hamble estuary in 1994 and was subsequently found in Poole in 2004. Looking green on the plate, with a slippery texture and subtly sweet taste, this can be used as an ingredient in miso soup. Wakame, named one of the most invasive seaweeds in New Zealand, is harvested in the cold temperate regions of Korea, China and Japan, and has recently been introduced for cultivation off Brittany. Over the years a variety of alien species will have found their way into the ecosystem of Poole Harbour. Some will have been intensely invasive, others lost as conditions did not suit their survival. Dredging to keep the navigation channels open, land reclamation for roads and housing, and pollution from various kinds are all human impacts that contribute to a changing environment. Assessing the baseline flora and fauna and watching for new incomers can be done by professional scientists and amateurs alike.

The Appearance Of Cordgrass, *Spartina*

There are very early reports of *Spartina anglica* in the literature from 1899 when Mansell Pleydell recorded a new stiff perennial grass in Poole roadstead. Then in 1905 some clumps were found near the Fever Hospital and by 1907 there were hundreds of clumps. Over the next 20 years colonization of the mudflats was rapid and by 1924 800 ha of Poole harbour was covered by Spartina.

The Spartina story had begun with the accidental introduction of *Spartina alterniflora* from the eastern seaboard of North America into Southampton water.

Spartina cordgrass

A native plant *S. maritima*, now extinct, used to grow around Hythe and the mouth of the river Itchen. A new species of Spartina was first noticed and collected around Hythe in the late 1870s. Something had occurred which favoured the spreading of the new plant. The biological evidence suggests that the new *Spartina townsendii* was originally a sterile hybrid: The something that favoured the spreading was chromosome doubling in the hybrid, which produced a fertile allopolyploid able to spread by seed, *Spartina anglica*.

R V Sherring writing in Vol VII of the BNSS Proceedings 1913–1914 tells of ...meadows where a golden brown sheen of ripe Spartina glows in the sunset and a similar pleasant brightness is visible in the early morning. Between Fitzworth and North point a generally luxuriant growth is marked. All areas of the harbour were invaded, only the higher reaches of Wareham Channel are free. In the past 16 years the grass has dominated the harbour causing a rise on muddy grounds and other salt loving plants are springing up in the shallower parts and will help to bind the mud into more solid grass land.

Between 1924 and 1952 there was a net loss of Spartina. In exposed locations marshes were subject to tidal scour. Since 1952 recession of the Spartina meadows has continued, most noticeably east of Arne peninsula around the inner harbour islands, i.e. Furzey, Green, Long and Round Islands. Reclamation of land for the Holes Bay Road has continued to reduce the area occupied by Spartina because of a reduction in intertidal area.

The dieback of Spartina continued from 1952 through to the 1980s as three distinct effects occurred. Firstly the break-up of marsh on intertidal mudflats, possibly due to increased boat traffic, secondly dieback where patches of Spartina sward degenerated from the inside, where badly drained highly anaerobic soils poisoned the rhizomes and thirdly from invasion by other species from the landward edge.

But the plant had been so successful that it was used for active reclamation of land and in the 1920s 40,000 plants were exported from Poole to Holland. From 1928–36 over 85,000 plants were exported to Ireland, UK, Germany, Denmark and Australia. (Raybould 1997).

The initial invasion of Spartina and the subsequent dieback has had an effect on the hydrographical regime within the harbour. Initially the accretion and sedimentation due to rhizome growth was stabilization of mobile sediment and led to a mass spreading of Spartina mudflats. This also had the beneficent effect of keeping the main water channels free of weed and sediment and deep. Later the dieback released sediment back into the water with subsequent shoaling of some of the water channels.

One of the reasons for the success of *S. anglica* is the colonization of the seaward edge of other saltmarsh communities. Spartina is able to colonize this vacant niche by a higher tolerance to salinity, flooding and sediment accretion, as well as a greater ability to oxidize toxins. Where once botanists might have feared a total invasion and swamping of other species by such an aggressive plant as Spartina, it can be seen with the hindsight of 100 years that natural checks prevent one plant from dominating the landscape and that in time a completely new plant such as this Spartina allopolyploid will find a vacant niche and exploit that. Since the early 1980s Spartina has become infected with an **ergot** fungus, *Claviceps purpurea*. There does not as yet appear to be any significant deleterious effect on either the individual plant or the stands of Spartina, but it is of interest that an evolutionary change is now occurring.

Ergot

Where stands of Spartina have died out it appears to have benefitted the internationally important flocks of wader birds in that there has been an increase in numbers possibly due to recolonization of bare mud by invertebrate species which provides food for the birds.

STUDLAND

A stroll along the beach at Studland might initially prove uninteresting save for a few shells of the **Common Periwinkle**, or **Netted Dog Whelk**, *Nassarius reticulatus*. Always there will be the ubiquitous **Slipper Limpet**, *Crepidula fornicata*, and washed up shells of the **Common Oyster**, *Ostrea edulis*.

A sandy shore holds fewer niches than a rocky shore for seaweeds to attach to and secondarily for animal species to hide in and feed on. The holes one might walk across are actually the burrows of a number of worms, big fat **Lugworms**, *Arenicola marina*, **Paddleworms**, *Phyllodoce* spp. and **Ragworms**. Sometimes a sand encrusted tube above the surface will reveal a **Sand Mason Worm**, *Lanice conchilega*, underneath. Diggers armed with garden spades have to dig up to 30 cm or more to unearth these worms tightly holding the sides of their burrow with a series of bristles or even forming a U tube and retracting away from the disturbance. Razor shells of both the **Pod**, *Ensis siliqua*, and **Common Razor shell**, *Ensis ensis*, have a very strong foot and can retract very fast to quite a depth.

Large mammal swimming off Studland

In the corner of the bay where a number of yachts anchor for the weekend can be found beds of the **Eelgrass**, *Zostera*, the only marine angiosperm. Beds of this long Eelgrass are the favoured habitat for a number of animals including the common shrimp and prawns and more unusually Pipefish such as the **Straight Nosed Pipefish**, *Nerophis ophidian*, the **Snake Pipefish**, *Entelerus aequoreus*, and **Nilsson's Pipefish**, *Syngnathus rostellatus* and their close relatives the Seahorses. Recently Steve Trewhella has found two different species of the **Seahorse**, *Hippocampus*, the spiny and the short snouted. Seahorses are unusual in that the male guards the young in a pouch until they are ready to be independent. A trial exclusion zone is being tried out in 2009 to exclude boats dragging their anchors and disrupting the eelgrass beds, in an attempt to try and protect these small and delicate creatures. The Eelgrass beds are also the home to spawning grounds for bottom dwelling fish such as plaice, dab, sole and even little lumpsucker fry.

Retracing one's steps along the water line the tiniest of crabs can be seen scuttling away such as the **Shore Crab**, *Carcinus maenas*. Just occasionally one might find a parasitic **Barnacle**, *Sacculina carcina*, on a crab, looking like a lump of polystyrene attached on the underside of the carapace, but having the unfortunate result of preventing the crab from reproducing. **Long legged Spider Crabs**, *Macropodia sp*, scuttle away or immerse themselves in the wet sand. A mass of Gammarid Shrimps provide a rich food source for birds and other larger predators. A rare find one day was the **Isopod**, *Idotea linearis*.

BROWNSEA ISLAND

The sediments of Brownsea and the other Poole Harbour islands are from the Eocene period some 50 million years ago; they are part of the Bracklesham Group. Near the waterline is the Parkstone Clay, deposited in a tidal flat estuarine environment. It is a dark grey **pyritic** clay containing lignitic fragments of plants and the occasional leaf fossil. Above the clay is the Branksone Sand, a fine quartz sand deposited as a beach barrier or estuarine channel sediment. Above this are areas of Pleistocene gravels of Terraces 6 and 8, there are also areas of Head, or hillwash towards the centre of the Island. Until recently Brownsea would have been a hill some 50 m above the rivers Frome and Piddle that flowed to join the Solent River across dry land as sea level was up to 140 m lower than today. At the end of the last glacial stage some 12,000 years ago the sea level started to rise and by 5–6,000 years ago Poole Harbour would have been created leaving the higher land as the islands we see today.

Brownsea Island

Brownsea has always been important for its mineral wealth. The Parkstone Clay being pyritic produces Jarosite and Melanterite, ferrous sulphates. Respectively yellow and green encrustations they were used as a constituent of Copperas or Alum which was used as a mordant or colour fixer in the dyeing industry and in the manufacture of inks and pigments.

Beneath the Parkstone Clay there are deposits of Pipe Clay, important in the fine china industry. In the mid nineteenth century the then owner, Col. Waugh, decided to try to mine the deposits and borrowed money for the mining equipment and a processing factory. The mine shafts were some 20 m deep before adits were dug but the clay was only good for terracotta ware and bricks and when the bank asked for repayment Col. Waugh fled the country.

Of course much deeper is the Sherwood Sandstone, the source reservoir for the Wytch Farm oilfield.

The Island has had a varied history from occupation by King Canute in 1015. In the twelfth century Cerne Abbey had 'right of wreck' and built a small chapel. Henry VIII granted the Island to John, Earl of Oxford and built a fortified castle to defend the entrance to Poole. Subsequently ownership changed hands regularly with 18 owners between the sixteenth century and the present owner. Brownsea is the largest of the harbour islands, about 500 acres, with a variety of different habitats; it is ideal for wildlife, and if it were not for one particular lady, the island would probably be like Sandbanks, covered with millionares' mansions.

Mrs Mary Florence Bonham Christie, bought it in 1927, and evicted most of its inhabitants. It was a private estate before and many people lived there. There was a large farm, a golf course, croquet, tennis courts, many houses and fields for livestock; even what is now the lagoon was pasture for cattle and horses. There were labourers of all kinds and a church and a folly castle with amazing contents, built by a previous occupant. It was a shooting estate for the royal and the wealthy. The birth of the Boy Scout movement started when Baden-Powell had his first experimental camp there.

The new owner was an animal lover and wished the Island to become her own nature reserve. She allowed it to become overgrown, re-flooded the fields, banned all hunting and shooting and had most of the houses demolished. She prohibited strangers from landing, and rarely opened up to anyone, except for a charity in the name of animals. She loved the sika deer which had been on the island since the beginning of the century (although many had escaped to populate the Purbeck landscape) and the squirrels, rabbits and rats, which she enjoyed feeding.

She added her own fowl in the form of Pea Fowl, which still inhabit the Island today. In January 1961, an oil spillage devastated the harbour and the islands, after thousands of gallons of oil escaped from the Holton Heath establishment, thousands of birds were affected. Mrs Christie died just a few months after this catastrophe, and her grandson inherited the island. It was put on the market. Everybody rushed to place their bids, Purbeck and Wareham councils opposed mass development, the hunting and shooting syndicates wanted it, and the place was vandalised. All manner of strange goings-on happened, along with mass trespass. Eventually the Treasury took possession in lieu of death duties and the National Trust agreed to take it over if £100,000 was raised, which it was by public and private donations including the John Lewis Partnership who repaired the castle and who now rent it from the National Trust.

The secretary of the appeal, Mrs Helen Brotherton, was also the secretary of the Dorset Wildlife Trust, which had only recently been formed. It was agreed that the DWT was to be responsible for maintenance of a large proportion of the Island. A lot of work had to be done over the next ten years, as firebreaks were made, lakes and derelict buildings cleared, paths made, and other buildings made as accommodation for DWT staff. The Island opened to the public in May 1963 with huge numbers of visitors. In the same year the island suffered a huge fire which may have opened up the heath areas, but they were quickly colonised by conifer trees.

Today there is a good mix of deciduous and conifer trees, some of the pines are quite ancient. The red squirrels depend on them, unlike the grey squirrel. There is much oak, chestnut, sycamore and birch along with gorse and several other non-native tree species that were planted during the nineteenth century. Beds of the **Common Reed**, *Phragmites australis*, carpet the bogs and ditches which meander around the Island. A large heronry has existed for decades. During the last twenty years, **Little Egrets**, *Egretta garzetta*, have nested alongside and now outnumber the **Grey Herons**, *Ardea cinerea*. Two large lakes and several smaller ponds hold a variety of dragonfly and damselfly species, and many other insect species. Several rare spiders occur and all the species of birds expected in such habitats occur, but with the bonus of the freshwater lagoon in which special islands have been formed for nesting birds such as **Sandwich** and **Common Terns**, *Sterna sanvicensisa* and *Sterna hirundo*, and **Black-headed Gulls**, *Larus ridibundus*. We also have resident **Spoonbills**, *Platalea leucorodia,* and all manner of waders can be seen during the summer months. But it is the winter when the Island is at its best as many species of migrants come, especially if cold weather has hit the north or Scandanavia. Black and Bar-tailed godwits, Dunlin, Curlew, Redshank, Greenshank and Oystercatchers come every year. One dead Oystercatcher that was handed to the author, was ringed and was twenty-two years old. Hundreds of wintering Avocets fill the lagoon from September onwards, and the three hides give amazing bird watching at very close quarters. Special bird boats are put on during the winter as the Island is generally closed to the public, yet in the summer it is open daily by the National Trust.

Little Egret

All of the islands host trees, mainly **Scots Pine**, *Pinus sylvestris*; some islands are covered with them, others have green spaces within woodland while others have spreads of heathland.

Some are grazed by the **Sika Deer**, *Cervus nippon*, that originally escaped from Brownsea at the beginning of the last century. They are good swimmers and regularly cross at low tide to some of the islands near the shore. Some islands are good for nesting birds having no ground predators such as mammals, although a few islands host **Red Squirrels**, *Sciurus vulgaris*. Brownsea is renowned for them, although they became so inbred that foreign stock had to be brought in from northern Europe. Brown rats occur on Brownsea and maybe on other islands sporadically; other small rodents are also present. Rabbits inhabit Brownsea. There are no large predators, but birds of prey such as Buzzards, Tawny owls, Barn owls, the occasional Goshawk and annual migrating Ospreys take mammals and fish. Hobbies take the great

Heron

Barn Owl

wealth of dragonflies, Brownsea has lots of water in the form of lakes, ponds and ditches with marshland, creating ideal habitats for insects. The large amount of woodland ensures that dead wood is left creating habitat for many species of beetles, wasps and spiders.

POOLE BAY

The visitor to Bournemouth will be struck by the miles of clean sandy beach stretching from Sandbanks to Hengistbury Head. Every night in summer the beach is raked and scoured of human rubbish. To the purist and ecologist this also removes the naturally decaying seaweeds and organic matter that would normally form the basis of a sandy littoral food chain. In some respects the beach at Bournemouth is quite empty of natural wildlife. However a saunter across the sand towards the sea will reveal a number of shells which in their living form are found out at sea underwater.

Shells of all colours, shapes and sizes are to be found on the seashore and often it is these pretty shells that are the first contact a small child will have with wildlife. Amongst the shells on Bournemouth beach are the round half moon Slipper Limpet, the long narrow shells of a Razor Shell, the curly spiral of a Dog Whelk, the typical scallop shape of a Cockle and the big rough uneven thick shells of the local Oyster.

Most numerous of these will be the **Slipper Limpet**, *Crepidicula fornicata.* On turning the oval half moon shell over the observer will note a shelf half way across the inside of the shell. It is an fact a snail and has the remarkable habit of changing sex during its lifetime. Often great stacks of shells can be found cemented onto one another, with the largest female shell at the bottom and younger smaller males on top. Technically its reproductive habit is called a protandrous hermaphrodite, meaning the young larvae will settle and develop as males, until another shell settles on top of them and then the underneath one becomes female. Often in a bungalow stack there will only be one female underneath and up to 12 males on top.

These slipper limpets do tend to accumulate mud around them and change the substrate that the shells are growing on. This makes the substrate less clean for Mussels, the beautiful black purple pointy shell that is the edible *Mytilus edulis.* The **Common Oyster**, *Ostrea edulis,* is recognised by its big thick rough shell. Poole Bay used to have a number of oyster and mussel beds, but due to overfishing and the pestilent nature of the slipper limpet, the beds have fallen into disuse and now no longer support a fishing industry.

The distinct long thin narrow shells are those of the **Razor Shell**, *Ensis ensis.* These molluscs are light and vibration sensitive and will quickly retract into the burrow where they live vertically. Just a small hole indicates their presence or sometimes a small siphon will protrude from the burrow. The razor shell can retreat faster than a man can dig and if the siphon is accidentally predated or snapped off, it can sometimes regenerate.

The pretty pink flat triangular shells are those of the *Tellina* genus. These are shallow burrowers in fine silty sands and muds and are suspension or deposit feeders with long extensile siphons that can forage for food.

The **Common Cockle**, *Cerastoderma edule,* can sometimes be picked up, different species have various more or less pronounced ridges and hemispherical markings.

A very different shaped shell is the **Pelicans Foot**, *Aporrhais pespelecani*, this has a definite spiral whorl with up to 5–10 whorls, each with a finely or thickly knobbed ridge. The outer lip of the aperture is opened out into a five pointed lobe, hence the name pelicans foot.

Out at sea and underwater there are a host of different living species, most of which cannot be seen by the casual visitor from the beach, but sharp eyed observers will catch a tern diving and dipping and occasionally the flash of silver in the bird beak as it catches a tiny **Sand Eel**, *Ammodytes tobianus.* The sand eel is in fact a fish. Divers report various sponges and soft corals under the pier at Bournemouth. One particular high tide after a storm in winter the writer observed a mass of sparkly scrubbing brushes on the strand line. On further inspection these were found to be the mysterious **Sea Mouse**, *Aphrodite aculeata,* a **polychaete** scaleworm, about 12–16 cm in length. Bristling with a mass of iridescent hairs and chaetae, these creatures burrow through or creep slowly along soft bottoms and feed on carrion, detritus or microscopic animals.

Since 1989 there has been an artificial reef laid in Poole Bay, to establish colonization patterns and to determine biodiversity. A team from Southampton University, Jensen, Collins, Fleming and Mallison have been recording observations on blocks of stabilized pulverised fuel ash. Fifty tonnes of blocks were dropped in conical heaps (1 m high by 5 m diameter) in a rectangle grid 35 x 15 m of seabed. These lie on a sandy seabed at a depth of 10 m at least 3 km away form any natural reefs.

Colonization of the reef was rapid. **Pouting**, *Trisopterus luscus*, shoaled around the structure from initial deployment. This has remained the dominant fish species , with shoals of over 200 individuals observed around each reef unit during the daytime in summer. Wrasse species were observed within the first month. Lobsters and Crabs also moved in. Initially **hydroids, ascidians** and red algae dominated the cover of the block surfaces. Subsequently bryozoans and sponges increased in abundance and within 5 years the epibiotic species composition was similar to that of neighbouring natural reefs. For a full species list please consult the references of Collins *et al*. Some wonderful tagging of lobsters was done to ascertain their behaviour using first acoustic tags and then electromagnetic telemetry. Results indicate that both lobster and crab find these artificial reefs a good habitat site. Though there is movement to and away from the reef of large crustacean, the reef provides a valuable habitat for many different marine phyla and has led to an increase in biodiversity greater than on some local natural reefs.

CHRISTCHURCH HARBOUR

Located between Bournemouth and Christchurch the Harbour covers 156 hectares. A large sprawling estuary it drains the rivers Stour and Avon, flowing into the sea through a very narrow channel, the Run, at Mudeford. Reed beds and flat wetlands surround the freshwater flowing through the Harbour and only at high tide does salt water flush into it. Salt water can push all the way up to Iford Bridge at high tide and **Grey Mullet**, *Chelon labrosus*, can be seen swimming in the water under the Bridge.

The reed beds of Stanpit Marsh are a haven for nesting and migrating birds and come right up to the backs of the houses of Christchurch. The mouth of the harbour at Mudeford is only about 20 m across and is shaped as an S, reflecting the pattern of a slow winding river. Across the harbour are differing patterns and gradients of salinity according to how close or how far to the river bed one samples. The harbour is sheltered from the sea by the promontory of Hengistbury Head and is an important SSSI wetland.

In 1987 a sediment infauna survey of the estuary was undertaken for the Nature Conservancy Council. A second survey was undertaken in 2007 to compare and monitor results from the previous survey. Five identifiable indicator species were selected to represent changes between 1987 and 2007.

The **Ragworm**, *Nereis diversicolor*, was present in large numbers throughout the estuary in both surveys. With an estimated population of 2 billion in 1987 and 3 billion in 2007 it is the most important species in terms of biomass and a food source for wading birds. There is possibly a change in density and density pattern with an increase in the upper estuary in 2007 and decrease in the lower estuary.

A **Mud Shrimp**, *Corophium volutator*, a crustacean amphipod was present in 2007 in about half of the 1987 sites but large fluctuations of this amphipod can be expected. Lower numbers in the middle estuary may be correlated with sediment changes there.

The burrowing bivalve, **Peppery furrow Shell**, *Scrobicularia plana*, was found in low numbers in the middle estuary in 1987. It occurred in similar numbers in 2007 with a distribution biased towards the lower estuary. This suggests a stable population over the period.

Chironomid, a non-biting midge, larvae were found throughout the estuary albeit in low numbers.

During 2006 coarse sand had been dredged from the middle estuary and deposited on Stanpit Marsh. Although the diversity of intertidal and subtidal habitats was not high, the infauna of the sediments was very productive. The environmentalists carrying out the survey agreed that the condition of the communities was well within normal limits and provided good evidence that the overall condition of the estuary was favourable.

A very active ornithology group the Christchurch Harbour Ornithology group list over 180 species of bird using this area for feeding, overwintering or just in passage. Otters and seals have been seen in Christchurch Harbour hunting the rich sources of fish.

Christchurch Harbour

Glossary

Acciptres	In 1914 this term referred to any bird of prey, excluding owls. Nowadays the genus *Accipiter* refers to short-winged, long legged members of the order *Falconiformes*. For example, sparrowhawk and goshawk.
Aeolian	Sedimentary deposits caused by wind action, e.g. sand dunes.
Agger	Raised military or public road with sloping drainage embankments.
Aggregates	Commercial term for gravels of widely differing pebble size.
Alien	Not native. Introduced by accident or design.
Allopolyploid	An organism with more than one set of chromosomes composed of two or more chromosome sets derived more or less complete from different species
Alluvium	Detrital sediments, muds, sands or gravels, deposited by rivers.
Amber listed	Species whose population is threatened is threatened in Europe but not globally considering the number of breeding sites, the percentage of the population in the UK and other criteria.
Anther	The pollen-bearing part of a stamen.
Artiodactyl	Even toed ungulate mammals, e.g. pigs, sheep, deer.
Ascidians	Invertebrate chordates, known as sea squirts
Auroch	A wild ancestor of modern domestic cattle, larger and heavier with lyre-shaped horns. The last known European population was in Poland in the early seventeenth century.
Benthic	Sea bottom dwelling rather than the open sea.
Bladelets	Shaped shards of flint, used in darts or other compound tools, typically 10 mm wide and 50 mm long.
Borehole log	Continuous stony record of sub-surface strata formed by mechanically boring into the Earth.
Bract	A leaflike growth beneath a flower.
Braided river	Stream characterised by constantly shifting interbraided channels resulting in transient sand-banks and islands.
Bryophyte	A plant of the Bryophyta, a division of photosynthetic, chiefly terrestrial, nonvascular plants, including the mosses, liverworts, and hornworts.
Burins	Stone flakes with a chisel like edge possibly used to carve wood or bone or engraving.
Calcareous	Containing a high proportion of calcium carbonate,$CaCO_3$, thus raising the pH.
Calcifuge plant	A plant that will not tolerate alkaline soil. As in alkaline soil conditions iron is less soluble the plant suffers from chlorosis due to iron deficiency.
Chelicerae	Mouth parts of some arthropods including spiders, pointed appendages for grasping food also for injecting venom into their victims.
Cloaca	Posterior opening that serves as the only such opening for the intestinal and urinary tracts of certain animal species. Also known as the anal beak. From the Latin meaning *sewer*. All birds, reptiles, and amphibians possess this orifice
Comminuted	Powdered or severely broken of lithic material or a fossil.
Concretions	A volume of sedimentary rock which has been cemented by a mineral, usually forming around a nucleus such as a rock fragment or fossil. They can be rounded or of irregular shape. If small they are known as nodules if larger than 0.2 m they are known as doggers. When containing calcite veins they are known as 'Septarian Nodules'.

Deltaic	Sediments accumulated at the mouths of heavily laden rivers when entering bodies of water. The sediment are commonly alluvial.
Denticulates	Toothed flint tool, prepared by retouching an edge into a multi notched length like a saw, but used for sawing meat rather than wood.
Detritus	Mineral particles derived from pre-existing rocks by the action of erosion or natural weathering.
Doline	A 'sink' or 'swallow-hole' which in limestone areas surface waters drain to proceed underground.
Elytra	A hardened, modified forewing of some beetles and true bugs
End Scrapers	Common stone tool assumed to be used to scrape fat from animal skins and wood working.
Epibenthic	Located on the surface of underwater sediments.
Ferruginous	Strata containing marked amount of iron or iron-rust as a chemical constituent.
Ficron	Stone tool with long curved sides and a pointed tip.
Fluviatile	Deposits resulting from the action of flooding river-waters.
Foraminifera	One of the groups of the geologically ancient Protozoans, small unicellular primarily marine animals known as plankton. They range in size from microscopic to about 10 mm the multi-chambered Nummulites flourished in early Tertiary times and have been discovered in the Eocene rocks of the area.
Gastropoda	An ancient group of marine, freshwater and terrestrial molluscs with coiled univalvular shells, usually a helical spiral but sometimes a plane spiral.
Glauconitic	Usually fine-grained marine sediments with a greenish colour caused by the presence of glauconite one of the mica group of minerals, e.g. Upper and Lower Greensand and various lower Tertiary sands sediments.
Hippomorphs	Odd-toed equine mammals, e.g. horses, zebras and many now extinct horses and rhinoceros-like Brontotheres.
Hoppus feet	1H. ft = 1.273 cu ft. Calculated for round timber by taking the Mid Quarter Girth (MQG) in inches, squaring it then multiplying by the length in feet and dividing by 144. MQG = girth at mid point of timber in inches divided by four. Most volume measurements today are in metric values.
Hydroid	Colonial plant-like animals closely related to jellyfish, with stinging cells.
Incursions	Temporary inundation of dry land by the sea at specific times. Either single or recurring events
Insolation	The word stands for 'Incoming solar radiation' of heat from the sun.
Ironstone nodules	See Concretions. Ironstone nodules were formerly collected commercially where present for extraction of the sedimentary iron-ore.
Isostacy	The process by which the Earth's crust adjusts by vertical movements to the addition or removal of crustal material (e.g. ice), so as to eliminate gravity anomalies by attaining a state of isostatic equilibrium.
K/T	The boundary between the Cretaceous and the Tertiary (See Table 2.1) famous for being the time of the mass extinction that killed the dinosaurs.
Lacustrine	Formed in or by a lake.
Lamellibranch	Geologically ancient moderately sized bivalve molluscs adapted to marine, brackish and freshwater environments. Many variations in shape and size with striking examples appearing in the area.
Leaching	Chemical process by which rocks are disintegrated and decomposed by atmospheric agencies, e.g. wind, rain and temperature extremes.
Lithic/ological	The characteristics of a rock or sediment usually at exposure.
Lydite	A very fine grained black variety of chert, a form of flint. Formerly used as a touchstone for determining the purity of precious metal alloys. Also known as Basanite.
Melanic	Having an increased amount of black or nearly black pigmentation due to the presence of melanin.
Microliths	Tiny flint tool, often less than 25 mm long, believed used as barbs for arrow tips or

	placed edge to edge in wood, bone or antler called a haft.
Mygalomorph	A suborder of spiders so called because their fangs do not cross but point straight down unlike the more common araneomorph suborder which cross.
O.D.	Abbreviation of Ordnance Datum.
Ocelli	An eye-like marking on the body, probably mimicry of light sensitive ocelli in insects.
Oologist	A person who studies and/or collects birds eggs.
Oology	The branch of knowledge that deals with birds eggs – their collection and description.
Orogeny	Greek for *'Mountain generating'*. The process of mountain building caused by plate tectonics and the collision of continents, e.g. Africa and Southern Europe.
Oxidation	A geochemical process involving the leaching, by loss of electrons, of iron (FE^{3+}) or manganese (Mn^{3+}) rich sedimentary rocks.
Palaearctic	The cold and temperate zones of the Old World. Thus, the regions of Europe, N. Africa and Asia north of the Himalayas.
Pannage	The legal right or privilege of pasturing swine in a forest to eat acorns and beechnuts. It is still practiced today in the Forest to reduce the poisoning of ponies from too many acorns.
Pedology	The study of soil in all its manifestations.
Pelagic	Living in the open sea not on the bottom.
Permafrost	Permanently frozen ground, associated with late Pleistocene ice sheets. Formerly more extensive than those today in northern Siberia and parts of Alaska. Existed in parts of southern Britain where scattered evidence confirms their previous presence.
Plumassier	A person who works or trades in ornamental feathers.
Polychaete	A class of annelid worms including mostly marine worms such as the lugworm, and characterized by fleshy paired appendages tipped with bristles on each body segment
Primaries	Any of the large flight feathers of a bird's wing.
Pyrites/Pyritic	A widespread mineral, Iron sulphide, FeS_2. Occurs as an accessory mineral in igneous rocks and associated hydrothermal ore veins. Also occurs in sedimentary rocks formed in anaerobic conditions. Also known as Fool's Gold.
Recession	Permanent or temporary withdrawal of the sea from intertidal stretches of coastline.
Rhizome	A fleshy underground stem.
Sarcoptic	Also known as canine scabies, sarcoptic mange is a highly contagious infestation of *Sarcoptes scabiei canis*, a burrowing mite. Can also infect humans and cats but not severely.
Sarsen	Large sandstone boulders or blocks apparently of Eocene age now found as eroded objects in younger strata. They occur both singly and in groups. Frequently used as megalith stones. Older literature referred to them as 'Greywhethers'
Sepals	The usually green and leaflike growths immediately surrounding the petals of a flower.
Sessile	Imobile, fixed in one place by its base.
Shouldered Points	A point made using a blade struck from a prepared core, which is trimmed by pressure flaking along the edges; probably hafted onto a spear tip or dart which could be propelled using a spear thrower.
Siliceous	A term referring to the presence of prominent amounts of silica, SiO_2, in specific strata.
Sintered	Bone reduced to a dry powdery consistency by the cremation process.
Solifluction	The slow downhill movement of surface soil, gravel or scree cover due to alternate freezing and thawing of its contained water. A form of natural gravity transport.
Stigma	The tip of the style (female part of the plant).
Strip lynchet	A terraced field usually found on hillsides. Comprising a flat strip of land, called the tread, and a steep, scarped lynchet or edge, called the riser.
Supercilium	An 'eyebrow' stripe of feathers that runs above a birds eye, generally of a lighter colour than the background feathers.
Tesserae	Small square or rectangular faced tile pieces of stone used to make mosaic floors.
Tunicate	Various chordate marine animals with a cylindrical or globular body enclosed in a tough outer covering includes the sea squirts and salps.

Turbary	The right to cut peat or turf from heath or bog as a fuel.
Type Section	The horizontal or vertical record of a particular suite of rocks at the geographical locality where their sequence was first recognised.
Umbel	Flowers arranged in an umbrella-like shape.
Unconformable/ Unconformity	Breaks in the stratal sequence where older rocks are structurally separated younger rocks by a break. This may be parallel to the younger strata, may make an angle to it or may be irregular. Such interruptions represent unrecorded time and may indicate temporary or permanent cessation of deposition which may last briefly or for some time. Can also occur due to erosion of the older rock.
Unfossiliferous	Lacking or devoid of fossils.
Urban	Plants frequently seen in built up areas.
Vascular	Higher plants. Contain specialised tissues for transport of water and nutrients, includes flowering plants.
Vestigial	Part of a plant now scarcely present, though previously well-developed.
Vice-counties	These are the divisions of the country as established by H.C. Watson in 1873. Still used today used by botanists to record plant locations within a fixed boundary. The Dorset vice-county almost equates to the County political boundary of 1974. The area covered by this book lies within vice-counties 9 (Dorset) and 11 (South Hampshire).

Chapter References

1 History & Archaeology

Allison, P & Drummond M 1997 *The New Forest, A photographic record 100 years of Forest life*, Brown & Son.

Beavis, John 2004 *Dorset's World Heritage Coast an Archaeological Guide*, Tempus

Bradley, Richard 1978 *The Prehistoric Settlement of Britain.*

Collingwood and Myres 1968 *Roman Britain and the English Settlements*, Oxford University Press.

Cunliffe, Barry 1993 *Wessex to AD 1000*, Longman.

Frere 1973 *Notes from Britannia.*

Historical Monuments in the County of Dorset, vol *East RC on HM MCMLXXV.*

Ilay Cooper 2004 *Purbeck revealed*, James Pembroke

Proceedings of the Natural History Antiquarian Field Club, vol *15 1894*

Putnam, Bill 2007 *Roman Dorset*, Tempus.

Tate, Peter *The New Forest 900 years after*, Macdonald & Jan.

Tubbs, Colin R 1968 *The New Forest, an Ecological History.*

Williams-Freeman, J P 1915 *Introduction to Field Archaeology as illustrated by Hampshire.*

2 Geology

GENERAL ACCOUNTS

Drummond, M & R McInnes 2001 *The Book of the Solent* (Thomas Reed, Chale).

Hawkins, D 1998 *Cranborne Chase* (Dorset Press, Wimborne).

House, MR 1989 *The Geology of the Dorset Coast*, Geological Society of London.

Hyland, P 1978 *Purbeck: The Ingrained Island* (London).

King, MP 1974 *Beneath Your Feet: Geology and Scenery of Bournemouth* (Purbeck Press,Swanage).

Legg, R 1984 *Guide to the Purbeck Coast* (Dorset Publishing Co.).

Legg, R 2002 *The Jurassic Coast* (Dorset Books).

Shepherd, W 1963 *Looking at the Landscape* (London).

Tubbs, CR 1986 *The New Forest* (London).

TECHNICAL ACCOUNTS

Arkell, WJ 1947 *Geology of the Country Around Weymouth, Swanage, Corfe, and Lulworth*, Memoirs of the Geological Survey of England ~ Wales (EMSO).

Bury, H 1926 *The Rivers of the Hampshire Basin*, Proceedings of the Bournemouth Natural Science Society, vol 19, pp 1–12.

Bury, H 1927-8 *The River Solent and its Tributaries*, Proceedings of the Bournemouth Natural Science Society, vol 20 pp 88–96.

Freshney, E C & C R Bristow, and B J Williams 1984 *Geology of Sheet SZ19 (Hurn, Christchurch, Dorset and Hants)*, British-Geological Survey Report, WA/84/9,

Hampshire County Council 1990 *Hampshire's Coast: Christchurch Bay - West Solent;Framework for Coastal Defence* (H C C).

Jones, DKC 1981 Southeast and Southern England, in Brown, EH and K Clayton (eds) Melville, RV and

EC Freshney, 1982 *The Hampshire Basin and Adjoining Areas: British Regional Geology*, Institute of Geological Sciences, 4th edn (HMSO).

Reid, C 1915 *The Ancient Rivers of Bournemouth*, Proceedings of the Bournemouth Natural Science Society, vol 7 (1914-15), pp 73-82.

Sparks, BW 1960 *Geomorphology* (Longman, London).

Sparks, BW 1971 *Rocks and Relief* (Longman, London).

Summerfield, MA & A S Goudie 1980 The Nature and Significance of Sarsen Stones, in D K C Jones (ed) *The Shaping of Southern England* (Academic Press, London).

Tavener, LE 1969 *The Geological Structure of the New Forest* (HMSO).

West, RG 1968 *Pleistocene Geology and Biology*, (Longman, London).

White, HJO 1915 *Geology of the Country near Lymington and Portsmouth, Memoirs of the Geological Survey of England & Wales* (HMSO).

White, HJO 1917 *Geology of the Country Around Bournemouth*, 2nd edn *Memoirs of the Geological Survey of England and Wales* (HMSO).

FOSSILS

Carreck, JN 1955 -*The Quaternary Vertebrates of Dorset, fossil and sub-fossil*, Proceedings of the Dorset Natural History and Archaeological Society, vol 15, pp 164-188.

Castell, CP (ed) *British Mesozoic Fossils*, Natural History Museum, London (HMSO).

Castell, CP (ed) *British Caenozoic Fossils*, Natural History Museum, London, (HMSO).

Delair, JB 1958–60 *The Mesozoic Reptiles of Dorset*, Proceedings of the Dorset Natural History and Archaeological Society (vol 19 – 1958), pt 2 (vol 80 - 1959), pt 3 (vol 81 – 1960).

Ensom, P 1995 *Dinosaur Footprints in the Purbeck Limestone Group (Upper Jurassic Lower Cretaceous) of Southern England*, Proceedings of the Dorset Natural History and Archaeological Society, vol 116, pp 11–104.

Kemp, D J 1990 *An Illustrated Guide to the Middle Eocene Vertebrates* (London).

3 Mycology

Courtecuisse R and Duhrem B *Field Guide to Mushrooms and Toadstools of Britain* Harper Collins.

Major A *Collecting and Studying Mushrooms, Toadstools and Fungi* Bartholomew.

4 Botany

Bentham and Hooker 1930 *Handbook of the British Flora*.

Blamey, Fitter and Fitter 2003 *Wild Flowers of Britain and Ireland*.

BNSS *Botany Field Meeting Reports* (1950 – 2008).

Bournemouth Borough Council *The Chines of Bournemouth and Poole*.

Bournemouth Borough Council *Tree Trail* (leaflet).

Bournemouth Natural Science Society 1914 *A Natural History of Bournemouth and District*.

Bowen, Humphrey 2000 *The Flora of Dorset*.

Dorset Environment Records Centre (DERC), 2008 *Plant Records for Badbury Rings, Old Harry & Ballard Down and Durlston Head to St Aldhelm's Head*.

Dorset Wildlife Trust 1997 *The Natural History of Dorset*.

Durlston Country Park Trail Pack, 2008.

Edlin, HL 1960 Silviculture chapter *The New Forest, A Symposium* London, Galley Press.

Edlin, HL The *New Forest* (Silviculture).

Edwards, B and Pearman, D May 2004 *Dorset Rare Plant Register*, DERC.

Fitter and More, 1980 *Trees, Collins Gem Guide*.

Good, Ronald 1984 *A Concise Flora of Dorset*.

Haskins, Lesley E 2003 *Heathlands*, Dovecote Press.

Heathcote, Terry 1997 *Discover the New Forest.*
Mabey, Richard 1996 *Flora Britannica.*
NF Forestry Commission, 1975 *The Ornamental Drives* (leaflet).
Pearman and Lockton, 2007 *Aliens and Introductions* Paper, Japanese Knotweed Alliance.
Phillips, Roger 1987 *Coastal Wild Flowers.*
Phillips, Roger 1987 *Wild Flowers of Roadsides and Waste Places.*
Ponting, Gerald 2006 *The New Forest*, Landmark Visitors' Guide Series.
Powell, Michael 1996 Christchurch Harbour (leaflet).
Pratt Edward A 2008 *The Wild Flowers of the Isle of Purbeck, Brownsea and Sandbanks.*
Proceedings and Records of BNSS, 1944 – 46.
Rose, Francis revised & updated Clare O'Reilly, 2006 *The Wild Flower Key,*
Stace, Clive 1999 *Field Flora of the British Isles.*
The Urban Heaths Partnership *The Dorset Heaths* (leaflet).
Webb NR, 1990 *Biological Conservation* 51:pp 273–286.
Woodhead, Felicity 1994 *Flora of the Christchurch Area.*
WEBSITES :
    www.communigate.co.uk
    www.durlston.co.uk
    BSBI Distribution maps.
    Centre for Ecology and Hydrology.

5 Invertebrates

Chinery, Michael 1993 *Collins guide to the insects of Britain and Northern Europe.*
Hammond, CO 1994 *The Dragonflies of Great Britain and Ireland.* Harley Books.
Harde, KW & Severce, F 1998 *Beetles*, Blitz Editions
Jones, Dick 1983 *The country life Guide to Spiders of Britain and Northern Europe.* For a good identification guide to spiders.
Manley, Chris 2009 *Moths of Trigon*
Marshal, JA & Haes, ECM 1988 *Grasshoppers and Allied Insects of Great Britain and Ireland* Harley Books. Also showing its age a little now, but there is a useful cassette of the songs available.
Ragge, D 1965 *Grasshoppers, Crickets and Cockroaches of the British Isles* Warne. Although now out of date where distributions are concerned, this book is a classic. The account of the life-history of the Wood Cricket is particularly good.
Ragge, DR & Reynolds, WJ 1998 *The Songs of the Grasshoppers and Crickets of Western Europe.* Harley Books. This scholarly tome is for the real enthusiast, but two high quality CDs are also available separately, which are superior to the above mentioned cassette.
Roberts, M J 1995 *Spiders of Britain and Northern Europe.*

6 Ornithology

County Avifaunas
Clark JM & Eyre JA (Eds) 1993 *Birds of Hampshire.* Hampshire Ornithological Society
Green, George 2004 *Birds of Dorset* Christopher Helm, London.

DORSET WEBSITES
www.dorsetbirdclub.org.uk   Dorset Bird Club
www.portlandbirdsobs.btinternet.co.uk   Portland Observatory
www.durlston.co.uk   Durlston Country Park
www.chog.org.uk   Christchurch Harbour Ornithological Group

Hampshire Websites
www.hos.org.uk   Hampshire Ornithological Society
www.hants.gov.uk/countryside/titchfield   Titchfield Haven

Reference Books
Prendergast Col E D V and Boys, J V 1983 *The Birds of Dorset* David & Charles Limited.
Flegg, Jim 2001 *Birds of the British Isles* Silverdale Books.
Cromack David (ed) *The Birdwatchers Yearbook and Diary* Buckingham Press.
Green George & Cade Martin *Where to Watch Birds in Dorset, Hampshire & the Isle of Wight* Christopher
    Helm (Publishers) Ltd.
Couzens, Dominic *The Birdwatcher's Logbook*. New Holland Publishers Ltd.
Bruun, Bertel Delin, Hakan Svensson Lars *The Hamlyn Guide to Birds Of Britain & Europe*.
Heinzel, Hermann Fitter, Richard Parslow, John *Collins Pocket Guide to Birds Of Britain & Europe*.

7 Zoology

Beebee, T & Griffiths, R 2000 *Amphibians and Reptiles*, New Naturalist Library, Harper Collins.
Bouchner, Mirosiav 1999 *Animal Tracks* Blitz Editions.
Collins Pocket Guides 1966 *Sea Shore of Britain and Europe*.
Harpur, Merrily 2008 *Roaring Dorset, Encounters with Big Cats*, Roving Press.

8 Marine

References
Hawes, Peter 2007 Christchurch Harbour SSSI *Monitoring of Infauna and Sediments 1987 & 2007* A Report
    for the Bournemouth and Christchurch Borough Councils and the Environment Agency.
Jensen, AC and Collins, KJ 1995 *The Poole Bay Artificial Reef Project* 1989 – 1994. Biologia Marina
    Mediterranea.
Mallinson JJ, Collins, KJ and Jensen AC *Dorset Proceedings 121*, 1999 pp113-122 *Species recorded on
    Artificial and Natural Reefs Poole Bay 1989 – 1996.*

Bibliography
Humphreys J and May VJ 2005 *The Ecology of Poole Harbour* Proceedings in Marine Science 7. Elsevier.
Raybould AF 1997 *The History and Ecology of Spartina anglica in Poole Harbour* Proceedings of the Dorset
    Natural History and Archaeological Society vol 119 pp147 – 158.
Sherring RV *Proceedings of The Bournemouth Natural Science Society* 1913–1914 vol VII.

Photographic Acknowledgments

Lady's Bedstraw. Mike Downing
Chalk Milkwort blue. Mike Downing
Page 71 Horseshoe Vetch. Mike Downing
Page 72 Pyramidal Orchid. Mike Downing
Fragrant Orchid. Mike Downing
Autumn Lady's Tresses. Mike Downing
Page 73 White Helleborine. Mike Downing
Field Pansy. Mike Downing
Bee Orchid. Mike Downing
Page 74 Common Centaury. Mike Downing
Yellow-wort. Mike Downing
Common Knapweed. Mike Downing
Musk Thistle. Mike Downing
Page 75 Grass Vetchling. Mike Downing
Wild Teasel. Mike Downing
Woolly Thistle. Mike Downing
Kidney Vetch. Mike Downing
Early Spider Orchid. Mike Downing
Wild Clary. Mike Downing
Sea Aster. Mike Downing
Page 77 Ling with White Bell heather. Mike
Faherty
Common Dodder. Mike Faherty
Oblong Leaved Sundew. Mike Faherty
Round Leaved Sundew. Mike Faherty
Page 80 Heath Spotted Orchid. Mike Faherty
Dorset Heath. Mike Faherty
Bog Orchid. Mike Faherty
Page 81 Great Mullein. Mike Faherty
Page 83 Southern Marsh Orchid. Mike Faherty
Page 85 Lesser Sea-Spurrey. Mike Faherty
Greater Sea-Spurrey. Mike Faherty
Sea Milkwort. Mike Faherty
Page 86 Sea Kale. Mike Faherty
Little Robin. Wendy Crossby
Page 87 Yellow Horned Poppy. Mike Faherty
Rock Samphire. Mike Faherty
Page 89 Hairy Birdsfoot Trefoil. Mike Faherty
Hare's-foot Clover. Mike Faherty
Tree Mallow. Mike Faherty
Common Broomrape. Mike Faherty
Small Flowered Catchfly. Mike Faherty
Page 94 Guernsey Fleabane. Mike Faherty
Page 95 Pitcherplant. Mike Faherty
Hottentot Fig. Mike Faherty
Seaside Daisy. Mike Faherty
Page 101 Dawn Redwood. Mike Faherty
Indian Bean Tree. Mike Faherty
Bournemouth Pine. Mike Faherty
Page 102 Chusan Palm. Mike Faherty
Page 104 Knightwood Oak. Mike Faherty
Conjoined Oak with Beech. Mike Faherty

CHAPTER 5 INVERTEBRATES
Page 106 *Araneus angulatus.* Jonathan McGowan

Page 107 Wasp Spider with Long-winged
Conehead. Jonathan McGowan
Page 108 Nursery Web Spider. Ray Chapman
Page 109 Cobweb Spider, *Tegenaria gigantea.*
Jonathan McGowan
Page 110 *Thomisus onustus* on Hottentot Fig.
Jonathan McGowan
Misumena vatia with Meadow Brown butterfly.
Jonathan McGowan
Page 112 Southern Damselfly. Jonathan McGowan
Blue Tailed Damselfly. Jonathan McGowan
Scarce Blue-tailed Damselfly, orange form.
Jonathan McGowan
Azure Damselfly. Jonathan McGowan
Small Red Damselfly mating. Jonathan
McGowan
Emerald Damselfly. Jonathan McGowan
Page 113 Golden Ringed Dragonfly. Jonathan
McGowan
Scarce Chaser. Jonathan McGowan
Keeled Skimmer Dragonfly. Jonathan McGowan
Page 114 Ornate Brassica Bug. Jonathan McGowan
Page 115 Dock Shield Bug. Jonathan McGowan
Sloe Bug. Jonathan McGowan
Mirid Bug. Jonathan McGowan
Short-winged Cone-head. Jonathan McGowan
Large Cone-head. Jonathan McGowan
Great-green Bush-cricket. Mike Skelton
Page 118 Grey Bush-cricket. Mike Skelton
Roesel's Bush-cricket. Mike Skelton
Page 119 Large Marsh Grasshopper. Mike Skelton
Page 120 Stripe-winged Grasshopper. Mike Skelton
Mottled Grasshopper. Mike Skelton
Page 121 Common Field Grasshopper. Mike
Skelton
Lesser Marsh Grasshopper. Mike Skelton
Meadow Grasshopper. Mike Skelton
Page 122 Tortoiseshell Butterfly
Peacock Butterfly
Red Admiral Butterfly. Ray Chapman
Page 123 Marsh Fritillary
Page 124 Common Blue Female
Common Blue Male
Page 125 Silver-studded Blue Butterfly
Adonis Blue Butterfly
Green Hairstreak
Chalkhill Blue Butterfly
Silver-washed Fritillary
Page 126 Lime Hawkmoth Larva
Elephant Hawkmoth
Small Elephant Hawk Moth Larva
Page 127 Hummingbird Hawk Moth Larva
Page 128 Fox Moth larva
Small Eggar Larva
Page 129 Red-belted Clearwing

Cinnabar Moths
Page 133 Ruby-tailed Wasp
Sabre Wasp
Ophion luteus
Page 134 White-tailed Bumblebee
Page 135 Red Mason Bee. Jonathan McGowan
Page 136. Stag Beetles, male and female. Jonathan McGowan
Page 137 Longhorn Beetle, *Strangalia quadrimaculata*. Jonathan McGowan
Page 138 Green Tiger-beetle. Jonathan McGowan
Page 139 Minotaur Beetles, one unusual brown colouring. Jonathan McGowan
Dor Beetles. Jonathan McGowan
Page 140 Great Diving Beetle and Wood Ants. Jonathan McGowan

CHAPTER 6 ORNITHOLOGY
Page 143 White's Thrush. Alan Atkins
Page 144 Osprey. Alan Atkins
Page 148 Sand Martin. Kevin Carlson DWT
Goldcrest. Kevin Carlson DWT
Chiffchaff. Kevin Carlson DWT
Greater Spotted Woodpecker. Antonia Philipa
Page 149 Cuckoo. Alan Atkins
Page 150 Nightjar. Jonathan McGowan
Page 153 Cetti's Warbler. Antonia Philipa
Dartford Warbler. Alan Atkins
Page 154 Garganey. Alan Atkins
Spoonbills. Phyl England DWT
Page 156 Hoopoe. Alan Atkins
Wryneck. Alan Atkins
Page 158 Avocet. Phyl England DWT
Little Egret. Monique Vanstone DWT
Siskin. Kevin Carlson DWT
Page 160 Sparrowhawk. Geoff Hood
Page 161 Tawny Owl. Alan Atkins
Page 162 Red-footed Falcon. Alan Atkins
Hobby. Alan Atkins

CHAPTER 7 ZOOLOGY
Page 166 Grayling. Jonathan McGowan
Brown Trout. Jonathan McGowan
Page 168 Common Carp River Avon. Jonathan McGowan
Page 169 Slow-worm and Smooth Snake. Jonathan McGowan
Page 170 Sand Lizard. Jonathan McGowan
Common Wall Lizard. Jonathan McGowan
Page 171 Western Green Lizard. Jonathan McGowan
Page 172 Smooth Snake. Jonathan McGowan
Grass Snake. Jonathan McGowan
Page 173 Adder. Jonathan McGowan
Page 174 Common Frog. Stephanie Roberts

Natterjack Toad. Tracey Farrar
Common Toad. Jonathan McGowan
Page 179 Common Seal. Jonathan McGowan
Page 180 Polecat
Page 182 Red Deer. Jonathan McGowan
Page 183 Fallow Deer White Buck. Jonathan McGowan
Sika Deer Stag. Jonathan McGowan
Page 184 Red Deer Stag. Jonathan McGowan
Page 185 Roe Deer Buck. Jonathan McGowan
Page 187 Lynx Footprint. Jonathan McGowan

CHAPTER 8 MARINE
Page 189 Kimmeridge Bay Underwater ledges. M. Thornton
Ballan Wrasse. Jonathan McGowan
Bladder wrack *Fucus vesiculosus* with Periwinkle. Mary Thornton
Page 190 Coral Weed, *Corallina officinalis*. Mary Thornton
Lithothamnion and *Lithophyllum spp.* Mary Thornton
Laminaria hyperborea. Peter Tinsley
Green Sea Fingers, *Codium fragile*. Mary Thornton
Beadlet anemone, *Actinia aquina*. Mary Thornton
Snakelocks anemone, *Anemonia viridis*. Mary Thornton
Page 191 Dogwhelk, *Nucella lapillus*. Mary Thornton
Star Sea Squirts, *Botryllus schlosseri*. Mary Thornton
Sea Slugs. Jonathan McGowan
Page 192 Broad Clawed Porcelain Crab *Porcellana platycheles*. Mary Thornton
Common Blenny, *Blennius pholis*. Mary Thornton
Tompot Blenny, *Blennius gattorugine*. Mary Thornton
Rock Goby. Peter Tinsley
Page 196 Corkwing Wrasse. Peter Tinsley
Page 200 *Spartina* cordgrass. David Godfrey
Page 201 Ergot. David Godfrey
Page 202 Large mammal swimming off Studland. Peter Tinsley
Brownsea Island. M. Thornton
Page 204 Little Egret. Jonathan McGowan
Heron. Jonathan McGowan
Barn Owl. Jonathan McGowan
Page 207 Christchurch Harbour. M. Thornton

Index